In 2005 I went backpacking with 2 close friends, travelling through several different countries and countless towns and villages, walking, driving and travelling thousands of miles. This book is the first book of 2 that tells my story of my 6 months experience of what I did. I kept a detailed diary of my experiences at the time in the hope I would make it into a book, mostly for myself so I would never forget this part of my life, and to fortifying my own memories of this time as well as for anyone else who is interested in travelling in this manner. It wasn't until my return eight years later I started writing this book, where I surprised myself as to how much I had remembered and how much I enjoyed re-living it. There is so much information I had acquired in that time, that I have split my story into two books. The first book is of my three months in New Zealand and Australia, *Australasia*, with New Zealand covering both islands from top to bottom in 30 days, followed by spending 54 days in Australia where we covered a large portion of it in a campervan along the east coast, through the centre and then onto the south coast, before catching one of the most magnificent trains to Perth on the west coast. My second book covers Southeast Asia after I leave Australia, where I visited Bali and then onto Hong Kong, Singapore, Malaysia, Thailand, Cambodia, Vietnam, Laos and finally finishing in India.

Backpacking gave me a passion for culture and information, which I was constantly on the look out for. I must have read millions of words and visited countless points of interests to try and understand that culture. It would be an experience that would make me much more attached to history and culture, and more emotional and understanding to people and families from poorer countries.

You have the ability to change the path you take, so many times while travelling I could have easily not done something because I was tired, in pain or it was too much hard work to visit somewhere and sat around instead or waste away my days drinking and socialising. Everyday I tried to do something to understand the place I was at, even if it was just a walk. I took in the atmosphere and breathed the locals life as best I could, this would change the person I was and into who I am today. This part of my life was the most packed and detailed part of my life, differing every day for those 6 months. I became a traveller not a tourist and it will always be in my blood, it is something I will do and appreciate for the rest of my life.

I have tried to be as accurate as possible through out this book, my facts are taken from what I remembered at the time, also from my diary, brochures, pictures and film I took from the places I visited, also referring to my travelling companions Dale and Sharon as well as from many different websites across the internet, pulling information where I could from official websites and most often cross referencing my findings to other websites. Most of the more specific in depth details would not have been possible without the power of the internet, or the pictures and film that caught a moment in time that has been most valuable in some of these detailed descriptions.

There were so many small, which some people may say irrelevant parts to my story that I have remembered, but these small parts are what made my experience all the more interesting, and a reminder that while visiting these countries it's not just the places I visited, it's also what you make it, remembering the little things and taking in the atmosphere. I met real people and experienced strange occurrences that made that country what it is. I hope these irrelevant things portray my character and what I liked doing, as well as what I felt.

The Life of a Backpacker. Australasia.

First published © 2014. Brendan Cornwell. All rights reserved.
ISBN 978-1-63068-339-9

Acknowledgements

There are a few very important people and associations I would like to thank, that without them this book would not have been possible.

Global Village Travel was the travel company that we all went through who organised our route and tickets, they were exceptionally helpful to me when I booked my tickets to coincide with Dale and Sharon's. They were also very helpful rectifying a mistake on one of the tickets once I was travelling.

The biggest thanks has to be to my good friend Dale Thrower, although it didn't take much to talk me into joining him for the second part of his round the world tour, it was Dale that asked me to travel this 6 months with him. Also I referred several times to Dale and Sharon Richardson with many parts in this book that had escaped my memory or to expand on something I had a vague recollection of.

The search engine *Google* has been my main platform to research many of the facts and mileages that I have included, in turn this led me to many official websites for some of the more detailed information on places I visited. There are also many unknown people who had uploaded pictures and information that helped me in achieving my finished book.

Lulu.com is a free publishing, online book store that has made it possible for me to get started as an author, and is a great starting point for anyone who wants to write and publish their own book.

My last, and most special thanks is to my wife Emma, who put up with my daily tapping away at my computer that involved months of late nights and early mornings, while I dedicated a large portion of my day to my writing. Without her proof reading this book, it would have had many more grammatical mistakes, her skills in this comes from her office working background where this was very important. She had a difficult task doing this, as my instructions were to leave my character in my writing, and to make it as grammatically correct with this in mind. My character is not always grammatically correct.

Contents

Part I New Zealand

1	Planes and Time Travel.	6
2	New Zealand and the North.	9
3	Hobbit holes and sulphur pools.	29
4	New Zealand. South Island.	43
5	On without Dale.	55
6	The south and back up.	75
7	Reunited	81

Part II Australia

8	Australia. Sydney. What else do I need to say!	95
9	Off we go, in the campervan.	119
10	Drugs, Surfers and The Crocodile Hunter.	129
11	Four wheel drives and sailing yachts.	153
12	Northwards, and the rest of the east coast. It's been a long road.	199
13	The outback, it's definitely out there and a lot of it!	223
14	The town in the middle has no spring.	243
15	Dreamtime on the big rocks and dreaming inside others.	267
16	The tale of two cities, and many parts in-between.	293
17	The great train tour of the Australian desert.	333
18	The Final City of our Australian Journey.	347

Part *I*
Chapter 1
Planes and Time Travel.

Thursday 24th February.

The day I left felt like such a mad rush. I thought I'd packed everything until that morning, when I kept thinking about other things to throw in the bag. I went to my brothers to say goodbye and to see my nieces, it was then a quick visit to see Shaun, a good friend of mine that I'd known almost as long as Dale, to say goodbye and to get a picture of his new little boy that I hadn't seen yet, that had been born only a few days before. After that, I was getting more excited, the minutes were ticking away as it was getting ever closer to when I would leave. I was starting to get stomach-ache from the excitement, so I had something to eat which helped a little. My brother came over to mums again to the bitter end to see me off. We left at 2:30pm and made our way to London.

The trip to the airport wasn't as bad as I thought it was going be. I slept on and off for the most part of the journey as I was so tired from hardly sleeping from excitement the night before, making the airport in good time. I loaded my bags onto my shoulders and said my goodbyes to mum, feeling a lot less emotional than I thought I was going to be. I was a little sad, but I knew I would see mum and my family and friends again in 6 months, it just didn't feel like it was such a big thing now. I went into the terminal and after standing in the obligatory line for about 20 minutes, I had my heaviest bag checked in and I was then holding my first boarding pass of many in the next 6 months, and I was on my way to the gate. It was a short walk and I was there and just watching the world go by. I was watching the different people doing things, wondering or making up who they were and where they might be going, having the same thoughts when I moved to America that no-one passing me by would probably not be embarking on such a big trip. A little while later I thought I would walk around the shops and see what they had to offer, before I knew it I had looked at just about every item in every shop, and it was time to board the plane, not that we took off on time. We were 1 hour

45 minutes late taking off thanks to about 3 flakes of snow that froze the wings apparently. I've had more ice build up round my freezer door at home, which only takes a few seconds to sort out with a little chipping hammer. Amazing when you think about *O'hare airport*, in Chicago near where I used to live in the States never closes even in the depths of winter. England is crap at coping with cold weather. We finally took off but I did get a little worried to see water pouring out of one of the speakers and the overhead lockers, thankfully I was not under any of those and put it down to just being condensation in air-conditioning.

My first stop off point for the plane to refuel was Thailand, Bangkok, I met two people, who I sat next to on the plane. One lady was doing a trip similar to me but starting in Thailand, another guy who was also English, had married a Thai lady and had a child with her. This was his 3rd time doing this trip this year and he was bringing her back to England. In-between this I managed to get about 3 hours sleep. At Thailand we all had to get off the plane for some security reason. I was a little worried about finding my way round this foreign airport, thinking I wouldn't be able to read any of the signs and getting completely lost. Fortunately everything was well signposted in Thai and English. I had to walk around the airport, up the stairs and back to board the plane again while they refuelled. This is where I found that a pack of polo's will set an airport metal detector off really well. I got seated again to find two different people to talk to, one person was French but had lived in Australia since he was 8, he was a geologist and had been working in the mines in Thailand for 3 weeks where he had seen real gold in the rocks, what a job! I also talked with another elderly lady. We had both watched a documentary about the Second World War, which was based in Australia, then got talking about it after. It turned out that this lady was in Australia at that time and was going back to visit. We got talking a little more, she asked where I was going, and where I lived.
"It's a tiny little village in Norfolk, you'd never have heard of it." I assured her.
"Really!" she replied, "go on."
"Catfield."
"That's amazing!" she replied "My sister used to live in Potter Heigham!" That was just two miles from my mum's house!

Friday 25th February.

    The second part of the flight was a little boring, I slept a bit longer for about 5 hours, it had been night time for quite some time again at this point so I could manage to trick my self into thinking it was time to sleep, even though it was only 8pm in England. Travelling to New Zealand on the other side of the world is like time travel, the flight took 28 hours to get there, I left on Thursday and got there on Saturday, the extra 12 hour difference going through the time zones made this day disappear, maybe never existing at all. The best explanation is probably the days travelling were just shortened as I flew over the timelines.

Chapter 2
New Zealand and the North.

Saturday 26th February.

As my flight from England was delayed because someone couldn't work out which way to point the de-icer! I missed my connection flight to Sydney, thankfully the airline were very efficient at sorting the connection flight before we landed, we were well informed on the plane and there was a little table just outside the gate with some *Quantus* representatives to point us in the right direction, this put me back just two hours late which would make my total journey to New Zealand 28 hours.

I finally got on my way to Auckland, where I was to meet Dale and Sharon. I passed all the checkpoints, and was through the gate by about 2:30pm, with very few problems to see a sea of people, I wondered how the hell I was going to find Dale and Sharon, as I was doing my meerkat impression, not seeing them at all. Luckily they saw me and I heard a voice shout "Oi, moosh.", I knew it must have been Dale with a phrase like that! After a quick hug with the pair of them it was like being back at home and just picking up where we left off, Sharon and I didn't say anything about starting a relationship, we didn't need to, she just held my hand for a moment and gave me a little smile. After sorting out bags and belongings I had for Dale, I exchanged some money up at $2.6 to the pound, it was then a mini bus into the centre of town to book into the *Queens Backpackers Hostel* to do a bit of relaxing. It was a fair sized room with 3 bunk beds, a table and a sink. We looked at pictures and video messages I had taken for Dale and Sharon, I had been round to Dales parents to get a little message from his mum and dad for him. My mum gave a little message too for them both, mainly focusing on Dale not getting us into trouble. Dale also showed me some pictures of his from the last 6 weeks. In the evening we went out in search of food, we first stopped in a pizza restaurant that was looking a little expensive, I was worrying how much this part of the trip was going to cost me, it would take 3 months to go through New Zealand and Australia, eating at those prices every night would put a huge dent in my savings. As it happens it was taking forever to get seated so we moved on to find a much cheaper alternative. We ended up at a Korean restaurant, with a little help from Dale and Sharon I choose something and was surprised at how much I enjoyed it considering I'd never been to one before. My variety of different foods had been expanded considerably in the past few years and I knew I would have to get used to it, as I would experience a whole lot more by the time this trip was finished. We had a little walk round stopping off at a bar for a beer, We barely started our drink, when we were all told to get out as there was a fire, along with all the people in the theatre, 5 fire engines turned up but still we couldn't see any smoke. Dale was really shattered so decided to go back to the hostel while Sharon and I went for another drink. Sharon and I were making a real connection again while we chatted over our final drink of the evening, as I was starting to feel really tired myself from the jet lag we went back to our hostel for a restless sleep.

Sunday 27th February.

Jetlags a bitch when you travel across 12 time zones, I woke at 3am and was wide awake, what do you do at that time of the morning in a country you've never been to before, and only spent half a day at, in the dark? I wandered around the room for a few minutes looking for something to do, after looking out the window to the street finding nothing particular to amuse myself with, I looked over to Sharon on the top bunk with her arm hanging out, I walked over and gave her hand a little kiss which woke her. That's all her body clock needed to keep her awake with her jetlag, it wasn't all bad as I then had someone to keep me company. We walked downstairs to the common room in the foyer, there were a few other people milling about looking a little zombiefied too, most probably suffering the same problem as us. I gave mum a call to try out the calling card she gave me, we then sat around downstairs chatting for a while until Dale got up. He joined us downstairs to write his diary up, a guy poked his head in the door and said. "Anyone want some casual work for today?" Of course Dale was up for that as he was constantly worried about running out of money. Dale disappeared while Sharon and I went for breakfast, consisting of a pie and coffee in a local café, which would become a common place for us and breakfast.

We walked to *Albert Park*, a nice little park with a massive tree in the middle that I could easily stand inside with its large laying branches. As we walked out heading towards *Auckland Domain*, we found several scary hand made masks and lanterns hanging from trees, which were for a Chinese celebration.

Auckland Domain was another nice park with lots of tall trees and ferns and lots of winding paths that we seemed to get lost on at every turn. Back in town we visited *St Mary's* church, a wooden building that for some reason many years ago had been moved across the street to where it sits now. There were pictures in the church of the move, the building all boarded up being rolled across a big path on logs, dwarfing the several dozen workers around it. It now looks like it's been in this position from when it was built with its well-established greenery round it. The outside reminded me of the many buildings of this style I saw in America, with its many high pointed windows outside with the gothic style architecture. The inside was just as familiar which looked very old even though the outside was modern, with its dozen or so low chandeliers that were all well lit up, this part did not resemble the churches in America, they were more like the old churches in England with the long wooden pews and wooden rafters.

We walked to Parnell to have a drink in an Irish pub, *The Bog*. After our drink we walk from here completely the wrong way so decided to get the bus back. We hooked up with Dale after his days work at the hostel and heard of his stories of the day laying the floors in a massive marquee, he had to man handle these large boards and slide them into place, one guy thought he was clever by dropping the boards into places saying, "Nice one." with every drop until he broke one in half. We took a 10 minute walk to the local supermarket to buy dinner, Sharon and I bought food that could be eaten out of the packet, Dale bought a pizza not checking first if the hostel had an oven in the communal kitchen, which it didn't so he micro waved it because he didn't want to waste it, as he was tucking into his soggy pizza, he told us how his brother did this same cooking method before and made himself ill.

That evening we went to a bar close by to the hostel, it seemed to be full of backpackers which would also become a common sight close to hostels, in fact it was packed to the limit which made walking round near impossible. 3 girls had a good idea for clearing a path, one pretended to be wanting to throw up with the other two putting their arms out to make us aware she was coming through. She was very convincing and cleared a path like someone with the plague was walking through. They had a few drinking games for our entertainment, one of which was limbo for drinks, the other was random people would nominate themselves to take a drinking challenge, which was quite simply to drink a full shot of beer from a plastic cup. 3 people sat on the stools to compete with each other on stage with their cups, two little pads from a tens machine were placed strategically on their fore arms, usually these are used as an alternative type of pain management, it sends a small electrical charge to these pads to numb the pain, they then turned it up to full. Most of the contestants chucked their drink over the floor or into their own face, as their arm contorted and convulsed involuntarily, the facial expression told us it was rather uncomfortable. Only one contestant managed to drink the entire cup without crushing it or losing the contents, which was reciprocated by the large cheers and applause from the crowd.

After the drinking games we walked back to *Albert Park* as we knew there was a fireworks display, but as we hadn't checked the time it was to start, we completely missed it, we found a few people milling about the park that was covered in streamers bits of paper giving you a sense of many people occupying this place a short time before, instead we went for one more drink near the hostel before turning in at around midnight.

Monday 28th February.

Jetlag woke me at 2:15am, but as I was so tired I did fall back off to sleep after a short while until 8am. It was Sharon's birthday, and I had brought her two bracelets from dads Native American bead work collection to choose from, she loved both of them so wore one as an ankle bracelet, neither would come off until she got home. Dale bought her a little stuffed black and white dog that she named one of Dales favourite beers, Guinness.

We had to wait around a while for the rain to stop before we took our walk to *Auckland Bridge*, Dale had been having a bad hair day for a week or so as he let a very over particular hairdresser cut his hair. Although he took forever trying to get the perfect haircut for Dale, it failed miserably, he had several uneven and sticky up bits. So being as tight as he is, thought he'd get Sharon to give it a little trim up, she done well, and she even looked like a hairdresser while she evened up his hair with her fingers.

We took the long stroll to the *Auckland Harbour Bridge*, and in a little information hut near it, we found out there was a tour of the bridge for $65 (£25), which we thought was a little expensive, and our money would be better spent on the *Sydney Harbour Bridge* instead, as it was much more of an iconic structure, and had a little more interesting surroundings. The *Auckland Harbour Bridge* finished construction in 1959, and has a total length of 1,020m (3,350ft), which is only 129m (423ft) short of *Sydney Harbour Bridge*. The view from the *Auckland Bridge* is a little dull to say the least. It's a fairly standard iron bridge with only the Auckland skyline to look at with the distinctive Sky Tower dominating it. We could also have taken a bungee jump from the middle of it for $85 (£32), I was very keen on this but Dale would never do it, as he's a little scared of heights, neither was it Sharon's cup of tea, with no spectators allowed on the bridge when anyone was jumping, which was something I really wanted if I was to do something at this level of ludicrousness, I certainly wanted some video footage of it. This is one of the very few things of my whole trip that I passed by and have regretted, as I would not get the chance again in the next 6 months to do a bungee jump.

We took a long walk back stopping to take a few group pictures of the Auckland skyline, making sure to capture the *Sky Tower* in the distance, as we would be visiting back there later that evening. It took us nearly 4 hours to walk back, stopping on the way at a shop and bought something that is regarded to backpackers as invaluable, it would be the backbone of the route we would take around New Zealand, a book that would have practical tips, locations of sights, with a little history as well as maps of most of the cities. The most common book is the lonely planet. The one I bought was Fodor's exploring New Zealand. It was very good and was packed with information that guided us very well around New Zealand, with many facts from Fodor's book I have used myself in this book.

We changed and freshened up before heading out for dinner at an Indian restaurant, then took the hour and a half walk to the tallest building in the southern hemisphere, the *Sky Tower*. Completed in 1997, the tower stands at a height of 328m (1,076ft) to the top of the antenna spire and is the highest man made structure in New Zealand.

We got there a short while before sunset so we could get some daytime pictures as well as sunset ones. Our ascent was by a lift with a glass floor, at the top it really does feel high as you stand in the observation tower, it may be because there are very few other skyscrapers in Auckland that come anywhere near the height of the tower. You can walk all the way around the observation floor to view the Auckland skyline, you can see the entire city, the harbour and far out to sea, through the wall of windows that sloped slightly outwards. This was where one of those picture opportunity presenting itself to me, where I laid against the window. The floor on the outer edge was thick glass that you could walk over, which overhangs the footprint of the building allowing you to see straight down to the street below. I thought having my picture taken laying down on one of these glass floors with the street below would be fun, and it did make an interesting picture. We stayed for a few hours watching the sunset, taking pictures of the changing colours of the sky, as the sun disappeared behind the city skyline. I took the time to take in where I was and what I was doing. Feeling humbled by how far I had travelled to see such things as this, it would be a ritual I would do quite often in the following 6 months, which would shape my character a little more. We left here after dark in search of a bar for the evening, walking away we saw how the outside of the *Sky Tower* had changed unbeknown to us while we were sightseeing inside, it was lit half way up engulfing the observation tower and all the way up to the tip of the tower with a vibrant blue light, to make it stand out across Auckland as much at night as it did in the day.

We found a Karaoke bar much to Dales joy, we came in half way through a battle, which anyone could enter. Dale put his name down and did his usual song, which was *American Pie*. He didn't realise that the first contestant who ended up winning, had sang this one already. I'm sure there was a silent groan from the people who had already endured sitting through such a long song already. Even though Dale made everyone sit through this song twice he still managed to cop off with someone, so Sharon and I went back to the hostel for an early night.

Tuesday 1st March.

First thing after waking up we packed and locked our bags in the hostels safe room and walked a few doors up to the local pub so Dale could watch a Norwich football game before we moved on. I did something I don't do very often and I actually got into the game, I was even wearing Dales second Norwich city shirt that I had brought him. Of course he was wearing his as he did for most of the trip. Dale naturally was drinking a pint of Guinness because there was a game on, I can't drink at that time of the morning, so I went to the bar to order a coffee, I stood next to a guy that was looking very tired and seemed to be giving me a sideways grumpy look, I didn't care for his problem so I took my coffee, and sat and watched the game. Sharon came over to me and quietly said.
"You know who that is?"
"No." was my confused reply. How would I know this stranger who was still giving me a pissed off look?
"He was on our top bunk."
    I sank into my chair and hid behind my cup trying not to make eye contact, we did lump into bed a little in our half drunken state, and did a lot of tossing and turning trying to get comfortable with the two of us in a single bed, he must have thought there was an earth quake going on.

    I stopped by the doctors, to find out I didn't need a jab my local docs back home said I needed, Sharon and I then went onto *Auckland Domain Museum* to learn some of the New Zealand history, while Dale, the jammy git, got asked by a random passer by at the hostel if he would try out a web page and get paid $50 (£19) for it. At the *Auckland Domain Museum* there were a lot of items of the Maori history. The ancestors of the Maori were Polynesian and settled in New Zealand about 3,500 years ago. About 150 years after they colonised this country a warrior culture emerged, with this highly cultural and religious race. Today there are some 660,000 Maori living in New Zealand making up about 15% of the population. They are the second largest ethnic group in New Zealand after European New Zealanders. One item here in particular, a Maori war canoe caught my eye named *Te Toki a Tapiri*, which was one of the last to be built around 1836. Massively long at 25m (82ft) with a high bow,

I'm sure it was a formidable sight to any enemy with its 100 warriors on board. There were also some Maori huts, they must have been genuine as you had to take your shoes off to enter. We took our shoes off outside the door in front of the elaborate veranda with its native carvings. Inside it was some 12m (40ft) long and 6m (20ft) across. The roof and walls were made from straw like material with the beams of wood brightly decorated with traditional art. One chap was laying in the middle of the room and seemed to be doing something religious but I wasn't quite sure what.

There were also many small rooms one after another showing the different eras of New Zealand bars and shops in the last century, as well as several gun replicas and *World War 2* memorabilia.

We raced back to the hostel by 3:55pm as our rental car was being delivered to us at 4pm. After a bit of a wait we gave them a call and found they were at a different hostel. Our old Nissan Bluebird finally turned up which would be our transport for the next 28 days costing us $924 (£355). Dale drove us out of town heading west on highway 1 to Piahia, it was 156 miles of nothing but fantastic scenery of twisting roads, trees and rolling hills in almost every direction. We camped out on our first night in the car, with Sharon and I in the front and Dale taking up the back seat at the road side, on a random street, after our evening meal of a chippy.

Wednesday 2nd March.

After an uncomfortable nights sleep we took our morning bath, well, we stopped off at the Bay of Island for a swim to freshen up, we stripped off to our underwear instead of finding our swimwear, as our underwear needed washing anyway, much to the delight of the builders across the road, there was a lot of whistling and hollering which I'm pretty sure wasn't directed at me. It's a nice way to start the day, the cool dip in the ocean that is not getting whistled at, it certainly wakes you up.

We stopped in town at a café for breakfast, saw how expensive it was and found another much cheaper one. After a little walk around the shops, which had nothing to offer we thought we would check out Ngawha springs. These were natural hot springs, which are formed when in regions close to tectonic plate boundaries where volcanic activity rises close to the surface of the earth, when ground water runs close to these areas the water can get close to boiling point. Most hot springs used by the public are forged in to bathing areas like this one. The 9 different pools had wooden sides and floors that were built around the spring to make it look nicer, each pool was surrounded by old looking wooden fences and rockeries with a few plants, it somehow looked fitting for this place. The pools temperatures ranged from warm to scorching where you had to rub your legs to get your skin accustomed to the heat. There is supposed to be healing properties in this murky water, but you can't get the water in your eyes as there can be parasites, we were informed this by a another lady who was passing by casually telling us they could possibly kill us. It also didn't do much for my silver St Christopher, it turned a copper colour and so did Dales sunglasses. It cost $5 (£1.90) to get in and would cost me another $12 (£2.60) for some silver polish to fix my silver. It also smelt really bad like rotten eggs.

After about 3 hours sampling all the pools we thought we'd had enough of this healing eggy-ness and asked where the showers were. The owner directed us to behind the changing rooms with a little grin to which we found a hose, a cold one at that! We stuck the hose in every crevice to make sure no parasites had set up home, and headed out at 4pm north again on highway 1, then onto 1F through a lot of towns to reach the most northern point of New Zealand. We finally found a big shop that sold a bit of everything where I bought myself a pair of sandals and the silver polish.

We left for our final push to the north and didn't see another petrol station until we got to Waukiki Landing, the last town before the northern point, a further 12 miles which we didn't have enough fuel for. We asked in the café next door that was owned by the garage if we could get any fuel, "Yeah we'll open it for $20 (£7.70)." was the reply.
Dale was looking a little surprised and said, "Oh we'll have more than $20 worth."
"No, you give me $20, I'll open the garage, and then your fuel."
Dale recoiled a little, he'd never spend money unnecessarily and besides we'd already driven 146 miles that day, we were hungry and there was nothing else north apart from a light house. I had a very nice burger and chips and we camped out in the car behind the petrol station, we wrote up diaries and chatted a little before getting to sleep for about midnight.

Thursday 3rd March.

We managed to wake up at about 7am, refuelled at a cost of $1.37 (52p) a litre, which was much better than I thought due to how isolated it was, as most stations in the built up areas was about $1.19 (46p) a litre. We were then set to drive the last 12 miles of bumpy gravel road to Cape Reinga, which was quite hard work. From the car park the lighthouse, which is a tiny 10m (33ft) tall, looked like a speck on the very green hillside, we walked the last few hundred metres of pavement from the car park to see it. In front of it there was a signpost pointing to the major cities around the world and the distances to them, London was a mere 10,499nm (12,082miles).

The lighthouse here was first lit in May 1941, it was the last manned light to be built in New Zealand, and replaced the *Cape Maria Van Diemen lighthouse* which was located near to Cape Reinga, from there the shore line curved to make a small bay, at the end of this is the island, Motuopao island, where the first lighthouse was situated. It was built in 1879, however due to the difficulty in accessing this because of the turbulent seas that had also claimed 120 ships in this area, it was moved to Cape Reinga for safety. The complete lantern fittings from Motuopao Island was reused at Cape Reinga, the new lighthouse was fitted with a 1000 watt electrical lamp instead, powered by a diesel generator, that could be seen for 26 nautical miles (30 miles or 48 km). In 1987 the lighthouse was fully automated and the keepers withdrawn, it is now monitored remotely from Wellington at the other end of the north island some 655miles (1055km) away. By 2000 the original lens and lamp were replaced by a 50 watt tungsten halogen beacon, which is powered by batteries that are recharged by solar cells which dominates one side of the lighthouse today, taking away the nostalgic look of the rest of it. It now reaches a slightly lower distance of 19nm (23 miles) and flashes every 12 seconds.

It wasn't long before we were heading back, past the petrol station back onto tarmac and another 10 miles with a bit more gravel road to Spirits bay, I taught Dale the *'hey hey we're the monkeys walk'* down the beach as we ran to the crystal clear sea for our morning bath. The waves were almost 2.5m (8ft) high as we jumped through the crest as it crashed over us, on one of the waves I turned my back to it as it rolled over me, it was so powerful it just slammed me into the sea bed and kept me there until the wave had past. We got back into our eggy smelling car and drove back to the café from last night for lunch, the car and everything in it was still stinking of the hot sulphuric springs from the day before and would stay with us for sometime.

We started our drive back south again to Paihia, there wasn't much else going back this way as the top of the north island is not very wide. We came past Cable Bay, and we made a hasty stop as we could see a lot of something a hundred metres or so out to sea, they were dolphins, there are many places around New Zealand where you can see dolphins close to the shore. There seemed to be about a hundred swimming and some were playfully jumping rather high, Dale and Sharon were going to swim out after them to get a bit of free swimming with the dolphins, but they started heading out to sea out of their reach. We got to Paihia by 6pm, we stopped at a big *Woolworths* to get some fruit and biscuits, on the way in Dale got a holler from a random passer-by in the car park who was hanging out of his car window shouting Norwich as he drove away, even half way across the world people will recognise a Norwich City shirt. We went into town for food then to a bar for the evening, Dale and Sharon wrote diaries, and I read up on the guide to New Zealand to find places of interest we might want to visit. By the time we'd found our camping spot at the side of the road from the night before, we had driven 175 miles this day.

Friday 4th March.

We got up with the intention of hiring a sailing boat, and finding some dolphins of our own, there was a tall ship experience that cost $95 (£36) that would take you out to see the dolphins, but they couldn't find any the day before, so we thought if the experts couldn't find them we had little chance, and besides there was next to no wind. So we drove down the west coast to Waioterama to the *Labyrinth Woodworks & the Amazing Maize*, owned by an eccentric guy with wild grey hair and looked a little camp. After a few mind boggling and difficult games we had a walk round the Amazing Maize, which was not that amazing, for a start you could see through the maize so navigating your way around wasn't that difficult, it was also a little run down, we had to find 11 letters that were in great need of repainting and fixing up to make two words to get a prize. We found two letters relatively quickly and took more time working out the words. After a lot of head scratching and mosquito bites later we all came up with something different, so the old guy gave us all the prize we'd worked so hard for, a blue lollipop that turned our tongues a frightfully bright blue. That can't be good for your insides! The old guy then proceeded to show us several tricks from his array of items for sale that was stacked to the rafters in his little shop, one in particular he showed us was a simple small wooden tube about 3 inches long that had a similar length piece that fitted inside it with a ball on the end. He grasped the small wooden ball and started to pull it out saying there was a force pulling them together, the further he pulled it out the more it began to quiver and seemed to be wanting to snap back into its holder. I thought it must have some kind of ultra thin band attaching the two, so I passed my hand through the gap and the piece he was holding went shooting across his shop. Dumb founded I picked up the piece on the floor and handed it back to him, it was just a small stick with a ball on the end, the other piece was just a tube, I couldn't understand how it had happened until he pointed out the obvious, quite simply he'd pinched the ball between his fingers to ping it across the room. He tried very hard to sell us some tricks but it was time for us to move on, and besides once you know the trick it's not so fun. Leaving this strange mans grotto we made our way down the little gravel road with a good drop off on one side, as we came round the corner it was obvious I was driving too quick thinking 25mph was fine on this loose road, and it would have been fine if I was going in a straight line and not on a camber down hill and round a corner, it made the car fishtail quick wildly much to the joy and excitement of Sharon shouting 'yes', where as Dale was the complete opposite calling me several unkind names. As it happens luck was on my side and at 25mph my counter steering skills worked well and I straightened it up within a few seconds.

We drove south with no more incidents to Waimomaku, which was the next village to see *Hokianga Brewery*, New Zealand's smallest brewery, a little wooden shack that had a total of two beers, light and dark. We all plumped for the dark, which made me feel like I was going to shit a brick the next day as a result of drinking it. I'm glad I'd only bought a half as I found it a little difficult to get through it was one of those beers you chew. We ordered toasted sandwiches and the owner thoughtfully decided we might like some grapes to go with our food and beers and pulled a sizeable vine from the fence outside and plonked them in front of us. They consistency was like they were crossed between jelly and oysters, as I rolled the one and only grape I tried around my mouth, trying to swallow it without throwing up.

Sharon did a bit of filming outside this little pub, as she was panning around outside the pub and the surrounding area, she caught a couple of people in frame who were sat on their porch across the road, where they shouted they wanted payment for being in our film. We hastily got in the car and headed further south, stopping at Waipoua forest to see the *Tane Mauta Giant Kaur*, a giant tree. It was a little way off the road, which was a few minutes walk along a wooden walkway with railings, so not to destroy the vegetation. I was surprised that we couldn't see it until we were nearly there. And it really is a giant at 1200 years old it stands 51m (169ft) tall and has a girth of 13.5m (45ft). We set the camera up on the ground to try and capture the immense size of it that had some success, by placing the camera on the ground facing upwards along the height of the tree with us in the foreground.

Carrying on south we saw a sign for Piroa Falls so thought we'd check it out. Another 5 minutes of gravel track and a short walk and we were there. The waterfall had a drop of about 15m (50ft) in the middle of a rocky crevice that was about 18m (60ft) wide. It cascaded down through two fairly deep pools. It was in the middle of nowhere and not a sole about which is good for two reasons, you don't have to worry about getting changed into your swim ware showing your bits off, hell we could have swam naked if we wanted it was so isolated, but swimming naked with Dale isn't something I wanted to do. You can also shout as loud as you like and there was a lot of screaming going on as it was so cold, we swam across the first pool, then very carefully to climb the few metres up the rocky ledge to the next pool, to plunge into it to swim under the fall. It was so cold screaming was the only thing to get the air in my lungs and Dale was just as bad. I did look quite panicked swimming back, which was due to the cold cramping my muscles, I've never been a strong swimmer, the sheer cold that seeped into my core is probably why I managed to stub my toe on the way back and not even feel it until I got warm again.

We carried on south on endless twisty roads and countless quaint little bridges, it started to turn dark and I fell into a deep sleep and missed driving past Auckland in the dark. Dale had filmed it as we passed, most probably not for my benefit but at least I got to see the city lit up as we crossed the bridge out of Auckland. I finally woke up at Thames where we spent the night.

Miles driven – 359.

Saturday 5th March.

We were up late this morning at about 9am, our first stop was the mall for breakfast where I had a croissant, and to buy a cassette adapter for the car as we had Dales wide range of music on mini disc and no way of us all hearing it. We found one for $30 (£11), needless to say we didn't buy it and I called home instead.

We drove out on the ever familiar twisty roads east to Whitianga, Mercury Bay, here it's known for its hot beach from thermal activity, at low tide you can dig your own hole to make a thermal pool, but unfortunately the tide was coming in. Sharon and I were already there for a while as Dale had to find the toilets. After a while Dale came wandering up the beach drenched, "What happened to you?" I said. It did look a bit strange he was soaked through.

"I thought I'd have a look up the beach past those rocks and a wave crashed over them and soaked me." Strange again I thought, there just seemed to be several large rocks with several deep crevices between the sea and the cliff, with not much else beyond that. Sharon looked at him with an expression of knowing. "You were taking a shit weren't you?" Dale just nodded with a matter of fact look then casually said, "Yeah." As it happened he was having trouble finding the public toilets and this was his only impending solution. I did laugh to myself, and still do thinking of Dale digging a hole between two rocks, getting into position and then getting swamped by a big wave while halfway through... Well I don't need to go any further.

Of course we took a dip, there wasn't a gradual drop off in the water, more like a sheer drop! Dale and Sharon carried on swimming, they swam out really far while I just watched and hoped they'd be able to get back. Sharon got back first while Dale swam another 10 minutes. We spent the time reclined in the sand a short way from the lapping waves with our eyes closed dozing, forgetting that the tide was coming in. We had a rude awakening as the waves finally caught up to us lapping our feet and getting our towel wet, much to the amusement of a couple of guys a little further up the beach as we jumped up dragging our towels with us, no doubt they had been watching us for some time and was waiting for the inevitable. Dale joined us and decided to cover up, with way too much sun cream, and ended up looking like a snowman. A short while later we got dried off and changed as discreetly as we could in the car park and had lunch at a nearby café, while writing up our diaries.

Our next destination was Matamata, we got as far as Tauranga and stopped for our evening meal, we must have walked around the whole town looking for something cheap but ended up settling for a subway. Walking back we came across an Indian restaurant with a deal on for $12 (£4.60), which Dale was most upset about as he'd already feasted on a subway meal, most Indian restaurants were $18 (£6.90) for the same meal.

We carried onto Matamata, and found a bar to amuse ourselves for the evening, it was an old looking pub inside with a few round tables that seemed lost in that big room, with a piano and reception desk at the back, the front part and outside was much more modern looking. We got our drinks and played poker outside where there were a few tables, some locals on the next table mentioned they thought we must have been English playing cards in a pub.

We took a drive around looking for a quiet place to sleep, after about 15 minutes we found a nice quiet corner in a golf course car park.

Miles driven - 191

Chapter 3
Hobbit holes and sulphur pools.

Sunday 6th March.

We were woken at 8am to the sounds of toffee nosed twats noisily pulling their golf clubs out of the tiny boots of their sports cars, while looking down at us in our old car. We found a bakery for breakfast, this morning I was thinking I spend money too easily for breakfast and should ease up on it a little, but bakery food is so nice and probably the only healthy food I was having. Driving into Matamata you're greeted with a sign saying '*Welcome to Hobbiton*' as Matamata is the home to the '*Lord of the Rings*' film trilogy, a small area a short drive out of town on Alexander Farm was the set of 'The Shire' and the Hobbit's homes. The area was found by Peter Jackson spotted during an aerial search of the North Island for the best possible locations to films. A deal was done with the farmer that was to be kept a secret for some time, the New Zealand Army was contracted to build a one mile road into the site and the initial set development. There was also a 1,524m (5,000ft) no fly zone round the farm where pilots would lose their license if they were to breach this area, and at the end of filming, Hobbiton was to be demolished without a trace of the little fella's homes. They had already torn down a few of them after filming when it was decided to keep this area as a tourist attraction, the demolition team found out with seconds to spare before Bilbo's house was torn down, now there are just 17 out of the 37 standing.

We found the booking office for the tour, a little house with rounded doorways and grass growing on the roof to resemble the Hobbit holes. We paid our $50 (£19) and waited for our tour bus. Dale on the other hand wasn't going to fork out the money and try and sneak in instead, we took the half hour or so bus trip and as we turned into the thin road on the farm leading to The Shire we saw Dale drive past as he'd been following the bus, several hundred metres later we were at the set. We disembarked and carried onto the set by foot along the narrow path, rounding the first corner we came to an overhanging tree, where in the first movie Gandolf is on a horse and cart coming into the village, with the children running following close behind as he lets off some fireworks. The guide took us round showing us the various points of interest, there is a red marker a few hundred metres past the lake that is beside Hobbiton, where in the film Frodo and Sam stand and say it's the furthest a hobbit had been, before they take the brave step across it.

They showed us the area over the hill behind the hobbit holes where the animals were kept for the film, as well as the eating areas and trailers for the cast. There was a large picture on a board overlooking this area showing what it looked like during filming. We were shown the party field, before it was a field, it had a large stinking boggy water hole that was filled in to make this area, at the end of this is the party tree, a massive tree that was the centre of the Shire. Behind this there are all the hobbit holes, these were situated among several large mounds, there were also pictures here too from when it was filmed. We explored all the hobbit holes that were strewn over the hill on several different levels, separated by little gravel footpaths and stone steps. They are quite small, only getting half a dozen people crouching in each hobbit hole at a time.

At the time we went, all that was left of them was a plywood face to the house which was painted white which was pealing and sagging quite badly, as it was mostly untreated wood, the only resemblance to the film was the distinctive round windows and doors. Since then they have completely rebuilt the set as it was seen in The *Lord of the Rings* film trilogy. The Hobbit homes are only about 3m (10 ft) deep as the interior was filmed in a studio. We made sure to get a picture of inside Bilbo's house, there was also the oak tree that overlooked Bag End that was cut down and brought in from near Matamata. Each branch was numbered and chopped, then transported and bolted back together on top of Bag End, the tree itself weighed 26 tonnes and had artificial leaves that were imported from Taiwan and individually wired onto the dead tree. We were there two and a half hours before we were on our way back. On the way back to the main road they got a call on their radio from the farmer to say he had seen some people trying to sneak in. What had happened is Dale had parked his car and was being followed by another car with another two people in, Dale approached them and said it was obvious why they were there and decided to sneak in together, there wasn't actually any way to sneak in as there was a field separating Hobbiton from the road, this is where they came unstuck, Dale was covertly using bushes, banks and a ditch, where the other two made a run for it, spooking the cows and drawing the farmers attention to them.

We met up in the car park where we had booked the tickets and drove on to Rotorua, a volcanic, sulphurous town where there are several areas of hot rock and sulphur pools. Approaching Rotorua we could smell that familiar eggy smell that had been lingering in the car for a few days after our visit to Ngawha hot springs, wherever you go in Rotorua you can smell sulphur. We'd arrived just in time for Dale to find a pub to see a football match between Norwich and Chelsea, while Sharon and I went for lunch in the form of a massive piece of carrot cake. After the footy game we took a walk around the many sulphur pools, they ranged in all shapes, sizes, types and temperature. There were some in the middle of a grassed area with a simple wooden fence surrounding a huge amount of rocks that looked like they had been stacked on top of each other. You could walk up to most of them by boardwalks that were less accessible, one of which was a steaming, bubbling hot lake with large amounts of white steam drifting off that would make you think there was a fire that was out of control. Some areas had warnings that some parts it was possible that you could fall through, and no doubt to a scorching painful end. By the lake on the shore there was a sign that said '*no walking, danger, thermal area*' of course Dale and I thought it would make a good picture of him standing next to it, after a few careful steps he got to the sign without incident, we thought it must have been a safe bet as far as the sign, someone must have stuck that post in the ground there in the first place!

There were a few holes in these large grassy parks ranging in sizes with steam slowly escaping the brownish water in them, with some of them having a few large rocks coated in a little of yellow sulphur also emitting a little white steam. This is where Dale and I had a little bit of an inquisitive boyish test we wanted to try out, or should I say Dale did and I went along with it because it sounded fun, just like when we used to get into trouble as young children. So I shielded Dale from the rest of the park and he proceeded to pee on these hot rocks among this shrub and tree area to see if the white steam turned to yellow, which it didn't but it did get us in trouble. Although no one could see what we were doing it must have seemed obvious what we were doing, we found this out as a large woman on the other side of this park a good 30m (100ft) away, which I might add was the only person in this part at the time, expressed her disgust in our experiment. "Oi! What the FUCK do you think you're doing! You dirty fucking bastard! You're fucking disgusting doing that in public!" She started to make her way towards us at this point, which we got quite concerned about as she looked like the type of woman that could knock a horse out with one punch. She carried on her rant with a surprising second volley of swearing. "You dirty, filthy fucking bastard! Pissing in the open like that, I've got my fucking kids with me!" And she did, 2 children of about 8 years old were close behind her as she got more irate and swore all the more. Yes maybe not something you would want your children to see, which they didn't, but it was ok for them to hear every swear word under the sun. We made a hasty retreat round the corner and lost her, I was generally worried for our safety, she looked like she was about to explode how red in the face she was going. It may not have helped matters as we found it hysterically funny which she must have plainly been able to see. We also dug a hole once we were sure we were far enough away from the ranting woman, to see how deep you have to go until you get heat, after a few strokes of a stick to make a shallow hole in the ground we found it wasn't far before it starts to get nice and warm.

    I had another unhealthy meal of garlic chips and sausage but there just isn't any cheap healthy food when you travel like this. We sat outside trying to enjoy our unhealthy food while taking in the local air. After our full bellies we decided to work it off in the local park, well we walked through it and on the way back to the car to find no children playing there, so naturally the inner child in us came out and spent some times on the swings and slides and those strange animal things perched on a spring that are really put to the test when an adult swings back and forth on it. After our little playtime I drove out of Rotorua to Whakatane. We arrived at 9:45pm after covering 139 miles this day and found a nice, very dark area to sleep by the sea where we wouldn't get disturbed. Sharon and I left Dale sleeping and went for a little walk by the sea. It was so calm and quite before we went back to our car for the evening.

Monday 7th March.

We were up late again despite getting an early night, although I was woken by the rain as I'd got hot in the night and opened the window so I got a little shower, maybe I was tired from sleeping uncomfortably in the car. We found an expensive café for breakfast, quiche and coffee of $13 (£5), before we went to see if we could get a boat tour to White Island, an active volcano, which would cost $140 (£53) each, but all boat trips had been cancelled that day because of high winds. So we headed out of town to an air strip where we could be flown out for $450 (£173) for the 3 of us, Dale and Sharon haggled him down a bit until Dale pulled out his trump card as he did in most things that were a little too much for him, which was an elaborate story of how he had links to an organisation in the journalistic area, and he would be writing a book when he was back home of his experiences from this travelling trip of his. Dale is very competent with his writing skills, and he had great intentions of writing a book along with mentioning all of the companies that helped him experience many different aspects of travel, just as I have in this book. It was just that at the time he had not sourced the 'links to an organisation', although I was confident this was something he would accomplish somehow, it's an uncanny knack that Dale has of falling on his feet. In the end we got him down to $300 (£115) and we were shown to our plane.

We all got into our little 4 seater more or less straight away with Dale in the front and Sharon and I in the back, in no time we were taxing down the runway for our flight that was about 30 miles from the shore. We soon climbed to 900m (3,000ft) and got a good view into the distance. As we left the land and started our flight over the ocean there was a distinct colour change in the ocean, more or less a straight line between the two, maybe where the ocean got deeper. We passed over several small islands, one of which was Whale Island that I thought looked more like the Loch Ness Monster. After a short while I could see White Island in the distance, sitting in the middle of the ocean, as you approach you can't really get an idea on how big it is, but as we got closer I could see it was quite big, it was actually 1.2 miles in diameter with the highest peak at 321m (1,053ft). It's almost round with a few parts jutting out, there's a large crater in the middle with water in it with a ridge on 3 sides. I couldn't help thinking it could be a villains lair, and that water was just a cleverly designed roof that could slide open to expose his base, where a few helicopters would be sitting ready to take on any good guys that would be coming to foil their plan to take over the world. Back to reality it really was an active volcano, in fact it's one of approximately 452 volcanoes in the Ring of Fire that circles the world in a 25,000 mile horseshoe shape. You can see the presence of the sulphur seeping into the sea where there was a yellow sandy colour snaking its way out to sea, the water in the middle of it was also steaming, another reminder that it is active. At the booking office for the boat trip there were many photos of the hike on the volcano showing how hostile it is, it had been mined several times for the sulphur, the last time being in 1923. It still has machinery rusting away and suffering from the effects of the sulphuric atmosphere, a tractor stood as an example of this, the sulphur had stripped all the rubber off it, revealing the steel banding from the tyres loosely hung around the rims with no trace of the rubber whatsoever. There was also no casing on any of the wires so there were hundreds of strands of copper, green with corrosion strung all over it. It also showed pictures of some of the people hiking, one person at the end of the trip had taken off his backpack to clearly show much darker lines on his t-shirt where the straps had been, the sulphur had eaten away at the dye at the parts it could get to, in a way I was glad I didn't go on the hike, if it can do that to a t-shirt in a few hours and disintegrate rubber, who knows what it would do to your lungs.

After circling the volcano a few times the pilot said he'd fly over the centre of it to show us how the heat and thermals from White Island would affect the plane. We headed for the centre of it and the plane started shaking and bouncing about a little, "It can get a lot worse than that!" we got from the pilot. Dales face started to look a little disconcerted. "I'll make another pass and get a bit lower." The pilot said with an excited grin, which was the opposite reaction to Dales facial expression. Dale has never been a great flyer, as with most people who share this fear, it's not actually the fear of flying, it's the fear of crashing, if the plane's engines had failed at a dizzying height then flying is much more favourable. So we got lower still and passed over the volcano's hot centre with much more dramatic results, the plane shook quite violently bouncing back and forth with creaks and groans coming from every item that was attached to the plane, it was probably the most fun the pilot gets on his day to day flights, or maybe it was just payback and thought he'd shit us up for knocking him down $150 (£57) on the flight. We circled a few more times and we were on our way back, I had been quite excited about seeing this volcano and took over 100 pictures of it. As we approached the airstrip the pilot said, "I'm going to land on the grass, it prolongs the life of the tyres." as I said already, Dale isn't the best of passengers in a plane and I think he was probably still a little flustered from the erratic flight path over the volcano, we started our decent to the grass next to the tarmac, Dale was starting to fidget with his trouser leg whilst nervously babbling onto the pilot, as we got lower Dale was getting a little more frantic and was starting to roll his trouser leg up in an irrational way, until it was as far as possible up his thigh as we touched the grass and bumped to a stop.

We left for Otorohanga and stopped at *Woolworths* to get fruit for breakfast and then to a Chinese for curry a dinner. We thought the reason for us being so tired was because we were not resting properly at night being cramped up in the car, so decided it would be a good idea to try the tent out that we'd been lugging about in the hope of getting some decent sleep, in a position much more like laying down. We found a campsite that was quite small, it had pitches on either side with an office at the end, kitchen and bathroom, and no camp manager. Great we thought, we might just get a free nights camping. We pitched our tent, had our meal and spent the rest of the evening drinking beer and eating chocolate biscuits. We got into our little tent and in our sleeping bags for what I thought was going to be a good nights sleep.

Miles driven - 185

Tuesday 8th March.

Breny's philosophies in life:
Like the boy scouts, always be prepared!

I learnt a valuable lesson this morning, what I thought was going to be a good nights sleep ended up being the worst I have ever had. The first thing was I had no sleeping matt, which meant not only could I feel every lump in the ground, I also lost most of the heat from my body, I'm surprised I didn't get hypothermia! I must have got about 1 hour of broken sleep, I was so tired in the night, that when I did sleep I fell so deeply that I had several weird dreams. Not only did I have to deal with being freezing cold and seriously uncomfortable, somewhere behind the campsite there was a duck that I'm sure knew of my predicament and was laughing at me as it quacked all night, adding to my difficulty in sleeping.

We crawled out of our torture tent at 7am, took it down and hung it up to dry out while we showered, there was still no camp manager so I thought it would be a good idea to be as quick as I could. I came out and started the car for a quick get away, several minutes past, before Sharon came out, a few more minutes past and Dale emerged, leisurely wandering to the car, swinging his wash bag without a care in the world, "Come on get in the bloody car." I said hurriedly, he still didn't seem to bothered as he got in the car, not until we pulled up at where we had hung the tent to stuff into the car, when the camp manager pulled in behind us boxing us in. It cost us $8.50 (£3.26) each for an awful night, but he did give us some vouchers to get some money off for the Kiwi House, which we found out was behind the campsite. Sharon and I decided we'd take a look at the native bird as we hadn't had much luck in seeing one in the wild as they are nocturnal, we saw two of them in the indoor enclosure, it's kept dark in the day, so they're awake, and both were wandering around. They're a very strange bird, and relatively small, a ball of feathers on legs, with a pointy beak. One of them was quite old for a Kiwi, it looked a little scraggy with most of its feathers standing up on end with almost blonde highlights. They had named it Rod Stewart. Outside there was a duck pond and one particular angry duck with a distinctive quack, not only did it want to attack me, I'm sure it was the one from the night before that kept me awake. It's a good job it was so cranky not allowing me to get near it, otherwise I would have rung its neck! There was also a huge aviary, with lots of strange birds of prey, it was very high which gave the birds a good deal of room to fly about in.

Next was a 27 mile drive to Waitomo caves, a cave complex, which was formed from limestone at the bottom of the sea some 30 million years ago. There were many stalagmites and stalactites in various shapes, which were 1000s of years old. The most memorable thing here was the amount of glow-worms hanging from the ceiling of the caves, they looked more like LED lights.

The next stop was a further 90 miles to Taupo, which brought our mileage that day to 120 miles, I slept most of the way which isn't surprising because of how little sleep I had.

The first point of interest was a natural spring that was cascading down a small waterfall, into a shallow pond about 6m (20ft) across, before it ran down over a few rocks into a fairly fast moving stream. We managed to spend two hours here with a lot of the time talking to some nice German and Norwegian people. The small pond was nice and warm, as warm as you'd expect a Jacuzzi until a cocky little kid came along saying he could stop our nice warm bathing. "Yeah right." was my reply, with that the kid disappeared above us momentarily to where the waterfall was and then popped his head back up overlooking us, "There you go." He said carrying on his cocky attitude and then pissed off, then it did turn cold. The little shit really had done it! I went up to investigate to find a small stream from where the hot water was coming out of the ground, winding its way past our waterfall and disappearing off somewhere else, with a simple piece of corrugated iron and a rock which had been used to divert the hot spring water down to the river. After a minute or so of burning my hands and feet I got the hot spring water diverted back down the waterfall. I spent a little while longer soaking in this pond playing with a rock that floated, and feeling good about myself, that I was the one that had revived the hot spring, which I wasn't going to mention as it was my comment that resulted in it getting diverted and enjoyed my little ego boost. The rest of the time we spent in the river, it too was warm at the shore but unfortunately there were people who didn't care too much for protecting this environment, as there was litter laying around everywhere and Dale stood on a piece of broken glass, but managed somehow not to cut himself. It probably came from the likes of one chap who had been there that day with his girlfriend to drink beer, and thought the best way to dispose of the bottles was to sink them, then push them into the riverbed. Even though we were in the river, it was warm from the spring near the bank, as long as you stand in front of the little cascade of water that comes over the rocks. It's a strange sensation standing in a stream with the front of you really warm while your back is cold from the river. The German people got out a little before us and dried off on the high bank by the river, I was nicely surprised by the German girl who decided to strip naked, as she finished drying herself, she had a big stretch for everyone to see. Of course I alerted Dale right away as he was totally oblivious of what was going on, and for the record, not all German girls are hairy and don't shave.

We dried off and went back to the car that was next to the assault course, so Dale and I had to prove who was the most manly, something we do quite often, it's what guys generally do but we do it for fun. The most exciting part was the zip line that was some 100m (328ft) long it was even more fun when Dale and I went two up on it. We went into town for a meal at an Irish pub and as it was Irish I thought I'd try Guinness again and actually enjoyed it this time. After a stop at the internet café, which had the worlds slowest connection, we went back to the assault course to sleep as it was quiet and out of the way.

Wednesday 9th March.

We got up late at 8:40am, well I did, the other two were in no way enthusiastic to get up, we went to a super market for breakfast and was pleased to see they had free refills on the filter coffee. After getting all hyped up on caffeine we headed up Desert Road through *Tongarire National Park* to see the tallest mountain in the north island, it's an active volcano called Mt Ruapehu, which stands at 2,797m (9,177ft). We stopped on the way up to see Raukawa falls, which had about a 15m (50ft) drop and was surrounded by lots of greenery, it was a couple of hundred metres from the road as we peered at it through the tall trees. We carried on to the top of our mountain, but as we ascended, it got duller and mistier, we realized we were driving into the clouds as it started raining until we got as far up as we could. We really couldn't see a thing, visibility was only about 30m (100ft) at best, so we snapped a quick picture of us there and headed back down.

Dale drove back down out of the clouds, into daylight and onto Wanganui where we parked up and went in search of a pub for the evening, after passing by 2 expensive ones we found a more reasonable establishment. After a few Jack Daniels it was time to let a bit out, I was so surprised at what I saw I had to go back and get my camera, not something I usually take into the gents, but the toilets had something that was very much like a cattle grid in front of the urinals, it was a good 2 foot deep and the width of the line of urinals, makes you wonder how bad a shot the locals are. Walking a bit further in search of food we found *The Celtic Pub* with all you can eat pizza, and we really did eat all we could while playing on the round pool table with a few more drinks. We thought we were going to be here a while so we parked the car in a secluded corner of *Woolworths* car park bringing our mileage that day to 214, however we got thrown out at 10:30pm despite the board outside saying they were open until 1am, maybe it was because of the amount of pizza we were eating. Either way we were so full we had to lie down in the car for 30 minutes before we moved on. We found a club called *The Buzz Bar*, we were told if you wear a hat you get a free drink, didn't we look a bunch of walleys, when the person on the door looked at us blankly with an expression of bewilderment at such a question. We went upstairs to the *Moda Bar*, where I carried on drinking Jack Daniels, at only 20 cents more for a double, how could you refuse. The music really wasn't to our tastes but we danced all the same, the floor was mostly full of coloured people and it was very much more their type of music. The big hooped earring girls were doing the arse shake and shallow squat dance, with a sorta sideways look at each other, which we had no chance of being able to replicate, so we were just jumping around a bit instead and having fun, after we'd realised this was going to be what we were going to hear all night, Sharon thought it was time she made a request for guns and roses, a little while later it came on and all three of us cheered while the rest groaned, one girl actually slapped me on the arm at her disgust with our song choice. Within 20 seconds, everyone except us had vacated the dance floor at least we didn't have the problem of bumping into the big sticky out bum dancing. As soon as our song was over they resumed the same music for the rest of the night and turned down any other request from us. We left in the early hours and got to bed at *Woolworths* at about 3am.

Thursday 10th March.

Dale woke us up at about 10am thinking that we were getting towed, it was actually the manager from *Woolworths* knocking on the window, I'm not sure if he thought we looked unconscious, and was just checking we were alright. We got breakfast there before going into town, as we drove there I thought all the towns looked the same in New Zealand so you tend to forget which one you are in. We stopped in a betting shop for coffee and to write up our diaries, I thought it would be a good idea to check the rest of my airline tickets at this point with Dale and Sharon's, and I'm glad I did as I was missing the ticket from Hong Kong to Singapore, we also worked out how long we would be in each country so we could change our flight dates. There was nothing else to do here so we took the 124 mile drive to New Zealand's capital, Wellington, the most southern point of the north island, and where we would catch the ferry to the south island. We took a drive up to Mount Victoria lookout, it overlooks the sea and most of Wellington, it was a good view but after getting blown about for a while we went to a hostel where Martin had left a few of Dales things he'd borrowed, Martin had originally started the trip with Dale and Sharon but was finding it a little slow paced for him, and decided to go ahead alone. I also purchased a YMCA card here for $40 (£15), it's like a discount card that would get me money off several things like attractions, train and bus tickets. It did save me a small fortune in the end.

We thought we'd find dinner and watch a film to while away the evening. We parked up near to the cinema, got out and watched a guy rather awkwardly back into the space and into the front of our car, we all saw what was going to happen and shouted to him to stop, but he hit the front of our car anyway bending the number plate, he staggered out and it was quite apparent why he'd managed to reverse straight into us, by the inability to stand upright and the vague look on his face. It was a steel plate so I straightened it out and fortunately that was all the damage he done. After he staggered off probably in search of another bar I should've slashed is tyres. We found a chippy then went on to the lovely old looking cinema, the screen was small and only seated about 50 people but was very cosy. the film we watched was '*The Motorcycle Diaries*'. There were a handful of people there and even though it had subtitles, I very much enjoyed the film. Based on a true story in 1952, where a 23 year old man and his friend, take themselves on a trip through south America covering 1000s of miles, initially by motorcycle. The lead character discovers himself by his observation.

After the film it was getting late, we found a quiet street and parked up at the end for the night.

Miles driven - 170

Chapter 4
New Zealand. South Island.

Friday 11th March.

I got Dale and Sharon up at 7:30am, I'd been cold most of the night as it had been raining for most of it. I found out there was a *Quantus Airline* agent in Wellington so stopped in there to change the dates on the flights, when I booked them they gave me random dates on each flight and was told I would have to stop in a place like this to change them. I wasn't able to get my missing ticket here as the one in question was with *Thai Airlines*.

We had breakfast at another nice little café that was quite posh looking and was reasonably priced, we went back to the car and realised we'd been parked there for an hour without a ticket, so we then took turns in sitting in it while we sent emails home at another one of the slowest internet café in New Zealand.

We had time for one more sight to see before the crossing, which was *Old St Paul's church*, a lovely little church with bright white walls and a bluish grey roof. The inside was just as quaint with its low ceilings and made entirely from native timbers, the wooden interior was made much more vibrant by the red carpet. The beams that seemed to occupy every part of the roof space had some beautiful engraved wooden plaques, with stained glass windows that enhanced the already glowing interior. *Old St Paul's* is a fine example if 19th century Gothic Revival architecture. The church was built on land bought by Bishop Selwyn in Mulgrave Street in 1845, augmented with a Crown grant of Māori reserve from Governor Grey in 1853, with the church being completed and consecrated in 1866 after just one year of construction, and would be the second Anglican church in the area.

We picked Dale up and boarded the ferry, a massive catamaran with 4 huge jets that sprayed the water a hundred metres or so out the back to propel us along, it really was powerful, as we seemed to be getting a fair bit of speed up. Sharon and I had a drink in the bar, while Dale went back to the car to get his mini disc player. I was amazed at how the waitress could not only keep her balance as she poured our drinks as we skipped across the waves, but also how she didn't get nauseous by looking down and concentrating on the glass without spilling a drop. We stood in the bar pretending we were on a surf board, and by this time we were well into the crossing so it was a lot more choppy, you could feel it jarring your legs in all directions, one was so violent I nearly fell over. We headed to the back of the boat where it would be smoother where we bumped into Dale after his trip below deck, I have never seen anyone look so green before, of course my first instinct was to laugh at the state he looked, "I really think I'm gonna chuck!" was his greeting to me, I think he thought alcohol would make him feel better, as he was grasping a pint. What made him feel so ill was when he went bellow deck to where the cars were parked, there are no windows so you can't see the horizon and this will play tricks on you as your ears will be telling you one thing, but your eyes will not see this movement and make you feel sick, also the further forward you get the more you will feel the waves. Dale had been walking back as we hit a wave, probably the same one that made me nearly lose my balance, it actually sent him into the air. His green gills soon became their normal brown tan look when he got to the back with us.

When we got a little closer to shore and started our approach into the bay, that still took quite some time, we slowed to about a quarter of the speed so we found another higher up open deck where we could see more of the horizon. We were entering the south island with high rolling hills on either side quite some distance from the boat covered in vegetation. The skies were mostly clear with a few wispy clouds, we trundled on leaving two massive tracks behind us from the motors that stretch at least a mile behind us. It was picturesque and serene, this was another time I would take in the view and appreciate what I was seeing, watching the world go by.

Back on dry land I drove the rest of the way to Nelson, I think Dale had been quite traumatized by the crossing as he'd had a few drinks on board and got me to stop at a supermarket so he could get more beer, while Sharon and I got a chocolate éclair. We wound our way to Nelson, mostly along mountainsides with steep drops several hundred metres to the valley floor. I was quite horrified when the road double backed onto itself and we could see the road we had came along, I noticed a track in the greenery going from the road down the side of the mountain about 60m (200ft) or so, where the track stopped there was a car! A car pointing almost vertically down! It was so far away the car seemed like a speck, almost completely camouflaged by the overgrowth, I was so worried that there could have been someone in that car we stopped, then strained our eyes to try and see if there were any signs of life, but it was no use at that distance, I then had the great idea of using the video camera and zoomed in as far as I could, I was then able to see it had been there for some time, a neat square had been cut into the roof that was now rusting around the edges, I thought it must have been cut open to rescue the occupants. I couldn't imagine the terror you would feel going down that hill, waiting for something big to stop your decent before crashing into the valley floor.

We made it to Nelson making our mileage 127 miles for this day, we were going to meet up and stay at one of Dales friends, Simon. They had been friends for some time and he was staying in New Zealand for a year before travelling back to England, stopping off at a few places on the way. We finally found his house to find him out for the day, so we went into town to find somewhere to eat instead, Sharon and I settled for a Chinese meal, there were actually two restaurants, but Dale decided he wanted something from the other one, he was finished up before us so he took the car keys and waited in the car, a bad mistake when Dale is drunk. He did go back to the car but fell asleep in a drunken passed out fashion on the back seat. He also thought it'd be a good idea to lock the doors which made our life a lot harder waking him up when we had finished our meal. We got back to the car and tapped on the window for him to let us in, with no signs of life I knocked a bit louder, then started banging, hitting the door, rocking the car and shouting, how I didn't draw more attention to myself I don't know, I must have looked nuts abusing the car like that. He eventually came too long enough to let us in. We drove a little out of town and found a car park next to a lake to sleep the night, Sharon and I left the drunk Dale in the car and took a little wander under the still moon lit sky to the lake shore to take in the view, before we settled down for the night.

Saturday 12th March.

I was awake at 7am and ready to get going, but the other two were very unresponsive again, so I had to wait until 8:30am before they would move. After our normal cleaning of our teeth beside the car we headed into town and found a café with a revolving door for breakfast, this morning it was bacon and ham pastry, with a muffin and an Americano coffee, I loved these breakfasts!

Our first point of interest this day was the *Nelson Anglican Cathedral*. It is by far the most unique religious building I had ever seen. Walking up the slope at the front of the cathedral you're greeted by the giant doors in a wall of grey stone with 3 peaked roofs that came out only a short distance. The tower was just as unusual, at 35m (114ft) high it was not solid as most towers are, but had windows close together separated by a thin column of stone, from almost the base to the top making it totally see through. The small hill it sits on has a Maori name of *Pikimai*, meaning '*come up hither*', which I thought was an interesting coincidence. Inside the stone was just as dominating, the slabs of stone made definite edges from floor to the high ceiling that were originally going to be made entirely from marble blocks with the same intention to the exterior block. But after the *Murchison* earthquake this was deemed too risky as well as too expensive, and so the marble was ground up and made into a plaster, giving the walls this very unusual and unique appearance. It is a relatively new building as construction started in 1925 but wasn't completed until 1965. Inside the 350 seating capacity wasn't the only thing that stood out. The organ was also unusual, the 2,500 pipes stood alone towering up to nearly the ceiling on a wooden platform 2.5m (8ft) high that you're able to walk under, supported by 4 legs, The organ is spread over three manuals and pedals and has a detached electric-action console some 6m (20ft) away on a gallery opposite the pipes in the chancel, about 3m (9'9") high accessed by a spiral staircase.

We went back to Simon's house, he's a very pleasant guy and welcomed us in. After a short chat he was off out again to play rugby and we would meet again in the evening for dinner, Dale decided to go to the beach while Sharon and I found another unusual point of interest in

Nelson, The *World of Wearable Arts*, and just as unusual is that it also host a classic car section. The name of this place really is what it says, art that you wear, not only is it art but very strange art, it does amaze me what passes as art, and mugs like me will spend money to view it, and bigger mugs actually buy it! We came across one piece of art that I could have easily made in 5 minutes, it was a rectangular piece of rusting corrugated iron with the word *'through'* painted on it, that was it! Not only that, it was up for sale for a few thousand dollars! The majority of the exhibit was dedicated to clothes with several that just boggled the mind, like an outfit that resembled a chair when you were on all fours, dresses that looked like a bunch of crumpled up paper, a skin tight one the had extra long rigid arms with what appeared to be a paddle on the end, there was even one that was covered in tampons! At least the women wearing it would never be caught short with out one, maybe not a good idea to wear in the rain. We worked our way round to the car section where the oldest car was a 1906 Mercedes Benz, there was also a few American muscle cars, a mini, some rally cars and my favourite of all time, a Lamborghini Diablo. We stopped in a coffee shop before we headed back and I got to use my YMCA card for the first time, we had coffee and a filo pastry thing, and I got the coffee for free, which is something that I will always welcome.

We headed to the beach to find Dale which didn't take all that long, so we had plenty of time to take a little swim in the shallow sea for a while and then sunbath as we watched Dale trying to pull a German girl, we were there so long I ended up peeling a little from sunburn. We got back to Simons for 6pm and all went shopping so we could have a BBQ, we bought lamb, sausages, chicken, peppers and various salads between us and it was really good, I love BBQs, especially when it's cooked as well as that. We met the other girls that shared the house with Simon, one of them was not there that night and said she heard that there was a couple staying, so we could have her bed for the night. 'A bed' I thought, a good nights sleep at last. After a bottle of wine and feeling a little tipsy, we all headed out to the Victoria pub to see a duo singing to backing music, mostly old songs but they were very good, we danced for hours, I didn't feel too stupid as there were a lot of others dancing too. We then moved on to see another live band *Mean Fiddle,* which were very lively. As the night went on we were getting quite drunk and tired so decided to head back to Simon's house. The cool fresh air sobered us up a little and we started our way back, we passed 3 buildings before we came across another bar playing some fantastic rock music so Sharon dragged me in to investigate. The singer sounded a little like Ozzy Osbourne and the music was a get your blood pumping type of music. I danced until my legs ached, then watched from the bar as Sharon carried on, unbeknown to her there was a guy behind her eyeing her arse up, she was dancing a little provocatively sticking her arse out and wondered why she got it pinched, she looked around and scowled at him without a clue why he'd made a pass, I just watched and enjoyed the spectacle. It was about this time I got hit by a woman for the second time on this trip, there was a slight bump between us somehow and she actually punched me in the nuts!

    We finally got out at closing time much to my relief. I'd had more than enough excitement by this time and was looking forward to our bed. We got back to Simons and we all arrived somehow at the same time, getting to sleep soon after.

Sunday 13th March.

For some reason Dale woke us at 9:45am thinking we wanted to know that him and Simon were taking the girls home they'd pulled the night before, but we were enjoying the comfortable bed which was something we now realised we had really missed, as we had slept like a log, and didn't actually ache, so we stayed there a little longer before showering. When they got back we had a fried breakfast before Simon took us across the road to watch the local cricket match. A guy there took us in the pavilion where he showed us his generosity by giving us all two free beers at the bar. After a bit of lazing later and having a nice soaking in the sun, Simon got out a map to show us several places to visit on the south island, telling us lots of lovely places to go and some interesting attractions as he'd already travelled round much of it himself, before stopping here.

The cricket wasn't enough to keep our attention occupied all day so Sharon and I walked into town and unsurprisingly Dale stayed, probably the free beer was too much of a temptation although he only got one more beer before the owners appeared and caught on to what was happening. We visited a gallery that was small but interesting, among the pictures were also some Maori artefacts and a very memorable flute made from bone. After a leisurely coffee we took a walk down the oldest street in Nelson that has just 16 houses that were built between 1863 and 1867, they were really small as you would expect and quite close to the road.

As we couldn't find much else to do we went back to Simons and found Dale still watching the cricket, and it was quite sometime before it finished. We spent the evening back at Simon's house where we played drinking games and poker with two of the other residents, Ciya and Dover, I did exceptionally well, or I was lucky as I got the best hand of the evening with a full house at one point.

We finished the evening watching a film on TV, *John Q*, a drama with a shocking hard truth of a poor family in America with no medical insurance, who's child is in need of a heart transplant. We were quite tired and drunk by the end of the evening, but didn't have the luxury of the bed tonight as the owner was sleeping in it herself, instead we had to make do with the sofa cushions pushed together to make a bed.

Monday 14th March.

We woke up at 8:15am, feeling quite sore from the make shift bed, the cushions kept inconsiderately parting leaving us awkwardly lying with various parts on the wood flooring. We washed and had coffee at Simons before we left for our next destination.

It was a lovely drive to Kaikoura along the windy roads, past the coast and in to land, over the quaint little one car wide bridges that were old looking, with an elaborate network of wooden beams covering it which didn't seem secure enough to withstand the weight of our little car. But after a dozen or so bridges we got quite used to our fears and drove as leisurely over the bridges as the roads. I drove most of the way, Dale sat in the back with his coat over his head reading, the coat was to stop his motion sickness, he wasn't sick so it must have worked.

There isn't a lot at Kaikoura, it was cold and expensive and had two main attractions. It's by the coast, and you will find the Fyffe house. It was home to a whaler, Robert Fyffe, and was built in 1842. The house was made into a museum and hosted many whaling items with descriptions on many parts of it. The outside of the house was built on whale bones that looked like vertebrae that were used to raise the house of the ground slightly, with many other different types of bones strewn everywhere, even the gate post was made from whale bone. There was also one of the small rowing boats, which was used by Robert Fyffe himself for whaling. Inside was just as interesting, we wandered around the thin halls and low ceiling rooms looking at the many items and points of interest about whaling, as the house was made into a type of museum. There were many facts on whaling and how it was carried out, one particular old picture on the wall was of several guys standing on a sperm whale that had been killed and dragged to shore. There were sperm whale teeth with very delicate and elaborate scrimshaw engraving of large sailing ships, the detail was very impressive. Although the whole house was dedicated to killing these massive gentle creatures, I didn't feel any resentment to the whole idea of it or what it stood for. At the time when a whale was killed, most of it was used, its blubber was used for oil, the meat was eaten and as the house shows even the bones and teeth were used, yes it's a pity that such a docile creature is killed when it's minding its own business for the gain of us humans, but it's no different to you or I sitting down in McDonalds and having a *Big Mac*, cows are just as docile and we confine those animals to fields until we ship them off to be slaughtered, at least the whales got to live in their natural environment doing what whales do until they're hauled inland.

Our next stop was a seal colony where there were several of the big lumbering beasts sunning themselves, there was a distinct line on where not to go and warning signs not to cross it, so not to disturb their natural habitat. One guy thought he'd be clever and cross the line to get a close up picture of one of the seals, it started to get a little scared so several of us told him to get back, which he didn't seem too bothered about, I was just hoping that it was going to turn on him and eat a finger, something I know they are quite capable of.

Our main attraction for the next day was a boat trip to go whale watching, I was really quite excited about this one and very much looking forward to it, even though the tickets were $125 (£48) each.

The only thing cheap I could find to eat tonight was a burger and chips. After a while of sitting around writing our diaries we found a bar with some live music, it was one guy with an acoustic 12 string guitar, it was pretty good too, except for being a little tinny. We parked up at the whale watching boat trip car park for the night and had travelled 175 miles this day, I was still quite excited about the morning and was threatened by Dale and Sharon that I'd get tranquillised, not only this day but they thought I was too lively and was wearing them out, I was lively because I was finding everything so new and exciting and it showed, they themselves most probably were in a similar state of excitement when they first started 6 months before I did.

Tuesday 15th March.

I thought sleeping in the car park for the boat trip would mean that we wouldn't be late, and we weren't, but we did wake up late at 7:30am and had only 15 minutes to get in and have something to eat, I had a sausage pastry thing that the waitress forgot about and had left it in the microwave, I'd just finished eating when we were called for the bus. It was a short drive to where we would catch the boat, a twin hulled boat powered by two jets which allowed us to motor across the water at about 27 knots (31mph). We would be looking for sperm whales, and as we were seemingly wandering aimlessly across the water we had a very informative tour guide filling us full of facts about whales, many of which I had forgotten by the end of the trip. There were several screens inside showing us where we were, speed, directing as well as the depth of the water. The reason why you can view sperm whales here so close to the shore, is because it's one of very few places where the depth reaches 1,200m (3,937ft). The guides talk got cut short after 10 minutes as our first whale was spotted. I didn't know what to expect and what we saw was the long grey back of the whale poking out of the water, there is actually only 10% of the whale showing while the big animal floats and lumbers about in one place while it catches its breath, to dive down and do what whales do in the depths of the ocean. It sat there for a while then started to blow the odd puff of air out of its blowhole turning into a high jet of spray. Its head would then take a slow but definite dip into the water which then turned into a vertical decent, with a elegant arch of its back which looked like we were watching in slow motion, its massive tale then rose out of the water which glistened as a small waterfall fell off the end of it, as like the rest of the whale that too became vertical and slipped into the water as silently as the rest of the animal, as it disappeared into the ocean. The first swipe of its tale produces the equivalent to 300hp that leaves a foot print on the surface in the shape of a large circle that makes a definite calm spot, that can be seen for quite some time after the whale is far below the surface. We saw 5 whales in all, they usually see 1 or 2 and there is no guarantee that you could see any! With each sighting came more boats and also the odd plane circling above, we would view the whale from behind so they couldn't see us, as they have been know to smash boats.

After the whales we took a cruise around a group of rocks to see some seals basking in the sun, which we got fairly close to, but they didn't seem to bothered and carried on sleeping. On the way back they spotted about a hundred dusky dolphins merrily jumping out of the water, so we headed over to get a closer look. We really could not have got any closer as we neared them we were surrounded by the happy creatures as they swam under the boat. The guide told us how clever dolphins are, like how they will pay more attention to pregnant women, knowing they are pregnant even before the woman knows herself, they can also be a nuisance to divers as the dolphins know it's unnatural for humans to breathe underwater, and they try to push them to the surface, they have also been known to help injured people to shore. At this point Dale was getting a little excited about swimming with the dolphins, but I managed to talk him out of jumping in to swim with them, so as we headed back we agreed to drive round to where they were so Dale and Sharon could swim out to them.

We got back and drove around to where they were, parked up in a camp sight by the beach and I nervously watched Dale and Sharon swim out towards them. I didn't join them as there was no way I would make it out that far without drowning as I'm not a strong swimmer, I can swim well for a short distance but I have to exert so much energy to keep my head above water. It was a long way out, and as they got further out I got more concerned. It must have been getting on for 300m (984ft), before they got to the dolphins. Sharon turned back before she got to them from exhaustion, but Dale carried on until he was in the middle of them. A boat full of passengers, probably another tourist cruise sailed past him, it looked like he could touch them he was that close. After quite sometime, Dale made it back and was looking very exhausted in the 50m (160ft) or so from shore, usually I'm not too worried about his swimming abilities, but on this occasion I was thinking I was going to have to jump in to rescue him. I had done this once before for him when we were teenagers when he was swimming in the local river when he got cramp and went under the water. My rescuing attempt that day when I jumped in after him was to pull him out by his hair. Fortunately today he made it to shore by his own accord and I helped him out of the water, the cold and the long swim had drained him quite considerably but he did get close to the dolphins, within an arms length, they have this thing where they will always just keep out of your reach. We made use of the camp showers, which was a treat, as the last shower we had was at Simons a few days before I went back to the car to find Dale still shivering with the engine running and the heater on full.

We then left to visit *Hanmer Springs* in Hanmer, it's a much more commercialised public bath with the hottest pool at 41°c (106°f) and the coolest at 26°c (79°f) it's an open air pool and the water seemed just like a normal swimming pool that was tiled with only a hint of an eggy smell, as the heated water is sourced from a bore hole close to the complex. The largest pool was a least 25m (82ft) long so you could have a proper swim, the others were separated by bridges and walkways with some large rocks round them and even in the middle of them, with plenty of greenery making it feel very natural, it was very nicely done. We also enjoyed the waterslide there, Dale did his story bit of the writing thing again to get a free wristband to go on this water slide, that Sharon and I didn't pay the extra few dollars for, I think there were a lot of others who thought it was a little too much as we were the only ones on it on it. He managed to get it off with minimal damage so we swapped it between the 3 of us and all had a few goes.

We left here with Dale driving to Oxford as I dozed in the back, I think it was all that relaxing in the hot thermal water that had made me so tired, by the time we got there it was getting late covering 213 miles this day, we found a little gravel track to park up on for the night.

Chapter 5
On without Dale.

Wednesday 16th March.

    We were up about 8:30am, drove into town and found a bakery with some lovely ladies serving, who didn't charge me to warm my muffin. We got back to the car and Dale was looking a little serious and told us how he was getting short of money and was worried he wouldn't have enough to finish the trip, so he wanted to do some casual work in Christchurch. We weren't far from Christchurch and it would be where we would fly out from to go to the next country on the list, Australia. We tried to talk him out of it, I told him that I'd come on this trip to travel together and would miss him, but his mind was set on staying in Christchurch, and if he needed the money that bad I wasn't going to persuade him any further. We took the short detour to drop Dale off, while we were there Sharon had to find a doctors to get a typhoid injection, and she'd had a little eye problem that turned out to be just a slight irritation.

    So after Sharon shooting up and getting some eye drops we were on our own and on our way to Arthur's Path, a road that wound it's way from the east coast to the west coast, through mountains where we saw some beautiful views of valleys, hills and open fields that had several big rocks strewn over them. We made a stop in the middle of *Arthur's Path* to have a look at The *Devils Punchbowl*, which was a half hour walk from the road. It was a nice hike to the waterfall, it looked like some one had taken a big axe and put a dent in the 15m (50ft) high mountain range, where a torrent of water was flooding out to a bunch of rocks and a small pool at the bottom of its drop. There was a nice viewing platform to get a good look at this and for some reason it was fenced off, so you couldn't get within 9m (30ft) of it. There wasn't any reason that I could see for this, apart from the odd boulder you could turn your ankle on, there didn't seem to be any loose rocks or a cliff or holes you could fall down, so I hopped over the fence to get that all important dramatic shot of it, which I managed quite well except for getting a little bit of moisture on the camera, which would later on cause condensation on the inside of the lens, leading to an annoying small spot that would show up on every picture I took towards the sun, this would end up costing me £100 back home to get it fixed, at least I was pleased with the picture of the waterfall!

We carried on our journey to Ross, a small mining town that would be the end of our drive for this day and covering 240 miles by the time we got there. Our drive through the mountains became less exciting as it started to rain, the only other interesting thing was a water fall over the road, water was coming down the mountain and instead of going across the road, it was intercepted by a type of bridge in the form of large guttering that carried it over the road and shot it out down the mountain.

We only made one more stop on the way for dinner in a town that I have no idea what it was called, it was another nameless town like countless others we had passed. It was a pub advertising cheap food outside on a chalkboard. It was a lovely little quiet pub with very few people in where I enjoyed a rump steak special for $12.50 (£4.80). After the meal we were the only ones left, the landlord and the bar man played us at doubles, and best of all, the pool was free. We probably stayed a little later than we usually would have, but we didn't have to be anywhere anytime soon so it was a nice evening. Sharon drove the rest of the way with the only interesting sight in the dark was a thin bridge that also had railroad tracks.

We got to Ross late, and by this time it had finally stopped raining, we parked by the beach as we could usually find a secluded car park where we wouldn't be disturbed, before going to sleep we took a very dark walk along the beach.

Thursday 17th March.

We got up at 9am and took another walk along the beach, I was surprised we didn't break a leg when we took our night time walk when we arrived, as the beach was littered with deadwood. We drove into town for breakfast where I had a steak and cheese pie. We then did some research about the history of Ross to find it had extracted some $700 million (£269 million) in gold with a further $48 million (£18.5 million) under the town waiting to be mined. We went on the *Water Race Walk*, a little walk that took us a few hours passing by the old mining part of the town, past some old small shacks made from corrugated iron which hadn't been lived in for a long time and had only the bare essentials. The path wound on through the trees, up and down hills until we came to the top looking down onto Ross, as it's known today. There is still evidence of recent mining as there was an extremely large open mine, that covered several hundred square metres but was now filled with water. On the way back down we walked past a stream that you could find gold in, so Sharon and I spent some time looking very carefully in the bottom of the stream to see if we could get lucky. We didn't find any but we did meet a couple that had spent 4 days panning for gold and had accumulated enough to buy their wedding rings.

We drove onto *Fox Glacier* to book tickets for the next day, at $270 (£103) each for a ski plane to the top of the glacier, which was something I was very excited about. We then drove onto *Franz Josef Glacier* to take a two and a half hour walk to the foot of the glacier. Long before you get to the car park you pass several signs saying, 'in this year the glacier was here'. When we saw the first one, we thought we must have been close, but it still took us a surprising amount of time to get there. We parked up and took our leisurely walk to the glacier, passing greenery that turned into rocks and small waterfalls, we finally came to the end of the path, to a massive opening where over 1000s of years the glacier had cut a path in the landscape several hundred metres wide, it looked more like a dried riverbed, grey and scattered with rocks. In the distance we could see the bright white glacier that turned to black at the bottom of its long slow trek to the foot of the glacier, where it had picked up dirt and rocks as it rolled back and forth so very slowly. We walked onwards to the face of the glacier until we were as far as we could get, it was fenced off for our safety, as a glacier is always moving, being pushed down from the weight of the snow from the top. Large sections can give way at anytime resulting in boulders of ice the size of a car to crash down, this was quite evident by the car sized boulders sitting on their own a few metres in front of the face of the glacier, it would make a hefty dent in your head if it landed on you as the face stood about 9m (30ft) high. There weren't many people around so we decided to hop the fence ignoring the warning signs saying *'extreme danger'* in big capital letters to get a much closer look, I know it was stupid and dangerous but it wouldn't be any fun if we always obeyed the rules and it also makes for a much more exciting adventure, other wise this section would have read: *Walked up to the glacier, took some pictures, then walked back again.* We wanted to see the glacier up close and that's what we did, I walked right up to the face and actually touched it, I got such a feeling of how big it was, I felt so small and insignificant compared to this monster of ice that not even solid rock can stop, you can't believe that ice, which is nothing more than frozen water can actually cut a massive trench like that in the ground. I stood beside one of the fallen boulders of ice that was nearly as tall as me for a picture, before we ventured along the face to where water was flowing out from underneath it, this is part of the never ending cycle of a glacier, snow falls at the top and it melts away at the bottom and it moves forward slowly, the speed of the flow changes depending on the temperature in the summer and the amount of snow that falls at the top in the winter. It was about this time when we heard a bone-chilling crack of ice, it had a deep resonance that sort of echoed for a while and it was a sound that meant business, a sound that made you fully aware that something on a large scale had happened, Sharon instantly ran away murmuring a startled 'Oh shit', to the comfort and safety of the other side of the fence, I thought it was a better idea not to run blindly and looked up, my thought was that if a car sized lump of ice was to fall, I would see it lumbering down and then decide which way to run. As it happened there were only a few small pieces of ice that gently came tumbling down so I strolled out and joined Sharon.

    We took the walk back to the car park and then onto another walk that took us in a loop, ending you up where you started. We first passed *Peter's Pool* which was in all the guide books, which usually accompanied a picture of this dead still pool with the reflection of the snow capped mountains and the *Franz Josef Glacier* in the distance, I attempted to recreate this picture, which didn't turn out all that bad with just a few ripples on the pond. The walk then carried us on through woodland tracks and streams and over a suspended footbridge that turned out to be quite wobbly, which we exploited, seeing how far we could rock back and forth. After this excitement the rest of the walk turned out to be a little boring as we passed tree after tree through the woodland before we got back to the car park.

We drove back to town and went to the *Alice May* pub where we had dinner, I got a great bargain of chicken nugget and chips for $8.50 (£3.26). We heard of a band playing at the *Franz Josef hotel*, which really wasn't a band and only consisted of 1 guy and a backing taping, that he was singing to very badly. It wasn't too long before we made our way back to the *Alice May* where I had a cigar and endured a pint of Guinness which is a drink I'm not that fond of, but for some reason keep trying in the event I would really enjoy it one day and besides it was *St Patrick's day* so I thought I'd endure it for the sake of this day, I found out that I liked it a little more this time than the last time I drank it, I didn't actually spit it out. We whiled away the rest of the evening talking, watching the sunset and looking across the beautiful landscape where we could make out the white trail of the glacier we had visited that day in the distance.

We found a little un-occupied spot at the end of a road where we spent the night.

Miles driven - 142

Friday 18th March.

We were up at 7:30am and were pleased to be greeted by glorious sunshine, so we would be able to take the ski plane flight to *Fox Glacier*. However our first priority was to find the toilets. There are certain places you can't just crawl out of your car after a nights sleep to hang a leak, and this was one of them. We soon found a café, ordered coffee and muffin and took turns in using the toilet. When backpacking, toilets such as these aren't just used for what you'd expect, I quite often used toilets like these to have an all over wash, and to clean my teeth, this was one of those days.

We made our way to the runway for 9am and stood beside the little well kept tarmac runway waiting for our ski plane. Sometimes in life you're standing somewhere surround by lovely scenery minding your own business, watching time go by when something quite weird and unusual will happen that leaves you blinking in disbelief and a little speechless, this happened to me on this day. The quiet countryside was broken by the sound of a helicopter in the distance. A spec appeared with something dangling beneath it. As it got closer we could see that the object was some type of large mountain goat, dead, suspended by a rope around its neck. The helicopter landed on a little concrete pad 15m (50ft) from us that had a fuel pump at one corner. The pilot got out of his chopper, leaving the engine running and proceeded to casually fill it up with the high octane, and highly combustible fuel, he then gets back in and flies off into the distance and out of sight.

A short while later our pilot arrived, a very mellow chap who obviously enjoyed getting paid to fly people around this beautiful landscape. A short while later we took off and climbed rather rapidly, heading to the coast which wasn't far at all, we banked round and came to a channel that had been carved into the landscape a few hundred metres across, it had several shallow rivers that snaked their way from a glacier in the distance to the sea, crisscrossing each other as they went. We headed up the river onto round *Franz Josef Glacier* before we headed onto *Fox Glacier*. We followed several different snow covered peeks, banking several times to get a good look at scenery before we would get to the top of the glacier. We came to a massive wide clearing, it was at this point I had a type of realization that I had never had before, I saw a spec appear out of nothing to the side of this clearing but didn't take much notice, we seemed to be taking forever to land, feeling like we were at a snails pace when in reality we were probably travelling near to 100mph. We were fairly high above the glacier so I put it down to that, but as we got a little closer, and the spec got a little larger I could make out what it was, it really was a shock when I realized this spec was a helicopter that had brought some other tourist to see the sights. It was astounding as to just how big this was that we were going to land on. I found out some years later after researching it for this book, that the reason it seemed so big is because the glacier is actually 8 miles long! As we descended we flew past the helicopter getting ever closer to the snow and had a surprisingly gentle and smooth landing, the engine was cut and we got out onto the crisp snow. We were about 2600m (1.6 miles) above sea level, with the base of the glacier only 300m (984ft) above sea level, making this the only glacier in the world at this latitude to be so unusually close to the sea, ending its trek among lush green vegetation. It was more like ice we were standing on so you don't sink into it to much, the second thing I noticed is that it's quiet, not just quiet in a library quiet, but you're outside, there were no sounds of birds, insects, or the obvious, leaves rustling in the breeze, it was just eerily quiet. The only concept you have of the wind is the noise it makes in your ears. This was another one of those times in my travels that I felt humbled by the world, at this simple landscape, I felt so young and small compared to this 18,000 year old glacier that was left behind by the last ice age. The pilot told us not to wander off to far as there are some very deep crevasses, some of which are covered with snow and we wouldn't know they were there until it was to late. After about ten minutes we were back in the plane and on our way back to the airstrip. The pilot took us along another scenic route back along ridges and crevasses, some of these crevasses you could easily loose the plane in they were that big. We saw a group of people on a trek all tied together, making their way to a little hut on one of the rocky ridges. The whole flight was an experience that will forever be firmly imprinted in my mind and well worth it, there were several activities I did on this trip that I thought to myself, 'I don't care how hard it is to do or how much it cost, I was going to do it', I didn't want to have any regrets on anything I passed up for either of those two reasons.

Arriving back at our little airstrip we then headed south stopping at Haast for lunch, a very bare and desolate town with the mountains being the only great view to look at. We then continued south on *Haast Pass* where there were various sightseeing stops that we found out about thanks to the *Lonely Planet* guide book.

Roaring Billy Falls was the first stop, a short trek from the road, we came to an opening like a lake bed covered in white rocks, at the other side a high water fall that was not all that wide at the top, but cascaded down over many rocks and fanned out to some 30m (100ft) wide. The water at the bottom ended in a considerably large pool that was an unbelievable vibrant blue.

The next stop a little further along the road was *Thunder Creek*, another long, thin waterfall that accumulated into a rocky pool, then making its way down a gentle decent of boulders and into the far distance among the trees, which was more like a forest as it stretched as far as I could see. I guess the water was so blue and untainted, as we were in the middle of nowhere with very little civilization around. A little further and we came to the *Blue pools*, so named as these were the bluest waters we had seen, as it was so clear we could easily see fish swimming about. Then onto another waterfall, *Fantail Falls*, this waterfall idly rolled over a wall of rocks in the middle of a tree covered cliff face.

We carried on the *Haast Highway*, which neatly cut through the middle of two lakes, *Lake Wanake* and *Lake Hawea*, which like the rest of the day were very picturesque. Our final destination for the day bringing our mileage for the day to 196 miles was Wanaka, a little town where not much happened except for a lot of restaurants that charged way to much to the likes of us. We did however sniff out a bargain at *Shooters Bar*, themed with guns in front of all the pumps and lots of sexy posters of ladies in the toilets, which incidentally I thought was a little strange as I don't associate anything sexy in a toilet, neither did I want to be getting aroused when I needed to relieve myself.

After our spare ribs and pizza we went to the *Paradise Cinema*, Dales friend Simon who we had met in Nelson had told us of a few places to go and sights to see, this cinema was one of them, all he said was it's definitely worth going to and that it was very unusual, so our inquisitiveness got the better of us and we bought tickets to see *Touching*

The Void. A true story of two British climbers and their journey up the west face of the *Siuala Grande* in the Peruvian Andes in 1985, one of the climbers slips and is left dangling by the rope that is attached to his friend, dangling in a deep crevasse. After being in this hopeless position for some time, without being able to pull him up, with the other not being able to climb up, the rope is cut before they were both pulled to their deaths. If you want to know how it turns you'll just have to watch the film. The cinema really was unique, the foyer reminded me more of a village hall, we bought the tickets and a drink that came in a mug, not only that, every mug was different. We went and found our seats to find that the whole seating arrangement was as random as the mugs, there were sofas, arm chairs, deckchairs, airline seats and even a beetle car with some comfy seats, we chose a nice comfy sofa that we sank into like a bowl of jelly. The film really was good and will be well remembered for a long time, quite fitting because of where we had been for the past two days.

After the film we found a nice quiet car park by *Lake Wanaka* and went to sleep looking over the still water.

Saturday 19th March.

I woke to a morning as still as when I went to sleep, it was very relaxing just waking up and looking over a calm still lake early in the morning. A short while later I was sitting there writing up an email on my laptop, when I noticed a little figure come into view in the middle of the lake. He swam across quite effortlessly and out of sight then a little later came back again. We went in search of breakfast and Sharon had the biggest cup of coffee, it looked like it was served up in a bowl! We then went onto *Stuart Landsborough's Puzzling World*. As the name implies it's full of puzzling things. You're greeted at the gate with a clock tower balancing on one corner at 45 degrees. We entered the foyer, which had several tables filled with mind teasing puzzles, the kind that you have to fit several different shapes into a square, or separate two pieces of metal that's been twisted into a near impossible shape. After an annoying hour and a half we entered and decided to spend another hour and 15 minutes walking around the Great Maze. It was a large rectangle with strategically placed fence panels that wound its way back and forth to create a challenge, to which you have to find your way around the 4 corners, with which I'd like to point out we finished in an average time. We eventually went inside to marvel at all the mind boggling sights, a large portion was dedicated to rooms that were at various angles to trick your mind, you were in a straight room, basically the floor was at an angle different to the walls and there would be something that was level, like the pool table room, there was also a tap running down a chute that seemed to flow upwards. The pictures we took this day do not give the illusion anywhere near what we felt like while walking round, it even made me feel a little sick as my eyes were being tricked to what was level so they were getting confused with my ears, it has a similar effect as to why you get sea sick.

Further into the attraction we visited the toilets, now I wouldn't usually write about a visit to the toilet, although I have already mentioned 2 other of my visits so far in this book, except for this one was a little more disconcerting than my usual visits, I was glad I didn't need a sit down visit as the seats were made of a clear resin with which they had barbed wire and razor blades carefully inserted through out them. The last marvel we saw was a room with a checked floor and a door at each end, it was filmed constantly which was on a two minute delay so you could have a good wander inside and then see what it looked like after. Sharon and I went in to the odd shaped room, the end I went in at, had a very low ceiling, which got higher and further away from the camera as you crossed to the opposite corner where the other door that Sharon entered. The appearance from the outside is that one person is much taller than the other, and as I walked from left to right I shrank.

I think we completely exhausted Puzzling World and finished with a picture of us in front of the sign that was attached to another set of 4 small towers, which were all at peculiar angles.

We took the 35 mile drive to our next destination which was Arrowtown, a former mining town built on the *Arrow river* which was rich with gold in the 1860's, it had a lot of old looking houses which gave the town a quiet, sleepy feel to it. We were now near a road we had very much been looking forward to, since we were told by the hire car company that this was the only place we would not insured. When we got there, another 10 miles on from Arrowtown, we could see what they were talking about. Skippers Road runs along *Skippers Canyon* for about 19 miles, a road barely one car wide with sheer drops, blind bends and no barriers, many cars have been lost down these several hundred metre drops, so there is no wonder after a few insurance claims from careless drivers their insurers made this a no go area. It is known for one of the many places used in The *Lord of the Rings* films, the river with its steep cliffs either side was used in The *Fellowship of the Rings* where Arwen defeats the Nazgul by conjuring up a flood. The river however is more notably known for its riches in gold founded in 1862 by Thomas, Arthur and Harry Redfen, they found in *Shotover River* by what is now known as *Arthur's Point*, 4 ounces of gold in 3 hours, which would be worth about £1,500 in today's gold prices. It was thought to be one of the richest riverbeds in the world and they made no secret of their amazing find. So this area soon became swamped by miners, trying to make themselves rich quick. Soon after this discovery, the road was built by four contractors which was very poorly made with several people loosing their pack horses and supplies. This paved the way for hotels and schools, as this became a booming town. At its high point there was over 1,000 residents along *Skippers Canyon*, levelling out to around 200, and today there are no residents and very few signs that this was ever a bustling society.

We started our drive of *Skippers Canyon*, stopping briefly at the warning sign about not being insured, to take some pictures, we were sure Dale would be ok with us taking the drive on this treacherous road, after all it wasn't his card details on the deposit for the car. The road really was bad as it was made up mostly of compacted rocks but resembled a dirt track. Even with hugging the rock face there was only about half a metre (1'7") to the near vertical drop down to the valley floor. I felt quite concerned at one point when we stopped to take pictures, I stood near the edge and found it fairly easy with just my own weight to crumble the edge of the road away. Strewn along the way we came across ruins of the once thriving community. The first such ruin was the *Welcome Home Long Gully* Pub that was built in 1863, which was in use up until 1951, all that is left today is two chimneys in a grassy area. We wound our way along the cliff faces, waterfalls, landslides and various outcrops of rocky towers that had been given names to what they vaguely looked like. There were several parts the road cut through the hillside leaving what looked like a tunnel without a roof with names such as *Hells Gate*, some of these had a rather high incline where I had no idea if there was anything coming the other way. Fortunately most people adhered the warnings and we only saw two other cars on this drive. There are several activities available in this area with guides for walking, cycling and 4 wheel drive excursions, there is also a foot bridge you can bungee jump from which we drove past. A mile or two later we were at *Skippers Bridge*, spanning the gorge about 75m (250ft) above the river. Built in 1901, this was the third bridge built over *Shotover River* to reach *Skippers Point* safely. The first bridge was built in 1866 just 6 metres (19ft) above the river, and was prone to damage from flooding, this was rebuilt in the same place in 1871. The access to this crossing was difficult as the approach was very steep on both sides, so a much longer suspension structure was re-built and is what stands today. It hadn't changed much, the bridge was made of wood with two huge stone pillars at each end, long planks lined the way from end to end for your wheels, I guess to strengthen it so you didn't fall through the rickety old bridge, with the sides in a criss-cross lattice it didn't make you feel entirely safe, I had an urge to get across as quickly as I could, stopping briefly in the middle to take some pictures. On the other side round the next corner we came across a school in the area known as *Skippers Point*, it had been very well restored, you'd have thought it was new. We tried the door of the flint walled school to find it unlocked so we went inside and took a look around. A few benches and desks in the cramped little school were mocked up. I took a seat and sat quietly, taking the time to think about how many children had been taught in this school. How many peoples lives had been changed living in this area, children of parents panning for gold, so they would have been very wealthy, while others were still waiting for their lucky break if it came at all. Did parents pick their children up from this school with thousands of dollars worth of gold in their pockets that would change their lives forever? We took a few pictures and left quietly and respectfully, closing the door gently behind us, and drove up the hill further along Skippers Road. We didn't get very far before we realised the rest of the track was better suited for 4 wheel drive vehicles, as we bottomed out a few times and thought losing the exhaust might void our warranty, so we spun round without reaching the end and made our way back. It was a good idea actually as it was starting to get dark and it was hard enough to navigate the tight turns, it had already took us 3 hours to drive the 10 miles to where we were, so without stopping we thought we'd make it out in an hour or two. Driving was quite slow as the thought of one wrong move or over shooting one corner really could end in our deaths. As dusk fell, the nightlife started to emerge with ever increasing rabbits and hares jumping out in front of me.

I said to Sharon, "You know I'm gonna stop flinching when I see these animals, I ain't gonna risk killing us to save one little creature I'm afraid." Surprisingly she was ok with that remark and fortunately I didn't end up killing any little critters. I found the whole experience of *Skippers Canyon* exhilarating, and the drive was exciting, strange I know driving somewhere as dangerous as that, but it was a difficult challenge that I managed with some ease, although I couldn't let my concentration lapse for a minute. The views were fantastic, virtually untouched by man, there was no obligatory photo viewing area where every tourist would get the same picture, which would also have been found on a post card in some tourist information area that undoubtedly you would pay an admission fee, but instead I stopped where I liked and stood on cliff faces and sheer drops to get my breath taking pictures, the scenery was lovely and I had a constant thought on the history of this road.

We emerged from *Skippers Canyon* as darkness fell and took the short drive to Queensland, finding a Thai restaurant shortly after arriving. We parked up and I had a Thai green curry for the first time and thoroughly enjoyed it, the most memorable thing on this first experience was the taste of coconut, which gives it its classic taste. Coming out of the restaurant we heard a live band in the pub next door so spent the rest of the evening there, it was quite a good rock band except for the lead singer jiggling around in a peculiar fashion in rather a gay way.

Miles driven - 124

Sunday 20th March.

We started the day as we did like most others, we drove into town looking for food, but today we found every shop and cafe was closed, even though it was past opening time, maybe it was a bank holiday or something we thought. After a while the shops started opening and we visited the Muffin Man café, I ordered 2 different muffins and I was served up with something much more extravagant than you would think, my large plate arrived with strawberry sauce drizzled round the side with an a elaborate patterned and sweet sauce, that had been squeezed out in random loops onto a cold surface which hardened quickly, and then placed neatly between my 2 very fresh muffins. Finished off with some berries on one of them and the whole plate dusted with icing sugar. That was one hell of a sweet breakfast! We booked tickets for the TSS *Earnslaw* steam boat, as we had a few hours to kill we took a little walk around the town, stopping to see *William Cottage*, a little wooden shack and the oldest in Queenstown which was built in 1866. We didn't go in, as we weren't that excited about paying to see a little house, so we just peered through the windows instead.

We also visited *St Peter's Anglican* (Episcopalian church). Episcopal means, that it has a bishop that is an overseer in the Christian church. The church resembled a small castle from the outside with its flint walls, with a ceiling that is much lower than traditional churches and smooth, cream painted walls. Our next quick stop as we couldn't afford to eat there was the *Hard Rock Café*, I always enjoy visiting these cafés, not just for the good food but also for the memorabilia, with the most memorable item here on this day was a twin guitar. The *Hard Rock Café* was founded in 1971 by two Americans in London, where they opened this café and covered the walls with rock and roll memorabilia, a tradition that would be seen throughout the franchise that has now grown to 175 cafés in 53 countries.

We made our way back to where we would catch the TSS *Earnslaw* to find it not in the dock, must be running late I thought, in fact everything in Queenstown seemed out of sink to us until Sharon had a thought and said to me, "Cover up your watch!" what was she on about I thought feeling a little bewildered at her remark, as she turned to the nearest passer by and asked for the time, it was actually an hour earlier than what my watch said, a quick check in our guide book confirmed the clocks had gone back, so we actually had over an hour wait for our boat. We sat by the lake writing up our diaries and chatting, watching, a speed boat with a parasailer that had a big yellow chute with a smiley face on it, but the most interesting thing that happened next was that some one bungee jumped from the parasailer, that must feel strange! We waited in the sunshine a little longer and watched the TSS *Earnslaw* slowly making its way back from its first trip across *Lake Wakatipu*, which has a length of about 50 miles and with 112 square miles of surface area it makes it a thin and long lake. It was about this time I saw a photo opportunity as the old boat passed the parasailer, I noticed an elderly couple sitting on the bank admiring the steamer, I snapped one of my favourite pictures of this couple under a tree looking out across the lake at the *Earnslaw*, with the modern speedboat tearing off in the opposite direction with its smiley face parasailer in tow, the *old and new*.

We walked back to the dock to find a tipper truck full of coal dumping it on the ground as the *Earnslaw* was pulling up to the quay, a little tractor came round and proceeded to shovel it in a chute on the side of the boat. It can actually hold 14 tonnes of coal and will burn 1 tonne of coal in 1.5 hours at full speed of 13 knots (15mph). The boat itself sailed its maiden voyager in 1912 and was originally built in Dunedin, 175 miles away, then disassembled, transported to Queenstown by rail, which is where it has been since. It was built after the gold rush and was much needed to transport livestock and supplies to and from the farms along the lake, as well as public needs for foods, mail, transportation and tourism. It served in this manner for 50 years before it was decommissioned, renovated and re-launched solely for tourism.

We were using a piece of history today to visit *Walter Peak Station*, a sheep ranch founded in 1860 which has grown to 6,500 acres and is home to 1,500 sheep and 1,000 cattle, even today this farm is known for its isolation, besides the shipping access, the only other way to get to it is by a 77 mile unsealed road. We took the slow ride across the lake, admiring the scenery for the most part, the only other point of interest was being able to walk over to the engine room via a cat walk where you could see most of the workings of the engine and watch the crew men shovelling in the coal to feed the twin, triple expansion 500 horse power jet condensing engines, it was quite a sight seeing the massive roaring glow of the furnace getting stoked every few minutes. The rest of the boat was fairly basic, the front quarter of the bow was open, and the cramped bridge was a few metres higher with the bright red funnel behind it. The rest of the boat was a covered section for seating, two decks one of which were wooden slatted seats with the other having a little more comfort and modern looking. It was a great experience thinking we were actually using a boat that had historically been used for many years. There were pictures of when it was used for its original purpose of transporting goods and livestock, it was interesting to think that where we were standing, at several points in its life it would have been filled with sheep. I bet everyone on that boat on days like that, would have walked off with sheep shit on their shoes!

    We got to the beautiful farm, and we were able to moor up to a small jetty that was only a few seconds walk onto the farm. The little farmhouse was modern looking surrounded by many colourful plants, a little further on we came to several pens that had red deer, sheep and highland cattle, we were given feed for them which they were all to eager to eat, the highland cattle seemed to be the most friendly animals there, they lumbered slow and deliberately about and taking the feed surprisingly gentle with a little added slobber and snot, they also appreciated a good scratching round the face and ears. After I had finished making friends with the cattle we had a little snack at the café where some more over enthusiastic animals were taking food out of our hands, this time in the form of birds. The tour included demonstrations of sheep farming, the first being shown how the sheep are herded, Meg the sheep dog did a great job in rounding them up with the usual whistles which Meg obeyed without hesitation, at one point the farmer purposely let the sheep get away from here as she laid in the pen waiting for her next command, as they trotted off, the dog shot a look at her owner with a expression of 'what the hell are you doing!' She went to get up to stop their escape, but with another whistle from the farmer to stay, she reluctantly laid back down in disgust.

    The last part of the tour was to see how they sheer sheep, the farmer had a sheep, led and pushed onto a purpose built stage where the sheep were shorn, it didn't take very long but he was sweating a lot as he told us of people getting seriously dehydrated from sheering all day. At the time when we visited *Walter Peak Station*, the record for the amount of sheep shorn in 8 hours was by a New Zealand man, which was 719 at a rate of 1 every 40 seconds, it has been broken since then, when I was writing this book 8 years later, to 742 with 1 sheep every 38.8 seconds by another New Zealand man. But more surprisingly though is a 24 hour shearing marathon in New Zealand which helped raise $10,000 (£3,846) for the home and neighbourhood trust by two gentlemen, which was 2,220 at 38.9 seconds per sheep, I think New Zealanders like sheering.

After our sheering experience we mingled around with the sheep before making our way back to the jetty, as the boat chugged its way back with another load of eager tourists. The trip back was relaxing as we'd seen the boat at every angle on the way over, so we enjoyed the scenery and listened to the enthusiastic woman playing those old songs everyone loves to sing on the grand piano.

We arrived back and made sure to use our free drink voucher we got with our boat tour at the casino close to the docks, I played the 2 cent machines and won $5 (£1.92) but pumped it back in again and lost it, well what you've never had you never miss, I was thinking I might have won the big one forgetting the rule that in a casino the house always wins. Our next bar was the *–5 Bar* and as the name suggests, it's cold in there with the theme being that everything was made out of ice. The *–5 Bar* was a part of a normal bar which had a small window looking into the walk in freezer it was here we were to wait to be taken in. We made ourselves comfortable at the bar and recognised a couple that was also waiting to experience drinking in the cold, it's a funny thing backpacking, most people do the same route from New Zealand, Australia and through Asia, and so you end up bumping into people you've seen at some previous town, on this occasion we had met this couple once in a bar and then again at Kaikoura when we went on the whale watching cruise.

We were handed thick coats and gloves and stepped inside the massive freezer, it was a bizarre sight, only because you're just not used to seeing so much ice made into your everyday things in a room. We were first led to the bar, which was made entirely of ice where we chose our cocktail, I had a Cool as Ice as we were surrounded by the stuff, it was pretty good too so I followed that one with several more. Behind the bar there were several shelves for the glasses and various bottles of drink, the glasses themselves were also made of ice with a special chemical to stop you sticking to it. There were several ice sculptures, a pagoda, Pegasus, rabbit, swan and an elaborate table, there was also a two seater couch with only a fury animal hide for comfort, even the walls were covered with ice bricks. All in all it was an interesting experience, I think it is very much remembered and enjoyed by everyone who visits the *–5 Bar*. We finished our time in the fridge by smashing our glasses in a bin, as I'm sure they might be a little tricky washing them up to use a second time, as we exited into the warmth of the real world you get a little surge of alcohol as your body rapidly changes temperature, leaving us a little light headed and rosy cheeked.

Sometime later after we had sobered up, we headed out to Queenstown and a 177 mile drive to the west coast, after going the wrong way back to Arrowtown we doubled back and stopped after about an hour for fish and chips. I drove about half way before Sharon took over to drive, the rest time went a little quicker for me as I had a little nap, waking just before *Milford Sound*s. We parked up just outside the town beside a stream where we spent the night.

Miles driven – 213

Chapter 6
The south and back up.

Monday 21st March.

We woke at about 8:30am with a great view of the mountains and glacier, we may have been slumming it sleeping in a car, but what hotel had views like this for free! We noticed there was literally millions of mosquitoes so we liberally smothered ourselves with mosquito repellent in an attempt to get a little less eaten. To say the town had the bare essentials was an under statement, it had 1 petrol station, one café, a big car park and several boat tour operators, as the only attraction here is the fjords. The bottom west side of New Zealand has a stretch of about 130 miles of coastline of fjords, with *Milford Sound* being one of the most northerly inlets. It's about 9 miles long with sheer rock faces on either side reaching at its highest point of 1,200m, (3,900ft). We made our way into town for breakfast, which I had one of my most common breakfast meals, a croissant, but this one had ham and cheese instead of the obligatory jam and butter. We booked our tickets for the boat trip then sat in the car to write up our diaries and clear the pictures off the cameras to the laptop, just in case I got carried away taking photos on the boat. Time was slipping away and getting close to our boat trip so we made our way to the birth and actually arriving bang on time, I thought 'these things never leave on time anyway,' unfortunately on this occasion it left 1 minute early so we had to hang around another hour for the next one.

We finally pulled away in our little boat favouring the open deck to get the best view, and what a view we had, it wasn't one continual crevasse, but more like several overlapping crevasses, which looked more like rolling mountains. The cliff faces towered over us, I felt rather small cruising alongside these cliffs. There were a few waterfalls and rock formations that resembled animals, one of an elephant and another of a lion's head that I could vaguely make out. The captain had been talking to us for the entire two hour cruise on various bits, with information which I found very interesting at the time but have forgotten most of it by the time I got to write this book. With the captains cruising these waters several times a day they get to know what is where, we came cruising up slowly along an out crop of rocks where the captain was telling us that hopefully the seals would be here, he nimbly and quietly crept the boat round the corner and there were several seals basking in the sun. The bow of the boat was frightfully close to the rocks but I'm sure he knew what he was doing, it also aloud me to get some up close pictures of them. We finished our cruise at the mouth of the fjord where it met the sea, I say finished our cruise, of course we didn't get out there and swim back, the trip back was the way we came so we pretty much had finished the trip. We had a brief look out to sea before we turned around and made our way back, as we had seen most things on the way up it aloud us to sit back and enjoy the beautiful scenery. There was one very special treat we had on the way back when a pair of dolphins swam off the bow, elegantly keeping up with the boat, darting back and forth over each other and under the boat. I wonder if they just do it for fun, maybe they're really thrill seekers competing with each other to see how close they can get to the boat. It seemed to take a while getting back so we relaxed on the deck.

After getting back we went to fill up with petrol, we only had a quarter of the tank left and was sure it wasn't enough for the 74 mile drive to Te Anau, we found the petrol station to be dry with no idea when they were getting their next delivery, so we steadily and slowly made our way to the next town, driving as economically as possible. We stopped at a waterfall on the way, which was fairly un-exciting, then with another stop at *The Chasm* which was strangely warm, most streams like this usually come from the mountains and stay quite chilly on the way down. The *Chasm* is along a nature walk and is part of the *Cleddau River*, with the water basically running over several large rocks. Over time the water has worn the rocks into a strange pot holed Swiss cheese look. Several bits of debris were sticking out of the holes, mostly large sticks and branches that had also been worn unusually smooth. We carried on our gentle drive to Te Anau wondering if we'd make it, it seemed like a lifetime getting there. When we finally did our first priority was to find a petrol station, by now the petrol gauge was below the red as we searched the streets randomly for a petrol station. As we came to one particular junction, I saw one about 50m (164ft) away, I was so happy and couldn't believe we had actually made it without having to hitch hike to get some fuel, so I floored it with a little cheer from myself, with Sharon remarking, "You don't care now if you run out, do you?" and she was right, I was happy to push it that far if I had to.

We stopped off at an internet café to see where Dale was, to find him in Dunedin which is on the east coast, we had a few more places to visit on the west coast before we would meet up. We made a quick visit before dusk to the Wildlife Centre which had several aviaries set in big grass fields, there were many colourful birds of unusual breeds, one of the most brightly coloured birds was the Takahe bird, a small flightless bird indigenous to New Zealand with an average weight of 2.5kg (5.5lbs), a little strange looking that looked liked it had been crossed between a chicken and a tailless peacock, it was thought to be extinct when the last four known birds were taken in 1898, until the rediscovery of them in the *Murchison Mountains* on the south island in 1948 when there was about 400 birds. It was thought that they had been on a steady decline since the Polynesian settlers who arrived about 800 to 1,000 years ago, which hunted them for food. After their rediscovery they declined again to about 100 by 1982 due to Fiordland domestic deer, quite sadly this is now controlled by the national park that implements deer control by hunting them in helicopters. By 2013 the Takahe bird, had risen to about 260, but I wonder how many deer have been lost in that time.

We found one of the birds at the wildlife centre had escaped, and was wandering round one of the enclosures, with no obvious sign to where it had came from, we found a little house nearby which seemed to be part of the enclosure, so we knocked on the door and the guy just said ok and stood there a little awkwardly. We looked around a little more finding a friendly parrot type of bird that liked my finger, so I gave him a little tickle on his beak.

The only cheep meal for the evening was another chippy before we made our way south stopping at *Colac bay*, we found a lovely little pub to spend the evening with a fishing theme which carried on into the toilets. Another memorable item was a picture of a four tonne shark that had been caught nearby. The barman was a little strange, but with the pool table at 20 cents a game, it was worth enduring a little weirdness, but he was nice. We found a self sustain campsite, which basically means there is a field and a toilet which was the best we were going to do this late at night, it was quite nice, in fact much better than we expected, the toilets were clean which had another fishing scene painted on the outside, we really wanted to find somewhere with the full works so we could have a decent shower, I hadn't washed my hair or showered for a week.

Miles driven – 180

Tuesday 22ⁿᵈ March.

We were up at 7:30am and left soon after in search for breakfast, but with nothing close by we drove onto Bluff and stopped at *Woolworths* for a fruit breakfast. Our guidebook described Bluff as the most Southerly town in New Zealand, and with not much of a detour we gave it a look. There really wasn't much there besides a similar sign post to Cape Reinga overlooking the sea, it was 869 miles to Cape Reinga, but our route from Auckland had taken us 3,479 miles. The only other interesting item here was a rock that was named Shag Rock, we didn't try it out as the name suggested so moved on to the Southerly most point of New Zealand, Slope Point. It was about a 60mile drive, stopping on the way to see a Hooker seal colony at Waipapa Point. There were several of them basking in the long grass, some of them waddling about, we took a walk down the beach and came across a giant of a beast, but some how I always think they look quite cute and harmless, but with wild animals I'm always aware they are wild and unpredictable. We stood at a fair distance to admire and take pictures, far enough that if he did decided to take an over enthusiastic liking to us, we had enough of a head start to out run him, as it happened he wasn't that interested in us, he sat there looking around with the cute puppy dog look with those droopy eyes they have, he turned to us like he was going to blow us a kiss, but instead quite aggressively barked at us, you have never seen two people run so quick.

Another short drive and we were at Slope Point, the Southern most point of New Zealand, the road turned into a gravel track, then a further 15 minute walk to get to the little lighthouse and the signpost to signify, we were there. The signpost was a lot more sparse than the ones at Bluff and Cape Reinga, there were only 2 pointing in either direction, one to the equator at 3,465 miles, the other to the South pole at 2,984 miles. There really wasn't much here, so after getting bored throwing stones in the sea we headed east about 25 miles to Curio Bay, where there was a petrified forest. As I had never been to one I had no idea what to expect, the logs are actually 180 million years old fossils that were buried by ancient volcanic mud flows, then gradually replaced by silica. The sea, over time has eroded this away to expose the fallen trees and stump of varying sizes. The trees were ancient conifers that are related to the modern Kauri and Norfolk Pine, we had been walking round studying these fossils for sometime, walking on raised parts of it to keep out of the shallow puddles from the sea, we had no idea how big it was until we left, the route back took us several metres above the shore, as we looked back you could see the bigger picture, the whole area had much more fossils than we could see when we were up close to them, the raised parts we had been walking along were actually large felled trees.

We carried on our easterly direction another 100 miles, we were originally going to a waterfall, but with the light failing we went to Nugget Point for sunset to see Yellow Eyed Penguins, these birds are common along New Zealand where Giant Kelp protects the land and the forests. They pair for life and always return to their favourite nesting site among the roots of the forest trees. We couldn't get onto the beach as it was a protected area, but we still had a good view of the undisturbed penguins from a high advantage point.

We took a swift drive to Balclutha as it was getting late to have something to eat, it didn't take too long to find a cheap meal at $15 (£5.76) for steak and chips, which I couldn't pass up. With a full stomach we then found somewhere to sleep, our guide book listed a motor lodge here which had basic cabins with a toilet and a shower, we weren't to hopeful as it was 10pm by the time we got there. A few people were socialising outside their cabins, so after asking round we found out the owners actually were in one of the cabins and were nice and friendly, so we tapped on their door and was warmly welcomed by Mike who was also very amusing, I think the strong smell of the use a smoking kind of drug was why he was such a nice guy this evening, we handed him $35 (£13) and we had a room. The first thing we did was shower, it took 3 washes to get the grease out of my hair, all I kept doing as we settled down for the night was running my fingers through my soft hair.

Miles driven – 251

Chapter 7
Reunited

Wednesday 23rd March.

I woke early for some reason even though this was the most comfy sleep I had had for a long time, I was so warm and relaxed I went back to sleep until 9:30am, when I finally roused myself I made good use of the shower again before we left. We managed to get a cup of coffee with no milk, but managed to scavenge some off a nice New Zealand couple in one of the other cabins. We also met a nice South African couple with 2 kids that they schooled themselves. We went to town to find an internet café to see where Dale would be so we could meet up, he wasn't going to be at the hostel until 6pm so we decided to go back to motor lodge to do our laundry, for some reason there was no hot water so Mike did it for us with his own washing machine. While he was so generously doing that we went back into town so Sharon could post her journal and her camcorder mini DV tapes home from the last few months, I posted the pictures I had put on CD, as well as the leaflets I had accumulated, I thought I'd have to do this on a regular basis as I would probably need a second back pack just for extra crap I would pick up along the way. $17 (£6.53) later we found a convenience store so I could buy some fruit and pies for lunch, then popped back to the motor lodge to pick up our freshly washed clothes, probably the cleanest they had been since I left home.

We left to Dunedin at 2pm, it was only 49 miles, so it didn't take too long giving us plenty of time to have a look around the town. We took a walk around an art gallery, which had free admission, then to the *First Church of Otago* (Presbyterian). We could only look at the outside of this church as it was locked but was still well worth the visit. It reminded me of a typical cathedral with its 60m (196ft) pointed tower, it was gothic in style constructed in brick and faced with Oamaru stone. It was founded by the first major wave of settlement of *Otago* by Pakeha, under the auspices of the Free Church of Scotland in 1843, with the church being completed by 1875 after an architectural competition to design the new church for the *Otago settlement*, which was won by Robert.A.Lawson who lived in Melbourne, Australia.

Our next place of interest was *St Paul's Cathedral*, it is known as the mother church of the *Anglican Diocese of Dunedin*, and is the seat of the Bishop of Dunedin. It was built in 1862 – 1863 and was the first parish church of *St Paul*. It was originally built with Caversham stone, and could accommodate 500 people, unfortunately it was not constructed well and weathered badly resulting in the spire being removed after a few years. It wasn't until 1904 when William Harrop, a prominent Dunedin businessman died and left the bulk of his estate to fund the new cathedral, however the money was conditional on the chapter raising £20,000 towards the cost, it took 9 years to raise this money and it wasn't until 1915 when construction started of the cathedral. It occupies a site in the heart of the Octagon, an eight sided plaza bisected by the cities main streets with a paved area in the centre which has water features and a giant chessboard. The gothic style cathedral, which stands with a presence with tall whitish grey walls, has 38 steps leading up to the entrance made from Takaka marble, which makes it stand out. The inside is as eye catching as the outside with its large tall vaulted ceiling, the only one in stone in New Zealand. Another dominating piece here is the memorial window above the front entrance with a plaque that reads,

'This window was erected to the glory of god and in thankful and loving remembrance of those of the Otago and Southland who gave their lives in the great war 1914 – 1918.'

By the time we had finished our little sightseeing in the centre of town it was time to meet up again with Dale, he had some amusing stories consisting of drinking, girls and getting into places free with his writing links. After having a good catch up and a laugh at his entertaining antics we found a bar for the evening, Southern Break which had a 9 ball competition that we could enter in teams for the price of a drink and the possibility of winning the $50 (£19) bar tab. But the players were really good, this was immediately apparent as they all had their own cues, us on the other hand had to make do with the pub cues that were all slightly bent with wobbly tips. Needless to say I lost the first 4 games, Dale did a bit better but still had to purposely foul to get the upper hand but it was all in vain, and we lost miserably. We left the bar after midnight and went back to the car that was parked on a side street, Dale and I left Sharon to sleep in the car and went in search for a kebab as we needed something to soak up the large amounts of beer we had consumed during the pool games. After a slight altercation with some 18 year old lads, thinking they were big boys wanting to take us on, we got back to the car, getting off to sleep straight away.

Miles driven – 52

Thursday 24th March

Dale was up at 5:30am to work at a radio station he'd got some casual work at, leaving Sharon and I to sleep a little longer finally getting up at 7:30am, then finding our way to a café for breakfast and coffee. We spent the morning wandering round the *Otago Museum*, it was founded in 1868 and has a collection of over two million artefacts and specimens of natural history, most notably that of New Zealand's bird life and ethnography, (the study and systematic recording of human culture) It also has a display with the prehistory and history of the Otago region, there was also galleries devoted to the Melanesian's, a name that denotes an ethnic and geographical grouping of island distinct from Polynesia and Micronesia, a group of islands immediately north and north east of Australia, this museum also has the world's most extensive collection of Moa remains and many ceramics and cultural items. The place was really big and so we didn't manage to get around it all or take in as much information as I would have liked. We really needed an entire day to see everything in any detail but we enjoyed what we did see and left quite fulfilled.

We had already arranged to meet Dale somewhere, to find him not there, after a while I found him waiting in the wrong place just around the corner from us. Sharon and I had a great idea of visiting *Speight's Brewery*, much to our surprise Dale turned down this offer of accompanying us here as he had already been there, I thought he must have had something really good lined up. He dropped us off at the Brewery, where we took a 90 minute tour taking us round where we got to learn how these fine ales are brewed, although they describe themselves as brewing ales they are actually lager based drinks. *Speight's Brewery* has been brewing beer here since 1876 with one promotional branding based on being a real southern mans drink, they also have a series of Speight's ale houses, across New Zealand. We were educated on all aspects of brewing there is a natural spring under the brewery, which they use for brewing they also have a tap outside that takes water from this natural spring for the public, which we used. Inside at the start of the brewery there were several items that were used in brewing by Speight's in its early years, there were barrels of different sizes and items that were used in all the aspects of brewing, with several other Speight's memorabilia with an old large Speight's mirror. There was also a life size figure of a man dressed in period workers clothes in a mock up of the time period.

The tour took us round every part of the brewing facility, past giant copper kettles and we even walked through a lauter, which is a large cylindrical wooden vessel. Early in the brewing process it is used to contain the mash, heated and drained to make wort. At the end of the tour we were led to a small bar with 5 pumps that were finished in copper that reminded me of the copper kettles we had seen on the tour. We were told that in the 15 minutes we were there concluding the tour, we could serve ourselves, and drink as much as we liked, we wasted no time in picking up a 125ml glass and filled it to the brim and started drinking. Each pump had a different flavoured beer, my favourite being an apricot flavoured one, I managed 6 glasses, one and a third of a pint before the time was up, which is good going for me in the allotted time, leaving me slightly light headed for a short while.

Dale picked us up and we found out what it was that was more interesting than the brewery, a tall, beautiful Dutch blonde girl. We all went back to the museum, getting round most of the remaining part seeing mostly the animals, Mori boats and artefacts, and an impressive Fin Whale skeleton hung from the ceiling. It is the second longest animal in the world growing to 27m (88ft) and weighing in at 74 tonnes, this one must have been about that size.

After leaving here we said goodbye to Dutch girl, and grabbed a 12inch subway for dinner, before a short drive out of Dunedin to Baldwin Street, the steepest residential street in the world. Its overall length is about 350m (1,150ft) starting with a modest slope, then ascending dramatically for the last 161.2m (528ft). Its steepest part a 1 in 2.86 and an average of 1 in 3.41, climbing a height of 47.22m (154ft) making it an exhausting climb by foot and just as difficult for our little car. We started the drive up the hill with much enthusiasm with Dale at the wheel, but to be honest I was not entirely at ease with the thought of him driving us up this mini mountain, what if the car conked out half way up and he lost control? It's extremely hard to get out of a fast moving car safely especially on a steep hill if it was weaving all over the place. But fortunately the car and Dale did manage the climb, just. The engine whined and complained and strained every hard worked horsepower, shifting down in to first gear to make the last few metres over the summit as it was seriously running out of steam. We turned right at the top and turned round to tackle the decent, hopefully not becoming like a runaway train. As we neared the brow of the hill we got a huge sense of the sheer steepness of the hill, which was fortified by Dales procrastinating and I'm sure I heard his bowels loosen a little more. We rolled down the hill with just as little drama as on the way up.

The hill has been used for several charity events and visited by many people, some of which have got into trouble from not respecting just how unforgiving gravity is. In one case two students attempted to travel down the hill in a wheelie bin, it collided with a parked trailer and killed one girl instantly with the second student suffering serious head injuries. On a lighter side it has had balls, 30,000 jaffa cakes rolled down it, and running up and down it to raise money for charity. We parked up and took a walk to find out just how unfit we were, attempting the *Baldwin Street Gutbuster*, one of the charity events held annually, this involves running from the base, to the top and back down, even though there are steps to aid you it was incredibly exhausting, the record for this is 1min 56sec. Being the icon of physical fitness Dale and I thought we could get close to that so I set the little timer on my watch and went for it. I did really well, making the half way mark on the way up in 30 seconds, I kept pushing as hard as I could to beat the 2 minute barrier, it was only a matter of a few more steps after this when my lungs nearly exploded with a searing pain shooting though them and had to stop before I passed out.

After our fitness failure we headed north into the night to Akaroa, stopping on the way at Moerake, on the beach here, are some large spherical boulders, according to Maori legend they are the remains of food baskets washed overboard from a great canoe shipwrecked there on its way from *Hawaika*, geologists call them *Septarian Concretions*. I think this must be one of the best examples of these boulders as they are so amazingly round, there were several scattered over the beach completely intact with the heaviest at about 7 tonnes, some of them looked like they had been cracked open leaving a hollow shell, which made me think this was an ideal photo opportunity, it was dark but I could still vaguely make out the water in the bottom of the shell, I carefully eased my way over the water and sat on the edge of the basket for a great photo, after hopping off I asked Dale if he wanted a picture in the same place, not realising that he hadn't been as observant as me and walked into the middle of the boulder, getting wet up to his knee, I laughed so much at his dismay, we got the picture then found another similar boulder, which Dale did exactly the same thing, I couldn't believe it, I laughed so hard I nearly peed myself, I often find myself laughing at Dales misfortune, he didn't find it as funny as I did which added to my amusement. Dale and Sharon shared the rest of the drive to Akaroa, getting there at about 1:30am covering 317 miles this day, which by this time, Dales soggy feet and socks had festered nicely creating an odour that I really didn't enjoy sleeping with, at least I had the humorous thought of why they smelt that bad.

Friday 25th March.

We sleepily and reluctantly got up at 8:30am, making our first priority booking tickets for snorkelling with Hector dolphins, it is a very popular attraction as they are one of the rarest, as they are only found in New Zealand, and are the smallest dolphins in the world at 1.2m to 1.6m (3'11" to 5'2") in length. The only trip they had this day was at 3pm, with very little else to do in this little town we did everything at a much slower pace to kill the time. We started with breakfast at a café where the manager grilled us some hot cross buns, then slapped a 10% surcharge on it because it was a bank holiday, shops here also can't sell alcohol on bank holidays either. We then took a leisurely walk round the shops before lunch where the lovely lady who served us, forgot to charge me for my coffee. We idly killed time after lunch, Sharon called her mum while Dale found a public toilet where he washed his stinky socks, he washed them here like he was at a laundrette, it was something we all did to some extent, as backpacking quite often means you don't get the use of a washing machine when you have run out of smalls, the public that were using the facilities that day must have thought he was a hobo! While waiting for dale I went through my backpack taking stock of what I had and decided to throw a pair of old jeans out, I didn't realise when I packed them how impractical they are when backpacking as they take forever to dry.

Eventually our time had come to go for our swim with the dolphins. Arriving at the shop we had booked the tickets at, we were led to a room to squeeze us into a wet suit, then it was to the boat for the short trip out to the mouth of Akaroa Harbour. The little boat that had 10 of us on it chugged away for about half an hour before we caught sight of our first dolphin, at this time of year it was autumn so it wasn't particularly warm at 12°c (54°f), it was also a little windy which caused a little swell on the water that got increasingly choppier the closer we got to the entrance of the harbour, which also increased one woman's nausea until she chucked up over the rail. She ended up not participating in swimming, it was a expensive trip to make you chuck up, I still would have gone snorkelling even if I had to feed the fishes half way through. We cruised around slowly until we had attracted enough attention from the dolphins to warrant jumping in, we put on our flippers and stood at the back of the boat, as I had mentioned it was cold, the thought of the water temperature made every one a little reluctant to take the plunge as we all stood there looking at each other, I on the other hand had paid a lot of money to experience this and wasn't going to waste any time and jumped in, it was really cold that actually hurt my lungs which took my breath away, this took a few seconds to control, the *Gutbuster* Challenge from the day before had left my lungs quite sore which didn't help matters. I put the snorkel in my mouth and sunk my face into the cool murky water to see one of the dolphins swim past, the visibility was at about 3m (9'9") so it was difficult to zero in on the dolphins, I kept lifting my head up every now and then to try and see where they were. I did this for about half an hour with a good deal of success, with swell on the water, the temperature and my bruised lungs it was freaking my senses out making me feel a little peculiar, most of the dolphins had lost interest in us after this half an hour so I got out.

Back at the shop we showered while washing my socks and underwear, followed by a nice warming cup of tea before driving the 50 miles to our last destination in New Zealand, Christchurch, the largest city in the south island. We drove through some lovely scenery on the way along the windy roads, at one especially nice view I got a little over excited and wound the window down as we were going along to get that picture of the moment, completely forgetting about our drying technique. My underwear, socks and trunks were all jammed on the outside in the closed window to let the air created by the movement of the car dry them, and now they were all over the road with cars running over them. After dodging the traffic, reclaiming my clothes we continued to climb up and over a mountain, looking back I noticed that we had actually driven through and above the clouds, or maybe it was fog, either way it made for one of my favourite pictures which looked like a sea of cotton, I had to take 4 pictures side by side to get the entire scene in. It was getting late by the time we got to our destination, so we went in search for food and found one of the best priced meal so far at $6.50 (£2.50) for a chicken and rice curry. After emailing a few friends we drove out of town a little way to find a secluded bowls car park to sleep for the night, I was in the driving seat getting into my sleeping bag when the police pulled up to check what we were up to, I started to blurt out something other than 'we were camping here for the night', but it was a little obvious as it's fairly difficult to drive with your feet in a sleeping bag. They just said 'oh ok' and drove off.

Miles driven – 77

Saturday 26th March.

I woke at 5am with a big headache and dehydrated so I chugged some of my bottled water, it tasted a little nasty so thought it was best to be a little dehydrated than poisoned, tipping it all out and managed to drift back off to sleep until 7:30am, despite feeling groggy. After we managed to rouse ourselves we had our morning ritual in the skanky public toilets across the road, not my ideal first choice but we had no other option so we made do. I was feeling so tired I retreated to the back seat for another hour before we made our way into town to find a Starbucks for a coffee and a chocolate Danish for a pick me up. We then went into the city centre to take a look around the *Christchurch Cathedral*, an Anglican cathedral built in the second half of the 19th century, it had a greyish black look to it with a dominating 63m (206ft) spire in the front of the building, quite sadly more than half of this spire fell in the 2012 earthquake, resulting in the spire and the front of the cathedral being demolished and rebuilt, this would be the forth time since its construction it has been damaged from an earth quake. I didn't take any pictures of the interior here as it would have cost $4, which was only £1.50, but I thought it was just a money grabbing idea, so we decided to look round instead. It is gothic in style, as the architect was known for his revival in this style of building. The first stone was laid in 1864 but was not completed until 1904 after several set backs, mostly from lack of funds. The front of the building also had a large rose window that gave it even more of a distinctive look this also fell in during the last earthquake.

The arts centre was best of all, as it was free to enter! The first part of the building was started in the 1870's formally known as Canterbury College, with the front of the building dominated with large windows it did look like a typical old college. Inside is quite unusual as it is split into many rooms to include speciality shops, bars, cafés, restaurants, galleries and theatres. The shops in specific aim to promote the growth of Arts and Crafts in Christchurch, having many cultural items of many different types such as beaded, quilts, wood and pottery to name a few, with some shops having teaching classes. Each room was a compact size with everything stacked in neat to make the most of their shop space. They also have a weekend market, and it is the site of many festivals and special events. Unfortunately this is another building that suffered from the 2012 earthquake and was closed as a result for safety reasons, which I think is a great loss to the community which may also have an effect on the sale and cultural aspects from the businesses that were there.

Next we found another free activity to do which was the botanical gardens at *Hargley Park*, the gardens have 1000's of plants that have been gathered from around the world since 1863, with many trees that have been growing here for more than 120 years, some of which had twisted and looked very unique. There are several horticultural displays as well as conservatories, memorials, garden arts and walking tracks. It was so big you can almost forget that you were in the middle of a city, we did manage to walk all the way round, passing the Avon river where punting on the river here is as iconic as it is in Oxford and Cambridge.

We walked back into town, making sure to take our time to see all the sights of the different buildings, the city and buildings gave you quite an old nostalgic feeling with their large windows and stone walls. We came across several street performers, one of which was an old chap that was singing with a dog performing various tricks, which at one point got comfortably onto a skateboard and pushed himself along, dressed in its brightly coloured clothes. I brought my camera up to catch a sneaky picture, but this guy was a pro and saw me immediately, getting the dog to lift its paw in a pose that was very cute, which of course he knew would make me feel obliged to drop some money in his upturned top hat that was placed centre staged to his performance.

We met up with Dale to find that somehow the car battery had died, it had been a bit temperamental since we picked it up, as it had an automatic transmission so there was no chance of bump starting it, leaving us to wait around for the car rental company to come out to us to change the battery. For our evening meal I found an Asian restaurant getting a chicken, rice and veg meal for another great price of $6.50 (£2.50). After our fill it was back to the car to pack and tidy up as we were off to Australia the next day, then found the *Grumpy Mole Saloon* for a drink, this was a themed bar from the wild west and it truly is wild, with wood everywhere with items original and replicated from wall to wall, the walls were heavily decorated with totem poles, tepees, blunderbusses and cattle horns to name a few. I felt like walking up to the bar, asking for two fingers off their finest whisky and having it slid down the bar to me. We finished the night at a Karaoke bar where of course Dale sang but was out done by the 3 camp boys and someone else singing Bob the Builder. After leaving the bar it did take us sometime driving round before we found somewhere to sleep our last night in the car.

Miles driven - 20

Part II

Chapter 8
Australia. Sydney. What else do I need to say!

Sunday 27th March.

I was first up at 7:30am and finished packing my last few things before our morning coffee at Starbucks. We took the car back to the rental company, making my last note of the mileage as I had done every day since we picked it up, so I could see our total mileage by the end of it, we ended up clocking an amazing 4,182 miles during our stay in New Zealand, to put into perspective on how many places we went to, from the northern most point at Cape Reinga to Bluff, the most southern point of New Zealand it is 1,287 miles. It was quite fortuitous that we only had a half mile walk to the bus station and a 30 minute wait before we were off to the airport. We quickly checked our luggage in while Dale begrudgingly had to pay for another visa, which he persistently moaned and complained about to the guy on the desk, admittedly he had already paid for it once, but this had gone with his last passport along with the rest of his belongings with whoever stole his bag in Argentina. You would think in an age of digitalisation they could tap his passport number into their computer and see he had indeed already bought one. But this apparently was not possible and it was much easier to ask him to pay for another one. In airports it's always a good idea not to argue too much with the person who is going to let you through to get on your flight. They do, and have many times refused people on flights because of attitude or lack of a visa, which Dale really couldn't grasp. I did try and tell him that he wasn't getting on this flight without having to cough up, but this got him a little more irate, so as my swimming skills are not that good I thought it was time I slipped off through the gate and leave him to it, eventually he saw sense and joined us in the departure lounge after buying another visa. We sat around for a few hours listening to music and talking, I also had a lovely savoury muffin and a beer before we got on the plane.

The 3 hour flight to Sydney Australia was quite uneventful while I relaxed watching a film, it got a bit more exciting when we landed as the only thing I had to declare, was mud on my shoes that customs got a bit worried about as they went through a x-ray machine, so I got a free cleaning of the souls on my shoes. After being cleansed we exchanged some money at $2.4 to the pound then caught a minibus into town costing us $8 (£3.30) each, a little walking about found us a hostel in Chinatown that was cheap enough at $25 (£10.41) a night. By the time we unloaded in our little room I realised how much I was carrying, as my shoulders were really paying for it by this point, wishing I had bought a better backpack with a frame with some sort of support. We were given a room that was barely big enough for the 3 bunk beds leaving no room for our backpacks, so Sharon and I shared a bed and used the second one for our luggage. We were sharing a room with Dale, Frank the Dutch guy who was well toned and strutted knowing he had what the women wanted and what men wanted to be, but annoyingly a nice guy none the less, with the other bunks occupied by a pair of lesbians from the UK, one of which was a complete bitch that moaned about everyone including the incredibly nice Dutch Frank, they had been residents here for some time getting their bunks for free for working in the kitchens. They told us how a fat guy who had previously been in our bunk who slept in his underwear and no sheets, snoring rather loudly, they thought the best way of dealing with this was by throwing thongs at him. With all three of us frowning I thought, well her arse is pretty big but surely there was a better way than smothering the poor chap with her fishy knickers, the more mouthier one of the 2 then told us,
"Oh yes we know all the lingo here, thongs are flip flops."
I could tell we would not be making too much further conversation, with them and went to the toilet noticing there was no lock on the door, to the single bathroom and shower.

We all went out after settling in to our hostel in search of food, finding a chicken curry for $6.50 (£2.70) that was incredibly tender. Sharon and I wanted to take a walk round the city to finish off the evening, but Dale wanted to head back as he'd got some more casual work for 12 hours at a fair. We took a walk down to the harbour taking us about 30 minutes from our hostel, deciding to take in the iconic site walking round the park opposite Sydney Opera House and *Sydney Harbour Bridge* as we were excited about seeing these iconic and well known structures. I was a little disappointed at the Opera House initially as it looked much smaller and less magnificent than I expected, but we were quite some way off so I thought maybe I'd get a better feel for it when we visited it. We enjoyed our walk back through this city, it had a nice clean and safe feel to it, getting back to our hostel we climbed to the 12th of 13 floors and was very much looking forward to sleeping in a bed.

Monday 28th March.

We were up at 8am to find Dale had put his stinky shoes by the open window, I don't mean they were just airing as they were a little sweaty, but they stank like something had died, not surprising as he had been wearing them for most of his 7 months of backpacking. Much to my delight by chance he knocked one of them out, I was so pleased as I wouldn't have to smell that god awful smell every time he took them off. However he was not happy, after exclaiming 'Oh shit I've lost a shoe' several times he peered down the 12 floors to see it on the roof of the hotel next door, he was so happy as he was sure he could get it back. He disappeared to that hotel to find no obvious way of getting it himself, so he ended up asking the manager for it back. I personally would deny I owned such a worn and battered old shoe. However the guy said he'd see what he could do.

We had breakfast but only had one choice of beans on toast, slopped up by the lesbians, washed down with a not so nice powdered coffee. We left Dale to go to work at the fair where he was manning the stalls of various fairground games, I'm sure he did a good job enticing people to try their luck on his stall, as he had a great welcoming personality. My first task for the day, as it was the beginning of a new country for us was to send emails and pictures to our friends and family, finding it much cheaper at an internet café here, than in New Zealand. Sharon and I headed back to the harbour to get a closer look at the *Sydney Opera House* and the *Harbour Bridge*, stopping at a bar for lunch. We tried out a half and half pizza, topped with BBQ emu and crocodile washed down with a beer, which was very much enjoyed, the meat was not really no more unusual than any other meat we are used to, although it is a little leaner than most, more like pork, I couldn't comment on what it tastes like as it was smothered in BBQ sauce.

We first took a walk over the bridge, which crosses Port Jackson spanning a total length of 1,149m (3,770ft), It is known as a through arch bridge, nicknamed as '*The Coathanger*' bridge due to its arch-based design. The steel structured arch itself, spans 503m (1650ft) made up from 28 panel trusses reaching a height of 57m (187ft). The entire bridge weighs a whopping 39,000 tonnes, all held together by 6 million rivets, with the largest weighing 3.5kg (8lb) and 39.5cm (15.6 inches) long. The practice of riveting large steel construction was widely used at the time of construction in which started here on the 28th July 1923, and opening on the 19th March 1932. The rivets were heated until they glowed red hot, then inserted into the plates, then simply rounded off the headless end making a bond that would be nearly impossible to break.

The ends of the bridge are dominated by, two granite faced pylons that are 89m (29ft) high, which were constructed by 250 Australian, Scottish and Italian stonemasons. Quite amazingly they cut, dressed and numbered the 18,000 cubic metres (635,664cu ft) of granite at a temporary settlement 186 miles away, then transported by 3 boats to the harbour and assemble producing these magnificent towers that make it visually well known.

The bridge has attracted tourist to it even during its construction, where they used the bridge for climbs, first using the south-east pylon taking visitors 200 steps to see a 360 degree view which is still used today, it now also contains a museum and a tourist centre. It carried on with this tourist attraction up to World War 2 where it was closed to the public and taken over by the military, where they modified the 4 pylons to include parapets and anti-aircraft guns. The pylon was re-opened in 1948 as a tourist attraction until 1971 when the lease ran out and it stayed closed. In the 50's and 60's there were several newspaper reports of people illegally climbing the bridge, which gave rise to what is now known as *BridgeClimb*, a company that was set up after its opening once again in 1982. Today there are 3 regular climbs daily, one of which takes the climbers over the iron arch that spans from one end to the other. You get a real feel of the size of this structure when you see people walking along the top of the arch, it made them look like ants in comparison. I was very interested in taking the climb, today it is much safer than the illegal ones, with everyone being tethered to a safety line as well as wearing safety gear, also having to take a breathalyser which was all perfectly acceptable to me, but when I found I would not be able to take my trusted companion, my camera with me even though they took pictures for you, like with anything like this, they would have been extortionately expensive, so I admired it from underneath instead, I'm sure it would have been a fantastic view but I was happy missing this attraction on this occasion.

We next got an up close look at the *Opera House*, this time we were certainly not disappointed, it's huge! It actually covers 1.8 hectares or 18,000m², or 3 football fields giving you an instant awe of magnificence standing next to it. The reason to why it's so big is because it does not only support opera but is resident to many other performing arts, including the four key resident companies which are *Opera Australia, The Australian Ballet, Sydney Theatre Company* and the *Sydney Symphony Orchestra* which hosts some 1,500 performances with a total seating capacity of 5,738. This draws about 1.2 million people a year, 300,000 of which take a guided tour, where I would be one of them the next day.

The design itself is an expressionist design with a series of precast concrete shells, each composed of sections of a sphere 75.2m (246ft 8in) to form the structure of the roof, set onto a podium. It's 183m (600ft) long by 120m (394ft) at its widest point and is supported by 588 concrete piers that are sunk about 25m (82ft) below sea level. The shells themselves look very unique as they are covered by a chevron pattern if over a million glossy white and matte cream Swedish made tiles that give its unmistakeable look.

The construction of the *Opera House* is a very controversial one. Planning began in the late 1940s when Eugene Goossens, the director of the NSW (New South Wales) *State Conservatorium of Music* lobbied for a suitable venue to host large theatrical productions. At the time they were using the *Sydney Town Hall,* which was thought to be nowhere big enough and ill equipped. By 1954 Goossens succeeded in gaining support from the NSW Premiere Joseph Cahill, who called for the design for a dedicated opera house, so a competition was launched on the 13th of September 1955 to find an architect to build it. There were 233 entries representing architects from 32 countries. The winner was announced in 1957 and was won by Jorn Utzon, a Danish architect who won the £5,000 prize, although I think the thought of winning such a contest would be more of a prize to me than the money. He would move to Sydney to oversee the construction in 1963. He also won the *Pritzker Prize* in 2003, an architects highest honour.

Construction was started in March 1959 starting with the podium, but due to Utzon not having the final design completed because of structural issues, which were not resolved for sometime putting the project behind schedule. By January 1961, the project was 47 weeks behind schedule from an array of problems and unexpected difficulties beside Utzon's design problems, because none of the shells were identical, it put the budget under great strain, which resulted in 6 years and 12 attempts of research in how to precast the concrete shells economically, before a workable solution became apparent. The 14 shells and the outside of the *Opera House* was completed by 1965, even at this point it was over budget with the construction so far costing $22.9 million. The inside would be the more costly part, and it was about this time that Utzon resigned and was replaced by Peter Hall, who modified several of Utzon's interior design, with some of them being completely dismissed and re-designed. There was a string of reasons to why he resigned, many of which we may never know, but I think it was mostly due to the breakdown of communication between Utzon and his clients funding the project, with him wanting to share every aspect of it, but he was unwilling to compromise on some aspects of his designs that the clients wanted to change, along with draining money through bad decisions there was some pressure for him to resign. In the late 1990s the *Trust* began to communicate with Utzon in an attempt at a reconciliation, to secure his involvement in future changes to the building. In 1999 he was appointed by the *Trust* as a design consultant for future work. The first interior space was rebuilt with an Utzon design, and was opened in 2004 which was renamed '*The Utzon Room*' in his honour. Jorn Utzon passed away in November 2007.

The *Opera House* was formally completed in 1973 at a cost of $102 million. It was originally estimated to take 7 years at a cost of $7 million (£3.5 million) making its construction 10 years late and over budget by more than 14 times. Today it is one of the most iconic and well known, buildings in the world, I'm sure it has made its money back with just the amount of tourism it continues to generate.

Our day today was only to look around the outside and to look at prices of what was on. We then took a walk to the *Royal Botanic Gardens* that were near by, it was across the bay by the *Opera House* which gave us a good view of the *Opera House* and the *Sydney Harbour Bridge*, although it was starting to get dark it was still a good view. We wandered round the park on our way back to the hostel, admiring the *Sulphur Crested Cockatoos* that were jumping and dancing showing off their bright yellow crests.

By the time we got out of the park it was dark, on the way back we passed through *Hyde Park* to find the night life emerging here in the form of friendly little possums, at least that was what I was hoping for as I thought they could be vicious, but they did seem friendly enough and we got very close to them and kept all our fingers, so I thought they must have been quite used to humans here in the middle of a city and were nice to us, as they probably get fed by everyone coming through.

Back at the Hostel we got changed and asked someone there if they new of anywhere cheap to eat and what music was on, We went in search for our first recommendation back towards *Hyde Park*, stopping off at the *Ken Dud Gallery* which hosted several local artists paintings. One of which I could not believe he was asking $20,000 (£8333) for. Not because it was really good, but the complete opposite, it really was bad! I don't mean that it wasn't very good, it was terrible! It's the kind of painting you would do at primary school, when you're 5! The sky was 2 colours, the sea was a line painted across the middle, and a solid blue filled in below it, with 2 unidentifiable shapes each side, this too was painted in a solid colour. I could have done much better and I can't paint! Moving on from our disappointing visit we arrived at the Irish Pub, *Scruffy Murphy's* for a steak and chips that was surprisingly good for $5 (£2.08), topped off with some sweet chilly sauce. Our second recommendation was a short walk from here for some live music at the *3 Wise Monkeys*. They regularly host live bands here, which we only got to see by good manners persuading them to let Sharon in, as they mentioned their dress code. I was quite surprised as it was a place regularly visited by backpackers who were dressed much more inappropriately than what Sharon was dressed in. Anyway we spent the evening upstairs listening to a singer entertaining us to all ages, of soft rock and made a good evening, One old guy there was a bit of a dark horse, he danced most of the evening also managing to get the odd young girl up to dance with him.

We left at about midnight, back at the hostel we soon crashed out for the night rather quickly.

Tuesday 29th March.

We were up early at 8am despite our busy day yesterday and our late night, we made our way down for breakfast and caught up with Dale and Dutch Frank, (who Dale referred to us as fun Frank) who were there already, for another delightful helping of over done mushy beans and cold, almost burnt toast. Dale told us that last night he had asked next door about his shoe, but they still hadn't managed to get it back for him. He was going there again before he went to work again this morning.

We had to change our Thai Airline ticket dates to fit our schedule, well Sharon did I had forgotten mine, I'd left them safe and sound in my backpack at the hostel. We moved on towards the *Australian Museum* stopping off at a market type stall to buy some fruit and ending up coming away with a persimmon fruit, as we'd never eaten or even seen anything like it before, very strange taste something I couldn't even describe, it couldn't have been too bad as we ate it all.

We arrived at the *Australian Museum* to learn some history of this country, that it had been inhabited for at least 40,000 years by indigenous Australians, made up of Aborigine or Torres Strait Islanders. Aborigines are originally from Africa, who left their homeland about 70,000 years ago and made their way to Asia, before settling in Australia. Where as the Torres Strait Islanders are culturally and genetically Melanesian which arrived from much closer to Australia, as they occupied the group of islands between the northern tip of Australia and Papua New Guinea. It wasn't until 1606 a group of Dutch explorers discovered this country, with English settlers not arriving until 1770 claiming the east coast. Since then the population has thrived across the approximate 3 million square miles of country by 2013 to over 23 million, approx 410,000, or 2% of the population which are Aboriginal and Torres Strait Islanders, this number has declined from 1788 when it was approximated to be 750,000. Today Australians are mostly concentrated in the eastern states.

The museum itself looked like a typical old museum, with its high dominating off white front and its tall pillars and many windows. It is the oldest museum in Australia, after being moved from several locations, a permanent structure, was built in 1846. Since then, additional wings, floors and buildings have been added and now holds 14.5 million specimens and objects in its collection, run by 200 staff. Since the 1980's a number of interpretive items were introduced such as texts, diagrams, reconstructions, audio and videos, computers, hand on exhibitions as well as interactive ones, to include exhibitions of Australia's wildlife and history with several live specimens, focusing on anthropological, geological, and palaeontological collections.

Today we focused on a few of these impressive collections, because as we walked in, it was very apparent that it was massive! We got to see many aboriginal artefacts, mummies and one room was dedicated to minerals, there were hundreds of them displayed in glass cabinets. There were lots of stuffed animals with the most popular one being the Kangaroo, koala bears and camels. Many people are unaware of the over population of camels, about 10,000, mostly Feral camels were brought over from India, North Africa, Arabia, China and Mongolia in the late 1800s, to help carry supplies and explore the harsh central environment. Once they had finished with them, the majority were released into the wild, being able to double in population every 9 years this number has now grown to over 1 million, with measures having to be taken to keep this pest population down, as they can be responsible for up to 80% of plant degradation in areas where they are more populated. They are now culled and sold onto Saudi Arabia where camel meat is consumed, with the more unusual breeds captured and sold as livestock to many countries.

There was just so much information here that we read, most of which I can't remember now 8 years on, as I got a total brain overload and just couldn't take any more in. So we stopped for lunch in the museum with one of my favourites of coffee and muffin, we relaxed a little and chatted and made another attempt.

The second half was spent mostly viewing several live exhibits, which is a nice change amongst the skeletons and stuffed animals. One of our last stops was the Egyptian section, which had many artefacts, masks and jewellery, as well as the mummies, some rather more freaky than others, with many of them highly decorated with gold, and was surprised to see one decorated in a beaded type of blanket.

We left here without even scratching the surface and headed to see the botanical gardens, which we had already been to the day before, for a look in the daylight before our 5pm tour of the *Opera House*. There were much more wildlife scurrying around than when we had seen it before at night. Mostly birds foraging for food which were very tame, not paying any attention to us just a metre away in the undergrowth, as we strolled round the well kept paths in the very lushes, almost over grown greenery, which would every now and then open up into nicely spaced, well kept lawns. We also got to see several trees that were full of bats.

After killing enough time round the gardens we took our tour, surprisingly it was a really good tour, getting to see the playhouse and the 2 main theatres, where we were lectured on the acoustical values. However more recently the *Opera House* has admitted that the opera pit is an acoustical disaster as it was originally intended as a concert hall. The concert hall contains the Sydney *Opera House* grand organ, which is the largest mechanical tracker action organ in the world, with over 10,000 pipes. The 5 theatres are contained in the largest shells where we got to go through the hallways that ran along side the impressive glass wall, which has an elaborate design looking out over the bay. The hallways gave me a cold dull feeling with the stone floors, and iron lattice ceiling that seemed cluttered and over engineered, which made me not all that excited about the initial feeling of the *Opera House*, until you walk into one of the theatres, and what a transformation! Lovely carpeted, warm, even homely feeling, that made you want to relax and feel comfortable. Which is probably the look and feel they were going for as they would want people to stay and enjoy venues, but would exit quickly as soon as they were in the hallway.

On the way out we booked tickets to see *Die Fledermaus* for later that evening. As we didn't have too long before the show we rushed off to find something to eat close by at a Japanese restaurant, *Wagamama's* where I had a chicken and rice dish. No sooner had we eaten we were heading back to the *Opera House* again to see *Johann Strauss's Die Fledermaus*, or much easily known as *The Bat*, a musical opera story of a man who is jailed from mistaken identity, with other parts of the story containing his wife being seduced while everyone is trying to get to a party. I didn't take it all in as it was sung in German, fortunately for me there was a thin wide screen above the stage with translations. Our seating was obviously one of the cheaper seats to the right of the stage on a balcony, we actually had a good view with minimal obscurity from a pillar that was easily over come, by moving my head slightly to one side. I very much enjoyed the show, even though I wasn't sure what was going on half the time. Never the less, I had a great experience taking in the atmosphere of a live performance at The *Sydney Opera House*. How many people can say that?

After this 3 hour show, we took a leisurely walk back to the hostel feeling quite sleepy, enjoying the city air, getting back and straight to sleep again after another tiring day.

Wednesday 30th March.

We were up later than we wanted this morning at 8.30am, but the bed was too comfy and warm compared to what we had been used to. We had our wash and were getting ready to go out when one of the lesbians out right accused Sharon for using her shower gel. It wasn't, 'Have you used my shower gel? but more directly with, 'You've been using my shower gel haven't you!' I couldn't believe she came out with it like that, had she been measuring it every night? Sharon soon put her in her place and told her she hadn't and she was using her own. We were actually quite honest backpackers for the most part.

I could only manage one piece of toast this morning for some reason, but maybe it was a good idea not to have anything served up by our accusers, who knows what they would put in it.

Dale still had no luck in retrieving his shoe yesterday so asked again last night, he can be a little persistent! So was going to take matters into his own hands this morning by attempting to retrieve it himself. He was then off to work again and he left it in our capable hands to sort out the campervan we were going to travel around Australia in. Dale was up for buying one, admittedly it may have been a little cheaper, as long as we didn't break down or crash! I was adamant to hire one for the reassurance of a stress free campervan trip, I really was stubborn about it, I knew what Dales driving was like, and there's a lot of kangaroos about that have quite often written cars off.

Downstairs we booked 2 more nights at the hostel and asked where we could hire a campervan. We were directed to a lovely helpful lady, Alix who was just like a travel agent who was ready to unload a large amount of money from us. She knew everything about the different forms of travelling around Australia, she was there everyday sorting out people like us, which she did very well. We started of with booking 40 days with *Wicked campervans*, we got one of the older one as they were cheaper and slightly bigger, for $3,010 (£1254). It sounded a lot at first but at $75 (£31) a day, between 3 of us it was a cheap mobile hotel room that we could set up anywhere. Well almost anywhere, but we'll hear more about that later on in the book. She told us these campervans were excellent and one of a kind as they were all painted with a different theme on the sides. We would be driving up the east coast, then heading west to pick up the *Stuart Highway*, that would take us through Alice Springs and onto Adelaide and finally Melbourne where we would be dropping the campervan off, she helped us with our route and which trains to take. Once we would get back to Adelaide we would be getting the *Indian Pacific* train to Perth, which we handed over another $155 (£64) each for, which was about half the price as we had a concession for being backpackers. We also got talked into a 4x4 camping trip for another $200 (£83) each as well as a sailing trip round the *Whitsunday Island* for another $400 (£166) each. Well, I say talked into, we both agreed on the 4x4 trip quite quickly, and when she told me about the sailing trip I immediately said I was doing, then realizing I hadn't included Sharon in that one and said, "I really want to do that, you want to come with me?" As it happened she was also very interested and came along with me, which pleased me no end as I didn't really want to go on my own.

While all this was going on, we noticed some activity going on behind us, there was some people there with professional cameras then one of the staff came over and asked us if we minded being in a picture that was for a new brochure for the company we sat at. We didn't mind but Alix was a little put off as she hadn't paid too much attention to make up that morning not knowing she was going to be on some brochure. She immediately dived in her handbag pulling out her compact and had a quick wizz round her face, so in her eyes she looked much more presentable. We finished off our chat with Alix with planning out the route we would be taking with her pointing out several points of interest that would help us no end. After our 4 hours of information overload we staggered out in search of lunch to find it raining. We stopped off at a café for cake and coffee before finding *Thai Airlines* again to change my flight dates, this time remembering my tickets.

As it was raining we made our way to the *New South Wales Art Gallery* to take in some artistic culture. It was another old building, guarded by two, magnificent figures, they are a pair of Gilbert Bayes' *Offering of Peace* which was installed in 1926. This building was similar in design to the museum but not quite as old. There had been several buildings before this was opened in 1897 that had housed art exhibitions since 1871, and since its construction, it too had been extended to the size it is today. It houses many different types of art as it is also known as a *'museum of arts'* as it does not just house paintings, it is also a place to see and experience lectures, symposia, films, music and performances, and is visited by more that 1.3 million people annually. It includes the most obvious arts such as Aboriginal and Torres Strait Islanders art as well as, Asian, Australian, Contemporary, Pacific, Photography, European and Western art. We worked our way round the 30,000 or so items through its many rooms, some of which seemed overly spacious leaving us walking for 2 hours to see as much as we wanted. There was a massive amount of great stuff to see such as *Van Gogh* and *Monet* paintings along with several other artists, no one has probably heard of, as well as the more cultural Australian indigenous items. We also got to see a lot of weird and quite frankly crap items that made you think if they were actually sane, and someone did actually say to them, "You know what, that is really good, you should put that in an art gallery!" but it was interesting to look at some things trying to work out what they were.

By the time we had finished our cultural overload it had almost stopped raining, so we took a walk to the *St Mary's* Cathedral, church of the Roman Catholic Archdiocese of Sydney, and the seat of the Archbishop of Sydney. The front is dominated by its wide nave and three towers, having the greatest length of any church in Australia, and you do get that feeling of how long it is when you get inside, it seems to go on forever. Construction started on this building in 1868, and built in several stages until its completion nearly 100 years later in 1961, when the richly decorated crypt was finished which lies to rest many of the early priests and bishops. It is evident of the stages of the build in this cathedral, as there is a difference of colour and texture of the sandstone of the interior walls marking the division between the first and second stage.

After a marvel at one building we then went to another, The *Hard Rock Café*. I always tried to visit as many of these as I travelled, as they are so interesting with its rock and roll memorabilia, as it's a little expensive for a meal we only stopped in for a beer and take some pictures. You see a lot of unusual items in these places besides the guitars and pictures, the most unusual item here was a white Cadillac Eldorado convertible, with white and black cow hide on the sides with bull horns on the bonnet, and a drum set with several guitars in the car. That's not the unusual bit, it was actually suspended from the ceiling in a dome with murals of some of the greatest legends of rock, Elvis, Jimi Hendrix and The Beatles, the whole this was quite an impressive, and elaborate feet of engineering for a restaurant.

We moved on to find somewhere cheaper to eat, finding ourselves at *Scruffy Murphy's* for steak and chips again, at that price and tasting so good, why wouldn't you. We went back to the hostel to meet up with Dale, then had the intention of getting changed and going out to the *3 Wise Monkeys*, but we caught up instead with what we had been doing with the route, and exciting points of interest we would be seeing in the next 7 weeks in Australia. Dale told us how he had got stuck that morning trying to scale the building next door, much to the dismay of the manager. Considering he's scared of heights it shows you what lengths he will go to, when the possibility of having to fork out some money to buy new shoes is involved. He told us how happy he was that when he got back today to find the shoe had disappeared, so he went to get reunited with it. The manager did suggest to Dale that he should invest in a new pair when he saw the state of them.

We talked later than we would have wanted to as the lesbians were noisily packing everything into plastic bags till quite late, and I wasn't sad to see them go so let them keep us awake. They finished the evening of keeping us awake a little longer by having a cuddle and kiss before they retired to their respective bunks, which usually I would have found quite enjoyable to watch except that neither of them was what I would call attractive.

Thursday 31st March.

We were up at 8am, after a quick get together we had breakfast at the hostel with some new faces, serving up a slightly better breakfast. We chatted a little while before we all went and saw Alix to see what else there was to offer, where we decided to take the Blue Mountain tour, about 45 miles away, for the next day. We managed a 2 hour chat with Alix with the only other points of interest she told us about, was the locations of the *Home and Away* and *Neighbours* set, which to be honest I wasn't all that enthusiastic about, but I knew we would be visiting them as Sharon and Dale were fans.

We all hopped on the train to Edgecliff, where the Vietnam Embassy was to get our visas, a crucial piece of paper which would allow us to enter their country in 3 and a half months time, stopping off at a café for lunch of more cake and coffee. We had to apply for the visas ahead of time, as this was the only place we could get it easily. 4 stops later we were battling with the badly English speaking Vietnamese, I know they are Vietnamese but they would mostly be talking to English speaking people here, so you would think they'd know the language better than that. We struggled on and had to hand over an extra $100 (£41.50) for an express process, that's daylight robbery without a cloak and dagger! But we had no choice so handed over the cash and our passports, which thanks to the 'bribe', which I'm sure went in their own pockets, we were promised it would be ready in 24 hours, but they were most unhelpful after that, the $100 didn't seem to be enough to allow Dale to pick it up for us the next day, so we had no choice but to pick them up ourselves, foregoing our trip to the *Blue Mountains*. We called Alix who was very helpful cancelling it without incurring any cancellation fees.

After our bit of a headache we got back to the city centre on the train again, finding something on one of the carriages that lifted our spirits a bit. One of the signs on the train had been skilfully defaced, with a few cleverly selected characters scratched off to read 'At night, rave near the guard's compartment naked with a blue light' If you cant quite get what it means, rave and naked had been changed from travel and marked. We wandered around the *Opera House* and saw the sights of Sydney, enjoying each others company. Getting near our meal times we dropped our day bags off at the hostel, walking through *Hyde Park* again, to find the possums again who were really quite friendly this time, coming even closer sniffing our fingers, no doubt looking for food.

We went out for a bite to eat and some fun, back at *Scruffy Murphy's* again for food, finding there was a 6 round pub quiz on, with a top prize of money and the possibility of winning a jug of beer. We took our table in the already packed bar and the other 13 teams and named ourselves *'The Kids From Norwich'*. Which is better than some of the teams with names such as *Spit Roast, my cat's breath smells of cat food*, (which I think is a Simpsons reference) *4 Blondes and a Wog* and *South end Slags*. It was good fun, hosted by a broad Londoner that enjoyed finding ways of slipping swear words in wherever possible. The drinks were flowing and the quizmaster was very comical, and the swearing became matter of fact after a short while. He got us all into it, making everyone have a good time, which I think was their intention, as we were happy and having a good time the beer flowed quick on every table, which I'm sure made the landlord happy. The questions were varied including general knowledge, TV, movie and songs which were played and sang by the bar full of piss heads, with some of them having questions too. At several points we were encouraged to do something to win a jug of beer, one of which was to the table that could sing the loudest to a Beatles song, *Daydream Believer* that they played at a fantastic volume. It was about this time we were made aware of the amount of English people that were there, with a large proportion of them being football fans, as they sang the alternative version to this songs chorus;
'Oh what can it mean to a, fat northern bastard and a, shit football team'. As it happened no one won and Dale was taking desperate measures, including ripping of his Norwich city shirt and swinging it around his head, which didn't work either. We did manage to win one jug of beer for reasons I cant remember now maybe I was too drunk by then.

We left here in search for more drink, finding ourselves in the *3 Wise Monkeys*, where they were playing live music covering, all sorts which were very enjoyable. We had lost Dale more or less as soon as we had arrived, so Sharon and I had several more drinks without him, we guessed he'd either pulled or went somewhere else. We drank some more, probably more than we should have, which came quite apparent when on one occasion Sharon came back from the toilet with an oriental girl in tow, telling me that this was her new friend. At this point it was getting late and we'd had as much drink as we could sensibly consume, so I suggested we should leave. As we came out we found Dale outside, I said in my happy drunken state, "What happened to you?"

"Well it's like this," he started with. "I pulled this girl, I'd been snogging her for quite sometime against the wall when a bouncer put his hand on my shoulder. So I pushed him off, which he didn't like, so he threw me out."

I was laughing quite hard at this thought, Dale was always getting into trouble with a girl one way or another. And that isn't the first time he'd been warned for expressing his over passionate affection for someone in a bar. We were both taken back a bit at this point, when Sharon, quite angrily spat at Dale, "Oh that's a surprise Dale! You got chucked out! I wonder why that is!!"

We were a few steps back from her, so I whispered to him. "Don't worry about her, she's really drunk."

So Dale continued with his story. "As they were throwing me down the steps I tried threatening them with my journalistic story, which made no difference."

I wasn't surprised it had little impact. Sharon on the other hand in her inebriated state was not so happy at him talking his way out of things using this method.

"Oh really! There's a surprise, you used that did you like you always do to get yourself into things for free!" Dale just gave a sideways look and said "I'll see you later." And walked off in the other direction and disappeared into the darkness, leaving me standing there, thinking which one should I go to. Sharon seemed like she needed more help as she was really quite upset, and besides Dale was more than capable of looking after himself in a strange city. She started telling me how upset she was with him, how he had talked his way into places for free with this journalistic story of his, cheating people out of money, telling me a few of the stories that she had been thinking about. I agreed with her, it wasn't very nice cheating people out of money, if it was an individual person and a small concern, but these stories were from larger organisations, not that that would make much difference, but still, morally it was wrong. I pointed out how many times we all had benefited from this, but as long as I wasn't effecting any single person, and that organisation agreed on letting us in for a reduced rate or giving us something extra, then I was fine with it, it's not as if he was forcing them. We went round on the same argument for some time in the middle of one of the most well known cities in the world, when we should have been enjoying it as well as each others company. I told her if she was that upset about it then she should talk to Dale about it and put it behind us. Sharon could be quite volatile sometimes when she was pissed off with something, she liked to vent her anger and even more so in her drunken state as most people do. As we were still arguing about the same thing over and over again she was getting more upset. A group of lads walked past and flipped a comment to me, "She doesn't love you!"

Now, remember how I said that Sharon could be volatile under the influence? Well she didn't appreciate that comment, she turned to them straight away and said. "Fuck you!" The guy on the receiving end of Sharon's sharp tongue stopped with his 3 mates, he turned to her and defied her comment.
"What did you say?"
Sharon shouted back, "I said FUCK YOU!" with such vengeance lurching at him thrusting a middle finger an inch from his face at him. It scared the shit out of me as I grabbed her arm trying holding her back, like I was trying to control a rabid dog! At this point I was wondering if he had actually shit himself, or was contemplating something rather unpleasant towards us. I thought to myself, 'Well Brendan, you can either fight and hurt a couple of them before you get a kicking, or just get a kicking.' to be honest I don't think I was capable of fighting one of them yet alone 4 as I could barely walk in a straight line. Fortunately he just shook his head and carried on walking. Maybe he was as scared as I was.

I thought our relationship was over at this point, as I couldn't work out how pissed off with me she was for excepting Dale as who he is, thinking it was a good run compared to my past relationships. However she did calm down soon after this last bit of venting, and we talked in a much better frame of mind until about 3am, sitting on a kerb on a random street in Sydney, by this time we had found some common ground to agree on in our stubborn argument.

Back at the hostel we found no sign of Dale. I was hoping he was ok, I would have felt terrible if something had happened to him after he left us. I had got so wound up, by the time we got to bed, I had given myself a migraine. We finished the evening with Sharon and I making up again and got to sleep.

Friday 1st April.

We were up really late at 11.30am, which wasn't surprising. I didn't want to get up and face the day, with the inevitable chat with Dale with a migraine that most probably was a lot worse from the hangover, but I couldn't tell which was which, but I knew it hurt. Sharon had a long chat with Dale about the same things she had talked to me about. I think she just wanted him to be a bit more considerate more than anything else. I told him my thoughts that I couldn't comment on his antics before he met up with me. I did tell him however that he seemed to be doing this more than I was used to seeing him acting in this manner. He listened to everything, and thought we should all think about what had happened, then got up and silently walked out.

A while later I slowly made my way downstairs to pay for another night at the hostel before we ventured out into the sunlight, that would make our heads hurt all the more. We went back to Edgecliff to claim back our passports, stopping off for croissant and coffee. We had a smooth process in the Embassy, which was a bit of a shock to me. I thought they would have lost at least one of them, or got the date wrong.

We got back and took a slow walk to the *Royal Botanical Gardens* and laid down in the sun, for a while nursing my poor head. It was rather boring just watching the birds flying by, but it was just about as much as I could handle today. One bird that came into land so low over the top of us, I thought it was going to hit me as I laid there, I felt a good waft of wind.

After we had enough of sunning ourselves we went back to the hostel and laid on the bed and dozed for another 2 hours until Dutch Frank came in, excitedly telling us how he was going to an *REM* concert. He showered, strutted around in his tight, black posing pants, which were more like a thong. One of the times he was passing my bunk, I said I hope we hadn't woken him the night before in the early hours, he didn't hear me properly so came a little closer, almost thrusting his sizable manhood in his tight pants at me, as I was at eye level sitting on the bunk. He hadn't heard me after all. When he finally went we dozed a little longer before we started to feel better. We finally ventured out for our evening meal at *Scruffy Murphy's*, having a very filling, Irish stew, then it was back to the hostel to find Dale already asleep, Although I guessed he was faking as he probably didn't want another confrontation with Sharon. We wrote up our diaries and I was putting pictures on my laptop and burning a few to CD, when I noticed Sharon falling asleep writing her diary. We soon went to bed.

Chapter 9
Off we go, in the campervan.

Saturday 2nd April.

We were all up quite early in our anticipation of hitting the road in our campervan that would be our home for 40 days, well Sharon and I would be, Dale wanted to stay in Sydney for a few more days, as he hadn't seen as many of the sights as he would've wanted, so quite unhappily we would be travelling without Dale again. He was going to hitch hike to Byron Bay, which was one of our destinations on the list about 475 miles north. For some reason there was no hot water this morning, so we had a quick refreshing, cold water wash then checked out. We stored our backpacks in the secure locker at the hostel, which was actually a room, while we picked our campervan up.

On the way to the train station we spotted a shop that sold maps, getting a bargain map of Australia for $11 (£4.50). A short train ride and a 5 minute walk later, we found our back street garage where our campervan was. It was an organisation called *Wicked*, that had several of these locations round Australia that hired out said campervans, they are a very economical company, which was understandable how, as we were looking at the minimalist state of the workshop. The campervans are very well known round Australia for their iconic murals painted all over them, making them quite memorable. Our campervan may have been the most memorable for all the wrong reasons. As we stood there I saw a mechanic busying around one of the campervans, I said to Sharon, "I hope that ain't ours!" I was looking at the side of the campervan with a large portion taken up with a mural of Josef Stalin, a Russian dictator that was responsible for killing 1000's, and controlling his workforce under strict rules for minimal pay, in dangerous environments with the threat of being thrown into a prison camp if they did not work hard enough. We looked around a little more and realised this was indeed our campervan, as there wasn't any others that looked liked they were going anywhere. A short while later we were called forward to inspect our home on wheels, as we peered around to the other side, thinking it couldn't get any worse, to our horror we found another, just as iconic Russian leader, Vladimir Lenin.

Another high political communist dictator, that was equally as responsible as Stalin for a good deal of genocide. It wasn't as if we could pretend these were pictures of someone else either, as there was also the well known hammer and sickle painted on the front half of the campervan along with their names. Although the back was much more humorous with '*I was stoned, so I missed it*' painted across it. We were shown round the campervan to how everything worked, and shown how to keep the campervan mechanically sound and was left to get on with it. Before we left we had a rummage through their box of bits that people had left behind in the campervan, I didn't find anything useful but Sharon found a book, something I hadn't thought about doing. Up until now we hadn't had time to read, maybe we would have some slower evenings over the next few weeks.

I found the campervan unbelievably easy and pleasant to drive, on our way back to the hostel to pick our bags up, it was then onto our first destination to Palm Beach, driving across the *Harbour Bridge* on the way that we had walked over and looked at several times during our stay in Sydney. It took about an hour to get to Palm Beach 30 miles away, with the only point of interest here was for Sharon to see the *Home and Away* set. I didn't recognise any of it as I had only watched it a few times as a teenager, before I realised there was better things I could do with my life. It was getting quite dark by the time we got there, but Sharon could still recognise the ramp down to the beach, where someone would storm down after an argument, telling them to '*rack off*' which we did a little re-enactment of. We also got to see, the *Summer Bay Surf lifesaving club*, which is a centre point in the soap, a little shack that had roller shutters obscuring anything inside.

Driving out from Palm Beach we stopped off at a chippy for some garlic fish and ships, which we both had so we wouldn't smell each others garlic breath afterwards. We drove towards the *Blue Mountains*, an area of diverse scenery, and countryside, filled with Eucalyptus trees and rock formations. We got to the outskirts of the *Blue Mountain* region to a campsite at Katoomba clocking up 113 miles on our first day of driving, to a very basic camp site which was just a field and some toilets and one other campervan. We settled down for what we thought was going to be a cosy, good nights sleep.

Sunday 3rd April.

I woke in the night quite cold, the few blankets that were supplied were not as warm as we thought they were going to be, so we pulled out our trusty sleeping bags out of our backpacks and went to sleep a little warmer until 8.30am. Breakfast was lemon cheesecake and coffee at the local café before we headed into the *Blue Mountains*. They were originally called *Carmarthen Hills* and *Landsdowne Hill* in around 1788, until the distinctive blue haze was seen surrounding the area. The *Blue Mountains* is densely populated by oil bearing Eucalyptus trees, the atmosphere is filled with finely dispersed droplets of oil, which, in combination with dust particles and water vapour, scatter short-wave length rays of light, which makes the blue haze appear. Disappointingly there wasn't any sign of the blue haze today but it was still as astounding without this quirk of nature.

Our first sight to see today was *Wentworth Falls*, which we were initially quite disappointed with, as it was a slightly faster pace than a trickle, down a few rocks and out of sight. We continued round this large type of bowl in the ground to see the rest of the falls, which were a little more satisfying. The bowl was actually a massive chasm of a few hundred metres with *Wentworth falls* in the middle of it, with its first initial drop of about 30m (100ft), fanning across the cliff face, with a further 30m (100ft) or so zig-zagging over the rocks at the bottom, making several more smaller falls. It has been here for some time with it first being documented about 200 years ago. Maybe it was responsible for the bowl type of area it sits in today.

Breny's philosophies in life:
Always look down, you don't know what you might miss!

The path took us round an almost natural path, past cliff overhangs and dense trees to a great advantage point to see the falls, in the opposite direction there was a scenery that stretched for miles as far as the eye could see. A valley a few miles across covered with trees so dense you couldn't see the ground, with rolling hills of green over the valley into the distance without a single man made creation in sight. Makes you feel quite small in comparison. Looking down where we stood also gave us something to wonder about, just as amazing as the rest of the scenery, the advantage point we were stood on was solid rock that had been worn in the most unusual way. It was smooth with a few ridges, with the edges resembling equally smoothed out shell laid on top of each other without a single crack or seem. It must have took 1000s if not millions of years for the wind to erode this, or maybe the falls were so big once that it flowed off this area causing it to be so smooth.

Walking back we found ourselves much thirstier than we expected, as it was so humid it crept up on us, on average, a third of the time it rains in this area. After hydrating, our next stop was *Katoomba Scenic World,* an area mostly know for tourism, which I was one of the 4 million that visited here every year. This area was also mined for coal from 1878, which was the tourist attraction we were seeing next via The *Scenic Cableway.* We boarded our little cable car with about another 20 middle aged Chinese people, which soon became apparent they were fun loving people, or they didn't get out much. We were to descend the 545m (1788ft) ride into the *Greater Blue Mountains World Heritage Area* rainforest, of the *Jamison Valley*. As we took an almost sheer drop in our packed cable car there were excited cries, whooos and ahhhss, with a lot of chattering in their language from the Chinese behind us, it wasn't until we'd got about a third of the way down before they calmed down and enjoyed it. High above the treetops, we had one of the best views from this cable car, where several rock formations in this area had been named which resembled something. One of the outcrops of rocks could be seen from the cable car, which was in the shape of three statues, named The *Three Sisters*. Apart from the cable car pylons and the cable disappearing into the trees, the only other man made item that could be seen this high up was a rather large viewing platform that poked out of the trees that was full of tourists taking pictures.

Arriving at the bottom we were led by a boardwalk to preserve the environment, past termite hills, vines entwined with each other and unusual trees growing through each other to our next ride, which was the steepest in the world, with a 52 degree incline, or 1.27 in 1.00. The sign telling us this I found rather amusing, as it also said '*DO NOT leave valuables, infants or cameras on the seat beside you as they can fall off and may be lost or damaged*' It was actually the word infant in the middle of it that made me laugh, obviously whoever made this sign had a sense of humour. We boarded the little train and into the seats that were at a 45 degree angle, when seats look like this you know it's steep! These tracks were used to transport the coal out of the mine, then by rope in large buckets to the top at Katoomba. We ascended to the mining area backwards. The ceiling of the train was quite low with a chain link type fencing, which came apparent why it was needed as we neared the top. We started off much quicker than I thought, with it getting a little steeper as we were nearing the top as we plunged into darkness and entered the tunnel, it was so dark that we didn't know how tight it was until we came out the other side as daylight started to illuminate the tunnel, the rocks were a matter of centimetres from the roof, I'm sure if the roof was not there and you put your arms up you would hit the tunnel ceiling.

At the top of the tracks there were more boardwalks taking you round various coalmining tools, shacks and the actual mines. This area was mined for nearly 150 years for coal and kerosene shale, which powered the steam age, but now is used in power stations. A few shacks had been replicated to show how the miners lived back then, they were small wooden and corrugated iron buildings that you could barely get half a dozen people in. They had a primitive iron oven, which was fuelled by wood and coal as they were surrounded by it, along with a few large pots for storing water or cooking in, as well as a basic wooden table with wooden bench seats. It looked like quite hard living. Another amazing point of interest was one of the buckets that had fallen here 110 years ago, it was covered in rust and bent out of shape, it would have been carrying kerosene shale up the mountain by ropeway from the 1890s to where we boarded the *scenic cableway*. It was built, by, a German company, *Adolph Bleacher & Co*, which built many of these types of machinery, all over the world in hard to reach places. This ropeway had a significant problem with the buckets coming loose from the haulage rope and running out of control, hitting the one behind it, knocking it off and falling to where it lays today. I spun the wheel that would have ran on the rope and was shocked to how easily and smooth it turns, considering it has not been oiled, showing how good the water resistant lubricant that were used, and a tribute to the engineering skills of the German company, which is still seen in today's German engineering.

There were several other mining items scattered around from picks and shovels to the cars that ferried coal and shale in and out of the mines. Several openings to the original mines are still there with, mock ups of animated miners, that talked about the mines and mining in general. On the way out we stopped at a natural spring that came out of the mountainside, through a rusty pipe to fill up our water bottles. After our slightly less exciting climb back up to Katoomba on the cableway, we drove onto and into the night to our next destination, a little township called Tea Gardens 229 miles away, stopping off at Newcastle for an Indian meal where I enjoyed a chicken and rice takeaway, making our bed into a table to eat on in the campervan. We turned of the A1 onto the minor roads, making it nearly to our destination, seeing our first wild kangaroo a little while after a sign warning us they were in the area. We found a picnic area to spend the night with only huge mosquitoes for company and a little public toilet with no lighting, which we soon got over by directing the campervan lights into the doorway to see, We rearranging the table again so we could go to sleep, making sure to use our sleeping bags this time with the hope of a better nights sleep.

Monday 4th April.

We woke up late to the sound of rain, heavy rain! It really was awful weather so we stayed in bed, as most of our activities in this area would be walking and sightseeing. We dozed and chatted in the warmth of our sleeping bags until 11.30am, before one of us managed to get into the driving seat to head into town to Tea Gardens, to see if there was anything to do which didn't involve getting soaked. There is some confusion to why it is named 'Tea Gardens,' one account is that around 1826, the Australian Agricultural Company arrived in the area in their attempts to grow tea, which failed. With another account suggests it was the tea-trees in the area that gave it its name. We went to the information centre in search of something to do, where we met two nice oldies, which we asked the question, 'What is there to do in this area.' They looked at each other, then one of them said. "You on your honeymoon?"
"No?" I said as Sharon and I looked at each other rather puzzled.
"There goes that idea!" he replied with a little smirk.
Then I caught on as we chuckled to ourselves, as if people of our age needed that type of encouragement! He then moved on to something a little more helpful, instead of hiking trips they showed us some nice driving routes past lakes and the Mango Brush Drive, with a nice golf club to stop at for lunch that was close by, which was our next stop as it was nearing our lunchtime.

At the *Hawks Nest golf club* I was surprised at how many people were there, most of them seemed to know each other, so they must have been locals. We settled for a very reasonable mini roast with veg and a beer, after our satisfying meal we sat there writing up our diaries while, we finished off our drink, when we were approached by a rather cheerful middle aged gent, grasping a book of raffle tickets. "You wanna ticket?" He said in a way you couldn't refuse. "What can we win?" I asked hoping it was going to be something like alcohol. "A chook" was his excited reply. "A what?" I really had never heard of that word before, "A chook" he said again with just as much excitement. So this went back and forth a few times getting nowhere before he said "A chook, chook. A chicken." Obvious when you know. So we took a ticket and hoped we wouldn't get first prize, it would've taken much to long to cook on our tiny camping stove we had packed away somewhere in the back of the campervan, so

125

we were wishing for something more helpful in one of the runner up prizes, We finished up our drinks and writing our diaries and wanted to get going, even though it seemed like a good atmosphere there. We passed a happy group at one of the tables and gave them our tickets as the raffle hadn't been called and wished them luck, then headed north on the scenic drive on the Mungo Brush Road. It was a very narrow, well kept road that took us along the coast, which we could barely see for the amount of trees. 15 miles from the golf club we finished this part of our drive as we came to Bombah Broadwater, we rounded the top of this lake getting a glimpse across the water through the trees. At the top we found ourselves at the Bombah Point Ferry Terminal. The name doesn't compare to what we actually saw, it was a crossing barely 70m (230ft) wide separating Bombah Broadwater from Lower Boolambayte Lake. It cost us $4 (£1.60) for the privilege to cross this poor excuse for a lake. We boarded the little platform surrounded by white railings that you could hardly get 6 cars on to make our slow trek across.

From here via the ferry it was only 9 miles back to the A1, which gave us another experience of travelling and made a change. After a look out across a wet and grey Boolambayte Lake, we took another scenic drive on The Lakes Way down another narrow road passing trees and fields, it would have been a lot more enjoyable if it hadn't have been pissing it down so much. We joined the A1 again, which then joins The Lakes Way again to our next stop, *Coomba Parks* to see some kangaroos, and we weren't disappointed. They were everywhere! In fields, peoples front gardens, hopping across the road and everywhere we looked. I stopped so many times in this sleepy town to take pictures of them, every time I stopped they would raise their head and stare at me with their head cocked on one side, some casually leant back a little as they were eating to look at me instead. I didn't know how they would take to me so I stayed in the protection of the campervan and drove closer to a few to get a better picture. They were also very quick and would launch them selves without much warning, which also left me to believe they would be more than capable of pouncing on me if they wanted, I was enjoying seeing these strange creatures in the wild, although I'm sure the locals saw them as a nuisance, I was hoping I would not grow bored of seeing them.

We then circled Wallis lake and past Pipers Bay, joining the A1 yet again and onto Taree, about 50 miles from *Coomba Park* for our evening meal, of BBQ chicken and chips which we enjoyed in our campervan, It was already feeling like a home and an everyday occurrence, sitting up at the dinner table at the end of the day chatting. It was another 50 mile drive to Port Macquarie, which was a smooth run continuing along the A1, which is where we spent the night driving 186 miles this day. We stopped off at *Woolworths* for some fruit before finding somewhere to sleep. It took us a while before we found a cul-de-sac to sleep at near some woodland area. As it wasn't too late we thought we'd watch a film on the laptop, I had bought a box set of 10 old comedy films in Sydney for $10 (£4.16). I wasn't expecting much for this price and I think I picked the best one out of the bunch for this evenings viewing, Totally Blonde. It was ok but we didn't get to see the end as the laptop battery was nearly dead and I needed to connect the adapter for the power pack to the battery of the campervan, which I couldn't find, so we went to sleep instead.

Chapter 10
Drugs, Surfers and The Crocodile Hunter.

Tuesday 5th April.

We were up earlier this morning at 9.30am for a café breakfast despite the continuing precipitation. The lady serving us was rather a simple girl but interesting none the less, as she too had travelled a lot, mostly round England and Europe, although the more excited she got talking about her travelling the less we understood, we just listened and joined in when we could. We had told her our intended route, we would be taking in our campervan, so she thought she would give us useful tips on the outback, I could not have understood this part, as that is all I wrote on the subject in my journal.

We thought we'd give the Billabong koala and Aussie wild life park a look, with the hope of seeing some lovely little koalas. We parked up next to another *Wicked* campervan which was so much better than ours, it had graffiti on the side, and in dark pink spray paint on the back was, *'If you'd like me to put a gimp suit on you and spank you with my large pink slipper, HONK ME'* I wonder if they constantly got honked a lot, to the stage they wished they had something different like us. After admiring the paintwork we found out the park we were at was mostly outside, and as there was still no sign of the rain slowing up and at a cost of $12, (£5) we decided to give this one a miss.

We carried on north on the A1 to Nimbin, a little town well known for all the wrong reasons, 262 miles from where we were. We didn't stop for any sightseeing as it was raining for the entire journey, the only stop we did make was for petrol, where we swapped seats, when I proceeded to spend the rest of the journey dozing, making it seem a little quicker. We rolled into Nimbin at about 4.30pm and you couldn't miss the fact of why it is known as the drug capital of Australia, as many of the shops were colourfully decorated selling many drug related items. It hadn't always been this way, in fact up until the 1840s it was only inhabited by a few indigenous people, the *Bundjalung*, when loggers, were attracted by the Red Cedar trees in this forested area. By the turn of the century most of the land had been cleared and the land was turned over to dairy farming and growing bananas, unfortunately by the 1960s the dairy industry collapsed due to recession, and Nimbin went into serious economic decline, until 1973 when the *Aquarius Festival* was held in the village by a large gathering of mostly university students of alternative lifestyles, much better known as hippies.

This festival was arranged by the *Australian Union of Students* as a 10 day countercultural arts and music festival, which aimed to celebrate alternative thinking, and sustainable lifestyles. This was the third and last of its kind by this organisation, and it was also the first event in Australia that sought permission for the use of the land from the traditional owners. Hundreds of the festival goes remained in Nimbin after this festival, who formed communes in search of alternative lifestyles. It is a nice thought that 6 years later the community staged the *'The Battle of Terania Creek'* to protect the remaining local rainforest. They succeeded in this where the New South Wales government imposed a 'no rainforest logging' policy across the entire area. These type of people don't get the name 'tree hugger' for no reason. Nimbin and the surrounding area are known as the *'Rainbow Region'* and is of cultural importance to *Bundjalung* people. Nimbin is derived from the local *Whiyabul clan*, whose dreamtime speaks of the *Nimbinjee spirit* people protecting the area. Because of this spiritual culture it is also known as a place of healing with it also being the resting place of the *Warrajum*, the *Rainbow Serpent*.

I parked up in the main street quite badly as parallel parking is not my strong point especially in a campervan, as I reversed in I clipped the curb, so I pulled out and tried again with the same result. After another 3 attempts or so I gave up and basically abandoned it, once I was out of the campervan I found out why I was much worse than usual, I was on a slight bend and I was never going to be able to park straight against the curb. Feeling a little more pleased with my attempt at parking we took a walk down the main street of Nimbin, which is definitely an unusual place, every where you turn you are reminded of drug use and alternative lifestyles, with one of my favourite establishments being the Nimbin Hemp Embassy that sold every sort of item you would need in drug abuse, one of the signs outside to tempt you in was 'Jesus wore hemp.' Was it wrong that I found that funny? Most of the shops down this sleepy quiet street had brightly coloured facades with most of them having some part of a marijuana plant on them. Our first experience of the local community was definitely an impressionable one, there was a laid back guy with his heavily pregnant dog as another equally laid back guy walked up to the dog, which did not seem to be appreciated by the owner which told him to fuck off. The second chap retaliated with, "I just want to stroke yer fucking dog mate! Anyways, you're a cruel bastard keep letting your dog get pregnant, that's obvious by the way her titties are hanging down to the ground!" they didn't seem so laid back at this stage so we walked away as quickly as possible, this is one of those times I saw it as an SEP, 'Somebody Else's Problem.' It's amazing how many unrelated situations to yourself can be avoided by applying this 3 letter rule.

We strolled down the street admiring the shops and looking for a internet café, getting offered drugs many times by what we thought were random passerbyers. As neither of us were drug users we politely turned them down and was pleased that this was the end of the conversation, as we were not pursued or pressured to buy anything. All the dealers we met seemed like they would not push this way of life on you and they respected our choice. We found some internet access if you can call it that, it took me 10 minutes to read and reply to an email from Dale who was already at Byron Bay, the owner couldn't really understand me for some reason but didn't charge me for the use of his internet.

We next found a pasta restaurant with some seating outside which we took advantage of, to watch the Nimbin world go by. As we waited for our food we realised everyone really did know each other, which isn't surprising really as it has a population of just 320, a far cry from it's 6,020 residents at the height of the dairy industry in the 1960s. We got chatting to some of the locals in the café asking them for advise on what to do in Nimbin. Several people over the time in this café told us that The *Weeping Camel* was on at the cinema tonight, it seemed that everyone supported the local cinema and were all interested in seeing the film. Our tagliatelle with bacon and mushroom sauce was very filling and way too much for us, the most memorable part of this meal was the amount of garlic in it. It didn't have light seasoning of it, there were whole cloves in it, it was so well cooked that they were soft and not as harsh tasting as you would think, I ended up eating several of them, I was glad Sharon had the same.

We took every ones advice to see The *Weeping Camel*, which we had no idea on what it was about but wanted to be part of this regular social gathering. The *Bush Theatre* was a lovely homely, and in keeping with the rest of the town, a little strange building, with it's bright green walls and rusting tin roof. It was a place for locals and travellers to meet and socialise, as well as hosting gigs and music. The theatre was originally a butter factory and had not been converted entirely to what you'd expect a cinema to look like, I think they literally took out the machinery, blacked out the windows, put up a screen at one end and chucked a load of 6 seater deckchairs in there which weren't all that uncomfortable. It seemed like the whole town had turned up to see the film, the theatre was really packed to see this 2003 film, it was a little better than most of the films they showed here, as most of them were old school cult, offbeat comedies, classics, European and arthouse to name a few.

The film itself was a little slow but interesting how the nomadic Mongolian shepherds lived and how spiritual they are. The story follows a camel at the end of the calving season, after a difficult 2 day labour the mother rejects the rare white calf and fails to establish a bond with it. To restore the harmony between the mother and calf they call upon a group of Lamas who perform a ritual, however this method does not re-establish the harmony, so the family resorts to the services of an indigenous violinist for a Mongolian 'Hoos' ritual, which is secured by their two young sons who take a long journey through the desert on camels to the community marketplace to locate the musician. The Violinist who is more accurately playing a morin khuur, performs a ritual of folk music and chanting, first draping a blue cloth over the camels first hump which is to make a magical link between the mother and the harmony that is represented in the instrument. The musician plays his calming mystical sounds in the melody of the 'hoos,' ending the film seeing the mother visibly weeping and the calf suckling. I found the film quite moving and appreciated a little more of this type of belief, maybe it was because I was in a spiritual place, or the fact that I had been following and understanding other races and beliefs that made me feel this way. I'm sure if I had been given this film at home I would not have been so interested in it. This is one thing I liked so much about my backpacking experience, it forced and allowed me to do such things that I would not usually do, I am glad I got the chance to see this film here. A sad fact is that the *Bush Theatre* had to close its doors in 2013 due to lack of support from the community and patronage, as well as some disrespectful behaviour shown by some and complaints from neighbours. I think it's a great loss and I'm glad to have been a part of its history. Hopefully it will be missed and re-opened in the future.

    We drove out of town to find somewhere to sleep and across a one car wide bridge, made up of what looked like old planks with a few hundred large rivets holding the planks down which seemed a little excessive to me, the part that amused me the most on this bridge was the no overtaking sign, I suppose if you didn't read the sign you might have tried to overtake in mid air!

Wednesday 6th April.

We were up early at 9.00am to get a good start to the day with our first priority of finding a shower, after getting turned down from one campsite we found *Granny's Farm*, a well known hostel for backpackers who were much more helpful making an easy $2 (83p) from us. After a vitalising refreshing clean we went back into town to find a café for breakfast, we found one of Sharon's sandals on the roof when we got there and quite quickly realised the other one was missing, we took a slow 2 mile trip all the way back to *Granny's Farm* where we found it. With something to walk in we found our way back to the café for breakfast, stopping for a photo opportunity at the Nimbin sign with the slogan on the back of our campervan. After breakfast and catch up on our journals it started to rain again!

We decided to leave the rainy town and get to Byron Bay, hoping for a bit better weather 46 miles away, which a short while later, we were greeted with sunshine. It lifted me up no end and I was looking forward to seeing Dale again. I had a pair of walkie talkies which Dale had one of them so we could locate him better, I turned it on to hear the local police but no Dale. We knew he would be on the beach as he told me in the email a time span he would be there, so we went in search of him among the many others. It didn't take too long as he can easily be spotted in the sunshine, as he is very dark skinned and gets his shirt off at the first glimpse of catching some rays and it was really hot there, unbelievable considering the weather we were in a few hours before. We found him in his boxershorts sunbathing and reading, with everything a bit wet, apparently much to the amusement of the 60 or so onlookers, he was so engrossed in his book that he forgot about the tide coming in, this is why we couldn't raise him on the walkie talkies either as his one did not like water and squealed a lot when it was turned on. Dale had hitchhiked all the way with 3 different interesting men and enjoyed the experience, I don't know where he had slept and I don't think I wanted to know. He had also been swimming here and found out how strong the current was, when he was nearly grounded on an outcrop of rocks.

This strong current is probably why it is a magnet for surfers, since the 1960s longboard surfers have been using the natural breaks here to surf, since then Byron Bay has been much more of a tourist destination, with the surfing still having much of a strong presence here, as we saw while looking for Dale. This area also lends itself to the alternative living feel as it is so close to Nimbin, as surfers also seem a little laid back. Before the surfing industry here this town was known, like Nimbin, for its cedar tree logging, shooting the logs down the hill to the beach to be dragged to waiting boats. It has had several industries here since it was colonised besides logging, it saw the rise and decline of a dairy industry, as well as abattoirs, fishing, whaling and gold mining on the beaches, all of which diminished by 1963. At the time I was there, Byron Bay had a population of nearly 5,000, with an industry in this area today mostly dedicated to tourism and surfing.

After a quick catch up we took Dale back to the car park where we had parked, along with 5 other *Wicked* campervans and told him to guess what, was painted on ours, I was grinning in anticipation waiting for his disappointment. He was hoping for some kind of interesting picture or a film star, oh how his face dropped to see the pair of dictators he would be living with for the next 5 weeks. We knew we would be at a loose end this evening so we checked out what was on at the cinema, before a steak burger and chips meal at a pub.

Back in the campervan while we killed time until our film I attempted to plug the power adapter in the campervans cigarette lighter for the laptop, only succeeding to blow the fuse, so I was determined to find the campervan battery so we could come straight off that and not blow anything else. After a lot of rummaging I found it under the drivers seat, I thought it was obvious once I found it, as the engine, much to Sharon's surprise was under the passenger seat.

Our film at the cinema we were watching tonight was *What The Bleep Do We Know,* a head fuck to put it plainly, that combines documentary style interviews and computer animated graphics, while it tries to make a spiritual connection between the consciousness and quantum physics, with the story revolving around a photographer who begins to question her life and starts to see the world in a different way through this method of thinking, I'm not sure if I made any sense of the film or this section, if you were to watch the film, you'd be as confused as

I am. We finished our day driving 54 miles, ending up in a cul-de-sac to sleep.

Thursday 7th April.

We were woken at 8.00am by the hot and sticky atmosphere in the campervan, so we packed our sleeping bags away and got going. After filling up with petrol we had breakfast, at this particular café Dale somehow had a coupon for buy one get one free coffee, which I filled up on. We stopped off at *Woolworths* for fruit and body boards at $10 (£4.16) each. I also picked up a disposable waterproof camera, as I knew I would have the opportunity in the near future to use it.

We took the time to visit *Cape Byron lighthouse* that is near the peak of Byron Bay, I was happy to look around the outside as I didn't think I would appreciate this any more by going inside, but Sharon wanted to take a closer look at $8 (£3.33) while Dale and I took a look round the lighthouse exhibit. The lighthouse was opened in 1901 as it was much needed here, Cape Byron is the most easterly point of the continent, and with no first order light between South Solitary Island and Cape Moreton, a distance of about 250 miles, this was the most logical place to build it. When it was first built, an 8 ton optical lens which contained 760 pieces of highly polished prismatic glass was installed by a French company, powered by a concentric 6 wick burner producing 145,000cd (1cd (candela) is approximately the light of 1 standard candle). By 1922 this was replaced by a vaporised kerosene mantle to produce 500,000cd, today it now boasts to be the most powerful lighthouse in Australia, with a light source of 2,200,000cd, thanks to being converted to mains electricity in 1956. The lens is massive and can easily be seen from the ground, I don't think I would have wanted to look at it when it was on!

As it was a lighthouse, they tend to favour high ground and this one was no exception perched high on a rocky cliff face, we wandered round taking pictures of the lighthouse and the many magpies, which incidentally I thought the only resemblance they had to British magpies were the colouring, walking down the hill towards the beach we passed a guy with something rolled up in some sort of bag on his shoulder about 9m (29ft) long, he stopped and asked us if we wanted to go hang gliding at $120 (£50) for Sharon and I, Dale has had more than his fare share of anxiety with flying in a plane, yet alone something with wings and no floor or engine so it wasn't even an option for him. We had seen a hang glider circling quite high above the lighthouse, he was taking off from the cliff, flying about a bit before landing on the beach. We could have both been hitched up to the thing and flew about, I would have much enjoyed it and we were seriously considering it, until it became overcast and looking like it could rain at any moment.

We left the murky skies of Cape Byron and drove north 58 miles to Surfers Paradise, to check out the 2 mile stretch of iconic beach, off the gold coast area. It is well know for its beach and the hundreds of tourists it attracts from around the world, who also visit for the numerous attractions around this small city of 18,000 people, such as boating and the aquaduck, market place, shopping stores and attractions, as well as one of the biggest tourist attractions, the annual *Surfers Paradise Festival*. It is a celebration of local music, film, art, food and fashion. It's held across 4 weekends over March and April, which we would be missing. Like the name suggests we would be surfing here today, or more accurately body boarding, in fact it was more of an attempt in the sport, we were nowhere near advanced to surf, none of us had ever been on a board! So this was a great way of having some fun in the surf. We picked a spot up the beach where there were no swimmers or surfers, to save our embarrassment on just how badly we managed these bits of hard foam, and there was no doubt about it, we were bad! I think it was more about enjoying the warm sea than trying to look cool on these boards while we tried to wrestle them over the 1 to 2 metre waves (3ft to 6ft). We took turns sitting on the beach as we only had the 2 boards between the three of us, getting stung by the sand as it was a little windy which picked up the grains, carrying them down this long beach and bombarding me while I tried to relax and take pictures. By the time we left, there was a small sand drift that had piled itself up against our bags and towels, making it even more difficult to dry ourselves.

After we'd finished our repeated failed attempts at body surfing, and exfoliating with our sandy towels, we made our way up the beach back to the city. It was a short walk up the beach that had a consistent width from the shore to the long row of skyscrapers that border the beach. Coming off the beach we found a shower head in the open, just stuck there about 3m (10ft) up, so we all gathered under it with our soaps and got to work, it must have looked a sight, 3 people in swimwear soaping themselves up in every crevice including what was under our swim suits, we didn't really care how many people were walking past, we were dirty and our campervan didn't have a shower.

Time was getting on so we went in search for food, finding a reasonably priced chicken curry, which was more than enough for one person. It started to rain again by the time we finished our meal, Sharon and I were stuffed so headed back to the campervan while Dale went in search for more food. Dale finally returned and we got on the road again onto the M1 to Brisbane, which was a short drive of about 50 miles stopping off at a *Target* store in Springwood to see if it had any provisions we might need. The car park was a little different here with large canopies stretched over large portions of parking spaces so we didn't get wet, but that was the most exciting thing here as we all came away with nothing, I thought about buying a snorkel and goggles but thought I wouldn't get much use out of it and that would be a useless item I'd be hauling around with me. In hindsight it would've been an excellent item to have in my bag.

By the time we got nearly to Brisbane our total mileage today was 119 miles, we drove around for a bit before we found a suitable car park to sleep in. We thought we'd watch another one of the films from my comedy pack, which was *Copper Mountain* starring Jim Carrey. Now, I am a massive fan of this actor and I thought I had seen every one of his films and thoroughly enjoyed all of them, this however was not one of those films that I would enjoy, it was actually his second film he had starred in at 21 years old, 11 years before his big hits of *Ace Ventura* and The *Mask* which shows how much he learnt in those 11 years after watching *Copper Mountain*. The film was about 2 friends who travel to a ski resort, with one looking to ski, while the other spends time trying to pick up women. When it was more accurately just over an hour of film involving a few scenes with Jim Carrey, with the rest taken up with some old guy singing country music, badly! It was beyond crap and more like sewage. So to avoid becoming brain dead we skipped every song and painstakingly watched the bad acting of Jim, managing to cut the film down to about 10 minutes, can you class it as a film at a little over an hour?

The more than boring film was put away for some type of Frisbee fun in the desert somewhere at a later date, and for some reason we were all so tired and went to sleep quite easily.

Friday 8th April.

A headache inconsiderately woke me this morning at 8.30am, we ate our fruit and went in search of another target store as it started to rain again, I had my fill of coffee in the café and then it was time to take our campervan for a service as stated in our agreement when we hired it. We begged and pleaded with them to re-spray the entire campervan but slightly rough guy said he just didn't have the time today. Looking at one of the other campervans here that had been freshly painted made me feel a bit better about what we had on our own campervan. It was 6 days after Pope John Paul the second had died, one of these larger campervans had been painted with the image of the pope holding his well know cross which was painted very well in good taste, however the other hand and the slogan was the problem. He was giving the finger with a caption saying '*Screw you all, God needs me*'. We were quite horrified at it, but then again now I think of it, could it be one of the highest compliments as it could mean he was so good at his chosen path in life that the creator of everything needed his help? The opposite side could not be found tasteful in anyway as it had the pope laying down giving the finger with the caption '*Pope John Paul II Final Tour*' So we counted our blessing and settled for a new slogan on the back.

I came up with a great idea for the back of our van that read; '*Some like the highways, we like it up the dirt track*' the thought came from all the unmade roads we had travelled and of the many more I was sure we had to come, to see some of the more hard to reach places. The other 2 were not as keen as I was, so we pawed our way through a phrase book of these one line funnies and settled for '*Good girls get fat, bad girls get eaten*'. The chap who sprayed the dirty one liner, told us that the slogans on every campervan, were chosen by people like us who had hired them.

We went into town with the idea of looking round, and as in most cities it is always hard to find anywhere cheap or free to park, so I headed for the multi storey until Dale started to throw a tantrum as he was so tight with his money, even though we'd be splitting it 3 ways. So we wasted several dollars of fuel trying to find something to Dales liking, and failing, ending up back at the multi storey. We squeezed our campervan in there and went for a walk while Dale went to a radio station to try and get some work there.

We passed the *Shrine of Remembrance*, a small cream stone circular building made from Helidon sandstone with its roof supported by its 18 pillars, almost every city centre in Australia has a war memorial like this which citizens gather on 25 April, *ANZAC* Day (Australia and New Zealand Army Corps), to pay tribute to young men and women who have fought and died for their country to ensure their freedom. It was very well built as it is moulded over the subway where the shrine of memories are, that was established in 1930. I found out how much more was here sometime after the event, now knowing this, I would have liked to have spent more time here.

Moving on we found *St Stephens Cathedral* surrounded by a large modern building, built between 1864 to 1922. Gothic in style built with large, almost unfinished looking bricks with 2 thin towers each side of the large window above the front door. It's built on a platform a little higher than the street, accessed by several steps. Walking up to this we found a small chapel, which was open with a lot of activity going on. Inside there was a small room with some wooden art, one of which was large slats of old wood arranged to make a semi circle with some artistic expressive art painted on it, you know the type where you load your paint brush up and randomly flick different colours over something. There was also a wooden sculpture of Sister Mary MacKillop, which for most of us, have no idea who she is and why she would have a statue made in her honour. She is actually responsible for one of the greatest Australian stories in the religious sense, Mary MacKillop made several trips in to Brisbane after her arrival to Queensland in 1869, establishing many schools, convents and orphanages becoming a long lasting symbol of the catholic community. There was a college here today who were taking a tour and there may have been some interest to me as there, as the person leading the group seemed to know what he was talking about so I took a seat to see what would happen. What happened was, I got, chatted up by a lovely Australian college girl, she started with. "So where you from?"
Thinking she may have thought I was a student from somewhere else I said. "Oh I'm just passing through, I'm backpacking but I live in England."

"Oh, you're a pommy." she said with a little smile. At first I was a bit offended by being branded a name I had never used myself to describe English people, even though recently both the Australian and New Zealand government have ruled it as not an offensive term after complaints were filed. Funny! As like myself I was initially offended but that was obviously not taken into consideration. There are many explanations for this name calling, some of which have now been disapproved due to lack of evidence, it is most probably derived from the word pomegranate, as they believed that sunburn occurred more frequently among English immigrants, turning their skin the colour of pomegranates.

After a moment of thought of my comparison to a fruit I soon came to like the idea of being labelled and recognised as a Brit and I liked her a lot more, she was quite pretty too but I made sure not to get to friendly with her, as I was very aware that Sharon was watching every move, I don't think she was too worried so she gave her a little grin to make sure she new I was taken.

Our next tourist stop was the botanical gardens. It was first selected as a public garden in 1828 and it was obvious it is well established by the amount of large trees and shrubs there, despite being flooded 9 times in its history as the gardens border the Brisbane River. It is home to cycads, palms, figs and bamboo to name a few in its 49 acres of parkland. One tree in particular grabbed my attention. it was fairly large with overhanging branches with some part of the tree growing out of the branches and into the ground like a root or some sort of support.

On the way out of the park we joined George Street and came across the French style *Queensland Houses of Parliament* which borders the park, a lovely old building which was completed in 1867, it has an almost multi coloured look to its sandstone brick work as each brick is coloured slightly different. The front of it was dominated with windows and a 3 peak roof, the end 2 of which are hip style with the middle one of similar design but curved out on each side. We carried on walking along George Street seeing the modern buildings to be surprised by another old building, kinda strange seeing these old buildings along this road, stuck in the middle of a modern metropolis, seeing the newer high buildings towering behind them. This building was just as old as the last, *The*

Mansion was completed in 1889 as 6 terraced houses, however today, it's tenanted by shops, restaurants as well as offices. It's called *The Mansions* for a good reason, they are big houses! A three storey building with a balcony on each level with each house having 4 white arches on each level built into it, and 10 of the same size arches deep. They were expensive houses, at the time it cost £11,700 to construct, about a third of what it cost to build the houses of Parliament we had just seen.

Our next stop was the *Gallery of Modern Art,* that exhibited paintings and pictures as well as what some people class as modern art. It's a very spacious gallery with escalators to the first floor, which gave you a good view of one of these modern arts, a large shallow rectangular pool nearly full of metallic silver balls about 30cm across that were floating along some kind of gentle current and idly clanked against each other, it was one of those things we had to touch and help along its way. There were also many good paintings of varying degrees of complexity, one of which was, some ones faces that seemed badly painted from a distance, upon getting closer you could see many other faces painted into the portrait that made up the picture.

Leaving the gallery it started to rain, so we went in search for some shelter when we came across The *Treasury Casino*, it was another grand 6 storey building with architecture in keeping with some of the older buildings in an Edwardian Baroque design in sandstone ashlar, which was built in 3 stages between 1886 and 1928 and now accommodates 80 gaming tables and over 1,300 gaming machines as well as a hotel. The inside was as elaborate as you would expect from a casino, the centre of the gaming area was surrounded by a 3 storey building, and palm trees dotted about the gaming floor. It was heaving with gamblers which was surprising considering it was 5pm, we however were not here to gamble as we only wanted to get out of the rain so we had a beer instead. I settled for a pint of 4X bitter, which is just the same as the 4X larger back home, which on several occasions round Australia found that the locals don't really care much for it.

We sat there for a while listening to the live music before it was time to leave and meet up with Dale at the multi storey, we then found the closest pub for something to eat which we didn't have to go far to find, as there was one across the road from the multi storey where I had a $5 (£2.08) steak and mushroom meal.

Our next priority for the rest of the evening was to find some live music. We found ourselves stumbling over The *Shack*, which had another unusual theme of writing of random things all over the walls, some of the walls were lined with corrugated iron. I topped up with a bowl of chips with chilli sauce before moving on to find more music, only finding a little more live music in the mall, which was not bad at all. After this we had exhausted the live music scene here this evening but Dale wanted to find somewhere that had karaoke on, Sharon and I had done enough walking and said we'd meet him back at the campervan, Dale however thought he'd be in for a late one and wanted us to leave him there and he'd hitch hiking the 50 miles to our next destination, *Australia Zoo*. I was really unhappy with this again and I snapped at him a little, I didn't want him yet again going into the unknown when we could all go together. But he was stubborn in his confidence he'd be ok. After one more attempt at getting him to come back earlier telling him how did he think I'd feel if he got hurt or robbed by doing something stupid, probably involving to much alcohol. It didn't make any difference to his plans, but he did say if he wasn't back by midnight to leave without him. Reluctantly I left him knowing he really had no intention of meeting us back at the campervan at that time, and I was right.

After a 90 minute call to my mum and a little rest in the campervan, we drove out of the city with out Dale to find some quiet street to sleep on, stopping on a little back road just off the highway near *Australia Zoo* that was dead quiet driving.

Miles driven - 68

Saturday 9th April.

We were up at 8.45am and were at the zoo soon after, I'd barely pulled into the car park, getting my things together standing at the side door when I heard the eager patter of skipping then, "What you up to you pair of prats!" I knew it must have been Dale, not from his description of us but the skipping sound.

We got $5 (£2.08) off the admission as the ticket lady thought I was a student and I wasn't going to tell her any different, making my entry $29 (£12.08). The *Australia Zoo* at the time, was owned by Steve Irwin and his wife Terri, but tragically in 2006 Steve died in a rare, fluke accident when a stingray stung him on his chest. The site covers over 100 acres, much of which has been expanded since 1997 thanks to Steve's hit show '*The Crocodile Hunter*' as well as several other spin off shows, with all the funds raised by filming of this as well as merchandise they have funded new conservations, buildings and new exhibits. Since I visited here in 2005 the zoo has continued to expand gaining more land allowing room for an open range safari, also an animal wildlife hospital which is the largest of its kind in the world at a cost $5 million (£2.1m), Steve and Terri always maintained they did this as their animals came first.

But back to the time I was there when Steve was alive and was seen as the greatest expert in animals of all time, we were hoping to get a glimpse of the legend, asking at the entrance what the chances were of him hosting one of the crocodile shows, which I'm sure they got asked by nearly every admittance, they told us it is always possible if he's about.

One of the first enclosures we came across was of a giant tortoise, it was a big one and old at 174 years, there were 2 idly laying there with an assortment of vegetables that they didn't seem to bothered about, taking the odd bite. After a while they got up and strolled around in their usual slow manner, which is probably why they live so long.

We then made our way to the elephants, 3 of which were coming out to eat, standing behind a flimsy fence, there was a lot of us lined up for the feeding several rows deep. A few zoo keepers were walking back and forth along the line with a bucket of apples, we eagerly grabbed a few and I noticed the cores had been cut out, so I asked why, "It gives them gas, and you don't want an elephant with gas." is the reply I got. I enjoy meeting large animals like this, as they can be surprisingly gentle and precise, they were also surprisingly hairy which was very coarse. We were about to leave when I notice along the track the elephants had came, someone on a off road motorcycle came riding up with a child with him, chatted to one of the keepers then turned around and went. He was a little too far away to make out as he had a hat and sunglasses on, but I'm sure it was Steve Irwin.

Next was an animal I had never seen in real life, and this wouldn't be the last by the time I left this zoo. The Koala pen had an open area to the front with several eucalyptus trees guarded by a keeper, as there was one little dopey fella sitting in a tree here about 2m (6ft) up. Their main diet is eucalyptus, so as a result from this limited nutritional value they sleep for 20 hours a day, so it's most probable when visiting these creatures you will not catch them awake, and this was one of those times. Visitors are able to hold the koalas here if they're awake, but we had to make do with giving it a little petting on the back half of their very thick short hair.

We went to see a show that seemed a little lacking in other visitors, maybe not so many people like snakes, and fewer that like to pet them as you have the opportunity as they walk them along the rows. I for one love snakes and have only had the chance to touch them a handful of times, another one of those creatures I give a lot of respect to as they will always be a wild animal, which could, and have turned on their keepers. This one however was only a small constrictor so I was quite safe. There was also an educational part to this as they re-enacted what would happen if you were to be bittern by a poisonous snake and how to treat the wound, something I was paying attention to as we would soon be heading into the out back, knowing there are many poisonous ones out there. A bird show followed with several parrots and cockatoos, as well as a type of herring that was diving for its food in the pond. There were also a few eagles, and a kookaburra, which is another animal I had never seen before.

We next visited the crocoseum that had several shows with different animals, in this 5000 seat arena that is very spacious and another first of its kind when it was built, that showed such animals, with a high chain link fence to make sure there is no way for the animals to get out. Most of the area is taken up by a clear kidney shaped pond, which leads out at one end to a system of channels and gates to guide the crocs into the arena pond that is surrounded by a well kept grassy area. The crocoseum was one of Steve Irwin's lifelong dreams. He wanted to provide his visitors with the opportunity to see crocodiles in clear water, to help educate the public how crocodiles live and behave in the wild, as they will usually hide in murky water, which I think is one of the main reasons to their high success in catching their prey and it's no wonder they have been on this earth for at least 225 million years, the only reason for their decline now, with some breeds at risk of extinction is due to habitat destruction and poaching.

The first show was the tigers, I don't think they were full grown adults although they were as big as a human, and it was obvious they had a good bond with their keepers, as to start with they were wrestling and rolling around with them. They also were being given bottles of milk with a teat, they were more like babies how they suckled clasping their giant paws round the keepers arms, some sat on the ground in a begging position, while another stood on a low platform draping its paws over its keepers shoulder. They then wanted to show them in action, as it was hot they wanted them to get into the pond to cool down, but like their smaller domesticated cousins, they don't like water that much so needed a lot of encouragement in the form of a blue barrel and a string bag. The keepers do put their all into interacting with them which is apparent that this was not done just for the show, as the tigers had a real bond with them. They were very playful with the barrel and net bag, the keeper would shake it in front of them and then run off with the tigers close behind, then much to our surprise they carried on running and jumped into the pond, the tigers at this stage were not so keen until about the 4th attempt and they followed with what looked like a vicious pounce, even though the keepers knew they were playing it must seem a little scary jumping in then seeing a tiger or two jumping towards you.

Next was what we all new and loved about the *Australia Zoo*, the crocodile show. The gates were opened silently then, slowly one of the beasts came swimming effortlessly up the thin channel and into the pond. The keepers were now taking on a much more defensive pose as they proceeded to tell us about their natural habitat, how they hunted and moved among a few of the points we learnt this day. The feeding time came of which I remembered from seeing countless shows of Steve's. The most common way of feeding them here was by a platform that protruded out from one end over the water several metres and was about 1.2m (4ft) above the water. They would then shake a piece of meat over the edge of the platform enticing one of them over, as slowly as they had moved into the arena one approached the keeper, slowing to a near standstill as its head so very slowly broke the surface of the water, it would home in on its meal and with a sudden definite movement it stood about 1.5m (5ft) out of the water at an unbelievable height, then the meat was dropped into its mouth. They did this several times without the croc faltering once and were as definite as the first time. These are the types of creatures that do not make mistakes which is why you never give them a chance to get near you, because you will be eaten, or severely hurt if it's not hungry, you don't get second chances. They also encouraged them out of the water onto the grassed area to get a good idea on how big they were, they seem slow and cumbersome on land with only being able to achieve 12 to 14mph over a short distance, compared to in the water where they are much quicker and can launch themselves onto land much quicker than you or I could move. We got to see another croc show after this and still no Steve Irwin but it was still very good. The second show had one of the biggest crocs at 1 ton, that's 2204lb. Nearly 16 times, my own weight! Even though he was even more of a lumbering oaf, the keepers still kept out of his way and quick to jump as soon as they snapped at their raw meat treats.

Lunch consisted of fast food, which I was expecting to be extortionately priced, but I got a big burger and chips for $9.50 (£3.95), it also came with free ketchup that Dale squirted all over himself, to be fair I hadn't seen this design in ketchup dispensary either. The sauce came in a small packet with 2 rectangular reservoirs that held the sauce. It was dispensed by pinching these together, forcing the sauce along a channel on the top to a point, to me it was quite obvious, I had already used 2 of them when Dale decided to give it a go, pointing it towards himself, I don't know why I didn't tell him it was pointing the wrong way, maybe it was my strange sense of humour.

After lunch we saw another croc show at a different enclosure, this one seemed to be their own enclosure they stayed in, a large pond surrounded by grass verges and trees. They had another feeding session enticing them out of the water, dropping the meat in the mouth as they lurched forward to get it. This one was a lot more cramped and I was concerned the keeper could get caught out, but in some ways they showed the were a little safer as they could duck behind the trees as crocs can't manoeuvre themselves round tight corners. This one was a little closer to the action, as there were 2 fences with roughly 1.2m (4ft) gap between them with the seating a few feat from the fence, with a much smaller capacity than the crocoseum we still got a good view of them.

We took a walk through the kangaroo park that was so big you soon forget it's an enclosure full of roos hopping around, there were not so many big ones and they were all very tame, most probably because people like us were feeding them as they would gently hop up and take the food out of our hands. There were many lying down and were completely at ease with us crouching to pet them. They were so relaxed one let Dale lay behind it and put his face between its ears although I stopped him at trying to put his sunglasses on it. It calmly sat there while I snapped away on my camera. We also got one with Sharon's little stuffed dog next to it for one pose. I couldn't help comparing the facial features of kangaroos to that of a Great Dane.

There was a second tiger show at, another location, which was a little different as it was enclosed to the visitors side by a large window, allowing you to get much closer. The pond came up to the glass so you could see under the ponds water line, which made for a good view as the keepers enticed the tigers in the pond by jumping in like the last tiger show. One of the tiger's favourite toys here was a tractor tyre that was rolled into the water and then commandeered immediately by 3 tigers. Another came close to the glass where I was, so I was only a few centimetres away from it.

We viewed so many enclosures, to many to remember and we could have spent a day or 2 there to take it all in without being rushed. We also got to see some other native animals before we left like the Tasmanian Devil which is actually a marsupial and the size of a small dog which are only found wild on Tasmania, they became extinct in Australia about 3000 years ago by an unknown reason. The one we saw today was asleep so we only saw a small bundle of black fur curled up in a corner.

The cassowary is another unusual bird found in Asia and Australia, a flightless bird similar to an emu at 1.5m to 1.8m (5–6ft) with their feet like an overgrown chickens. Their necks brightly coloured, almost fluorescent with blue and reds, quite a shy creature but can inflict serious injuries if provoked.

We got to see many different snake and lizard enclosures, as well as two more animals, which was another first for me, the first was a pair of wombats. They are the most adorable little creatures at about 1m (40") long with their stubby legs and round face. The enclosure they were in was minded by 2 keepers which were telling us about them sitting on the grass making a fuss of them, just like you would a dog, they had a real character to them. After a short while they decided to take them for a walk! One keeper put a harness on one of them and exited out of the enclosure to where we were, much to the disapproval of his friend who grunted profusely until it too got to go for a walk, it was practically sulking. We got to pet these too, we were told to stay behind it in case they got a little enthusiastic.

Another first for me again a little further on was another animal on a lead, a dingo, which is basically a wild dog so it wasn't any surprise they could walk them around on a lead, although they are classified as a subspecies of the grey wolf.

We kept ourselves busy with the rest of the more common animals you'd expect to see at a zoo up until 5pm. We left here and didn't stop until we got to Hervey Bay covering 139 miles, which would be the town where we were going to leave from for our Fraser Island trip. We stopped in town for a takeaway before dropping Dale of at a hostel as he had an extra night with his trip, as he didn't book his Fraser Island trip with us, he would be with a different group although we would be on the island at the same time. We left Dale to have a sleep in a real bed while we drove to the outskirts of town to sleep.

Chapter 11
Four wheel drives and sailing yachts.

Sunday 10th April.

    We were up at 8.45am to drive into town back to Dales hostel, he wasn't there so we slipped into the hostels café for toast where we found Dale. After trying to find somewhere for Dale to watch a football match we took a walk along the beach then back towards town where we passed a bowls green and found we could hire balls for a game, as none of us had played before we had a game. We were vaguely familiar with the rules and started playing until we came across a difficult scenario on the scoring, Dale and I looked around for the oldest person there to ask for clarification, the frail old guy who must have been nearing 100 put us straight. Dale and I both won a game and it was time to move on, the heat was getting a little unbearable and Dale had to get back for his orientation for his 4 wheel drive trip.

    By the time we had packed our bags for the trip in the campervan among the ants that had set up home there, it was time for our orientation in a small room with 20 others. We all instantly started talking to each other and it seemed like a good crowd and got on well, which was good as we'd be spending the next 3 days together, except for 3 people that seemed to stand out. I got the feeling immediately that these Irish guys could be trouble, it's a widely known saying that Irish are good at two things, drinking and fighting. But I wasn't going to presume this stereotypical opinion of them and kept an open mind, the leader of the 3, Carl which I didn't mind that much, was an over confident joker you couldn't help but like. We were sorted into our 2 groups with 11 in our group, joining us were the 3 Irish with another girl Lynn who was dating one of them, Ralph the German guy, Becky, who was a rather drippy girl travelling on her own, two Dutch girls who were travelling together, Kirsten and Anmica (Ann) who were really nice, but I always do find Dutch people nice. The last person who was travelling on her own was an English girl Sarah, probably the most liveliest and good fun type of person of them all. One of the first things on the agenda was to nominate someone to stump up $750 (£312) on their credit card, in case of any loss of equipment or damage to the vehicle, I quietly said to Sharon not to mention she had a card for this deposit, the agreement is anything that needs to be paid for at the end was to be split between everyone, this was one of those SEPs for the only reason that if a large amount of money did occur from the result of one person, would everyone pay up? In that scenario the person holding the credit card would get hit for the bill, which I thought was a little unreasonable and a $100 deposit from each person would have been better. Everyone looked at each other with no one wanting to give up their details, until some persuasion from the guy who was asking for it, told us we wouldn't be going unless someone came up with a credit card. We were then saved by Becky, who reluctantly said, "I suppose it'll be me then"

We were also shown how to use the 4 wheel drive and what to do when we got stuck, with our basic instructions for sandy areas was to put the 4 wheel drive into low ratio and keep it at about 4000 rpm. They showed us a burnt out clutch for a visual on what happens when riding the clutch while getting bogged down in the sand. This would be one of those occasions where we would lose our deposit. We all chipped in $15 (£6.25) for food for the 3 days and a few were nominated to go shopping, while Sharon and I bought a couple of cheap boxes of wine and a few cans of beer before meeting up with Dale, it was then to an Irish pub, Hoolihans for our evening meal, where I had a very nice Guinness pie.

Sharon and I took an evening stroll along the beach while Dale went in search for a cheap drinking hole. We went back to our hostel we were booked into as part of the trip for a little lay down on our bottom bunk as we were feeling a bit tired. There was 8 of us in this room that were all going to Fraser Island, 3 of which were a mother with her son and daughter from America, incredibly nice in the typical American way that you couldn't dislike. We laid there until 9pm when Dale called to us through the window, to ask if we wanted to join him at Hoolihans to watch West Brom playing Aston Villa as they were screening it. So we took our diaries to catch up on and went for a drink, not so much to see the game but to get out and do something. After the game we were ready to turn in for the night and we all made our way back, meeting up with a few people from our hostel on the way. You seem to talk easier to strangers of like minded people who are backpacking and this evening was one of those evenings, we were chatting and walking down the quiet streets, as we crossed one particular road near our hostel several people were walking in the opposite direction, most probably going out on the town. We just all instantly stopped there right in the middle of the road and started chatting, one guy who had already had a few to drink started chatting to me saying how the pen behind my ear suited me and he thought he should try it, pulling out a pen and lodging it behind his own ear. It didn't take us long to exhaust this conversation so I turned to Sharon to join in with her, before we all dispersed to do what we were going to do. As we walked away Sharon pointed out the guy chatting to me was obviously gay, I hadn't really seen this at the time as I never feel threatened by homosexuals as some men do, I thought he was being nice. I felt pretty good about myself thinking someone was after me in that sense and I wasn't even trying! We slipped into our room and got off to sleep quite quickly.

Fraser Island. Day 1

Monday 11th April.

It was an early start at 6.20am, and we were the first up so getting washed at the communal shower block was quick as it was empty, I thought this would be the best wash I'd have for a few days. We had to check out before rushing back to the hostel café for a breakfast roll and coffee, we were starting to run a bit late, and I was getting concerned of letting the rest of the group down, I never like being late for anything so we rushed our breakfast down and got to the depot, where we would pick up our 4 wheel drives, to find we were one of the first there, with most of the others running much later than us. The Irish, had been heavy on the drink the night before and were one of the last there and quite quiet as they were probably hung over. Carl was the designated driver to drive to the quay, and had to drive back after the trip, he told us this was the only driving he was going to do because he would be drunk for the rest of the time.

We were introduced to our vehicle, a 4 wheel drive Landcruiser and it was massive at about 5m (16ft) long and a ground clearance of at least 50cm (20"). We loaded up the campervans with all our backpacks, with the camping equipment and food in the storage cage strapped onto the roof bars, we climbed in with 3 in the front, and the other 8 of us on bench seats in the back either side of the Landcruiser, which was very snug. Quietly I was slightly concerned, as I was the only person there who had driven a vehicle this size, along with the weight of the 11 people, and the weight of the equipment and food on the roof it would make it fairly unstable and handle unpredictably, which I'm sure most of the others were unaware of. To date 3 people have been killed and many more have been injured severely enough to be airlifted to hospital from Fraser Island, on tours such as the one I was on today. Just 5 weeks before, nine backpackers were airlifted to hospital after their vehicle overturned at high speed on a corner that we would be passing the next day.

Carl drove satisfactory enough to the ferry that would be taking us to the island, along with the second, 4 wheel drive behind us that had the American family in, who I would have preferred to be with. We boarded with several other 4 wheel drives, with some on other similar tours like us, with some families that went to this island regularly, as well as a fuel tanker and a couple of lorries. We got out and went up on deck to take in the view on the 30 minute crossing, grabbing a coffee and muffin on the way. We thought we'd get our suntan lotion on too, only to have the wind blew it off the wall on the top deck, so I had to make an unscheduled trip back down to the car deck to retrieve it.

Fraser Island is approximately 75 miles long and 15 miles wide with a population of 194. It has been formed from sand accumulating on volcanic bedrock over the past 750,000 years and has a diverse plant life and rainforests, mangrove forests and eucalyptus, due to an abundant of naturally occurring mycorrhizal fungi in the sand, which release nutrients in a form that can be absorbed by the plants. There is evidence here that shows Aboriginal Australians occupied Fraser Island at least 5,000 years ago, with a permanent population of 400 to 600 that grew to as many as 3,000 in the winter months due to abundant seafood resources. The arrival of European settlers was the start of the end for the *Butchulla* people. European settlement in the 1840s overwhelmed the Aboriginal lifestyle with weapons, disease and lack of food, and by 1890 the Aboriginal population had been reduced to just 300, with the remaining Aborigines leaving the island in 1904, to where they were relocated to various missions across Queensland. Only a few families stayed behind and worked in the local logging or fishing industries.

We arrived and disembarked down the ramp with Carl giving it a bit of welly onto the unmade sandy road, hitting a large bump which seemed to signify the adventure had started to a few cheers and ouches from us in the back. We wound ourselves along the unmade deep rutted tracks to the other side of the island, parking up a little way from the coast to see our first place of interest, Lake Wabby. It's one of the smallest freshwater lakes on the island, which is also below sea level and is one of the deepest at about 12m (39ft). Its main supply of water is from a natural spring beneath it and it has formed a lake by the natural depression in this area, with dunes fortifying this, that were formed by sandblow blocking the waters of this natural spring. It was about a 1.5 mile trek along narrow paths cramped by overhanging branches and was quite steep in places to the lookout point, high above the clear green water, this lake along with most of the other lakes on Fraser Island are clear, which is mostly due to the white sand acting like a filter. The view was great from this advantage point, looking out across the hills filled with trees. It was another half a mile down the steep dune to the water where we found it a little too cold to do too much swimming, but refreshing all the same. We lazed here for a while watching the odd large fish swim by, this is one of the few lakes on Fraser Island that are not too acidic to support life.

    We made our way back to the 4 wheel drive for lunch, spreading various lunch items across the bonnet and we all tucked in. I made myself a peanut butter and chocolate spread sandwich I took a seat on a log next to Carl. We then got a visit from a rather long monitor lizard, we had seen him hanging around earlier on one of the trees, and it had obviously been waiting here for our return, as I would think many people like us ate food at this car park after visiting lake Wabby. His body was about 2 foot long with a tail just as long, he first came crawling under the Landcruiser flicking his long tongue searching for scraps, snatching a few bits of food on the way to where Carl and I were sitting, although they are meat eaters and catch live animals such as mice, I was sure he wouldn't attack me so I sat there calmly taking pictures much to the dismay of everyone else who were jumping at its every sudden move. It scavenged around the log where I was and stepped over my feet and licked a toe as it passed, again I didn't flinch as I didn't want to scare him, I quite like lizards and owned a chameleon at one point which I often handled. After it exhausted this area it disappeared into the trees and we finished up, packed everything back in the Landcruiser and left for the beach.

    We got onto the beach about a third of the way up the island onto *75 mile beach*, it is so called as this is apparently how long it is, when in fact this part that is very straight along the east coast is more like 60 miles with the total length of the east side of the island at about 75 miles. It is always about this length as it is constantly changing due to the movement of the sand from the sea. It's an informal highway, and in Australia highway rules dictate that road vehicles must give way to aircraft. We parked up on the high side of the beach where it was quite sandy as the aircraft favour the wet smooth sand near the water line. There are regular trips here by plane for the much better off people who just want to see it from the air and take a walk round the *Maheno* ship wreck which we were on our way to.

We first had a quick stop at Eli Creek, but as we were running short on time we had to make a quick stop to take a few pictures, which was a bit of a shame as it is the largest fresh water spring on the east coast of the island, formed by a natural spring and held in a rock basin about 30m (97ft) below sea level, with about 80 million litres of water a day being deposited in the sea, which has wound its way from several miles inland and has cut its way down to the volcanic rock. By the time it reaches the beach it has formed some large chilly ponds and channels that we splashed about in.

Further along the beach we reached the shipwreck *Maheno*, this luxury 5,323ton passenger ship was built in Scotland in 1904 and held the *Blue Ribbon* in trans-Atlantic crossing for several years until the first world war, where it was used as a hospital ship in the English channel. It was then purchased, by a Sydney shipping company, which was then used for the Trans-Tasman crossing, the area between Australia and New Zealand until 1935 before it was sold as scrap to a Japanese ship breakers. On the 25th June 1935, while it was being towed to Osaka, she was caught in a strong cyclone about 50 miles off of the coast of Queensland. The towline broke, beaching it on the east coast of Fraser Island 14 days later. You would think in 14 days they would have been able to get another towline on it! There were several unsuccessful attempts to re-float the ship until it was abandoned. Today, more than half of it is below the sand with many parts rusting away with other parts of the hull completely gone, which was evident as we approached from behind seeing a small part of the stern protruding above the sand, then dipping away to join it about a third of the way down the ship to where the hull is either rusted away or bent out of shape. There are many parts of this old steamer that have stood the test of time that can still be made out today 70 years later, only the steel remains where you can easily make out such things as cleats, pulleys and the bridge cabin. There are several other jagged twisted pieces of metal that were once a crucial part of the ship that can be barely made out. We took a walk around it peeping through the rusty portholes to the open expanse inside, with the odd wall or support beam that once housed all the cabins that have long been rusted away. There's a sign saying *'for your own safety access on or around the Maheno is not permitted'*. And for once I actually obeyed the rules looking at how deadly the jagged metal looked if you were to fall on it.

We drove on further down the beach to *Beaches Base Camp*, which is about three quarters the way up 75 mile beach, this was where we would be staying for the 2 nights we were here. Carl was still driving when we got to base camp, it was deep dry sand and quite quickly on the incline up to the camp we soon started to get bogged down, to save having to dig it out on the first day, we all got out and Carl backed up only just being able to get it out of the deep ruts by expertly steering left and right to get some kind of grip. He finally picked his spot and took a run up, slowly but surely he roared past with ease and up the hill, leaving us to walk the rest of the way, for some reason I found it quite funny at the time. We pitched our 2 tents, which were supposed to sleep the 11 of us, but it was soon apparent it was nowhere big enough, it could easily sleep 4 or 5 but not 6, so 2 nominated themselves to sleep in one of the Landcruisers. I had a quick shower at the toilet block, which was well kept and clean, we were spoilt with hot water showers although there was a meter you had to supply with coins. As I checked them out I realised the third one was not hooked up to a meter as it was just a pipe coming out of the wall with no sprinkler attached, which I was happy to use at no cost.

Our evening meal was cooked on 2 large gas fired barbecues with all of us helping in some way, I got to chop up the onions and veg to go with our sausages, chops, with the veg, and chicken on skewers that were also BBQ'd, The BBQ area was in a large outside shelter, which was basically a roof supported by posts a few metres in the air with 4 picnic tables that seemed very sturdy which would be the centre point for the rest of our evenings activity.

With our bellies full we proceeded to drink large amounts of wine and beer along with every one else. Sharon succeeded in beating me by the amount we drank so she had a lot less inhibitions than myself, but we both were very much into the swing of things with some singing and drinking games. For an hour or so random songs would appear from nowhere and we'd all start singing, some of us were on the tables which didn't completely withstand the bombardment of our drunkenness dancing, some becoming quite rickety. I thought the 22 of us were singing pretty bad, but not bad enough to scare any animals, a dingo came walking through our camp at one point near the tents, we gave it a cheer, it took a cursory look over its should and kept on walking.

Carl had been getting a bit of peer pressure from his friends to do his re-enactment of something, which he kept saying he wasn't going to do, even though you could tell he really wanted to. After a few refusals we had all caught on and collectively persuaded him to do it. He took centre stage on one of the 2 picnic tables which were pushed together almost like a catwalk. Cigarette in one hand and a bottle of beer in the other, he started his act. It was the scene from *Braveheart*, just before the 13th century William Wallace lead his men to fight the much larger English army, at what is known historically as *The Battle of Sterling Bridge*. It's an inspirational speech to persuade his men to fight with him for Scotland's independents, after one nervous Scott shouts, how there are to many of them. This was Carl's rendition in an over exaggerated Scottish accent;

"I am William Wallace. And I see a whole army of my countrymen, here in defiance of tyranny! You have come to fight as free men. And free man you are! What will you do without freedom? Will you FIGHT?"

As he threw down a pointed finger, with a wholehearted feeling of passion, as he shouted the last word. He then mimicked trotting on a horse as it was portrayed in the film in an amusing manor, then switched his voice to a slightly more common sound to symbolise one of the soldiers now speaking.

"Eh? Fight, with that? No! We will run, and we will live!"

He continued with more funny trotting, as William Wallace galloped back in front of his men in the film. His character then resumed that of William Wallace once again.

"Run and you will live at least awhile. But many years from now, dying in your BEDS, would you be willing to trade all the days from this day to that? For one chance, just one FUCKING CHANCE!"

He got so enthusiastic at this point with his acting he had to break character in an instant to apologise to Becky, as he flung his arm down losing his grip of his cigarette, hitting her with it along with several globules of spit that she was totally oblivious to.

"That they may take our lives, but they will never take, our freeeedom!"

He ended with his nearly full bottle raised, that hadn't lost a drop then took a bow to the cheers and clapping of the whole camp. It was very good and I'm sure it was his party piece and I'm glad he shared it with us, something I will forever remember with such clarity.

After the camp manager came to tell us to keep the noise and swearing down we moved onto the drinking games, one of which was *man in the moon,* which I'm not entirely sure on how it was played as I was well on the way to the non remembering stage, but there was something about a story we had to make up that we all took part in, one after another in our circle around a few tables, although we were restricted in how many words we could say chosen by the previous person. I'm sure drinking was involved somehow.

Another game arose called *I never have* which is really more of a test of how often you can take a swig of alcohol as the game is fairly fast passed. The game is basically a truth game but by answering with a swig of your drink, maybe this was to make it easier to ask the more unusual question. You form yourselves into a circle and one by one you ask the question, 'I never have' followed by something like 'Kissed the same sex.' If you had, you take a drink. So if you have experimented a lot then you're getting drunk pretty quick, like Sarah. The poor girl must have took a drink to almost every question to which one was 'I never have used anal beads' with Sarah being the only person who drank to it, "What are they like?" was the following question by several inquisitive drunks of both sexes, she just casually said "Yeah, they're ok." Becky was struggling with her turns as she wasn't all that clued up on the more adult things in life, coming out with the more tamer questions that everyone was taking a drink for.

We played this until the early hours and generally had a good time socialising before we made our way into the tent with the lovely Dutch girls for a surprisingly good sleep. As we were drifting off to sleep the silence was broken to the sounds of Carl shouting asking for anyone who had a lighter.

Fraser Island. Day 2.

Tuesday 12th April.

I woke at 5am with some serious dehydration, I chugged down a litre or so of water and was able to doze a bit longer until 6.45am before I, with several others, roused ourselves much to the unimpressed Irish. A quick wash and a sandwich and coffee for breakfast later, we managed to leave 45 minutes after we got up. I took the driving seat and drove along 75 mile beach to Indian Head, a high rock formation that came up to the sea cutting off the beach highway, so the only way forward was up another deep sandy rutted incline named the Indian Head Bypass, more like the Indian Head sandtrap! I sent everyone out of the Landcruiser, put the gearbox in low ratio and took a run up, driving how I was told in the orientation, getting stuck rather quickly along with 4 other jeeps, one of which the poor chap, had a trailer buried up to the axles. We let the tyres down a bit for extra grip and a little digging out later, I pulled it back to the safety of the firmer wet sand. Ralph came up to me trying to help, giving me some directions in our dilemma, "I will walk up and make sure everything is ok and clear and I will give you a sign."

I let him walk a little way and thought how much I could see here as 2 of the jeeps had now got through, I could see it was safe enough so I put my foot down and waved Ralph out of the way. I got a bit further this time before I dug a bit of a hole for myself, so stopped before I got any deeper or burnt out the clutch. Ralph came back to give me a telling off. "Why did you go? I did not give you the sign, there was no sign!" I didn't want to argue so got out and helped everyone dig it out and kept quiet. We had a few more feeble attempts to get it through with a little pushing from everyone else which I thought wouldn't be of much use, but I let them try anyway. Once it was out again a very nice middle aged, guy approached me to ask if I needed any help. He'd been coming to the island for sixteen years and was very familiar with the hazards of getting through this part, "You want me to get it through for you?" he asked. So I thanked him for his help saying he obviously had much better skills at this than I had and appreciated his help. He got in, backed up and turned around driving round the corner out of site, I got a little nervous thinking I'd just let someone get in our Landcruiser that I didn't know and let him drive off, I was quite pleased to see him bounding round the corner, thrashing the engine in 3rd gear. I don't think I would have had big enough balls to drive that hard, he got to where we had got stuck and quickly shifted down into 2nd gear as it slowed down dramatically from the thick sand, then pushed on out of the deep sand. I was so impressed with his driving and it showed just how hard it is to get through it, which was a great learning curve for me that prepared me for this for the rest of the trip.

We parked a bit further up and I hiked to the top of Indian Head with Sharon, Kirsten, Ann and Ralph, it was a little awkward as Ralph was still in a huff with me for not waiting for his sign. Indian head is the most easterly point and consists of rhyolite, which is a 50 to 80 million year old volcanic outcrop of rock. At the top it gave us a 360 degree, view of the area, it was a sheer drop down to the sea from here and it was quite a dizzying view when I looked down at the jagged rocks below where the waves crashed against it. We took the time to take in this view before taking a 1.5mile walk to the Champagne Pools.

Our walk took us along the beach further north when I came across the most peculiar sea creature, it was about 25mm (1") in length, bright bluey silver with blue lines down its back and large, with features that looked like hands with long fingers with frilly cuffs. It looked like it had been inflated making its skin tight and shiny, its head was also short and dumpy with patterns on it that made it look like a face. I had never seen anything remotely like this, and I watch a lot of rubbish on the Discovery Channel. I touched it with my camera strap and it moved a little but I wasn't going to risk picking it up to put it back in the sea just in case it was poisonous. I was right not to, I now know it is a Glaucus Atlanticus, or more commonly known as a Blue Foot, Blue Angel or Blue Dragon. It is actually, a sea slug but I couldn't imagine it as a slug because of how pretty it was. Its life is a rather boring one as it just floats about in the sea until it bumps in a Phsalia, the Portuguese man-o-war or Bluebottle which is it's main food source, and are very venomous. This sea slug is able to store this venom, and use it to its own advantage. They have also been known to carry some of the long venomous tentacles, which we found on another stranded one further along the beach. I left these little guys hoping the tide would take them back out into their home.

Before arriving at the Champagne Pools we were greeted by a sign that said 'Danger – Waves frequently break over rocks around pools and may cause death or serious injury.' Spurred on by this prospect we took the boardwalk to the pools for a dip, the wooden path wound its way around and brought us out above the pools where we could see many others already enjoying them. These pools are named so, as they are another out crop of rocks on the beach, slightly higher than sea level that form 3 sandy pools, the champagne affect is caused by the waves crashing over these rough rocks making it bubble and froth giving you an almost Jacuzzi like feel and was very refreshing. As the sea was quite calm today we enjoyed this bubbling massage that was really quite nice without death or injury for a while until it started to rain, bit strange why we decided to go because it was raining, we were laying in water! On the way out we sheltered behind a small cliff face when Dale passed us on his way to the pool, we had a quick chat, he was having a good time as much as we were. I told him about my little problematic driving situation to find he'd been having similar problems, although his tuition was a bit better than ours and would have worked, they were simply told to thrash the nuts off it. Our chat was short lived, as he wanted to catch up with his group to enjoy the pools, as by this time it had almost stopped raining.

We then left our shelter to find that Carl had driven the Landcruiser along the very bumpy road to where we were and as a result smashed one of our large jars of pasta sauce in the roof rack cage, which was now running down the windscreen and had spoilt much of our food that was also in the roof rack. He was very apologetic to everyone saying how we all knew how bumpy it was and he had no choice but to thrash it through. We all knew it was more likely his bad judgment as he had been drinking since 7am. Not willing to take anymore chances and learning from my driving mistakes earlier, I took the driving seat back along the bumpy road which was navigated without any drama or dislodging supplies in the roof cage. We went on to the sand pit I had got stuck on earlier where I let everyone out, it was downhill so I knew it would be much easier this time. I gunned it like our savoir did earlier and thrashed the nuts off it. escaping the sandy slope with ease.

    With everyone back on board Sarah, wanted to have a drive along the easier part of the beach but she was a little nervous, as she had never driven anything this big, so she asked for my tuition. I took a seat in the back behind her and gave her the encouragement she needed, It was nice she asked for my help and I enjoyed teaching her, which hopefully she will remember as a happy experience. When it got a bit more difficult she quit while she was ahead and asked me to take over, I got several excited loud cheers from everyone every time I had to navigate a sandy slope, that I was now finding easier as my technique improved each time, although it was a little scary at times with it swaying as I fought with it over the many sandy crisscrossed ruts of countless 4 wheel drives before us, I found it quite fun and challenging.

    Carrying on down 75mile beach, another one of the Irish guys, Sammy wanted to have a drive which was a bad move in hindsight, even I was scared as he took us on a potentially suicidal roller coaster ride. I wasn't sure if he was doing it on purpose or was just a really bad driver, maybe he was a little drunk too. He kept weaving back and forth violently rocking the Landcruiser, which was exaggerated immensely by the low tyre pressure. Lynn was very scared shaking her head in disbelief at his inappropriate driving, he had 10 other peoples lives in his hands and it wasn't as if he didn't know how dangerous it can be to flip one of these, as he had the same briefing as I did. I was bracing myself with my foot on the opposite seat and holding on to my own for the entire 3 mile journey of his, as it's not so much of the crash that causes injury, it's Newton's third law of motion that 'Every action has and an equal and opposite reaction' and there were no seat belts in the back. So at what ever speed we would flip over at, anything in that steel box that was not strapped down would keep going at that speed, until it was stopped by something, and I'm pretty sure the human body is much weaker and fragile than the Landcruiser we were in.

    Sammy finally gave up driving after a short while, as he said he was having to concentrate too much, really! I could have driven better with my eyes closed! I think everyone was a little shaken from his driving, so with no one wanting to take over, I took the driving seat again and everyone seemed to become a little more relaxed, with a few telling me they thought my driving was the best out of everyone, I wonder if it was said more for Sammy's benefit. We stopped off at base camp to put a bit of wind back in the tyres, to find the other group had been having similar problems today, they had also let some air out of their tyres and after inflating them, they backed over the airline gauge breaking it. So we had go to *Happy Valley campsite* about halfway down 75 mile beach a 20 minute drive away, to get some more stability in the Landcruiser making it much safer for our drive into the island, along the more harder sandy tracks.

Sharon took the driving seat along the beach and onto Allom Lake, I was quietly impressed with her driving skills as well, as she also had never driven anything this big, she took it in her stride with only one incident which scared Lynn again witless, maybe she was still suffering from Sammy's driving earlier. We had been driving on solid sand when we came to a raised sandy part that formed a small hill, but before I could tell her to counter steer from the slope and get the revs up she stalled it, slipping sideways a foot or so. We were sitting on one side of the slope listing slightly from the weight of 11 people making it feel a little top heavy. Lynn was practically shitting herself thinking we were going to tip over and we should all get out, which if a vehicle was turning over it is the worst thing you can do, as there is a good probability of getting crushed by the vehicle. I calmly said to her, "We've completely stopped, we're not going anywhere!" reluctantly she sat back and allowed me to talk Sharon through the best way to safely get out of it. The truth was that if there was any cocking around at this point there was a possibility that we could've toppled over, but that didn't happen and we drove on with no more dramas, to the lake.

Lake Allom, or more commonly known as Turtle Lake is about 3 miles in from the east coast of the island, down a tight bumpy track with a further 500m (1,600ft) walk to the lake, hidden and surrounded by Melaleuca trees. It's a freshwater lake like most of the other lakes, but that is where the similarities end, it is quite murky and filled with reeds round the shoreline, with no beach in sight. I got into the water knee deep to find tiny little fish feeding off my skin, it felt quite nice as I was gently pecked by these little fellas for free, people these days pay for that. As I stood there having my fishy manicure I got some very curious kreff freshwater turtles popping their head above the water, having a look then dipping back under and swimming away, only to return again for another look a little while later.

It wasn't long before we left here and back to our camp, Ralph was now in a better mood and drove the track back to the beach, Ann took over next for the easier part as she was not as confident either but she was far from incompetent. She drove with ease and at one point nearly got stuck in some deep sand, she stopped, put it in low ration, I think then some evil spirit must have possessed this lovely calm, kind hearted quiet girl, as she then floored it like she was in an off road demolition derby without a hint of hesitation, she wasn't worried in the slightest, which the same can't be said for me, driving out of the deep sand with room to spare. We got to see our second dingo after this along the beach, wandering alone as we drove past.

Back at camp Carl announced he'd left his wallet at the Champagne Pools and had to go back to get it, taking the Landcruiser with the other 2 Irish. Everyone was aware they had gone, with us all thinking to ourselves the same thing, the deposit. All of us were sure none of them were sober enough to drive and it was nearly high tide. This was a very relevant reason for not going out, as many parts of the beach highway could get flooded by the sea. This was one of the hazards we were warned against in the briefing, as the salt water will corrode or damage many mechanical and electrical parts of the Landcruiser, which was another way to lose our deposit, or possibly more than our deposit depending on what damage is done, not to mention if they crashed it while they were driving without us.

Breny's philosophies in life:
If you have to involve yourself in an SEP, do it quietly!

Everyone was concerned at this fact, and wanted to disassociate them selves at this point, to avoid the possibility of getting hit with a massive bill. But what were we to do? Everyone wanted something done about it but didn't know how to go about it and kept talking about it, so I took the matter into my own hands, as drink driving is something I feel very strongly against and very upsetting. One of the camp managers was introducing a new group onto the campsite, so I waited until she had finished her campsite rules and walked over to tell her I wanted to talk to her. "Where's your Landcruiser?" She asked, I wanted to be away from the new group before I said anything, "That's what I wanted to talk to you about." I replied, trying to keep it quiet. As we walked to the rest of my group, I told her what had happened and she was obviously aware of when high tide was. She seemed as pissed off as the rest of us saying she wasn't going to have that, then getting in contact with the islands police to keep a look out for them. Sharon then pointed out to me she was sure that she saw one of the new group talking to the Irish before they left. 'Great' I thought 'Just what I was trying to avoid'

An hour and 15 minutes after the Irish left they returned, supposedly with the wallet, somehow with the amount of people there after 6 hours I'm sure someone would have walked off with it. Firstly I don't think they could have made it there and back in that time, also there was no way they would have got through the deep sand at Indian Head Bypass without letting some air out of the tyres, the locals had hard enough trouble getting through and they had to let their tyres down first! The police hadn't caught up with them either so I'm sure they had not gone where they said they were. I watched Carl as he was called over by his friend with the new arrivals, it's obvious what the conversation was and in a matter of seconds he was heading straight for me with a great deal of anger in his body language. I was sitting down at one of the picnic tables facing out surround by the rest of our group, I think sub consciously we were all together for support knowing something like this was going to happen. I never like to fight over an argument as I find it quite pathetic, especially when another guy is only doing it to prove he is the biggest or more of a man.

"What the fuck Brendan, why did you tell them we had gone out!" That comment fortified our concerns, because if he was going to where he said and wasn't drunk, why was he so upset about me telling anyone he had taken our Landcruiser. I stayed sitting down keeping calm for two reasons, firstly by taking the more vulnerable position of sitting down showed I was not intimidated by him and hopefully would come off much braver than I actually was. Secondly if I had stood up to confront him it would have been an act of aggression and most probably ended in a fight, which we all know his Irish friends would have came and helped him out, I'm sure I would not have came out on top. I just replied, "It wasn't just me, it was everyone." as I gestured to the rest of the team around me, before I could say anything else he walked off just as angrily muttering and swearing about me under his breath. I talked to his mate Sammy a little later about it and he was surprisingly ok about it, and was going to try and smooth it over with Carl. He was a little better with me for the rest of the evening, but it was obvious we were a little awkward in each others company.

As our food had been spoilt earlier in the day, the other team offered to help out and was sure they had more than enough, which they did, loading everyone's plate up with a mountain of pasta. The American family were doing most of the preparing and quite confidently made sure to let us know how well it goes when you're organised. We were organised until the Irish took a drive!

After our donated pasta meal we had another drinking session for our evenings entertainment, and it wasn't long before another drinking game came into play called Fuzzy Duck. The game is started in your circle with the first person saying 'fuzzy duck' with the next person to say the opposing words of 'ducky fuzz' and then back to 'fuzzy duck' and so on. To throw a little more confusion into the game, at random someone can reverse the direction of the circle by saying 'does he?' You can see how spoonerism plays a big part in this game, which is when you take a drink. Sammy was the best at failing at this and it wasn't to long before he quit and went back to regular drinking.

We had many other fun parts to the evening, like one of which Sarah showed us how to scare off an emu if it was threatening you. If you wanted to know, you make yourself as high as possible with one arm pointed like an emu's head, and then make large whooping sounds, I have never tested this anti emu method so if anyone wants to use this, please do at your own risk. It could have been a drunken joke for all I know.

Our last game of the evening was the box game, which I was familiar with and had some practice several times before this evening. Taking an empty box placed on the ground you pick it up with your mouth, without using your hands to move the box or to steady yourself.

Then once everyone had taken their turn, about 2cm (1") of the top is torn off making it shorter. You'd think being drunk would be more of a hindrance when in fact it was a great help, as the alcohol more than loosened our muscles and ligaments allowing us to stretch and bend much further than any of us thought possible. I was able to manage a 5cm (2") high box with only the American girl managing the very last piece, which was just a flat piece of cardboard.

We had another one of Carl's renditions again which was nowhere near as good as his *Braveheart* one. This one was from *Pulp Fiction* where Jules recites *Ezekiel 25:17* from the bible before he shoots someone. He took his same position as the night before on the picnic table;

"The path of the righteous man is beset on all sides by the inequities of the selfish and the tyranny of evil men. Blessed is he who, in the name of charity and good will, shepherds the weak through the valley of the darkness. For he is truly his brother's keeper, and the finder of lost children. I will strike down upon thee with great vengeance and furious anger those who attempt to poison and destroy my brothers. And you will know I am the Lord when I lay my vengeance upon you"

He finished as in the film with his fingers as a gun, but pointed at me making gun shot noises. I don't know if it was a threat, but it far from scared me. It lacked much more feeling this time as half of the camp were either not watching or reciting it before he had said his line, which I'm sure was stealing his limelight making him feel a little less liked.

By about 11.30pm it was becoming a little quieter, I think the night before may have affected the amount most of us could drink along with the lack of sleep, so Sharon and I slipped off into the night and down to the beach, we decided we were going to tell everyone we were looking for dingo's, when really we wanted some time alone and enjoyed the evening moonlight.

We got back an hour or so later to find the Irish sitting at the edge of camp still smoking and drinking, with most of the others already asleep in their tents. We grabbed our shower gels to wash the grit and grind off from the days activities before getting a good nights sleep.

Fraser Island. Day 3.

Wednesday 13th April.

I was up at 7.00am and packed our tent ready to go, so we could get the most out of our day to hear the Irish moaning it was too early, followed by it was all my idea they had to get up early, when it was actually everyone as others were stirring before us. We finished cleaning the now encrusted pasta sauce off the roof cage and were on our way south down 75 mile beach to Lake McKenzie, 6 miles away by 8.10am. No one seemed too happy to drive so I thought I had better rather than be at the mercy of someone who was hung over and not wanting to drive. We followed the other team making it much easier as I didn't have to think where we were going. We turned off the beach after a short while onto the fairly wide track. It was peppered with large deep holes filled with water. I was driving responsibly as we approached each one, slowing down and manoeuvring round them or slowly driving through them in case they were too deep or rutted, as this may have sent me out of control, I thought everyone had, had enough of getting scared by a few of the other drivers. This sedate professional driving didn't last for long as I got the odd comment I was driving to slow and what was the point of having a 4 wheel drive, one by one it mounted until everyone was against my driving style so I said nothing and slowed down to let the second team get ahead, I then punched the throttle through a rather large puddle, resulting in a good deal of bounce and the entire contents of the puddle to be thrown into the air and over the Landcruiser. It was a great success as everyone was cheering as the unsecured bench seats settled back into position. I got spurred on more and more as each puddle came and then went over the Landcruiser, I was having a great time abusing the 4 wheel drive like this, and I think I may have won back a little respect from the Irish.

The last piece of the journey to Lake McKenkie was a very rough and bumpy road, to which I had to take really easy as it made the Landcruiser sway and rock that made your butt hole pinch up a little. Arriving here our first priority was breakfast, or should I say what ever was left to stop me feeling hungry, which was a peanut butter sandwich with no butter followed by a few biscuits. We then walked down to the lake, which is one of the most popular lakes here on Fraser Island for its beauty and tranquillity, well it would have been tranquil if it wasn't for all us tourists. There were a lot of people there but the beach is so big there was plenty of room, the lake itself has a surface area of about 370 acres (1.5 million m^2) and most of it has a clean white sandy beach, with the water a beautiful clear colour and changing rapidly to a very dark blue several metres out where it gets deeper to its maximum depth of 5m (16ft). We lazed and dozed on the lovely white sandy beach for about 2 hours, with a good deal of the time with my hand on Sharon's shoulder, the sun had been going in and out from the clouds all this time so we thought there was no need for sun cream. It was quite obvious that this was the wrong assumption as Sharon had turned a little pink from the sun except for where my hand, had been, I hoped everyone was not thinking I had slapped her.

Once it got a little warmer we took a dip in the lake, there was almost a straight line in colour as it changed to the deeper part and also got a lot colder so we favoured the shallow crystal clear part. Dale came here about the same time so we got to have a good chat with him to see how he'd been getting on, we also found out he would be getting back earlier than us and we all had growing concerns that Carl was over the drink drive limit already, and he would be driving back. So as this would directly affect me I was quite happy to do something about it, but this time I was making sure no one would over hear what I was asking Dale, we came up with the idea that he would go to our hostel, to tell them that he'd seen this Carl drinking and driving in their Landcruiser.

We left Dale again to enjoy the lake whilst we made our way back to the ferry keeping very quiet about our little plan. I drove to the ferry terminal after several of the team thought I was the safest, with the others not caring who was driving. Arriving there Becky started getting all panicky that we were at the wrong terminal, which had become a regular thing with her panicking at everything, so I found the picture I had took 3 days ago on my camera when we had arrived here and showed her, just to shut her up. Our ferry was 15 minutes late, while waiting we saw some activity near us with some young lads trying to get something very big out of the mud, it was a treat to see what he pulled out, he was rescuing a turtle that was about 60cm (2ft) in length and caked in mud, it had got stuck in the deep mud and these couple of lads dug it out. Hard to believe a turtle could get itself stuck, but it looked very happy by the speed it swam away at.

The ferry finally arrived to find Carl had lost the return ticket so we left him with it and all walked onto the Ferry, watching from the top window, to see him get on anyway noticing he had a beer in his hand drinking as he drove on. Everyone except the Irish after seeing this said they weren't going to get in the Landcruiser with him. I wasn't too worried as I knew what would be waiting the other end so I kept quiet and watched it unfold, with the crossing long enough to have coffee and chips before we disembarked. Arriving at the mainland we walked off and waited for Carl. As he pulled up no one got in, and several of us confronted him about the amount of alcohol he had consumed this day, to which he responded to, and started to get a little irate.
"I'm not drunk!" He protested, "I've had one drink all day!" one of the Danish girls replied quite bluntly. "You're lying! You were drinking when you drove onto the ferry! We all saw you!" As this was going on we saw a police car pull into the car park, swing round looking straight at us, then driving back out. It was obvious to me why they were looking at us but everyone else thought it was a coincidence, including Carl, so he said, "Well I'll go and find out, someone drive me down there and I'll prove it" no one wanted to as we were all under the impression no one else was insured to drive on the mainland. He then ran to the nearest person that was then leaving for a ride to where the cops were a short distance down the road. A few minutes later a sheepish Carl came back and was actually apologetic as he was over the limit. Several asked me again to drive, but as this was in my mind an SEP, I would have walked if I had to, so I refused, I don't know what the fine would have been for driving with no insurance here and I didn't want to find out.

The Police had said Sammy could drive which he did fairly well, although everyone in unison shouted 'slow down' as he approached a roundabout to quickly. Arriving back after the hire company had been through our items, found we had a few cups and plates missing with us all having to pay $3 (£1.25), it was nothing, a little annoying but I paid my part right away while some of the others moaned about it before giving in. While this was going on the Landcruiser got thrashed a bit outside to make sure it was ok and we all left without any more fines.

We had a lift back to the hostel and then checked, into a 10 bed room with the Irish and Sarah. We met up with Kirsten and Ann at Hoolihans with 5 others they had met before the Fraser Island tour, for a steak special for $14 (£5.83) We left after a nice long chat back to the hostel to retrieve our laundry we had washed, to dry them and shower. The most astounding thing I found as I entered the shower block was my little soapbox along with the soap inside was still where I had left it before I went on the Fraser Island trip. We filled in our Journals for the last 3 days and got to sleep in a much comfier fashion, for a well earned sleep.

Thursday 14th April.

We were up at a respectable 9am to pack the campervan with Dale meeting us shortly after, to find he was still drunk and immediately started drinking much to my disgust, I thought we'd probably have a tough day with him from this. I usually enjoy his drunken antics but I have to be in the same state to appreciate it. He did tell us however of a nice place to go called '1770' which is the site of the second landing by James Cook and his crew of HMS *Bark Endeavour* in May 1770. He had originally named it Round Hill after the creek it sits on. To commemorate the bicentennial of Cook's visit in 1970 the name was changed to 1770, with the community here holding the re-enactment of this historic landing each year as part of the 1770 festival held in May.

It was a little out of the way but we wanted to see this piece of historical village. There really wasn't much there except for the nice scenery out to sea where somewhere Captain Cook had landed and set foot here at a once uninhabited place. It was more exciting watching Dale climb along the rocks dangerously close to the edge and would've been in serious trouble if he fell, I tried to scare him into coming back up by telling him I wasn't going to rescue him if he fell, which worked eventually. I had already told him he must be an alcoholic and he had a problem, to which he replied that he was already drunk when he woke up and continued drinking to stop getting a hangover, he thought if you were sober when you woke up and then started drinking, then that is a problem. There was some logic to it so I couldn't really argue with him anymore so I thought I'd have some fun instead. When we stopped for lunch here for coffee and pie, Dale fell asleep which made it possible to draw all over his forehead and nose much to the amusement of the rest of the café.

We left here after Dale had a little confusion in the mirror in the public toilets, and were on our way again to see how far we could drive today to Ailey Beach, our next destination. Sharon took over driving while Dale slept off his drunken state, not waking until we got to Ilbilbie to fill up with petrol for the third time today. It was a boring drive as there was very little civilization, we thought we were going to run out of fuel at one point as we hadn't seen a petrol station for the last 60 miles to

Ilbilbie. It was getting late and we had already driven 482 miles today so we drove to the outskirts to camp.

Friday 15th April.

We were up at 8am and drove back to the garage where we had been to last night for muffin and coffee. Dale drove the rest of the way to Alley Beach, another 152 miles. A town of nearly 8,000 people with being one of the many departure points to the Great Barrier Reef, and for us it would be the departure point for our Whitsunday Island sailing trip. This little town and the islands were both named by James Cook, with the Whitsunday Islands named so, as he was believed to have passed through here on the Christian Festival day of Whit Sunday.

We checked in with Prosail chatting for a while about this exciting trip, we hired out stinger suits as it can be extremely painful getting stung by jellyfish, and can be fatal if you get stung by the Box Jellyfish. It didn't look all that thick and would stop such a thing but we took their word for it and coughed up the few dollars to hire them.

Our next check in point was at *Beaches Hostel*, it was close by and nice as well as clean with an en suite bathroom. We had lunch at McDonalds and bumped into Becky there from the Fraser Island tour, then made a rapid departure with Sharon going to find sunglasses while I sent emails. It was the first time we had been apart for this long since I met her in New Zealand, which felt quite strange.

We met in a bar near the hostel once we had finished where we caught up with our diaries before taking a walk along the beach, while Dale went to another sailing company to see if they had any work so he could get a free trip. We met again a bit later at the bar for some live music, Dale had no joy in getting any casual work, so he would be staying in the campervan finding something to do in this area while we were out sailing.

We were back at the hostel for our evening meal for a pasta dish, then packed our bags after for our sailing trip, taking it slow and easy to recover from the last 4 tiring days. There was one last item missing from our luggage for our trip, which was alcohol, we drove about until we found a drive through, off license, which seem a little contradictory and was a first for me. We bought a box of wine each that would sustain us for most of the trip at $13.90 (£5.80) before heading back to the hostel for an early nights sleep. Even the loud music from the bar outside our hostel wasn't enough to keep me awake, slipping off to sleep more or less immediately.

Whitsunday Islands Cruise. Day 1.

Saturday 16th April.

A 7.30am start ensured us to be one of the first to shower before heading out. We checked out of the hostel and had Dale drive us to Shut Harbour about 6 miles from where we had stayed. We said goodbye to him for another 3 days and found our boat. It was beautiful sitting there in the dock looking very long at 25m (82ft) showing its deep maroon hull with the deck that looked very close to the water when in fact it was a few metres above the water line. This optical illusion may have been caused by the massive, aluminium mast that dwarfed the boat, as it must have stood about 36m (120ft) high, with 4 spreaders down the mast with several thick cables to withstand the immense load from the sail. Looking at the size of the mast it's not hard to see why it's one of the fastest maxi yachts in the world, and that's no exaggeration! It was specifically built for racing, designed by Ron Holland from New Zealand, and built in 1981 at the *Penury ship yard* in Cornwall. It had many firsts built into it which may be the reason to it being so successful, it is light and strong as it's built from Kevlar with an aluminium space frame inside it that gives it an amazing amount of rigidity, this was the second yacht to have been built in this way where the hull itself is so strong it can support the enormous loads that are generated from the massive mast I had already mentioned, at the time it was the tallest single spar mast in the world. All this has made it fast, in its 7 year ocean racing campaign it won every major event twice! And it's the only one of its kind to have achieved this.

We were met by one of the deck hands to find we were one of the first there, she took our names and then looked down the list and said, "Oh, the lovely couple!" We sorta frowned at each other which until she followed with, "That what it says here." I thought it must have been from the lovely lady Alix in Sydney that booked this trip for us. We decided to grab a coffee at the café nearby until the bus, with the rest of the group turned up 15 minutes late. We all boarded the boat and immediately were told to take off our shoes that were put into a large bag for the entire trip. We were then shown to our sleeping quarters, below deck was accessed by steep steps through a small hatch leading to the spacious cabin thanks to its unique space frame leaving most of this part open. The kitchen is in the centre with the cooker, sink and various other cupboards, along each side were the bunk beds with the odd protrusion of the tubular bracing across them, which was about 15cm (6") in diameter. Towards the front were the 2 toilets that were a mission in itself to use, the toilet was pushed up against the curved hull with the seat about 1m (3ft) off the ground with one of the huge tubular space frame on the other side that came into the cramped space half way up behind the toilet and down to the floor, making no floor space to speak of, as you had to also step over the bracing of the 2 massive cables as soon as you walk in that held the mast in place. The next cabin past the toilets was where we would be sleeping, quite spacious compared to the rest of the bunks, there were two double beds one on each side with a partition of rain jackets in the middle, we also had much less metal parts of the hull and space frame taking up our bed space. We were sharing the cabin with an older couple, Ron and his wife who were very pleasant to chat to and the oldest on the boat.

    We got under way out of the harbour by engine power, while we had the safety instructions with all the dos and don'ts, this was put in a nice way showing it would be a relaxed trip. One of the most memorable dos was the rule on walking about up on deck, which was, at all times on deck you always have one hand for your beer and one for the boat.
    The captain of our boat was Mr Kirk, that's right, we had Captain Kirk as our skipper, he's good fun, friendly and very knowledgeable answering all the questions he was asked, as he had been sailing for many years all over the world. At the time of writing this book in 2013 he is still the captain of this boat. Really, what a lucky bugger to have landed this job, getting paid to sail such a famous boat twice a week in one of the most beautiful places in the world.

    We cleared the bay and once we were in open water the engines were cut and we were ready to start sailing. All the way round the edge of the deck was a low rail about 60cm (2ft) high with 2 horizontal wires strung though it, the deck is mostly taken up with rails, hatches, cleats, ropes, pulleys and 5 handles, also known as grinders, these are used to hoist the sales. 3 of the grinders were used to hoist the main sail, 6 people took their places in pairs opposite each other at the grinders with Sharon and I eagerly taking the end grinder. I wanted to know what it was like to be a part of the crew, imaging what it would be like in a race when you see them furiously cranking the handles at a blistering speed. Jess took her place in one of the hatches on the end of the rope that was looped several times round a large round cleat to stop the sail from falling back down, as well as to tie it off. It was her job to give us the orders on what to do, the first part winching the sail was the easiest with the 3 pairs cranking the grinders fairly quick, compared to the speed we were spinning the grinders, the sail rose a lot slower from its hidden compartment along the boom, which was as thick as a girder. It rose steadily to about three quarters of the way up, by which time it was becoming a struggle and slowing down dramatically, as the weight increased from the amount of sail that had been hoisted, Jess told us to stop, shifted the gear in the winches and commanded to go again in the opposite direction. Again it was much quicker to crank the grinders as the sail neared the top, only to be struggling again a few moments later, one more gear shift with a bit more frantic cranking and it was completed, with the last few turns very tight as the sail was stretched to its highest point. After this experience I can say with some certainty that the people who race these boats must be fit to raise these sails as quick as they do.

The jib, the little sail at the front was next to be winched needing only 2 grinders to hoist it up which was much easier as it's a lot smaller. We were then well on our way where we would be mostly sailing around the 2 largest islands that are part of the 74 tropical islands known as The Whitsunday Islands. The biggest is Whitsunday Island followed by Hook Island to the north, they are surrounded by the other smaller islands covering an area of 9,213 square miles with most of them deserted, with only 8 of the islands inhabited having a variety of first class resorts and accommodation, with the great barrier reef on its doorstep. It wasn't long before the sails were filled and we were gaining a fair amount of speed with the boat listing at an unbelievable angle at times. The deck that was usually a good 2m (7ft) above the water line, now had the water lapping onto the deck as it dipped into the sea, to help keeping the yacht level we all took our places on the high side of the yacht with our feet dangling over the edge, it look very high as I peered over the side looking at the bottom of the hull. I don't know how much difference it would make if we weren't there, but it was the most comfortable place to sit as choosing anywhere else on the deck was a little tricky, having to prop yourself up on one of the many pieces of equipment that made up the deck, as slipping off the deck was very probable, considering we were at about a 45 degree angle, not to mention painful as you were bound to catch one of the protruding pieces of metal, if you avoided all those then landing on the low rail that was being thrashed by the water would have also been rather uncomfortable.

After a short while heading north to avoid the Mole Islands we headed in a north easterly direction towards Hook Island, by then we were heading, downwind so the boat was now levelled out and much smoother, letting us, relax a bit more. We rounded the top of Hook Island to get to the east side leaving us with very little wind as the island was blocking most of it, the sails were dropped and we made the rest of the journey to Hook Island Reef by motor, picking up a very amusing Scottish diver on the way.

James the Scottish diver, rounded up the ones that wanted to do the dive for $75 (£31), with me being one of the first in line. There were a lot of instructions to go through, with much of it explained in a light hearted manner, although diving can be dangerous even at the maximum depth I was permitted to do without further training of 10m (32ft), much of it was not applicable here as we would not be very deep at all. After our briefing we enjoyed the rest of the leisurely trip to our dive site sunning ourselves on deck, when the hum of the engine was overpowered by Captain Kirk shouting, "Dolphins of the bow!" we sat there in a disbelieving manner to see the odd person looking a little excited at the front of the boat, I gabbed my camera and joined them, much to my happiness I found the captain wasn't joking, he had actually seen them swim past him at the stern and knew they would be heading to the front of the boat. There are many theories to why they do this, but it seems that most of them point towards that they like doing it or it takes them less effort to swim in the wake of the bow. There were about 5 of them keeping up with ease with the boat as they jumped in and out of the water to grab a breath to carry on swimming with each other dashing left and right. And as suddenly as they arrived they veered off and disappeared as quickly.

I excitedly arrived at Hook Island Reef where we dropped anchor a little way off shore by about lunchtime, where we had served up a potato salad which I'm not usually too fond of but for some reason this one was particularly nice. After a short rest I climbed into my sexy blue stinger suit as there are many kinds of jelly fish here with some being quite painful, and on 2 occasions while snorkelling here it has resulted in death from Irukandji jellyfish stings, it was then a short trip in the little yellow dinghy we had been towing since we left the mainland, to ferry us into the shallower waters by the beach. The Whitsunday Islands are on the fringe of The Great Barrier Reef about 30 miles away, so there was an abundance of coral and tropical fish which we were promised to see. We were sorted into 2 groups as we were met with another dive instructor once we were on land, then kitted out with our masks, air tanks, inflatable vest, regulator, flippers and weight belt. This was the first time I had been diving but I was no stranger to swimming underwater, being able to free dive with some confidence. But this was much different in the way I was a little unfamiliar with all this equipment that would let me do something humans can't usually do. It was all incredibly heavy as we waded into the water which was like stepping into a warm bath. It was hard to believe I needed an inflatable vest with a bit of air in it to make me buoyant, I thought I would have sunk strait to the bottom with all that. We came to a stop in the waist deep water with a few more instructions on how to use the regulator, with this being the last of the instructions we were asked to put our heads in the water using the regulator to get a feel for it. It only took me a few seconds to get over the unusual feeling of breathing underwater before something caught my eye, a brightly coloured fish swimming round us. The water was so clear there was no problem seeing for quite some way, I came back up to find several of them going over what we hard already been told which I felt I had remembered all what they had told me and taken enough in to dive safely. I popped my head back up then asked James. "There's some fish right here, can I just float about and watch them?"

"Sure, why not!" He replied which was all I needed to get my head back under, I floated around the group for about a minute or so in amazement of what I was doing finding it incredibly easy before the other instructor asked who had told me I could start, she yanked me out of the water and filled my air vest to stop me going under until everyone was ready.

They finished up the irrelevant questions and we got underway in my group of 4 with James. With us all holding hands, we descended slowly a few metres with James adjusting the air in our vest to keep us buoyant, my world now was an alien one, I could move in any direction like I was flying with such ease. It was so brightly coloured and vibrant and I didn't know which way to look, it was so exciting swimming with the many fish and there was a lot of them, schools of grey fish with bright yellow tails, maybe a hundred swam past and seemed to ignore us. Everywhere I looked there was coral covering the sea bed growing like strange trees, some with thick branches with others thin and spiky looking, rocky types of coral were dotted about with others growing on it. One of the most intriguing coral that we could touch gently under James's supervision resembled a brain with short tentacles, it felt and looked like wet chamois leather swaying in the current. There were fish everywhere I looked, I probably saw 1000's on this dive with so many different kinds varying in size and colour, some that really stick in my mind are the bright blue and black striped fish, small bright yellow ones that mostly hang around closely to the coral and a dark green fish that had several different bright colours on its fins.

I got so complacent looking at this beautiful scenery that I wasn't paying attention to where my group was, I thought I was following them when I felt a tug on my flipper to find James behind me pointing to my group, swimming in the opposite direction. We spent about 30 minutes diving before our air was nearly gone with it feeling like a few minutes, it is by far the most enjoyable thing I have ever done, I was glad my first diving experience was there as it is one of the best places to dive in the world for the most colourful and varied coral and fish. Anyone who has the opportunity to do anything like this should not hesitate, as it is one of the most amazing experiences you will ever do.

We finished our dive near to where we had started, with the short 30 minutes of weightlessness we stood up in the shallow water and began walking to shore, as we rose higher out of the water the heavier I felt finding it much more heavier than before, I was also feeling a little light headed which was normal according to James. We had a short time on the shore which I was going to use for snorkelling in the shallow water to find it leaked, as I sat there in the shallows steadied myself against a rock, I had already been warned about how sharp coral is, and that's exactly what I had leant against. It was as sharp as a razorblade slicing into 2 of my fingers causing a great deal of blood to leak out of me.

Back aboard we spent a bit longer resting when Captain Kirk came out from below deck presenting a large hotdog, then proceeded to wave it high above his head and started whistling. He told us how he had for quite a while been calling these juvenile Pacific Sea Eagles, enticing them with these sausages. It wasn't long before one of these young birds appeared, circling our yacht until Kirk threw it 20m (65ft) from us, the eagle then dived towards it with its claws leading, snatched it precisely from the water and flew off to eat it with several happy shrieks. Kirk did this again a short while later in the same manner as another one circled us, it was joined shortly after with a second one. As the first plucked the sausage from the water, the second eagle clipped one of the cables attached to the mast with a hard thud, the dull noise rang through the boat as it spiralled out of control and crashed into the water. I don't think swimming is one of their strong points as it thrashed in the water trying to get airborne, it almost looked defeated immediately, maybe it was shock, I was more concerned that it had broken a wing, as it laid there with its wings spread out trying to fly on the water. Kirk must have had the same thoughts as he jumped overboard into the dingy to rescue it with several panicked 'oh shits' under his breath. He was a brave man, I don't think I would've wanted to do it as it is well known how powerful these birds claws and beak are, they are also massive being the biggest breed of eagle reaching a wingspan of 2.5m (8ft). Luckily he wasn't to find out, as he was starting the engine of the dinghy the bird got enough height to fly away.

Our evening was spent at Nara Inlet on the west side of Hook Island, as there was still very little wind, we made our way there under the power of the motor. On our way we came side by side with another sailing yacht, the *Apollo*, a little smaller and winning several of the same races as the *Condor*, but not as many times. As we raced with each other we approached another maxi yacht, the 18m (60ft) *Freight Train* that was motoring at a slower speed, as we passed either side of it. We edged a little further ahead, as our boat was slightly quicker, as we gained distance I noticed some familiar faces on the *Apollo*, the Irish from Fraser Island. Could've been worse, I'm just glad they hadn't picked the *Condor*!

Arriving at dusk several hundred metres into Nara Inlet we dropped anchor just in time for our evening meal of chicken curry. We soon came around to some drinking games with our captain starting us off. Gripping his glass with his thumb and one finger he said "Captain Kirk had his first drink of the night" and it would then be the next person in the circle to then hold their glass but with 2 fingers, and say "Captain Kirk, had his second drink of the night" and so on to 3 and 4. If the number of fingers or the saying was wrong you took a drink. It was recited quite quickly with most of us getting it wrong at some point with the Irish guy failing the most giving everybody else some great entertainment. I wonder if all Irish have problems with this type of game? Our evening ended up a fairly tame one, with everyone winding down and asleep without too much drama around midnight.

Whitsunday Islands Cruise. Day 2.

Sunday 17th April.

We were up at about 8am, breakfast was a very refreshing fruit salad with a coffee, before we were to make our way to Whitehaven Beach. We motored out of our sheltered inlet then raised the sails with a few other volunteers working the grinders, hard and as furiously as we did the day before. We had a side wind again which gains the most speed and allows for the more exciting sailing as we were again at a near 45 degree angle. We sailed between Hook and Whitsunday Island, only having to tack 3 times over the 12 mile or so trip down the east side of Whitsunday Island. The islands are made up from volcanic eruptions from over 100 million years ago, but it wasn't until the last ice age 10,000 years ago which flooded the continent, this isolated the peaks of the island from the mainland. The beach to where we were going to today is a 4.5 mile beach of nearly pure white sand and is very clean, recently winning the cleanest beach in *'Keep Australia Beautiful'* as well as being named the top *'Eco Friendly Beach'* in the world by CNN.com. As a result dogs and smoking is prohibited on this beach.

As we got closer nearing the beach, the bright white sand that stretched on into the distance was very impressionable, dropping anchor about 200m (650ft) from shore with the many other boats of all types. Two boats caught my eye that I liked varying in style dramatically. The first was the *Camira* catamaran. Purple with a giant sail with 2 jibs and considerably larger than the *Condor*, this is one of those luxury boats with more than enough room to move around in, inside it has a spacious room decked out in wood, chairs and tables for relaxing and eating. On deck is very similar with comfortable long chairs and a few tables with easy access off the back of the boat down a few easy steps to sea level. The second boat was an old style tall ship with 2 masts with multiple sail and 3 jibs, the *Solway Lass*. At 37m (121ft) long and a breadth of nearly 6m (19.5ft) it was a little larger than our own yacht but much older being built in 1902. This boat has had a varied life being used to transport many different cargos, as well as working in both world wars and being seized by the opposition in each, as a *'prize of war'*. While under the command of the Germans in WW2 it hit a mine damaging it quite badly, but was repaired as it was of some value to them. It was beautiful with its rigging, cabin and rope ladders up the masts. It was great to see that health and safety hadn't stopped this ship from sailing as there was someone standing precariously about 20m (65ft) on a rope, parallel to the spar to tie the sail off. It had much more rigging than our own yacht and I'm sure it's a wonderful sight to see it sailing with all its sails in use. I hope that one day I will have the opportunity to experience sailing on a ship like this.

By this time it was lunch, where we were treated to sausage, pasta with veg and some very nice bread. We boarded our little dingy then were ferried 6 at a time to the white sands of Whitehaven beach which is visited by roughly 75,000 people a year. We took our towels and for the most part, we laid there soaking up the sun without a care in the world. The sand is incredibly fine making it a hazardous place for electronics which I found out after I had taken several pictures, but luckily I didn't cause any damage to my camera, but it is fantastic for polishing jewellery which did wonders for my St Christopher, that was still a little dull from the sulphur pools in New Zealand despite my best efforts to shine it up with purpose bought polish. The sand is bright white due to it consisting of 98% pure silica. Local rocks do not contain silica so it is theorised the sands were brought here by prevailing sea currents over millions of years. It's also strangely much cooler than regular sand making it much more comfortable to walk on in extreme heat. I had a short swim in the clear water, which looked clearer from the white sand but that was about the only exciting thing here. As I was sunbathing I noticed another tourist boat, which had a unique way of getting their passengers to the shore, it must have been a relatively flat bottom boat as it beached itself a few metres from the shore, a ladder was then dropped off the front allowing them to walk to shore in ankle deep water.

After a good sun soaking and polishing, we were ferried back to our yacht, then taken a little further north past Hill Inlet to Tongue Bay which didn't take to long. We were let off here to take a 1 mile hike to a lookout point, being allowed our shoes for the first time since we had boarded the yacht, which seemed a little strange at first as we walked to the lookout point, it was a great view across Hill Inlet with the shifting sandbanks that swirled back and forth, with Whitehaven Beach in the distance stretching away for us and out of sight. Inland it was a scene of uninhabited thick forest as far as the eye could see looking completely untouched. It wasn't long before we were walking back and on board our yacht to where we motored to the top of Whitsunday Island to Scrub Hen Beach for the evening.

After a while chatting and general socialising we had a meal of a deliciously good steak and mushroom with veg and some of that really nice bread again, finishing off with a few glasses of wine. After a bit more chatting and socialising followed by some more wine, we thought we'd sort our bedding out before we got to drunk to manage it. We then laid down for a moment for a little alone time, chatting between ourselves enjoying each others company, which was a little to nice and relaxing and I felt myself drifting off, I suggested we should get up before we fell asleep, but Sharon was enjoying our time and insisted on a few more minutes, this was just long enough to fall into a deep, slightly drunken heavy sleep. We woke with a start a few hours later hearing the rest of our shipmates up on deck singing *'You've lost that loving feeling'* several times. In my groggy and still slightly tipsy state I took a big swig of wine before I realised we were just too tired to manage joining in with the rest of them, which was a shame as they sounded like they were having a really good time, looking back I wish I'd made more of an effort to get back into the swing of it, but I didn't and we ended up going back into a deep sleep to the sound of more drunken singing.

Whitsunday Islands Cruise. Day 3.

Monday 18th April.

I was up a little after 8am with only a few others that were looking a little hung over and heavy eyed. I felt fine and as most people first thing in the morning I went to have my morning wee, to find someone had not remembered one of the first things we were told about the toilets, is that boat toilets work on a pump to take away the waste and they cant handle vomit. To be fair in a drunken state navigating through the yacht and up the steps to puke over the side, was probably not the easiest thing to do, luckily the other toilet hadn't had the same mistreatment. I was feeling a little hungry and couldn't wait for the rest to get up for breakfast, so I found some Weetabix and made myself a coffee while everyone else was stirring. Sharon joined me shortly after my breakfast on deck where I was greeted with someone else stomach contents, on the deck and down the side of the yacht. We were slowly followed by everyone else, with a few people still dozing on deck and under the canopy on the fore deck. A little later once everyone had finally pulled themselves into the land of the living, breakfast was served which I had a little of, as croissant and fruit sounded too good to turn down, I'm sure it also helped many unsettled stomachs and was nicely refreshing.

We made our way up the east coast of Hook Island to Manta Ray Bay at the north of the Island near to where I had dived on the first day, I don't think anyone was in a fit state to hoist the sails, so we used the motor all the way there. The ones that were suffering most from last nights activities, had been playing some game where a glass was filled with a shot of what ever the person was holding after answering some riddle or question right, it was then passed on to the next one, which would also put their shot in upon a correct answer, this went on until someone got it wrong and had to down the contents. That's where the song '*I've lost that loving feeling*' came in whilst they were drinking this concoction, which also explains why a few of them couldn't keep their drink down. Arriving in the crystal blue waters it was soon apparent how many fish are here, as Kirk started throwing pieces of bread in which soon attracted several big fish that excitedly spun and splashed about snatching the bread. Several of us got masks and snorkels off the boat that were kept in a large chest full of some liquid, which I think was some type of cleaning agent. I climbed down the side of the boat and started swimming among the many fish. It wasn't long before I realised my mask was leaking but with all the masks already in use I had to improvise, this was accomplished by blowing out of my nose to fill my mask with air blowing out the water. It was a little difficult, as I had to tilt my head to one side to allow the water to settle near the edge, without it getting in my eyes. We had moored in very deep water, but as I neared the shore it became a lot more consistently shallower allowing me to see much more of the coral and the ever increasing fish, there may have been so many here due to the no fishing zone in this area. After a while of blowing water out of my mask I managed to get some in my eyes making them sting and unable to see the main attraction here, so I swam to the beach that was quite a short one, nestled between some large rocks and backed by thick hilly woodland. I rested here to take my mask off and let my eyes recover. Sharon joined me after a short while and once my eyes were back to normal we swam together for quite sometime enjoying the underwater scenery, showing her which type of coral we could touch. We also did some free diving which I'm quite good at as sinking comes quite naturally to me, swimming is always quite a chore and tiring as most of my energy is actually keeping my head above water, snorkelling is much easier for me as my head is in the water and I float quite well then. I really enjoy free diving and it seemed quite effortless, Sharon on the other hand is very buoyant and can swim for miles, literally. From my point of view it was quite amusing watching her trying to dive, getting her head under the water was not too difficult, but no matter how hard she swam downwards she couldn't submerge the rest of her body. We swam around for quite sometime, again I was just as amazed with how bright and full of life this area was, at one point there were so many fish I actually touched a few of them, I also unintentionally touched one of the many jellyfish I had seen which fortunately wasn't one of the poisonous ones.

Back on board we found Jess and another deck staff in the water scrubbing the well encrusted vomit off the hull, personally I would have made the culprit do it as well as unblocking the toilet. Jess was in a surprisingly good mood considering what she was doing, when she was joined by someone from a neighbouring yacht, who new her that made her even happier. He had made his way by an underwater propeller scooter, which is a hand held diving aid like a small torpedo with a propeller in it that helps the diver to exert themselves less, resulting in less oxygen used and so longer periods can be spent underwater. He was diving underwater travelling some distance at a time, grabbing a breath of air and then diving again until he popped up next to Jess much to her delight giving her a big happy hug, I so wanted to have a go on that diving aid, how cool would that be gliding over the coral with no effort at all?

After lunch we motored a short while until we raised the sails again for our final push home, as we entered the open seas we had the most amount of wind since we left. For most of the time on this final part, the wind was hitting us side on which made us list over more than we had for the entire trip, with a good metre of the deck submerged with the water covering the low rail. We hit the waves with such force making the water crash over the front and soaking many of us. I went below deck at one point to retrieve Sharon's camcorder, which was a great experience with no windows to see the horizon, and the floor at an unbelievable angle made my route to the front more than difficult. The only reference I had on the angle of the yacht was to see the waterproof jackets in our bedding area swinging left and right on its rail.

We were back to shore by about 3.30pm, we had a quick questionnaire on how good the staff were on this trip before we left, and Dale was there waiting for us to take us back to the hostel. After we checked in Dale took us to the *Lagoon* by the sea for a swim, a 4.5 million litre (990 gallons), fresh self chlorinated saltwater pool, which is up to 2m (6.5ft) in depth. It is a lovely place with a bridge over the middle of it, a shallow sheltered area for children with a rockery, a picnic area with grassed parts round most of it as well as a beach area, allowing a jellyfish sting free area to swim in all year round. Ann and Kirsten from our Fraser tour were using this facility here too, so it was nice to catch up with them. After about 10 minutes of swimming Dale and Sharon wanted to learn how to dive, I'm not the worlds best diving expert but I new a little more than they did so I tried my best. Sharon picked it up quite well but Dale managed to kick his legs out as he hit the water creating a big splash behind him, rubbish diving but amusing to watch. After 10 minutes of diving, or just jumping in and splashing in Dales case we noticed a sign not to far away from us we had completely missed saying 'no diving,' around the same time we were approached by the lifeguard who wanted to point out the fact we had been doing this right next to this sign, he found it funny and I don't think he really cared as it looked like he was then going off duty, to leave us with no lifeguard. We carried on diving a little further up where the lifeguard had told us we could do this, only to be sworn at by some dickhead at the other side of the lagoon. Firstly there was no one else where we were so injury to anyone else was not an issue. Secondly quite often in life, I find that complete strangers get worked up that someone else is doing something wrong, and feel the need to put them right, even though it isn't effecting them in the slightest, as in this situation. What's it got to do with him I thought, it was only ourselves that would be getting hurt if we stuffed it up.

We had a quick shower before we went out to a bar for bangers and mash and to have a drink with the crew of the *Condor* with the rest of our group, a little strange I thought as we had been drinking with them for most of the 3 days we were at sea. Anyway it was a nice evening and we had several drinks with the others with some good live music. We had been joined by Becky from the Fraser island tour who happened to be in the same bar when we arrived and chatted to us for a while, she was a bit of a drip and a whinger and a little naïve, but none the less we still made polite conversation with her as she wasn't actually unpleasant at all. Unfortunately for Sharon she had taken a liking to her and had attempted to exchange email addresses several times, until she cornered her in the shower block after the Fraser tour and practically demanded it. One of the guys on the *Condor* trip who was quite unattractive and a bit of a loner who didn't really make any friends for the entire trip, had been giving Becky quite a bit of attention as soon as she joined us, at one point she exclaimed to Sharon how attractive she must have been as she had pulled already, Sharon replied back, "What him? But he's not very nice!" Sharon had to back track quickly as she soon realised she was enjoying the attention. They say beauty is in the eye of the beholder and it must be true for this pair, it was nice to hear they found something in each other, as several months later he proposed to her in Australia and they are now married, and at the time of writing this book in 2013 they are still together and still living there.

We had only bought one glass of wine each, then kept going back to the campervan nearby to top up our glass with the rest of the wine we had left over, from the tour. By the time we had finished it off we were rather drunk, I had been getting a little bored so made a point of making drunken conversation with the others and got some dancing in which made me feel a lot more lively and started to enjoy myself much more. At closing time I was ready for bed, but Sharon was more interested in going to a nightclub a few doors up that we were told about. She talked me into not going, as I wasn't really interested, when Ron from the sailing trip realised she had gone alone he told me I should never go home without my pretty lady. He was a very dear fellow but I assured him she would be ok, she had been in much worse places on her own on this trip before I met up with her than here. I said my goodbyes and walked back to the hostel, I hadn't even got half way there before Ron's words started playing on my mind, I kept thinking how I wouldn't be able to forgive myself if something happened to her. I spun round and went back towards town, past the bar and looked for the nightclub, I didn't know what it was called so I was basically looking for any nightclub. I don't know in my drunken manner if I took a wrong turn or missed it but I couldn't find this nightclub, after about 20 minutes of walking about getting nowhere I reluctantly headed back having the misfortune of bumping into Carl and his buddies from Fraser with one of them shouting at me, "Brendan you fucker!" then making a rugby tackle move towards me, to which I jumped up and pushing his head away from me which I'm sure was more luck than judgment that I didn't fall on my arse, I think, thankfully this was all I needed to do so they then left me alone, which was a good job as I think anything more aggressive and I would have been failing miserably. Typical I thought, I bump into the only person I didn't want to see again but couldn't find my girlfriend. I found my way back and went to sleep hoping I would wake up sometime soon to Sharon getting into bed.

Chapter 12
Northwards, and the rest of the east coast. It's been a long road.

Tuesday 19th April.

I didn't wake up until 9.30am and to my relief with Sharon, we showered and packed up our belongings but I couldn't find the campervan keys, I was quite worried that I had lost them in the evening of drinking the night before. I went back to the campervan hoping to find Dale and I did, he was in it so I asked how he'd got in and that I'd lost the keys. "I didn't think you'd remember" He replied, "I came into your room last night looking for you, I woke you up and asked for the keys and you got them out of your shorts pocket and gave them to me. I said then, were you going to forget this and you promised me you wouldn't and you were wide awake," I find that really worrying that I did something and have absolutely no recollection of doing so, I thought, what else did I do?

I took my waterproof disposable camera to be developed before we left Airlie Beach, as I couldn't wait to see the pictures I had taken. We had a bit of a wait as they were having some technical difficulties with the transference onto disc, so we went and found Dale at the *Lagoon* his favourite place, where he was sunning himself and reading. He introduced us to a spider drink that he'd enjoyed several of while we were away on the yacht. These were known to me as floaters when I last had one at middle school, this is basically coke with ice cream, although today I was having something a little extra with it, a cappuccino. I know it sounds a bit wrong but it was good, and refreshing being such a hot day. After our cooling drink we had a look for sunglasses, postcards and books until my pictures were ready, which I certainly wasn't disappointed with as I had captured many of the bright fish and several coral I had seen. The only downside to pictures underwater is that it seems much more cloudy and darker into the distance, with the coral looking much more alive and interesting in real time as it swayed in the current.

We started our long drive north on the A1, it seemed like we were always on this road, in fact we were one of a million that travel this road every day. It's quite difficult not to travel this road at some point while in Australia, as it circumnavigates the continent joining all the mainland state capitals and is the longest national highway in the world at over 9,000 miles long. I drove the first stretch of 116 miles with Dale taking over for the rest of this very straight boring road to Innisfail stopping off at Ayr, a small town that we found some out of date chocolate that happened to be very nice for 30 cents (12p). As this was the only exciting thing here we carried on to our next stop about an hour or so later at Townsville for our evening meal, which we would have found a lot quicker if it wasn't for the guy in McDonalds who gave us directions sending us the long way round to an Irish bar, *Molly Malones,* for a lamb madras, which was excellent. We had a little entertainment on the big screen while we ate watching something I thought was a little unusual for a bar, drag racing. Not something you'd think would pull in the customers. Walking back to the campervan we found some very unusual public chairs that were made from some kind of cast metal, which we saw as a photo opportunity trying to make ourselves blend in and be part of it with varying degrees of success, one of which was a mans legs as the legs of the chair and the arms with one of them holding a bottle. The other was female orientated with the torso and bust for the back of it and 4 legs with high heels on, although that bit did look a little weird as all four feet pointed inwards.

Sharon then took over driving for the rest of the way to Innisfail bringing our mileage today to 341 while I sat in the back of the campervan writing up an email on my laptop and loaded and named all my pictures, from the last few days. At Innisfail we found a nice secluded side road to camp on feeling rather hot for what I was sure to be a restless night.

Wednesday 20th April.

We were up after a hot and sticky night by about 8.15am, we drove into town to find a bakery for breakfast, this particular one we found sold very few cakes, this may have been due to the fact they boasted to use no animal fats. After my fill of Danish pastry and coffee we went to *Palmerston National Park* and took a walk to Johnson River, it was about a 2.5 mile round trip with steep descents and inclines making it very hard to hike through. Not only did we have to contend with the steep grade, we had to duck and dive under and through trees with some interesting routes. This park contains over 500 species of rainforest trees, and there certainly were a lot of them that we had to navigate round and over. One strange type was flat on one side stretching up very high, with others having several vines hanging off them, which I could have done a Tarzan impression on. Several trees had also fallen into the path making the winding path even worse than it was already. It was challenging but much more interesting than your regular walk.

We came to a lookout point where we could see the river a few hundred metres down and into the distance, and we realised it was gonna take forever, well that's how it felt anyway. From here the river was from left to right nestled in a valley, it didn't seem all that deep as we could see rocks protruding above the water line across the stream at one part, everywhere we looked there were trees covering the mountains. Quite sometime later we got to the bottom seeing some interesting items on the way, I kept finding leaves that were loosing its actual leaf, leaving behind its veins like a skeleton. I also found a large seed husk, dark brown, thick and long which resembled a large penis, breaking it open I found 6 conker like nuts neatly lined up inside. Because of the damp conditions and such a large area of diverse plant life, there are many varying types of animals and insects, which alluded us for much of the walk, the only wildlife we saw was the odd small lizard and a few spiders.

At the bottom we found some parts deep enough to swim in between the platforms of rocks that surrounded the stream and rock pools, Dale and I stripped down to our boxer shorts and took a dip in the cold refreshing water. When we got in the water we found there was much more of a current than we had first thought, with the real possibility of getting swept downstream if there weren't so many rocks to hang onto. We took this opportunity to have a bath, as we were never sure when a real bath or shower would present itself.

We made our long zig zagging trek back up to the campervan and back into town for lunch in a café themed with wood with the toilets named bulls and steers for the men and cows and heifers for the ladies. There wasn't a great deal on the menu so I had to plump for a burger that broke a large portion of a filling from one of my back teeth, this left me quite concerned. Firstly I don't have good teeth with the biggest problem being an accelerated decay, so it doesn't take long for a cavity to turn into something more painful or worse. Secondly I knew it would have to be fixed before I got to Asia, imagine dental treatment there!

Our next stop was Lake Eachum where the main attraction here were turtles that can breath through their bums, the Saw-shelled turtle is named as its oval shaped shell flattens out to its edge which has a serrated appearance. The secondary breathing ability is possible as it circulates water in and out of its rear ends where thousands of tiny blood-rich projections absorb oxygen. This allows them to stay under water for prolonged periods but cannot be dependent on this form of breathing and still has to surface for a breath via their lungs. This lake is an enclosed catchments and is also home to several fish which as well as the turtles are a complete mystery to how they arrived, as it is isolated from any other watercourse. It didn't take us long to see a few turtles at the edge of the lake, swimming round the felled trees that were submerged in the shallows.

This lake was formed approximately 12,000 years ago from volcanic activity that heated the water table, which in time caused a massive explosion through the build up of steam, this created the lake as its known today which is practically round, it then slowly filled with water that is now at an average depth of 65m (215ft). There are no streams or natural springs to feed this 158 acres (640,000m^2) lake with the only water loss from soakage and evaporation and can only be replenished by rainfall, the level can fluctuate up to 4m (13ft) between the wet and dry season. The local Aboriginal have a much different story to how this lake was formed, according to this 12,000 year old oral record, after a failed attempt at hunting an animal where the spear hit a tree to reveal witchetty grubs, in the process of chopping the tree down to get more out of it, they angered Yamini (The Rainbow Serpent) which turned the sky orange and opened the ground and swallowed the men, which then formed the lake they called Bana Wingina.

While here we found a floating short jetty surrounded by tubular railings with an opening at one end where a ladder entered the water for swimmers. A few others were diving here and swimming, so Dale and Sharon thought they'd have another practice at diving. Sharon had managed to retain her new skill, but Dale had seemed to be starting from the beginning again, and was still resembling the skills of a small child as his legs were going off in different directions. I tried various ways to show him with various degrees of failure, he was a little apprehensive as he was worried he would hit the bottom of the lake. One of the guys swimming there told us it was really deep and we had no chance of doing that. To prove this to Dale I then climbed to the top rail of the metal railings, from where I was standing there must have been at least 2m (6.5ft) to the surface of the water, at this height I am competent enough to pull a dive off, I launched myself as high as I could and dived vertically into the cold crisp water. I went so deep my ears actually popped and that's something I had never been able to do before, so I must have been quite deep, it felt like forever to get to the surface. After I climbed out Dale then did his best, with try after try, trying not to over think it, managing a half decent dive in the end.

After our second bath of the day we made the last part of the journey to Cairns, stopping briefly close to Cairns as we saw a sign saying 'Cairns lookout point.' Several miles away we could see Cairns below us as well as far out to sea. The other interesting item here was a circular plaque with many place names on it with a line pointing in its direction with how far it was, one place particularly caught my eye, *Yorkey's Knob*. Arriving at Cairns a short while later, our first stop was at *Peterpan's Adventure travel agent*, for another 'must do' before I die and checked out the different scuba dives at the Great Barrier Reef. This travel agent was really good with many different tours with information on leaflets and posters round this large open plan office.

While Dale went looking for an internet café I called my mum, as I was standing in this booth chatting, Sharon was nearby at a picnic table writing up her diary, when a lady sat beside her and proceeded to chat with her. Sharon liked chatting to people in different countries to get an insight into their culture and life in that area, which was something I also adopted which was a great experience. However on this occasion she wasn't so keen on the topic of conversation, after my call home I joined her to hear this strange lady opposing her view on Sharon of the queer Australian government. It wasn't too long before we made our excuses and went looking for Dale. After his unsuccessful hunt for a internet café that was open, we had a great success on finding a cheap Thai meal for $5 (£2.08) that left us satisfyingly full.

After this we came across an Aborigine shop that sold an array of native items, with the most common item, a boomerang that was one item I had on my list to buy, I had always wanted one ever since a family friend had brought one round one summer to our house when I was a small child. There were so many different ones to choose from, it seemed a little strange from never seeing a boomerang in a shop, to coming here where they were a common item. I chose one with typical native markings and paint, with many different coloured spots in circular patterns with lizards and some type of fish. It was supposed to be, and I hope it has, been painted by native people. It is a sad fact that a high percentage of Aborigine items for sale in Australia, claim to be painted by natives when they are not and are a mass produced item. It is a treasured item I will always have that is always on display in my house. There was also just as many didgeridoos lined up in racks, which were also brightly coloured and decorated with traditional symbols and styles. An unusual fact about them is that they were only used in the north of the continent and as far down as Alice Springs. The traditional didgeridoos are primarily made from the hollow branches of different types of eucalyptus trees of varying sizes, although they are usually about 1.2m (4ft) in length. Some were straight while others have an interesting kink or bend in it as they are from natural branches that can be any shape. Originally the branches would have been taken from trees that the centres had been eaten out by termites, they would clean it out making the main part of the instrument. Today this method is not used as much as it can lead to imperfections, which will affect the acoustic quality. These imperfections can provide an inherent uniqueness in the didgeridoos acoustic character, but can also mean that many eucalyptus didgeridoos if poorly made, don't have the correct internal shaping form making the correct sound. The didgeridoo is thought to have been used for the past 40,000 years, with the oldest written record of cave drawings dating back 2,000 years. We were allowed and shown here how to use one, we pushed our lips up to the wax moulded mouth piece, then basically blew a raspberry. More technically you use a loose lip technique while blowing into it to create an evenly sustained fundamental tone, with the different sounds created by tightening and loosening your lips and cheek muscles, as well as moving your tongue around to change the shape and the way the air flows to your lips. For us we managed something a bit like a wet fart with the odd sound that was similar to the sound it should make.

After leaving here light headed and tight cheeked, we wandered round the shopping area and market style places, until we came across *Johnnies bar* that had some live music on, so naturally we went inside to take a look and stayed there for a while. It wasn't long before Dale uncharacteristically went back to the campervan early, leaving Sharon and I to enjoy the rest of the band on our own, but more amusingly we got to see most of the people there dancing nearly as bad as me.

When the live music finished we also went back to the campervan, and found it to be a very difficult job of finding a quiet place to park up for the night to sleep, after some great deal of time we found somewhere we thought was safe with very few cars about for the night.

Miles driven - 156

Thursday 21st April.

I woke to see a female ghost in a long wave white dress walking towards our campervan, she then carried on walking straight through it, as she was walking away, she gave me a glance over her shoulder, I watched in disbelief as I sat there on the bed with Dale and Sharon who were still sleeping. Thankfully I woke up at that point at roundabout the same time as Dale and Sharon to the sound of school children. School children we thought? What the hell! Was our silent, collected and panicked thoughts. I crawled out of my sleeping bag in nothing but my boxer shorts and took a peek out the curtains, to see we were parked outside a middle school! Something we had totally missed in the complete darkness the night before. We were quite horrified of what people may have thought about people sleeping in a campervan with a pair of dictators across the side of it. The campervan wasn't what you would call inconspicuous, so I immediately jumped in the front grabbing a t-shirt on the way to look a little more normal if that was at all possible. I drove round the corner away from the school route so we could get dressed and clean our teeth, I don't think it would have been appropriate spitting toothpaste in the gutter outside a school.

We drove into town stopping off on the way for breakfast at a café where I enjoyed a Cornish pasty and coffee. After parking up in the centre we went back to *Peterpan's Adventure travel agents*, but this time finding a snorkel and dive for $89 (£37) on a high speed catamaran for the next day which was much cheaper than the quote the day before, which seemed like it would be one of the more quieter ones as at that point there were still 45 spaces left.

After booking our trip Dale went to do his emails, while Sharon and I waited in the campervan chatting until Dale had finished. We went in search of lunch, narrowly missing out on serving time at a bar & restaurant, so we had to find something to eat at *Woolworths*, as well as another disposable waterproof camera. After eating our lunch sat outside the shop, we carried on walking and exploring when we passed the *Reef Casino*, where Dale wanted to have a quick flutter. The casino was a tall square white building surrounded by palm trees and window type boxes full of greenery with some of them circling the building, it also had a glass double pyramid type of roof to top it off. At the time I wasn't the gambling type at all, so I watched Dale from one of the balconies to get a good look at what he was doing as well as the rest of the floor. He made one bet on the roulette wheel making the odds more in his favour by betting on 2 of the thirds, this came in to his favour winning him $5 (£2.08). He took his winnings and that was our time in this casino.

Dale gave us his internet card that he had a few minutes left on, so we could send our emails while he picked up the dive trip tickets. We went to meet Dale after emailing when I did a good deed for the day, while walking along the path, a bird flew into a building right in front of us, nearly knocked itself out. It laid there stunned, so I picked it up and encouraged it back from its sleepy look. I think it still didn't know where it was as it just sat there quite happily in my hand looking around, I put it in the safety of a bush and hoped it recovered completely before something else ate it.

After meeting with Dale again we went to a talk recommended to us by *Peterpan's Adventures* called *Reef Teach*. This 2 hour 15 minute talk was taken by an amusing Irish guy that really knew his stuff, telling us all about the reef and how it lives and thrives, what not to do with live coral getting a little over enthusiastic at times but interesting none the less. Fortunately we had a break in the middle for coffee and biscuits, which was good as I found it very wearing from the amount if information I was taking in, and this gave me a little perk to get through the second half. In this section we got to touch several different pieces of dead coral that had been taken from the sea where it was already dead. After this, we were in search again for food, finding an *Asian food court* to find a more than you can eat plate for $5 (£2.08) which left me feeling a little ill from the sheer amount of grease coating it. We stopped at the *Woolshed* for a drink, and then onto *Johnnies*, not staying too long here as the live music was a bit to clubby for my liking, but we were in there long enough for one person to notice Dales Norwich city shirt.

After our short stay here, it was a drive to the outskirts of town where we found a lay-by that seemed adequate enough, until we got out to clean our teeth to get eaten by some large mosquito's who were congregating in their thousands, which unusually made me come out in large blotches. We quickly pilled back in the van to find a less crowded place, finding one near to the airport for a much more satisfying place to sleep.

Friday 22nd April.

For some reason I woke at 5.45am, maybe because of the excitement of the day, so instead of waking the other 2, who I'm sure would not have shared my excitement and not be best please with me, I managed to doze of again until 6.30am. As it was, we had to rush to where we would be departing on the supercat, arriving 6 minutes early we had just enough time to pick up our goggles and flippers, with Sharon and I opting to hire the stinger suits that Dale decided to save his money on. He kept saying how he thought he'd be ok and would find it funny if he didn't get stung at all. He reminded us of this several times on the 2 hour trip to the reef, which by that time I was hoping he was going to get stung. The chances of a deadly sting here are quite slim and was more likely to be nothing more than uncomfortable, so I would have very much enjoyed seeing Dale with several stings all over his body, then I could've reminded him how he could have had a stinger suit for a few dollars. Admittedly it was only for the snorkelling as they favoured the surface of the water and I think he was hoping he would see one before he was stung.

We soon cleared the harbour and were skipping across the waves quickly to our destination at the reef. Due to the high speed and the choppy water many of the passengers were suffering from seasickness. I had taken one of the crews advise during their funny speech as they handed out ginger tablets, I don't know if it helped but I wasn't sick. Unlike 3 friends at the back of the boat who had been out the night before and had consumed large amounts of alcohol, they were now paying the price for it, I think they all threw up at some point. We were sitting inside for the most part, which can also be one of the worst as sometimes this obscures your line of sight to the horizon, which is one way of getting seasickness. I watched several people from here retreat to the back of the boat to try and level out. One unfortunate chap was sitting there for quite sometime, leaning back in his chair with his eyes closed and turning whiter by the minute. By the time he was ready to chuck he staggered up out of his seat to battle with the motion of the boat as it crashed over the waves, he was stumbling and grabbing onto everything while it was quite obvious he was struggling at keeping his breakfast down. He made it to the door at the back before his cheeks suddenly filled, fortunately for him, and for us, he was next to a pile of sick bags which he grabbed one just in time and promptly filled it as he got to the back. I felt a little ill after a while, most probably more from the other people looking queasy, so I joined the rest of the pale and green faced people at the back, as this offers the least amount of movement and minimises sickness. After a short while by 10am I started to feel better as we were nearing our destination, and time for our scuba dive briefing. I stayed inside for the most part before I started feeling ill. Probably because we were still moving at a fast pace and I was concentrating on the dive instructors giving the briefing, I turned to Dale and told him I was starting to feel quite rough. I noticed he was staring out of the window and the horizon, telling me to just keep my eyes there and I'd be ok. But it was too late for that, so I retreated again to the back of the boat to level out again.

Unfortunately by the time I was feeling better I needed to pee and change into my trunks, which was a problem for many reasons, the biggest was that we were still travelling at a fare rate of knots and the toilets were at the front of the boat with no window, so there was no chance of seeing the horizon. Unlike the back of the boat where it is the smoothest, the front is the worst so there was no chance of standing up to pee, then I had the arduous task of changing. Believe me, in hindsight, and a tip for anyone else who does anything like this, put your swimwear on under your clothes before you get on the boat! When I had finished stumbling about in the toilets I was feeling a little green around the gills again and went straight to the safety of the stern.

As we neared the reef, we started to slow down taking our position among the many other boats taking similar tours, it became much calmer as the coral that we could now see just below the water, breaks the waves up making it calm in the surrounding areas. Our first reef we would be diving at was *Saxon Reef*, which is one of about 3000 reefs that makes up the worlds largest coral reef system, along with approximately 900 islands, making it one of '*The Seven Wonders of the Natural World*'. To say The *Great Barrier Reef* is big is an understatement, at over 1,600 miles it's longer than The Great Wall of China, and with it covering an area of 133,000 square miles, this makes it the only living thing visible from space. Although I was one of the 2 million people a year that visit here, I still very much felt like a part of this industry, to me it was a life changing experience to say I had been there, as it was something I had always wanted to do from my first memory of learning of this reef. There would be several more occasions in my 6 months of travelling I would have the same feelings. Tourism here pulls in around $4 billion (£1.7 billion) per year from a diverse range of tourism operations in the *Great Barrier Reef* area, via approximately 820 operators and 1500 vessels which include day tours, overnight tours, snorkelling and scuba diving, long range roving tours, aircraft tours, self-sail, glass-bottomed boat viewing, semi-submersibles and educational trips, cruise ships, beach hire and water sports, passenger ferries, whale watching and swimming with dolphins. There is also fishing trips, although now there are many no fishing zones to promote fish population, after several places were suffering depletion and possible extinction of certain species. The teachings we had which I believe is common for most diving excursion, is that everyone is very respectful of the coral, and the fish that inhabit it. However, the majority of damage the reef sustains from this tourism comes from the seagulls landing on the ships and platforms and shitting in the water, this causes an elevation in nitrogen, phosphorus and mercury, which can cause up to 12% of the coral to become diseased, where as in areas that do not have this problem the diseased coral is as low as 1%. The major cause of pollution and declining water quality however is from farm runoff on the mainland, caused by overgrazing and excessive use of fertiliser and pesticides. Even with all this devastating and damaging pollutions the reefs can increase in diameter by 1 to 3cm (0.4" to 1.2") per year, and grow vertically anywhere from 1 to 25cm (04" to 1") per year, which supports over 2,000 different plant species.

    We were lined up on the seats at the back along with the line of air tanks, and slowly we were given each item getting heavier with each apparatus to make us a diver and looking forward to getting into the weightlessness of the sea. Once we were completely kitted out, one by one we stood at the back of the boat and took a long step out into the water, we had been put in groups of 4 with me and Dale managing to stick together, the first great thing I noticed is that once I had submerged, all my sea sickness disappeared leaving me to enjoy my dive. One of the first scuba diving lesson we had to do a metre or so under the water, was to take our regulator out, throw it over our should, blow a few bubbles and then retrieve the mouth piece to carry on breathing. If I was down several metres I would've been a little freaked out by this thinking of the panic not being able to breath, but as I could almost lift my hand out of the water at this depth I was calm enough to perform this and managed fine, this is one of the most important lessons as if this happened deeper and you were unable to retrieve your mouth piece you could be in trouble, as a rapid accent at depth can cause physical damage to your lungs. After a few other easier parts of this lesson we were on our way, linking arms and descending into the lively water. One of the first fish we saw was one we had already been told about, although he was named *Wally* I'm sure this was just a gimmick, and which ever *maori wrasse* that came along they'd say it was *Wally*. He was enticed over with a few fish treats our instructor had in his pocket, we then had the chance of petting him, yes I petted a fish! It is such a dopey thing with them growing to 2m (6ft), which this one must have been almost that size. The instructor gently put his hand on its bony forehead and guided it towards us, it slowly turned and swam past me allowing me to run my hand along it's body as it went. It's unfortunate that these gentle fishes inquisitive nature has been its downfall, allowing them to be easily caught and sold as food greatly depleting their numbers. Once they were protected their numbers started rising again, which is good for the coral, as they protect it by eating sea hares, boxfish or the crown of thorns starfish that attach the coral. Although the coral here wasn't as bright as the *Whitsundays Islands*, it was still bright and full of life with fish everywhere I looked, more than 1,500 fish species live in the reef, with 30 species of whales, dolphins and porpoises, 125 species of shark, about 5,000 species of mollusc including the giant clam, this is just a few examples of the devise life that inhabits here.

Dale and I got to swim together for most of the 30 minutes we were under making sure to get a picture of us together, the instructor also found a sea cucumber that we were able to stroke its leathery skin, being careful not to startle it as it can squirt out a toxic fluid. Another great sight for me when I was exploring a reef with the instructor close by was a *whitetip reef shark*, these guys rarely grow over 1.6m (5'3") in length and are not aggressive to humans. They are recognised by a white tip on their dorsal fin, I saw it slowly and effortlessly glide past along a channel a few metres deeper than I was near the seabed, and disappear off into the distance. There were many different coral, like I had seen before at the *Whitsunday Islands* but on a much greater scale, there were so many different types of coral with various species of fish living in them mingling together round this underwater home.

Before I knew it my air was used up and it was time to go back, but my time was not up completely for looking at this underwater haven as I still had plenty of time to snorkel, while the rest of the groups had their scuba dive. I got into my stinger suit and laid in the water and idly floated about, fortunately this time everything worked fine with my snorkelling gear with no leaks so I could enjoy my time much more. I feel so relaxed in the water most of the time, this time however it took me a little while to get used to the small amount of swell as you aren't used to looking down with the sea bed as the fixed point, whilst moving up and down seeing it rising and falling. I saw more fish and coral snorkelling as with the scuba diving, which was amazing, I also got to see a turtle about 1m (3'3") long go gliding past on its own. When our time was nearly up for this part I got back on the boat and had some food, grabbing the last best bits of sandwich fillings.

We moved onto our next site, *Hastings Reef*, about 2 miles away after lunch, much bigger than the last one with just as much life but with more of a swell and a stronger current that proved difficult to navigate the sharp, and jagged coral. The fish were in massive numbers here too, with schools of fish swimming in all directions, with one of the biggest shoals I saw must have been nearing 100 black fish, as they darted across in front of me, I also got to see another *whitetip reef shark*. The current was proving too strong in places, when I was trying to swim against it I got nowhere, at this time I noticed several jelly fish and the inevitable happened and I was stung, thanks to my stinger suit it only effected one ear, I didn't even see the one that stung me, most probably because it's the long trailing tentacles that sting you that can be quite thin. The one I was stung by was not dangerous at all and more of a nuisance, I swam for a little longer before it became too uncomfortable so I swam back to the boat for a dose of vinegar spay, which has varying degrees of success depending on which type of jellyfish you get stung by. After about 5 minutes the pain had subsided considerably and I went back in the water and swam with Sharon for the remaining time, I had one scare with the current when it swept me over part of the coral that was very close to the surface, to avoid getting cut to shreds the only thing I could do was to stiffen my body and let the current take me over the top of it, narrowly avoiding several a nasty cuts. Another woman didn't have the same luck when we were back on board, as she had a sizable gash on her thigh which usually looks worse than it is, as it causes a fine cut, also being wet spreads the blood making it appear much worse. Sharon and Dale were one of the last back on board, and much to Dales joy Sharon also got stung on her ear but didn't get it treated as I did, so it was glowing bright red and was very painful, Dale the jammy git without a stinger suit didn't get stung and relished in the fact we both had.

The way home was much more enjoyable than the way there as our sea sickness had gone and a free wine was being served, after this, and the relaxing swim and the fact we had been up quite early left Sharon and I sleepy, to which we managed to rest our heads together and sleep for most of the journey home.

Back on dry land it wasn't so dry as it was now raining, Dale had took a liking to a German girl, Sandra he had met on his Fraser Island trip, and had arranged to meet up with her when we got back, where we got to meet several of her friends as well. Sharon and I went for food where I found a steak special and it was then to *PJ O'Brians*, an Irish pub to meet up again with Dale and his new friends. We got a tip off, that there was another live band on at *Johnnies*, which turned out to be the same one as last night, but with a different type of music that was much better. There was more bad dances and funny people, one particular big guy was swinging his stuff on the floor with another random woman who was much smaller, she thought it'd be fun to swing her stuff about and bumped hips with him, after the second time doing this move the guy though he'd swing back with all his weight sending her flying into our table, *Newton's* law of motion again! We left by about midnight and waited for Dale back at the campervan expecting him to be quite late, we had already striped to our underwear and in our sleeping bags when he arrived back. I got into the front with the intention of driving out of town to our same sleeping spot we were at the night before, while Sharon stayed in her sleeping bag with Dale adopting the same idea getting undressed and snuggling down while I was driving. I didn't bother to get dressed, as I would soon be jumping back into my sleeping bag. I drove out of the city and came to a dualed road that had no turning and noticed the traffic coming to a stop. As I got nearer I realised it was a police road block which is an idea I think should be brought to England, they were stopping every one to check their papers and a breathalyser test with no exceptions. Great idea but a bit inconvenient in my current situation, as I was rolling to a stop, Dale rummaging in the dark for my shorts and t-shirt, throwing them into the front which I then found a little tricky getting on while driving without crashing or drawing to much attention to us, as I'm sure we would have had a fine for people in this vehicle not wearing seatbelts, or in a seat for that fact. I managed to get dressed while Dale and Sharon hid in their sleeping bags, I passed my breath test and they ran my plates to find I had no tabs and was told to pull in at the side. I was sure I was going to get caught but I kept my cool and chatted to the cop as to why I was missing this and it was a hired campervan which I'm sure he probably knew anyway. I couldn't believe he didn't look closely in the back, I suppose at a glance it looked like a load of bedding. As it happened my missing tabs wasn't a problem as it was hired and *Wicked* would get a letter to update their tabs on this vehicle. With a sigh of relief I said thank you and we got to our camping area for the night.

Miles driven – 22

Saturday 23rd April.

We were up at 7.15am and picked Sandra up shortly after. As she was going the same way as us, we all thought it would be a good idea for her to travel with us which worked out a little better, as the fuel was now being split 4 ways, and we still had a few thousand miles to drive, so I was very happy with that. We drove north to Port Douglas as there were a few sights to see here, and there is another town on this coast that was once a thriving gold community, soon after it was established in 1877 with its population growing to 12,000 quite rapidly. This was short lived as the construction of the *Kuranda railway*, and a cyclone that nearly wiped out the town in 1911, saw the rapid decline to about 100 by 1960, by then it was nothing more than a fishing village. Today the population has grown to nearly 5,000, with the *Daintree National Park* being one of the tourist attractions that help keep this town a stable and beautiful place to visit.

Our first stop was at the beach, it was at this point that Dale realised he had lost his camcorder, or more precisely my mums camcorder, that had been loaned to Dale as he had his stolen back in south America just before he met up with me in New Zealand. We pulled the campervan apart taking everything out hoping it had lodged somewhere out of sight, but to no avail. There were many places it could have been mislaid with our first thought, it being on the supercat that took us to the reef the day before. We called them when we got a chance to find it hadn't been handed in, so it was something we have to take on the chin and put it down to bad luck. Something I was constantly aware of every time I left a city, town or place, as I knew it was very unlikely I was ever going back there, and sometimes I would not have the possibility to back track to retrieve anything after I had left. I would often think of everything I had while leaving anyway and try to remember if I had it packed away. Dale however was taking it quite badly, most probably because it wasn't his to lose in the first place and he didn't really have the money to replace it.

Picking ourselves up from this, we took a walk down the beach to where we saw palm trees growing onto the beach, and in some areas they were growing on the sand. Apart from some nice palm trees there wasn't much else here besides an overly large lady swimming naked and a man throwing a fishing net into the surf and retrieving nothing but leaves.

We went back to town grabbing an ice cream on the way from the 42 flavours on offer at this particular parlour, we all had different flavours and I found Sandra to be a little adventurous at this point, not from the type of ice cream she had, but from sampling one of her ice creams with a spoon, licked it clean, then gave the spoon to me to sample the same one. We then visited the *Rex Creek suspension swing bridge* which took us over a side river to the *Mossman river*, this shallow rocky stream had just as much impact cutting its way through this forested area as the *Mossman river*. This bridge was quite easy to walk over as it was very stable even though it sagged a bit in the middle, there was something quite unique and nicely fitting to the area, even if there was a waist high chain link fence running the length of it to stop you falling in. It had a wooden arch as you entered it with thick rustic cables that were buried deep into the ground that goes up and over the bridge to the other side to support it. It looked old and felt part of the area, since I visited here though, this lovely old bridge has been replaced at a cost of $450,000 (£187,500) with a steel one that is much stiffer with vertical bars where the chain link fence once was.

    We were then at the river that was quite fast flowing that I was a bit apprehensive of swimming in, not only because I didn't think I would be strong enough to swim out of the current if it swept me away, but there was also a sign as we approached it, warning of the dangers of swimming here, and that drownings, had occurred there. After seeing Dale and Sandra swim without drowning, admittedly with some difficulty, along with 2 teenage girls I went in and joined them. It was refreshingly cold and a good workout with the current that I was able to swim against, but this may have been due to it not raining as this can bring on flash flooding. There was also a shallow area knee deep in the middle that I used for a rest a few times. We dried off on the riverbank to change which we usually do quite discreetly, and this would be the second time today I would see a pair of boobs, also the second time on this trip I got to see a German girls boobs, I think Germans must have much less inhibitions than us English.

We were then on our way to Cape Tribulation, another town named by Captain *James Cook* when on the 10th of June 1770, when his ship scraped a reef, running around damaging the hull on what is now named the *Endeavour Reef*. It was beached until the next day before he could refloat it, to which he named the north point as Cape Tribulation, because here, is where all his troubles began. This would be the most northern part we would visit in Australia, a little town still within the *Daintree National Park* 42 miles from Port Douglas. It wasn't until the 1930s Europeans started arriving here with several failed ventures such as farming vegetables, and livestock, fishing and cutting timber.

Today there is little in the way of activities in this small town with a population of 100, the close proximity to the *Great Barrier Reef* sees 2 boat charters a day leave here, with other activities here such as 4WD tours, horse riding, kayaking, trekking, crocodile cruises and jungle surfing, which if I knew about at the time, I would have gone in search of it. What a great experience flying through a jungle on a zip wire, something I have never done! The road to this little town is the last sealed road north which wasn't finished until 2002 thankfully for us, campervans aren't to good on muddy tracks, we had to cross the *Daintree River* along the way by ferry at a cost of $20 (£8.30), I think the ferry operators sit there hoping for someone to come to break their boredom as we didn't have to wait too long.

At Cape Tribulation we took another walk along the deserted beach that had more palm trees growing out of the sand, with them shedding several coconuts on the beach. It was quite warm when Dale and Sandra had a great idea of getting a free refreshing drink from the coconuts. These giant fruits that seem more like nuts to me are incredibly hard to get into without any tools, but Dale managed it by throwing them at rocks until they cracked, he can be so resourceful sometimes, thinking up solutions that many people wouldn't give a second thought to. He gave one to me, I put my lips up to the coarse fury exterior to drink the refreshing milk, which is high in several vitamins and helps in hydration. Once the milk was gone I broke it in half to munch on the interior, what a great experience, sitting on a tropical beach eating cocoanut. Walking further down the beach I found a small, cute, little plastic 3 eyed alien, from the *Toy Story* films that I picked up and it would travel with me for the rest of my trip. I had seen many areas on the beach that had little round balls of sand dotted around in large quantities about 10mm (3/8") in diameter, which made an interesting natural abstract photograph. I was a bit bewildered for a while to how these were formed until I saw the little creature caught in the act. It was a sand blubber crab no more than 25mm (1") across that was scurrying out of its burrow onto the beach, then working furiously scooping sand through its claws into its mouth to extract all the nutrients out of the sand, and what was left is this ball of sand. Quite some way down the beach we found a small mound of several large rocks that we laid upon finding a surprisingly comfortable position while we sunbathed for a bit, along with my new 3 eyed friend. It was amazing that for a while we were in glorious sunshine and warmth sunbathing, until all of a sudden it started raining, a bit unusual to us but normal for a place like this that is part of the *Wet Tropics World Heritage Area*, so we made our way back to the campervan, sheltering under the palm trees as it got heavier.

We drove back in town and found a *PK's* for our evening meal. This establishment had several amenities from hotel rooms to back packers, hostels and camping. The bar was typically Australia, open planned with a restaurant and seating outside with several long picnic tables under a roof to shelter you from the elements. It had a lovely feel to it, and a lovely roo burger and a beer for me. I hadn't long finished my meal as we sat there chatting outside, as the amount of customers increased to enjoy this meeting point, when I started to get a headache, which didn't take long before the others noticed I was unusually quite. I told them about my growing headache and was sure it would not turn into a migraine, something I had suffered from in the past. Something I should not have talked up, it was a matter of minutes before I felt my head pounding harder as the noise of the excited evening of people drinking came more difficult to tolerate, and more of an annoying echo that hurt. By 8pm it was getting too much to handle, without any painkillers I staggered back to the campervan in the car park to lay down in the dark away from the noise and lights, in the hope it would soon subside enough to be able to stand again. I fell asleep rather quickly and woke with a start an hour later to someone entering the campervan, I launch myself up out of my sleep and got as far as peering over the front seat before I collapse again from the pain that shot though my head, to see it was Sharon looking for the map. If it had been someone breaking into the campervan there was no way I would have been able to stop them taking anything in that state, I think I would've just laid there and said 'help yourself'. They had been talking to some of the locals who had said we could get further north if we wanted to, and was going to show them the route to take. As it turned out the road was to rugged for our vehicle and the idea was soon abandoned, besides there wasn't much north apart from more tropical rain forests. I vaguely remembered the others getting back into the campervan much later as I was nearly comatose by then, I found it quite scary that I was in such a state but couldn't have cared less at that moment as I was in so much discomfort.

Miles driven - 115

Sunday 24th April,

By 8am I was awake and surprised to have most of my migraine gone, I got some painkillers and had an egg and bacon muffin at *PK's*, using the showers here before leaving and taking a boardwalk trek close by. It was really good and full of life, tropical rainforests are extremely green and this one was no exception as the boardwalk took us along a track a metre or so above the ground, making it possible to walk through this wet, damp and boggy area to see this area in comfort. There were trees growing on trees, several different palm trees, ferns, reeds, and vines hanging from trees while some chocked others. As it was so damp, there was also many different types of fungi and an abundance of spiders, some in webs and some walking on the water. The boardwalk took us over small rivers with much of the forest well established round the walk and growing over the wooden path, which meant we had to duck and navigate the overhanging forest. It was an enjoyable walk that looped us round to where we started, and it was then time to move on, we got back into the campervan with Sharon driving us to Cairns back the way we came, as this was the only route possible to head west. On leaving this area we got to see our first and only wild cassowary that ran in front of us and into the forest.

Back in Cairns we reported our missing camcorder to the police, which was a complete waste of our time with Dale still holding someone else responsible for steeling it. We stopped at a fruit market where I got a great bargain of a big bunch of grapes for $1 (41p) and some bread before we made our way to Townsville for the second time, where we were then able to head west into the outback. At Townsville we had to wait a while as Dale wanted to watch a football match, I was a little irritated at this as it wasn't even a Norwich match and the rest of us wanted to get going as we had a great distance to drive. To waste some time Sharon and I went walking through a park and back to the pub, on the way back to the pub we passed 2 guys that were quite drunk. As we passed them one of them got up and followed us for a while until he asked us to join him at his house, I wasn't sure which one of us he was interested in and I didn't want to find out, so we made a hasty retreat to the safety of the pub where Dale and Sandra were.

We left Townsville as soon as Dales game had finished leaving the A1 and joining the A6 *Flinders Highway*. We were now leaving the comfort of towns and greenery to the sparse wasteland of the outback into the darkness. Dale drove on and into the night and past Charters Towers, which would be the last major town until we reached Alice Springs. It wasn't far from Townsville, it was about 80 miles of nothing to here and we would soon be coming to an abrupt stop. We passed Charters Towers and its 8,000 inhabitants on to more nothingness, we were wondering how far we could go until we were in what was classed as outback, as we were not insured for driving in the night due to the amount of kangaroos that have written off cars. It wasn't long before we got our answer as Sharon and I were dozing in the front, to be suddenly awoken by Dale saying no several times in rapid succession and swerving across the road, followed by a large thud that rolled down the side of the campervan. Sharon took it badly with her first words being, "What the fuck was that!" Dale trying to pretend it was nothing wasn't very convincing so we thought it was about time to pull over and camp for the night after managing 397 miles. The outback is great for camping, as most of the roads have a large unmade area along the side of it, so no more driving round for ages looking for a quiet spot to sleep.

Chapter 13
The outback, it's definitely out there and a lot of it!

Monday 25th April.

We were up a little after 7am, with our first stop at a petrol station that was nearby to use the toilets and get our gas bottle filled. It had masses of room round it and occupied an area about 200m (650ft) long, which we soon realised why it had to have so much room as there was a road train sitting in the middle of it filling up with diesel, under the lone canopy with 2 pumps in the middle of it a fare distance from the shop. This lorry was pulling 2 trailers carrying machinery, a short one compared to how long they can be. After my jog to the toilets, which were at the other side of the building as it was so spaced out, we found our gas bottle was already half full so they only charged us $4 (£1.60) to top it up.

I drove from here, not getting too far before we stopped for something to eat for breakfast. Pulling onto the side of the road we opened the back of the campervan to expose our kitchen, this comprised of a small worktop that we used more for storing items on, a cooler box we kept our fruit in, saucepans and plates as well as a sink that was rarely used, as it meant carrying extra water and we were tight on space as it was. Dale propped a shelf from the campervan beside the rear wheel to shield the stove from the wind where he was making himself a hot, all in one breakfast out of a can, while I stretch my legs eating my banana. A quick swish round the plates and saucepans, using a little of our bottled drinking water and we were ready to go again. We were now buying water in large quantities, as it was getting very hot in this area and was sure to get hotter, the further inland we got. The average temperature for this area at the time we were there is from 21°c to 32°c (70°f - 90°f) so we made sure to keep plenty of it. As we were clearing our kitchen ware away another road train passed by, it had 3 trailers carrying large concrete blocks, with each trailer rolling on 20 wheels, it was big at about 50m (164ft) long, but it certainly wasn't the biggest road train that is used in Australia. The world record, for the longest road train is 113 trailers at a length 1,474.3m (4,836ft), the equivalent of 143 London buses. This was achieved with a single Mack Titan prime mover, driven by an Australian John Atkinson. Although this is the record it was not for general use and was to only break the record, as it was only towed for a distance of approximately 150m (490ft) in an event sponsored by *Hogs Breath Café*.

We were now on our way, well and truly into the outback, and it really is unbelievably empty apart from the trees, which are surprisingly thick in this part of the Australian outback, whenever I think outback I had always thought of it as mostly desert. Anywhere along this road between towns, you could go a mile away off it into the distance, build a shack and set up a home for yourself and never be found or seen again it is that remote. We drove for about an hour before a bridge took us over a railroad which was *The Inlander Line*, a 560 miles railway that stretches from Townsville to Mount Isa, which was our goal for the day. We walked down to the tracks that we thought would make a good photo, and it did. The long shiny tracks reflecting the bright blue sky with the odd kink in it, which I was sure wasn't to good for the trains. Sharon also took a picture of me on the tracks, which is one of the very few I have of myself that does me any justice that I'm please to have in my collection. It was only a few hundred metres later and we came to a lay-by that was about 150m (500ft) long, most probably for those long road trains, at the end of this was a sign about 4.5m (15ft) high saying '*Welcome to Queensland outback*', which we saw as another photo opportunity and all did our own pose for the picture. Sharon leant against one of the posts while Dale hung off it with his feet in the air behind Sandra who was doing a half squat, with me tagging on the end as I had to hit the 10 second timer button on the camera and get into frame before it snapped. We then thought we could get a better picture with the campervan in front of it showing Stalin, with us sitting on the roof with our arms in the air which made a good picture, that one was difficult as I had to run up the side of the campervan using the open window as a foot hold, making it to my posing position with a second or 2 to spare. We then couldn't leave Lenin out so I turned the campervan round, for this picture Sharon and Sandra laid on their sides on the roof looking quite relaxed, while Dale and I stood either side behind them holding on to the edge of this massive sign, I only just made this one in time so I looked a little flustered, with

Dale having time to work on his pose, looking like a huntsman standing on his prize kill with his chin in the air.

It was 152 miles from Charters Towers to the next town, Hughenden with very little in-between, a town with a population of just over 1,000, stopping for petrol and moving on. How does that many people inhabit and find enough work to sustain this town in the middle of nowhere, a question I asked myself at every town along this road. Another 72 miles down the road we arrived at Richmond, this town was smaller still with a population of about 550. It was like a ghost town driving through, the A6 takes you through the centre of the town where each house had a generous amount of land, making the buildings well spaced apart. We came to the crossroads that had an extreme large and spacious turning space without a car in sight. It was incredible how few cars we saw on our drive through the outback, there were so few that after leaving Richmond, that when Sharon wanted a picture of herself driving the campervan, I got out and stood in the middle of the road to take several shots of her, driving past me without a single threat of another vehicle. We kept at a steady speed of about 60mph and I don't think we were overtaken once, although we overtook several slow moving vehicles.

We stopped again shortly after this to stretch our legs at a picnic area, if you could call it that, there were 3 concrete moulded picnic tables under a small, corrugated roof 10m (32ft) apart in this large sandy area next to the road. The trees were now getting less and generally dryer so there were some sandy areas, but plenty of grass covering the ground although it was now becoming patchy. The northern part of the outback is surprisingly green as much of this part is scattered with many small streams and ponds. Three road workers were also taking a break here throwing bread in the air for the Wedgetailed eagles that were circling above, to which they were swooping to catch it before it hit the ground. Ironic they were feeding them as they had a smashed windscreen from hitting an eagle, how can they spot a piece of bread in the air to catch it but not a small truck? We pushed on and 25 minutes later we came up behind something we had not seen for 5 hours since we were eating breakfast. It was the road train with the 3 trailers carrying the concrete blocks. I was amazed it had taken us this long to catch up with it even though we stopped a few times. These massive trucks have several tanks, which allows them to drive non-stop for many miles. They are also legally able to travel at 56mph, with that much weight behind it, hitting anything at that speed would be devastating as the kinetic energy would smash through anything and barely slow down, just think how long it would take for one of those to stop! It can be up to 170m (557ft) to stop at 56mph as some of these road trains can reach 200 tons (448,000 lbs), although they are usually around 79 to 118 tons (176,960 to 264,320 lbs). We passed this road train with some ease, as the roads here have long straights of a mile or two so it is much easier to get past them than you would first think.

It was 91 miles from Richmond to Julia Creek where we stopped for fuel again as well as swapping drivers which is something we did a lot, as it made sure that one person would not get overly tired and stop us getting brain dead from the boring road. We passed the smallest town so far on this stretch, Maxwelton that has a population of a little over 100 people, it was so small we didn't actually realise it was there, as there was only a cross roads and a small sign to signify that there was any sign of life. While filling up at Julia Creek in this town of 360 people we saw another road train, this time it was a Mobil fuel tanker pulling 3 very large fuel tankers, what a bang that would be if it went up!

It was then a final push to Mount Isa, 160 miles from Julia Creek stopping only once more about an hour later to try out my boomerang. We pulled into what seemed to be a farm entrance as there were a few wires strung along the fence with a wide iron gate to mark the boundary of this grassed field, that spread out in all directions as far as the eye could see, so I was sure I would have enough room not to lose it. Throwing a boomerang is an art, or should I say it's an art to make it come back to you. Boomerangs were originally never intended to come back to you, they were originally used as a hunting tool. They were shaped in this way to make it easier to throw it at a high velocity with a flick of the wrist, into the air at a passing flock of birds or horizontally hovering just above the ground to kill smaller animals. They would be thrown in excess of 150m (492ft) with some boomerangs as wide as 1m (3ft). Although used mostly by the Aborigines, boomerangs have turned up all over the world, with the oldest one found in Poland made from a mammoth tusk roughly 25,000 years ago. The Aborigines are credited for inventing the returning boomerang which is what we know them for today, they are much more fun than seeing how far you can throw a stick.

To make a boomerang come back to you, first you have to stand facing the wind, turn to the right, if you are right handed, about 45 to 90 degrees, and throw it with an elevation of about 20 to 30 degrees and physics works out the rest, with a little help from a few strategically placed bevels and the aerofoil shape, along with the spinning action to keep it centred and stable. The idea is, to snap your arm forwards and at the end of the throw you flick your wrist, this creates more force along with the angled boomerang, you can get it spinning very quickly, the more it spins the more lift is created by the aerofoil shape. My first throw was ok, it spun well but it seemed like I was trying to see how far I could get it away from me. The second throw did come back to me but a little to far, ending up behind me by several metres. The third throw, had too much elevation and it went to high, stalled and came straight down sticking in the ground. The forth was my best one, it was near perfect and if I had run a little faster I may have caught it, falling about 5m (16ft) from me. I was so astounded that it actually came anywhere near me that I stood there and barely moved. Everyone had a throw with the girls failing the best, their throws ended up falling on the ground a few metres away.

After our native experience we were back on the road getting to Mount Isa by night fall covering 482 miles today, passing one more town with a much larger population, than we had been seeing of about 2,300 at Cloncurry, where we moved onto another road, the A2 *Barkly Highway* that would take us all the way to Mount Isa. Upon entering this town we got stopped by one of them in the form of a policeman for a random breathalyser test, fortunately I was dressed this time, but like the last time I was carrying passengers in the back of the campervan, Dale and Sandra took the same hiding technique that worked last time and the cop didn't see them. After passing my breath test I found a phone box to call a life long friend of my mothers, Paul. He had emigrated to here sometime ago and was living in Adelaide, as this was another city we would be visiting I wanted to spend some time with him as I hadn't seen him for at least 15 years. He is a family friend I had grown up knowing spending many of

227

my childhood summers with him and his children, I had always enjoyed his company even as a child as he's the type of fellow that fits in with all age groups and people. My call to him was to let him know when we would be hoping to pass through to visit, as well as him finding a dentist for me to fix up that crater in one of my molars.

We drove round town a little before finding a spot near the outskirts by a railway line that had a lot of activity. The off road area we stopped in had another large area of firm gravel and reddish sand, the same type we had seen since we entered the outback. While we were getting our cooking equipment out to start making our evening meal, we were aware of a group of Aborigines walking past on the other side of the road, they looked like regular people really, but were incredibly dark skinned. As they passed us we heard one of them shout, "Up the Ozzies" followed by the others laughing just as loudly, it was obvious it was directed towards us but I was a bit unsure why, I had several guesses why, but I didn't like any of them, as all my thoughts revolved around animosity towards Australians, and anyone who was helping their economy. I was hoping this would not be a common occurrence for the rest of our time here in Australia. We all took our turn cooking our evening meal, for some reason I must have been desperately hungry as I had a pot noodle. I also had a pie that was much better than my starter I had bought from one of the garages we had stopped at on the way here. We spent the evening watching the trains come and go while writing our diaries, with most of the train drivers giving us a little toot, to which we started to see how much of a toot we could get from them which turned out to be not all that much. Sharon won this contest hands down, as one train approached, Sharon was waving and whooping at the driver to get a couple of short toots, until with one swift movement she lifted her t-shirt and bra to shake her boobs at him, this he very much enjoyed to the excited toots and several long blasts as he was hanging out the window, I really thought he was going to fall out as he passed us with a big grin.

We spent the rest of the evening watching another film from my bargain box of comedy, the 1994 film of Chicken Park, amusing in places as it's a parody of several films including Jurassic Park. We were all ready for bed after this with Sandra sleeping in the front across the seats, making it a lot less cramped in the back for a better nights sleep.

Tuesday 26th April.

    I woke up at 7am but gave myself a good half hour to come round enough to manage crawling out of the campervan, to perform my morning ritual of cleaning teeth and splashing a bit of water on my face at the side of the road, followed by an all in one breakfast in a tin we heated up on our stove, after having great difficulty opening it with the dodgy can opener that was among the utensils, supplied in the campervan. After our filling yummy breakfast we drove into town to find out what there was to do here at the information centre in town. In our guidebook we found there was a guided tour of the underground mine here at Mount Isa, unfortunately we found out at the information centre this was a mock up of the actual mine with no trace of any precious metals as the real mine had stopped doing guided tours, so we gave this tour a miss, which was a shame as learning about a real mine here first hand would have been something I would've enjoyed. Mount Isa is one of the top 10 suppliers in copper, Zinc, silver and lead that has made way for this town to grow to its 23,000 residents, although that number has started to slowly decline from fears of the mining of these precious metals drying up. Currently it is estimated that the underground mining will be exhausted by as early as 2019, although there is a possibility of another 40 years of mining if the plans for the open mine pit had not been put on hold. Most of this towns economy is directly or indirectly attributed to mining, there are several other activities here that pulls in recreational revenue that is only there due to the number of people that live there. There is a family fun park, aimed at children and families as well as retail shopping, the *Mount Isa Rotary Rodeo* and water sports at the nearby lake we would be visiting later that day, all of which is good for the economy but would not be there if it wasn't for the mine.

    I found this fact very sad that this town could easily become a ghost town like the ones we had already passed in the outback. It was also saddening to learn that this whole area was once home to thousands of indigenous Australians, the *Kalkadoon* (or Kalkatunga). This Area was first realised for its mining properties in 1861, with a township established by 1923 after John Campbell Miles stumbled over one of the worlds richest deposits, which then the mining community gathered momentum to the size it is today, to be soon exhausted of its use and discarded like a piece of rubbish to become an empty town of no value.

It is unclear the exact story behind how the native people to this area were eradicated, one of which is that the settlers cattle had depleted the feed for the native animals, and with a lack of food for the *Kalkadoons*, they had killed some of the settlers cattle to survive, which led to the stand off at *Battle Mountain*.

Another version, or maybe as well as, is one of the first settlers in 1866 was able to get some of the *Kalkadoon* people to work for him in his mine, but around this time friction grew after many more white settlers came to the region, which was responded by the *Kalkadoon* with attacking them in guerrilla style warfare with murdering specific people. As more settlers came, more *Kalkadoon* tribes were pushed further out of the region, which resulted in more attacks, with the owner of *Calton Hills Station*, 40 miles north of Mount Isa, was speared to death while he was tending his cattle. The new settlers had forged a police force shortly after the first settlers arrived here when signs of trouble arose, to protect them against these types of attacks. Following this they tracked the tribe responsible and trapped them in a gorge, where the tribe was massacred along with their women and children. But that wasn't the end of this sad story, after another shepherd was killed in 1884, one of the stations owner gathered a large number of men to join forces with the police, where they made a stand led by Sub Inspector Urquhart against 900 *Kalkadoon*, which repelled their attacks for some time, on what is now known as *Battle Mountain*. After a failed attempt of 200 men on horse back, Urquhart split his troops to flank the mountain and force them out of hiding where they were gunned down, putting an end to 40,000 years of their nomadic life, with this last assault weakening the tribe and made their land more vulnerable to the settlers to push them out completely.

Near *Battle Mountain* is a memorial obelisk to commemorate this battle, which is engraved with:
"*This obelisk is in memorial to the Kalkatunga tribe, who during September 1884 fought one of Australia's historical battles of resistance against a para-military force of European settlers and the Queensland Native Mounted Police at a place known today as Battle Mountain - 20km*

(12 miles) south west of Kajabbi. The spirit of the Kalkatunga tribe never died at battle, but remains intact and alive today within the Kalkadoon Tribal Council. Kalkatunga heritage is not the name behind the person, but the person behind the name."

So does the conscience of the organisation who placed this monument here, make any difference to this horrendous act of how this land was claimed, turfing them out like an unwanted weed in your garden or bugs in your house? Does it forgive the settlers who killed those Aborigines whose forefathers had lived on this land for more than 40,000 years undisturbed? Wasn't it their land? All this obelisk stands for is a reminder of how cruel humanity can be over something so materialistic, as some metal in the ground they wanted to make them rich with. It is a reminder not to repeat history. It makes me wonder if the negativity towards us when we arrived here was something to do with this piece of history. If this was the case, then this is a prime example of racism that needs to be let go, because it wasn't us, or any of the people who lived in this town who shot their descendants on *Battle Mountain*. I didn't have any negative thoughts against Aborigines and I still don't, for what happened during those times when people were settling here. Although I do feel for them that they were moved on from their lands they lived off, that they had used for centuries by someone else who wanted it. I know how I'd feel if someone just walked into my house and said they were going to live there because they liked it. But that was then, and this is now and hopefully attitudes have changed or will do soon.

We then moved on to the underground hospital built in WW2 after fears of the bombing of the Darwin Hospital, even though it was nearly 1,000 miles away. However they wanted to take precautions to protect the Mount Isa district hospital in the event of an air raid. In 1959 the underground hospital was damaged due to construction of the new hospital. It wasn't until recently the underground hospital was restored and has since received a prestigious award from The *National Trust* of Queensland for heritage restoration. After arriving here we first visited the museum, there were several items and equipment from the WW2 era here. From books to oxygen breathing equipment, and a few beds with skeletons laid on them, isn't that a little wrong? You would think the patients wouldn't be left on beds that long to deteriorate this much, I know medicine was bad then but I'm sure it wasn't that bad! As I was reading about this facility I also found that the underground hospital was never used, as the Japanese did not reach Mount Isa, therefore the underground hospital was not needed. Although it has been used in the 1960s by night shift nurses who would sleep there, as it was cool and quiet. It was another mock up and so we moved on, not venturing into the tunnels under the mountain, to look at a few beds and memorabilia of medicine from that era.

Our final stop in town was at the Mount Isa *RFDS Base (Royal Flying Doctors Service)* visitor centre. The flying doctors are a major part of the sparsely populated outback life, as they have been used all over the country in the hard to reach places from emergency flights to regular clinics. Founded by John Flynn in Cloncurry in 1928, who had a vision with his single engine aircraft, of the innovative use of the emerging technologies. His idea must have saved thousands of lives and brought medical supplies, to unwell people of thousands. The museum was factual with many pictures and items used in those first days of this new practice, there were several pictures on a board of the countless pilots and planes that have served this cause showing several that had landed on the natural runways that connect all these places, those long big empty roads. There was also a short documentary video on the good work of the flying doctors and operations in Queensland. There were no staff manning this museum, and it was nice to see that without someone there that this facility was still treated with the utmost respect, with a donations box at the end asking for a mere $2.50 (£1.04), that quite amazingly I saw Dale contribute to as he fed a load of coins into it, although I suspect it was all the lose change he had in his pocket that may or may not have added up to this small amount.

We drove 10 miles out of town to *Moondarra lake*, a man made lake that was constructed in 1957, with a dam on the *Leichhardt river* that runs through the town upstream, although in town it is dry for most of the year, it was officially named by a winning contestant from Mount Isa. By building this 9 square mile dam it provides water to the town and mining industry all year round, as well as being used recreationally for bird watching, sailing, watersports and angling, as the lake has been stocked with several different fish. Today we were using the grassy picnic area and using the cool lake for swimming, ensuring an all over wash for the day although it did smell a little like the Norfolk Broads, so I wasn't to sure on how clean I would get. Dale and Sharon were expertly and effortlessly swimming leaving me behind as I was a bit worried about getting out of my depth, not being able to swim as strongly as these two fish people. I got my body board I had used at *Surface Paradise* at the gold coast. This was where Dale found he was missing his lilo he had been sleeping on as an air mattress, so he had to make do without it which wasn't really too much trouble for him. I used my board to help keep me afloat with ease as we swam out to a buoy for the only reason for something to do. While floating around by the buoy I started cocking around, trying to stand on the board for fun, making sure to attach the cord to my wrist in case it got away from me, which was my downfall to losing one of my most important items, I was still wearing my sunglasses as it was incredibly bright and I find myself getting tired if I don't wear sunnies as I tend to squint a lot. While trying this stupid move that I knew was never going to end well, the board popped out from under me, garrotting my mid section in the process causing me to convulse in a few peculiar positions followed by nearly drowning myself. When I surfaced I realised I was missing my sunglasses, looking down I saw them sinking into the depths by which time they were out of my reach as they disappeared, and with a maximum depth of 11m (36ft) I was never going to get them back. After our swim we found a tap by the grassy picnic area over a drain that we used to wash our clothes. There were several Galahs Cockatoos here, a small pink parrot with grey wings that were very inquisitive, or most probably interested if we had any food, so we got some of the bread from our campervan that was becoming a little hard and fed them, although they had a little competition from the seagulls, 800 miles inland there were seagulls here! They kept swooping in to steal the bread off them and sometimes taking it from them when they already had it in their beaks. They got fairly brave coming very close to us at times but were just a little bit to skittish to take it from our hands.

After cleansing ourselves as well as our clothes, Dale wanted to check out where we had camped, in case his lilo was there, I thought it was a complete waste of time, even if it had fallen out there someone would have stolen it, or threw it over the fence onto the tracks or something, to only have to eat my words when we pulled up, remarkably it was still there, exactly where we had been. With Dale happy finding his little mattress, which he doubled up as a floatation device, we left Mount Isa as our time schedule was tight.

We drove until nightfall only managing 132 miles, where we found an open area at the side of the road by a 13m (42ft) windmill, with sails about 6m (19ft) across that was turning at a fair speed in the slight breeze. These windmills are used all over the Australian outback where water is hard to come by, these windmills are attached to a pump that pulls water from deep in the ground at the water table. It's a very slow pump due to the manner of how the water is retrieved, so there will be a large tank nearby for water to be used by the public and water for the animals and crops.

As it was still very warm, with a night time average temperature around 24°c (75°f), we hung our washing out to dry on several posts that seemed to be here for no reason. We fired up the stove and I had another meal in a tin, lamb hot pot that didn't turn out too bad. As we were wandering around the campervan clearing up, Dale stopped in front of us in the way someone does when they are about to make a speech.
"Is there something any of you have missed that should be here?" Was his puzzling question. We frowned at each other trying to work out if we had left anything behind at Mount Isa, until he finally pointed out there was no moon. We all looked about in amazement, we knew sometimes the moon doesn't come out as soon as night falls, but coming from a country that mostly has cloudy and foggy days we don't usually take notice of it, but here in the outback there wasn't a cloud in the sky and all the stars were out. Sharon started to freak out a little to where the moon was, getting worried something was really wrong. It didn't take her to long to work it out and all was calm again. It was a short while later when we noticed a glow in the distance as the moonrise came into view. Also something most people in towns and built up areas don't get to experience with the obstruction of buildings, trees and light pollution. It was eerily strange there in the middle of nowhere, quiet with the odd squeak coming from the windmill. It looked like a small glowing ball of light that grew as it rose like a miniature sunrise, that seemed to be moving at an incredible

speed up into the sky from its hiding place. After this little bit of unusual excitement I was sitting in the well illuminated campervan, as it was well kitted out with several lights, writing my diary up for the day with the door open minding my own business, when some kind of flying insect hit me full pelt in the face, then jumped off onto the dashboard of the campervan to recover. It looked like an overweight stick insect with wings that was roughly 10cm (4") long with 6 legs. It shuffled about a bit while I took a few pictures before it flew off again and disappeared into the night. I had several interesting items here that made good photography to which I exploited the best I could, before I left England I had bought myself a good point and shoot Sony camera, that was in a high class of cameras at the time. I had always had a good eye for photography but I was only self taught, so before I left I spent several hours with a good family friend, Helen, that I have probably known for most of my life, making sure to get some more detailed tips on how to set pictures up with some guidance on manual settings, which I think I picked up quite well and enjoyed very much. This trip was a great platform for teaching me these skills, as I would have the opportunity to capture something interesting through my viewfinder every day, which is really the only way you get better at taking good pictures, and sometimes you have to seize an opportunity to get that special picture, with one of the last pictures of the evening arising in this manor. The outback is a quiet and lonely place at night, with very few cars as no one wants to play chicken with a kangaroo, I heard a car in the far off distance and in an instance I saw a photo unfolding, which is another one of my favourite pictures that I will forever remember. I only had a few seconds to set it up so I ran to one of the post my clothes where hanging on, popped the camera on it and plumped for a 30 second exposure which turned out to be the perfect number. I snapped the shutter just before the car came into frame to capture the car headlights as a streak of light along the road, with the windmills blades near the centre of the picture with its sails blurred into a disc, the long exposure also brought out the sky, stars, trees and my laundry on the post. That was our peaceful evening, relaxed and quiet.

Wednesday 27th April.

We saw another great wonder of the world when we got up a bit before 7am, something that happens every day without fail that we take for granted, but find so beautiful to watch in a place like this, we watched the sunrise as I had another breakfast in a tin.

We got underway early in the end as we wanted to get to Alice Springs today, I got a little concerned if we would get there at all as Dale turned the key to here the engine turn over very slowly and then stop, it appeared that we had used the campervan lights a little too much the previous evening and I was wondering how easy it would be to bump start it. While I was pondering this Dale said, "We'll give it a few seconds." as anyone who has had the misfortune of a dodgy battery will know that by a quirk of physics, the battery will gain a few amps back if it's given a chance to rest, and by a stroke of luck about 30 seconds later this miracle worked when Dale tried again to which it sprang into life as the battery struggled turn the engine over one more time. With Dale at the wheel for the first 3 hours of our drive we were underway with a big sigh of relief, passing only one small town of a 180 residents after about 40 miles. Soon after this town we reached the border of Queensland and entered the Northern Territory where our road name also changed to Route 66, which would be the second country I had been to, and travelled on a Route 66. This border was marked with another big sign to signify we were entering it. As big as the last one we saw as we entered the outback, this tall white sign had an eagle flying across a red sun with *'Welcome to nature territory'* We wanted to get another photo of us doing something memorable in front of it. It was surrounded by a low tubular rail, that we would balance on, I set the camera on its 10 second timer and ran to my position on the end and we all took a step up and balanced 50cm (1'7") in the air with me losing balance just as the camera snapped that moment in time, capturing us all balanced, just! We carried on to see nothing for the next 280 miles apart from the odd airfield in the middle of nowhere.

I took over from Dale after 3 hours as he was getting a little brain numb. Driving these roads makes you feel a little lethargic from the boredom of seeing the same thing with very little to do in the drivers seat except keep it in a straight line and the needle on 110kmh (68pmh). We had made a few cads with the limited amount of digital files I had on my laptop, after listening to them several times in the last few days on the campervans CD player I really didn't want to hear it again, so I listened to my minidisk player for the time I was driving, The most exciting things I came upon on this stretch worth mentioning were 2 different things on the road. We saw some large birds landing on something in the distance, as we got closer, I realised that these were wedge tailed eagles, the largest bird of prey in Australia with a wing span as wide as 2.3m (7'5"). Two of these birds were taking it in turns to pull a piece off the kangaroo road kill between the cars going past. A little different compared to back home seeing crows picking at a dead rabbit. After about 2 hours the boredom was settling in and I was more or less just sitting there almost in a dream land, I didn't need all my brain cells firing to manage this level of driving when in the far off distance, across the heat haze of the road I saw a large stick in the middle of my side of the road. There was nothing behind or in front of us at that point and I could've easily gone round it but I just didn't, I stayed there in a straight line towards thinking I'd go over the top of it, I got closer and thought 'yep that's a big stick' and this went on for sometime with various thoughts of thinking it was a stick with different combinations of words that described the same thing as this was the most brain stimulating thing I had done for a while, until I reached it. I mean I was on top of it lining it up to go between the campervan wheels when I realised it was a large lizard sunning itself on the road! I only got a moment to take in any recognition of it but I think it was a monitor lizard, I looked in the mirror to see it hadn't moved and I hadn't squished any of it, I was hoping it would move after that, it might not have been so lucky next time.

We arrived at the end of this road to a T-junction at a garage called *Threeways* where I was glad to have a rest, as my eyes were really hurting from doing nothing. All that is here is the services for fuel, food and hotel with no town to speak of. We filled up with fuel and Sharon took over driving, leaving this garage and turning left onto Route 87 *Stuart Highway* to Alice Springs. There was only 2 ways you could go from here, Katherine, near Darwin was 500 miles to the right and Alice Springs was 330 miles to the left.

15 miles past *Threeways* was another town I could not believe, on this 830 mile stretch of road that has nothing of interest at all is a Tennant Creek with a population of 3,000 people. What do 3,000 people do there I asked myself? As we passed through it looked like any ordinary town, with shops, bars and restaurant with an airport. It was originally founded as a town in the 1870s as it was once part of the *Overland Telegraph* that ran through the middle of the country. It became much more popular when gold was found which became the third largest gold producer in Australia pulling more then 200 tonnes of it out of the ground. It mined here until 1999, until 7 years later when it opened another mine 60 miles away that is processed here. Apart from this the town relies on farming, tourism, sporting venues and Australia's premier street circuit go-karting event.

Half an hour later, after I had a little nap to rest my eyes we passed an area that was strewn with several, large round boulders that we could see a little way from the road, that looked interesting but didn't stop at as we didn't know of their importance. It wasn't until about 10 miles later at a rest stop at Wauchope when we stopped at a petrol station, we found out it was the *Devils Marbles* or *Karlu Karlu* as they are known to the Aborigines. It is falsely thought that the Aborigines believed the marbles to be the eggs of the mythical *Rainbow Serpent*, when they are actually a number of traditional dreaming stones making this a sacred site. These round granite rocks that reach a size of 6m (19ft) are a result of hardening magma within the earths crust under thick layers of sandstone, which lead to them lifting to the surface from the folding of the earths crust, with the wind and rain eroding the softer sandstone away over millions of years, and this is what's left. What happens in the spiritual dreaming is a mystery as the stories are kept among the traditional owners who pass the stories down from generation to generation.

All that was at this petrol station beside fuel was a hotel and refreshments so I don't think it could be called a town it was so small. While we were there, the owner started chatting to us about the area, she was very hostile towards the Aborigines swearing about them, telling us how there was a different law for them and seemed to get away with much more than Australians.

Moving on we took turns in driving the last 240 miles to Alice Springs stopping off at our smallest town yet, Barrow Creek, although it is hard to say how many people live there, as it ranges from 4 to 11 people. The main use of this town and the reason for it being here is it was chosen as a site for the *Overland Telegraph* repeater station that was opened in 1871, which was one of the 11 repeaters (excluding the *Telegraph Station* at Alice Springs) built to span the distance across the desert from Darwin to port Augusta. All that is there now is the old telegraph building and a roadhouse with accommodation. The old pub here was built in 1926 with the current publican of 25 years, Lesley Pilton, initiated what he terms the '*Barrow Creek Bank*', travellers post on the wall a signed banknote of their native country, to be used in a later journey in case they need a beer and have no money. We didn't leave a bank note but Dale and Sharon did blag some free coffee as they were driving and this was some stay awake and safe program. The lady minding the pumps and coffee was a very nice old gal, sat crossed legged on a fold out chair in the shade with a fag on chatting to us, while Dale and Sandra used the bathroom, which they were interestingly handed keys as the toilet were locked for some reason, Dale's key was a massive fork and Sandra's was a massive spoon. While they were playing around using them as swords the attendant was giving us some good advice as she idly wafted her hand passed both sides of her face to keep the flies off her. She advised us about driving at night because of how much damage the kangaroos can do to your car. One unlucky fellow she new in the neighbouring town, had bought a new pickup truck straight out of the show room, the next morning he was driving to a garage to have a set of roo bars fitted to protect the vehicle from these suicidal bouncy things, one of these fellas was unusually hopping over the road this early morning just as the proud owner of this pickup came round the corner, totalling his pickup truck. So I thought it would be a good idea to take note of this one as it shows how easy it could happen to a local.

We arrived at Alice Springs by nightfall bringing our total mileage for the day to 648 miles for a well deserved rest, although I had been resting in the back for most of this last part as I was getting bored of seeing desert, there was no civilization of any kind after the tiny town of Barrow Creek.

Our first stop at Alice Springs was to top up with petrol as we were getting low, with our first impression of the Aborigines in this area very poor, as a bunch of them across the road were shouting and swearing a lot, I wasn't sure what it was about but the attendant of the garage was worried they would give us hassle. As it happened that's as far as it went with us, then finding somewhere to park and find a bar. Walking the streets here the first thing we noticed, is how many Aborigines were walking about as we looked for our drinking hole, they actually make up 19% of the population of Alice Springs, that's about 4,600 Aborigines with most of them out this night on the streets. It was good to see that they hadn't been pushed out like so many other towns we had seen along the way, although a large portion of them that live here are unemployed. Which a is difficult subject to comment on, as before the European settlers came with their working ethics, money and an economy, 100% of the Aborigines were unemployed, and had been for 40,000 years.

The first bar we came to which was one of the most interesting and different bars I had ever been to. The first impression I got of *Bojangles Saloon* when I walked in, is the amount of empty peanut shells on the wooden floor. We made our way across the room to the bar with a crunch in every footstep to order a drink. We then admired this strange bar and its contents to great lengths, as everywhere you looked there is something what you wouldn't expect. The ceiling was lined with corrugated iron with boots nailed upside down to it of all different kinds, most looked like cowboy boots, there was also old cart wheels, boomerangs and antlers to name just a few strategically placed round the boots. One of the most single dominant items hanging from the ceiling was the hide and skeletal head, of a 60 year old crocodile that must have been at least 4m (13ft) long. The peanut shells that were every where in abundance, came from the tops of large wooden beer barrels and bowls dotted around the bar that had the nuts in the shells, pilled up for us customers which we ate several of, dispensing the waste on the floor in this unusual manner that you're not really used to. I found a tank with an old rusty motorcycle that had no rubber or wires on it, with a human skeleton riding it with stuffed snakes round it. The tables were just as rustic, these picnic style tables fixed to the floors were made from at least 10cm (4") wood of slightly different thickness' with fury cow hide wrapped round the seating part. Another interesting seating area was at the front windows that overlooked the street, at a high narrow table built with the same kind of wood where the seats were saddles, complete with stirrups. We also noticed some sort of radio gear here, to which we found out they actually broadcast from this bar.

Sandra had seen somewhere she thought looked like a good place to camp, but as it turned out it was too busy so, someone suggested the safest place to camp was to drive out of town to camp there, but another said there was a football field near by that is used sometimes by campers, after a few wrong turns we found our evening spot at the footy field and set up for the night.

Chapter 14
The town in the middle has no spring.

Thursday 28th April.

We were up around 8am, after another cooked breakfast and my second nosebleed since arriving in Alice Springs, brought on this time from turning myself upside down as I was inside the back of the campervan, looking under it for my sandals, the sudden rush to my head came straight out of my nose, not the best way to start the day. I had suffered with spontaneous nosebleeds most of my adult life, but 2 in as many days from bending over was a little unusual, but I wasn't going to get to worried as they only lasted a minute or 2. In town we stopped in a café for coffee and breakfast and to use the toilets, to which we were handed a key on a large piece of wood to access the toilets at the back of the café. Dale went first in the gents that had one toilet and a sink, while Sharon naturally took the ladies and was out before Dale, there were 2 ladies toilets and I was getting desperate to go so I took the ladies key off Sharon and slipped in to wash and use the facilities. After my wash as I was finishing up on the toilet I heard the door open and someone came in to the cubicle next to me. I finished and made a hasty exit.

We left Dale to go in search of a video camera while the rest of us took the campervan for another check up at a garage, and then it was off to an information centre where we found lots of things to do at Alice Springs. Our first point of interest was at The *Alice Springs School of the Air* this was the first one of its kind established in Australia. It is a primary aged correspondence school that utilises various communications technologies to have daily contact with students, home tutors and teachers. The first broadcasts were made from the *Royal Flying Doctor Base* here at Alice Springs in 1951. You can watch live lessons during school time, or a recorded one of the school's teaching program. There were many items related to these teachings from its first broadcast to present day, with one item being a radio that was used until 2005 when the high-frequency radio lesson was conducted. Today, the school utilises *Interactive Distance Learning* (IDL) technology, including satellite and broadband internet to broadcast lessons to the students over half a million

243

square miles. The children really make a community in this school and several of them have friends hundreds of miles away, with one girl in the broadcast we watched, told her friends in the class as well as everyone else on the air of the birth of her parents new child.

Sandra wanted to go and do some stuff on her own while Sharon and I visited the *Araluen Cultural Precinct*, first stopping at its café for lunch where I had a coffee and tried some bush muffins. I had wild plum and blood lime muffins. I can't say I disliked them, as they were like nothing I had ever tasted, I think my overall impression was good for both of these. While eating I could feel that familiar building pressure in my nose that was becoming uncomfortable which became worse as I stood up to leave, Sharon popped to the toilet while I rubbed my nose a little too vigorously as it had also become quite itchy, causing another quick nosebleed that stopped by the time Sharon rejoined me.

This tourist attraction was a fascinating glimpse into the art, culture and heritage of central Australia, and some of the local identities that helped develop the region. We started with the *Yeperenye Sculpture*, a 3m (9'10") high rusting metal sculpture several metres long, that we were able to walk through along the multi coloured tiled path. Across the ceiling of this giant caterpillar we found lots of information and artworks on circular discs detailing the caterpillars habitat, life cycle and cultural significance. The sculpture has been developed by metal artist Dan Murphy who worked with students from the Centre for *Appropriate Technology's ATWork program*. Mentoring based workshops with school children and local artists developed and made the panels to decorate this caterpillar. It is a fantastic example of collaborative public art work. The project celebrates the *Yeperenye (Ayepe-arenye)* caterpillar, the most important of the three caterpillars that are the major creative ancestors of Alice Springs.

I found the rest of the garden outside a little boring due to its sandy and arid complexion as the average temperature here at this time of year is in the low 30s and is extremely dry, which maybe why I started to get nose bleeds here. We then moved inside to the museum which has many informative exhibits describing central Australia's unique natural and geological history, the exhibitions follow the evolution of the landscape and the creatures that inhabited it, up to the present day of central Australian birds, mammals, reptiles and insects. There is also a large part dedicated to meteor craters as there are approximately 26 confirmed impact sites in Australia, ranging from a few metres to 55 miles in diameter, with some of them still being discovered in recent years. There are also many meteorite fragments, fossils and interpretive displays to detail the geological history of central Australia. There is a replica of the ancient *Alcoota waterhole*, which is a major scientific site in the region, this displays some of the megafauna fossils retrieved from Alcoota fossil site, including a giant freshwater crocodile and the largest bird that ever lived.

Back outside we took a look at the aviation museum where there was one of the twin engines, flying doctors plane, and the *Kookaburra memorial*. In a little shed are the remains of this little old plane on its side, as it was found in the desert, on the wall beside it is a picture of it when it was recovered 49 years later. It is dedicated to the memory of Keith Anderson and Bob Hitchcock who perished after their aircraft, the *Kookaburra*, made a forced landing in the Tanami Desert on the 10th April 1929, they were part of an air search rescues party to find Charles Kingsford Smith and Charles Ulm. They were found fourteen days later, the wreck was abandoned until 1978 when it was recovered by aviator and adventurer Dick Smith.

We visited the memorial cemetery that had 2 points of interest in this bare sandy expanse, the first is a very noticeable grave that has a statue of a short dumpy man with a beard, sat down with a gold pan in his hand, in memory of Lewis Harold Bell Lasseter. Born in 1880, Lasseter was made famous by his sensational claim, that he first alleged in 1929, that when he was at Alice Springs sometime around 1897, he had supposedly found a fabulously rich gold reef lying somewhere west of Alice Springs, of which he had retrieved several gold nuggets from it. Since then there has been several, well equipped expeditions to relocate this gold reef to no avail. Lasseter perished in the desert near the Western Australia and Northern Territory border in early 1931, after he separated himself from an expedition that was mounted in an effort to rediscover the supposed reef. His body was found later in 1931 by a central Australian bushman, Bob Buck, a pastoralist sent to search for Lasseter.

In recent years it has been thought that Lasseter may not have found anything and it was all a con to acquire money from his investors, as many of his facts have been proven untrue or questionable. One of the many disproved facts that have arisen with modern technologies, is the area has been tested with magnetometers, geological mapping, satellite imagery, seismic testing and remote-sensing, which shows that it is geologically impossible for gold to have ever formed in the areas where Lasseter alleged that it was located. Also the gold Lasseter had supposedly taken from this reef has been tested chemically, analysed and determined to have originated near Kalgoorlie, a thousand miles away. There is also some question to whether or not it was actual Lasseter's body that was recovered, as it is noted that Jimmy Nosepeg, an Aboriginal tracker who assisted Bob Buck to find his body said. 'The corpse was so decomposed, it could have been a black fellow."

The second grave was of Aranda tribesman, Albert Namatjira, the first significant aboriginal artist of Central Australia. His work of beautiful, watercolour, landscapes paintings from the west of Alice Springs are known internationally and have become extremely expensive. His grave was marked with a polished rock headstone, with a terracotta mural in the middle of it, which was created and led by his Grand-daughter Elaine through the members of the *Hermannsburg Potters*, to produce this picture of a landscape combining three sites in the MacDonnell Ranges, which were one of the subjects of his paintings.

Sharon and I then moved onto our next activity, which would be much more interesting than I first thought. I was initially attracted to this as I have a great love of all animals and I had never rode a camel. We arrived a little early and were led to where they were kept and waited for the rest to join us. I took a few pictures and carefully got to know them, I tried touching one of which was almost willing to contend with me, but I knew to be wary of them as they can be terribly bad tempered, hard to believe when they look so docile with that dopey look and long eyelashes that make them look sweet. As I had backed away, Sharon was trying to make friends with one of them when I noticed it in the process of moving its lips and head in a way that I was sure it was going to do something nasty. With Sharon completely unaware of this, I had just enough time to duck behind her, allowing Sharon to take the entire contents of this camel's mouth with a big grunt. Sharon was ok about it and we both laughed it off, although I didn't think I wanted to kiss her until she had washed. The rest of our group arrived and our handlers introduced us to our camels, with Sharon and I sharing the same camel, which was Kakadoo, who would handle our combined weight with ease as a small camel is capable of carrying about 400kg (880lbs). Kakadoo was encouraged to lay down by folding their legs under themselves and sit quite happily until you want to get on. The tandem style saddle was very secure which was a good job too considering how you get on. To stop them getting up prematurely while doing this, the handler stands gently on their front leg pinning it to the ground, which Kakadoo complained about profusely until he took his foot off. It's then a good idea to lean back as far as possible as they stumble and rise quite rapidly, arse first while grunting profusely. And there we were sitting comfortable about 2.5m (8ft) up. We were then attached to each other in a sorta diagonal method and were led onto the Todd River for an hour trek. Although camels can swim this was not happening today, the Todd River is an ephemeral river that begins in the MacDonnell Rangers and through Alice Springs. The river flows about every 2 years when heavy rain falls in the catchment area to the north of Alice Springs, which causes the river to start flowing through the town around 6 to 8 hours later. The dry riverbed can become a bank-to-bank flowing river in 15 minutes, but as the riverbed has a gentle gradient, that makes it possible to follow the leading edge of the flow at a fast walking pace. This rare event attracts many of the residents of Alice Springs who flock to the causeways and the *Telegraph Station* to watch and play in the water, although some places are hazardous with the combination of trees, waterborne and man-made debris. The river can cut off roads and railways during these times, with some of the roads built across the river that looks a little strange, with its raised paths beside it. The *Henley-on-Todd Regatta* has been held at Todd River annually since 1961, makes you wonder how they manage that considering there's no water in it, well they accomplish this as there is no bottom to the boat and they run the race, with it only having to be cancelled once in 1993 due to flooding. This is a big event and pulls in up to 20,000 spectators, quite amazing since there is only 25,000 residents at Alice Springs.

Our slow rhythmic plod down the river on Kakadoo was quite uneventful but very peaceful, there were barely any other sounds except for the little insects chirping away and the odd grunt from a camel, as our tour guide did the best he could to entertain us with some facts of the river and the camels we were on, as he led us along natural tracks that make you think you were somewhere in the desert. We rounded a 200 year old gum tree with roots that go down 20m (65ft) into the ground looking for that illusive water. It was in the middle of the riverbed that marked the halfway point of our trip, but this wasn't the oldest gum along this river, I found reports of some as old as 500 years. Across this 75m (250ft) riverbed, it is littered with these trees that looked half dead with the leaves mainly growing at the top of the tree. Most of them had bright white trunks and branches that made it look like it was dead, like dead wood that has dried out in the desert for quite sometime. Our camels were well behaved for most of the trek, with the only time with our camel having a little dance is when the young guy in front of us started petting Kakadoo, which he obviously disliked.

Back where we started, we said goodbye to Kakadoo and went in search for food, finding *Melanka Backpackers* bar, and tried out a roo steak for $9.60 (£4). It was a busy night and you're given a beeper to be beeped at when it's ready so they don't have to employ a waitress. I took the bleeper and said, "I'm going to take a seat out here" to which she replied. "Ok" It was still very warm and we didn't want to be in the stuffy hot and sticky bar. After half an hour of chatting I'd had enough of waiting and went back to the lady at the counter to find out if they were having difficulty in catching the kangaroo, but I put it much politer than that, to which she said,
"We paged you, it must not be working." She then pressed the test button and it performed fine.
"I was sat just over there!" I said as I pointed over to Sharon.
"Oh sorry about that, sometimes it doesn't work outside, it would have been thrown away if your meal doesn't get collected." I reminded her of the conversation I had with her when I ordered it, reciting to her once again I was going to sit outside when I ordered it, and suggested she repeat the order that I wasn't going to pay for, and sat a few metres away from the counter and watched to make sure I didn't miss it a second time.

After my fulfilling meal with nothing else to do we went to the local cinema with the intent of meeting Dale there, as there was a newly released film from a book both Dale and I had read and very much enjoyed, it was the remake of The *Hitchhikers Guide to the Galaxy* that was a huge leap forward from the original and a great way to spend the evening. We met Dale and Sandra at the end at the back of the cinema, with Dale pissed out of his head. I don't think he could even remember the film or even being there. As I have said before I don't mind Dales ridiculous antics and manner when I'm in the same state, but difficult to contend with when I'm sober. I did quite well guiding him to the campervan with no problems, for him to slump in the back on his lilo, and basically pass out. I drove us to the football field we camped at the night before, to find Dale semi comatose and unresponsive to my demands for him to vacate the campervan so I could make some kind of bed to sleep on, so instead of persuading him that I didn't think was going to be a quick process, I grabbed his lilo he was still perched on and in one swift movement dragged him out, landing in the dust in a pile of sheets and a lilo. This was one of the moments that I have exploited my friend much to my own amusement, I hadn't hurt him though as he managed to find his way back in without too much trouble.

Friday 29th April.

I was up later than I wanted at 8am, but I was feeling quite comfortable, with Dale not bothered about getting up either as he was unsurprisingly, hung over, hot countries and large amounts of alcohol never work together well. We cooked our breakfast and then to *Coles* supermarket to get a good stock of water and some food. Sharon and I were in and out and ready to get going way before Dale and Sandra, although I was sure it was Dale that was being the old women getting slowed down from the huge weight of his hangover. He eventually emerged and it was then a quick stop to get my underwater camera developed from Cairns for $16 (£6.60), before we picked Dales new camcorder up from another and it was then finally off to the MacDonnells Ranges.

This 400 mile mountain range was a short 14 miles drive from Alice Springs, consisting of parallel ridges that runs from east to west of the town to create these spectacular gaps and gorges, with it also having several areas of Aboriginal significance. Findings here of the valleys and range contain fossil evidence of the inland sea, which once covered central Australia and a quarter of the North East. This range was named by, John McDonnell Stuart, the governor of South Australia at the time in 1860, after Sir Richard MacDonnell, whose expedition reached them in April of that year. The first stop on our list today was *Simpson Gap* 12 miles out of town, getting to it was made easy with a road leading us close to it, to a small carpark that was a short walk to the gap. We walked along a dry riverbed that gave it all the more feeling of an old and ancient area. The old stream was narrow with good soft sand in it with a few large rocks and lined with gum trees either side. I think it must have water on occasions, or someone has a dry sense of humour as there is a warning sign beside this empty river, warning against swimming with a little no swimming symbol with a red line through it. A little further and we came to the water hole that is here all year round, all be it a shallow one, and no doubt is part of the river in times of flooding, this may have also been the remains of an ancient river, as it is known that a 60 million year old creek is responsible for carving this gap through this mountain. The gap can be seen from some distance, seeing the gentle slope from years of erosion down to the cold creek. The MacDonnell Ranges here is a great example of the folding, faulting and movement of the earth which happened here about 350 to 300 million years ago, as the red quartzite pushed its way out, leaving this very prominent layered jagged rocks, that shows its trek to the surface with its layers of rock at a 45 degree angle, that looks like they had been laid on top of one another. We took a little paddle in the shallow pool to the other side of the gap, it was so unbelievably cold it actually made my feet hurt. I found it a little unusual standing in air temperature in the low 30s to stand in water, I was sure was just above freezing, you'd think it'd heat up a little! Leaving here we got treated to seeing one of the many illusive wildlife in the form of black footed rock wallabies, these cute little critters love hopping over rocks where they forage for food. They're like miniature kangaroos that can grow up to 60cm (2ft) with a tail just as long. We were very lucky to see these guys, as they are nocturnal.

It was a 25 mile drive to the next tourist spot along here at *Standley Chasm*, which is owned and ran by the *Iwupataka Land Trust* and operated by an Aborigine family that charged us $7 (£2.90) for the privilege to see this natural site. The walk was a little longer than the last one, down an uneven path that was thick with rocks and gum trees, some growing while others were fallen across the path, on what seemed to be another riverbed, this gorge was also cut by water as surging flood waters over thousands of years are responsible for this beautiful site. There was more evidence of the movement of the earth as there were more light yellow and black, layered rocks, popping up in areas around the site at various angles to each other. The best time to see this gorge is when the sun is at its highest, and luckily we happened to arrive there at 1pm, at this time of day the sun captures the chasms grandness of these high walls that towered above us, with the bright day displaying many different colours and the formation of the rocks. The chasm itself is formed at an almost vertical angle that narrows to a thinner gap towards the other side. Water has flown through here as there were several areas of the chasm walls that were smoothed over and fluent like, it also must flow sometimes in more recent times too, as amongst the dry rocky terrain the odd old and weathered gum tree stood, with a sign of leaves nearing the top showing it wasn't dead, unlike the appearance it gave. Through to the other side of the chasm, the natural formation leads you along a track type that was most probably the original stream. The boulders got larger and the incline got steeper with Sharon and I stopping to rest on one of the large boulders not wanting to go any further. Dale and Sandra were a little more adventurous and climbed up further to what I thought would soon become too difficult. After quite sometime of waiting I was half getting concerned that something might have happened to them, and half expected to find him cocking around doing nothing. Which I was right on the latter, after several minutes of clambering up the rocks I found them also sat resting in the ever increasing difficult climb, with Dale doing most of the talking to Sandra that could have been done while walking back down. I was a bit pissy at first as my initial thought was of the daylight we were losing, making our time exploring shorter and missing something if we had to cut our day short, I grumpily snatch the campervan keys off him and snapped at him to get back so we could move on. I know I was a little harsh, but lets just say there was room for improvement on both sides. I strutted back down to the campervan and soon got out of my initial grump by the time Dale joined us, maybe it was the tranquil scenery that had the calming effect.

After we were joined by the wandering couple, we then had another 37 mile drive further along the range to a lake, which I used this time to eat my lunch, I had already prepared some sandwiches that were nice and soggy by now. This lake is more commonly known as *Bighole, Ellery Creek*, that has been formed from thousands of years of flooding, the water comes down from the hills, the water is then forced through the small gap carving out this waterhole, which is recognised as an internationally significant geological site, creating formations throughout the whole area, with the now well recognised angled rocks of different colours slanted into the ground. Arriving here an Australian made a point of chatting to us with an opening line to Dale of, "Hello mate, how yer going?" in that lovely broad stereo typical accent, followed by, "It's an outstanding vehicle you got!"
Dale sheepishly replied. "Yes, it's certainly outstanding for all the wrong reasons I think!" He was then curious to who picked it, to where Dale did his best to disassociate ourselves, from the art work on it. "Oh we didn't get to pick!" He said to a few laughs from the nice chap.

"I don't suppose you would!" He replied and then wished us luck. Seriously, except Russians dictator lovers, who would want that on the side of their campervan?

A short walk later and we were at the creek. High walls similar to the others we had seen with plenty of greenery and trees all round it, that were kept nourished thanks to the constant presence of the creek. I made my way onto the small beach and dipped my toe in to be shocked again on how cold it was, and debating on weather to go in, Dale was a great encouragement taking the first brave step so I seized the moment and thought how I would never get to do this again. I took the plunge that took my breath away making it even more difficult for me to swim, it really is cold which is due to the depth, at only about 50m (164ft) long, it has a steep drop off to 28m (91ft) making it this cold temperature. Hypothermia is a real possibility and you are warned not to spend to long at a time in the water. Dale was relaxing on his lilo like he was at a pool in some hotel resort when I joined him. We swam across to the other side, which I found incredibly exhausting, for a little walk further on where the creek turned into a shallow stream that became a bit marsh like, that then snaked its way off into the distance that would become a trickle, and then a dry bed, that no doubt would become a flowing stream again when rain falls further north like it has for 100s of thousands of years, that is responsible for sculpturing this area into what it is today. We made our way back after a short while, with Dale kind enough to give me his lilo for support as I had a worrying concern of not making it back. After a group picture in the water we were off to the next rocky formation a further 25 miles away.

The *Ochre Pits* are formed in a long cliff face of several metres high with many layers of different coloured ochre. This area like most of the MacDonnell range is property of the local Aborigine *Arrernte* culture, with this area being a registered sacred site, so the removal of the stone is forbidden under this rule. We walked along the many tight colourful layers of ochre with reds, purples yellows, browns and whites, which have been used by the *Arrernte* for ceremonial purposes and decorating and protecting their wooden tools and hunting items. The rocks are in perfect lines with some of them that look like blocks stacked on each other, in an unnatural way that didn't seem to work with nature. We wanted to feel what the ochre felt like as a paint, in the same way as the *Arrernte* used it. The ochre was soft and was easily made into a paste with a little water on our fingers, as we rubbed a finger up and down on the grooves that were obviously made by many tourists, and maybe Aborigine before us. Sandra painted a blazing sun on Sharon with myself painting a circle above my eagle tattoo to also simulate a sun. We were actually breaking traditional *Arrernte* laws, as touching or taking it is enforced with severe penalties. Most of the time I obey traditional and sacred laws, but I feel sometimes it's taken too far, in this case not only do they use it for traditional purposes, they also trade it in an economic sense to other tribes, I thought if it was that sacred, it wouldn't be used as a trading item. Also there is a lot of it, there are masses amounts of it that is several metres high and hundreds of metres long and probably a lot further into the rockface, it has been used for around 40,000 years by thousands of Aborigines, with still thousands of tons left that would never realistically be exhausted in the small amounts taken in the manner we were today. I'm sure natural erosion will destroy it way before man will in several million years or so. It seemed to me that someone is being a little selfish and doesn't want to share. After our risky body art attempt we took a walk further down this path amongst the major infestation of flies, they really liked my hat which was a typical Australian hat without the corks, but I would have very much appreciated this ridiculous look for the relief of them not landing on my face, they sat in their hundreds on the top of my hat, I thought I'd relieve humanity every now and then hoping I didn't unbalance the ecosystem by slapping the top of my head, taking a few dozen flies out with each swipe, although my black hat wasn't populated as much as one lady who walked past with a brown one. Dale didn't have a hat so resorted to wearing a pair of his Simpson boxer shorts on his head to which they took no notice of, with the odd one actually suicidally flying into his mouth, he didn't like that either. They were also many of them hitching a free ride on his black bag but staying away from his yellow Norwich city shirt.

Our last place of interest for the day was Ormiston Gorge which had a much more rugged scenery, with a much wider gorge. Dale and Sharon had broke out their fly nets as they'd had enough of eating them on our last walk which made them delightfully attractive but worked very well. There was also another small lake here that I opted out of swimming in, a little shallower than the last at 14m (45ft), leaving Dale and Sandra to test out the temperature, which Dale assured me it was better than *Bighole*, I took his word for it and wandered round taking pictures of this interesting and diverse landscape instead. Although it had similar aspects like scrubs, coloured rocks and gum trees with some of their roots exposed, it was still just as breath taking and humbling to walk round such a historical place where people had been visiting for tens of thousands of years. One of the gum trees I took a picture of was the most unusual I had seen, its trunk was twisted with two distinct colours, silver and black. Another interesting picture I captured here was, of a creatures burrow, only a small hole disappearing into the ground with a silky substance round its edge. I got some great close up pictures and different angles which I was pleased with and went away happy. It wasn't until I returned to England, watching the Discovery channel one evening, that I found out what that little hole was home to that had interested me so much was. Imagine how cold my blood ran when I found out it was home to a funnel web spider, which is the 4th mostly deadly spider in the world and the most deadliest spider in Australia. It was interesting to find out it's the 7th most deadliest animal in Australia with the saltwater crocodile beating it by one place. With a good bite from one of these it can lead to coma in 15 minutes, followed shortly after by death, if I was bitten while taking that picture I most probably wouldn't be writing this book now.

    I'm sure we could've continued along here to see many more places, but it was getting dark so we started on our way back with Dale at the wheel, not seeming to be worried about the wildlife that could say hello to us at any time, admittedly it wasn't completely dark so no one had said anything. All of a sudden Sharon shouted at Dale to warn him of a kangaroo he hadn't seen to which he narrowly avoided. He kept on driving despite this near miss and didn't seem to want to stop, from Ormiston Gorge it was 86 miles back to Alice Springs, so not too long after this with my fears of losing our deposit or worse still, crashing after hitting something and hurting ourselves, I reasoned with him, pointing out that we wouldn't get back to town before it was pitch black so we might as well pull over now. Which to my relief he did with out any more arguments with our final mileage for the day at 173. We cooked up our evening meals and settled in for a nice evening relaxing and chatting.

Saturday 30th April.

I woke early, so early it was still dark and busting for a pee, I snuck out of the campervan in only my boxer shorts, getting a little way from the campervan, to make sure I wouldn't contaminate anywhere we might be walking or cooking when we all got up to start the day. In hindsight it would have been a better idea to walk across the lovely flat road and pee on the other side well away from the van, as I had no idea what I was walking on or into. But no, I walked further into the bush among the dry coarse grass and shrubs when suddenly pain went shooting through the souls of my feet. I nearly pissed myself on the spot it was so painful, I could feel what felt like a few thousand, very fine needles sticking in my feet, with my first reaction to brush them off with my hand which wasn't the smartest thing to do, as what was in my feet was then in my hand. I peed using my other hand to make sure I didn't transfer any of those horrible things to my Johnson, then hobbled back to the campervan with great difficulty on the edges of my feet to try and avoid pushing the needles any further in, while in a great deal of pain. I sat on the road to inspect what it was, to find 20 or so little balls covered in these thin spines like a miniature sea urchin. I picked most of them out with great difficulty but was still in a good deal of pain, I could tell I still had many of them in my feet but could do nothing about it until it was light as I didn't want to wake everyone up with lights and rummaging though our kit for some tweezers. Remarkably I slipped in and out of sleep until everyone else got up, with Sharon kindly tending to my dilemma as soon as she woke up and operated on my feet, pulling the remainder of the tiniest needles out.

We made it back to town that was only about 30 miles or so and did our errands, Dale got his camcorder warranty stamped, and I got my underwater pictures back from the developers with only 3 dud pictures. We then split up with Dale and Sandra going to the internet café while Sharon and I went looking for sunglasses with the intention of meeting back up 30 minutes later. Unusually we were late meeting up from me this time, as I was in desperate need of a coffee after finding a great pair of sunglasses I liked for $20 (£8.30). Dale and Sandra obviously got bored of waiting for us, so we presumed they had gone somewhere else, so we took ourselves to the *Telegraph Station*, walking the 2 miles there along the Todd River.

It was a strange way of getting there along a riverbed but it was most probably the easiest route, as we got further away from town it became more arid with rocks. Arriving we found an older gentlemen sitting there in the hot midday sun who approached us asking if we wanted a tour guide. There wasn't anyone else there when we arrived so I think he was pleased for the company, to which he eagerly got up to our acceptance. He was a very good guide and full of local history and lived there all his life. He talked in great depth of the Aborigine heritage here, as he was half Aborigine himself. He told us how he was taken from his parents at the age of 2 by the government in what is known as the '*Stolen Generation*'. From 1909 to 1969 children of Aboriginal and Torres Strait Islanders decent were removed from their families by federal and state government agencies and church mission. There are several documented evidence, such as newspaper articles and reports to parliamentary committee's that suggested a range of rationales. Their motivations for this crime include child protection, beliefs that given their catastrophic population decline after white contact that Aboriginal people would 'die out', and a fear of miscegenation by full-blooded Aboriginal people. None of this seemed rational in the slightest to me, no wonder there is a good deal of bitterness towards the Australians. As it was abolished after 1969 I hope most people now see it as wrong and I hope this is a moment in history that will be learnt and never repeated.

This *Telegraph Station Historical Reserve* marks the original site of the first European settlement in Alice Springs, in 1862 explorer John McDouall Stuart led his third attempted expedition through the centre, to the north coast, navigating and mapping the country for white settlement. As arguably Australia's pre-eminent explorer, the Stuart Highway honours his remarkable feats of exploration and leadership. Following in Stuart's footsteps, the construction of the *Overland Telegraph Line* from Port Augusta near Adelaide to Darwin was completed 10 years later, this was in service for 60 years relaying messages. This is also the best preserved of the 12 stations along the *Overland Telegraph Line*, probably because it is the most visited, and in turn receives the most funding to maintain the site. Alice Springs takes its name from the waterhole a short distance to the east of the stations buildings, where the settlement optimistically named it as a spring as when the Todd River was in flood, they could see water coming out a cave along this rocky part of the river, when in fact it was the surging water filling the void to full capacity before it would be expelled back into the stream, to give this appearance of a natural spring. The first name of the town is taken from the former postmaster general of South Australia Sir Charles Todd's wife's name, with the river named after himself.

The grounds themselves had a decent amount of grass for the area, encouraged by the sprinklers, with much of the ground around the buildings bare with that familiar sandy look. Each building had been preserved well with telegraph poles across the station, leading to the building where the Morse code was received and sent, unbelievably the messages were sent and link this desolate place to the rest of the world by a single galvanised iron wire. The thought of a nation connected by this wire was quite amazing, the work involved do this in those times, across such a long distance that would take us several days to travel in a vehicle, it must have been a massive undertaking involving many people. One of the problems was the supply of food, especially meat as there was no refrigeration, so the 12 telegraph stations had to be supplied with live meat, Alfred Giles who had previously worked on the *Overland Telegraph Line* became involved in supplying the telegraph stations with the meat. On his first trip he successfully drove 7,000 sheep and some horses from South Australia to the northern stations, taking just over a year to complete the job.

Our route round the station first took us to the Post and Telegraph Office, like the rest of the buildings here, it was a small brick building with a tin roof and a small veranda, where the sign is over the top of the door. It was staggering to think that from 1872 after a submarine cable from Java in Indonesia was laid, every word of world's news passed through this station, although it did take an unbelievable 7 hours for a Morse code message to reach London via this *Overland Telegraph line*. Up until 1932, the town's people had to come to this post office to post a letter or to collect their mail. The building became a hospital and clinic when the *Telegraph Station* became an Aboriginal children's home in 1932. Inside there was great care taken to recreate the buildings first intent with several of the simple on off machines that were used to send messages and a solid wood counter with a few pigeonhole storage units behind it with a dozen or so holes. On the wall hung a wooden box that was one of the old fashioned telephones that had an earpiece you would've held to your ear and spoke into a small funnel in the middle, a great tribute to the era. I went up to it and held the earpiece to my ear and spoke into the little trumpet like mouthpiece. Some may have thought I was pissing around or being disrespectful. In reality I wanted to know what it was like to be a part of this history, imagining what it was like to be connected only at this point to someone else, instead of how we now rely on a little handheld device that is kept in our pockets that we can use anywhere and anytime.

All the buildings were well spaced out making it a considerably large area, so a short walk was necessary to view each building. The next quick stop was the Blacksmith's Shop. For obvious reasons we were not permitted to enter this building due to the amount of heavy and sharp items associated with this trade that filled this room, from billows to anvils and a large forge at the front filled with coal.

Another quick stop was the stables, a long building with half of it housing wooden carts from the era. Inside here were many whips, collars and stirrups, in one corner of the stable were leather saddles with bags that look old and very different to modern saddles.

The barracks was also an interesting building, it's the oldest building in central Australia with a long bench outside and a veranda at the front. It was designed like a fortress with gun holes built into the walls that were never used. This was because relations with the local *Arrernte* people were very good in the early days. It's sad to believe that the people who constructed this building, built it in mind with the intent of killing the locals. Inside were a few long tables with long bench seats with an old piano in the corner, and a tall black board with several relevant pieces of information on it. I quietly seated myself at the front to take a moment to appreciate the room and its history, and to read the information on the board. It was headed with '*The Barracks Building*' followed by what it had been used for in its lifetime. *It was a multi purpose room, divided into five sections with parts used for the first telegraph office, school, dining room and battery room.* This was as much as I could read as the rest had been rubbed off leaving only part words, which was a little unfortunate not to mention annoying.

The last building was the kitchen. It was dominated with a large green, cast iron oven with brown and black scorched areas round the ill fitted doors, 2 large ovens each side with a small door in the middle I expected to house the hot coals. It also had 2 large caldron style pots that could easily have been 100 years old, on the heavy slab top. There were many utensils and plates they would have cooked on, making you wonder how this room actually looked when it was being used, neat and clean and tidy I'm sure. My immature boyish humour came out here when I spotted an unfortunately named rusty metal box of biscuits from the time. The label was a little difficult to read from the corrosion, but you could still make out the name, Climax Biscuits. I know what you're thinking, biscuits in a metal tin isn't a new thing!

After taking in this piece of history, Sharon bought our guides book he had written and asked him to sign it, completing her experience with a picture taken with him.

We got back to the campervan in town, with my first job to finish writing up an email on my laptop, while sitting there with the door open, an Aborigine came begging for money to which he said he needed to make a call with. I always refuse charity to beggars especially in a place like this when there are so many of them, as you can easily get overwhelmed with others in close proximity. If you give to one, what makes them so special to deserve it rather than the next person? It's a harsh and extreme view to abide to but vital in areas such as this. It didn't mean I had no feelings for this persons unfortunate situation and by the look of him, he was definitely poor and in need of several good meals and a wash. I would have liked nothing more than to help him and all his unemployed friends in Alice Springs, but then I would have to help every poor, deprived person in south east Asia when I got there too, which would surely have left me in poverty myself! I refused his pleas several times, having to get a little firmer after he started tugging on my foot and he eventually left.

I sent my email at an expensive internet café, before we went to Anzac hill. Walking the streets towards the lookout we walked past another group of Aborigines, they also seemed liked they were poor and unemployed, maybe even homeless. This time we didn't get any begging, but for some reason one woman grabbed at Sharon digging her nails into her arm. I have no idea why this hatred to us was shown, we were far from being hostile to them, with both of us the kind of people who accepted cultures as they are. The unemployment among the Aborigine is high in Alice Springs, with reports from an aboriginal employment company has put it down to poor literacy and numerical levels, making it difficult for businesses to hire Aboriginal people in Alice Springs.

By sheer luck we bumped into Dale and Sandra on the way to the lookout point, so they joined us there near the outskirts of town about 1.5 miles from the town centre. Anzac Hill was the second such monument I had visited in Australia, dedicated to the men and woman of the armed forces. Much different to the one in Brisbane, the one here is much simpler but has just as much impact as the elaborate one I last saw. A single white obelisk at the top of the hill on a stepped platform, with bold letters engraved with '*Lest we Forget*' it stands alone so quiet but speaks volumes.

From this lookout point, I could almost see the entire town, but the most astonishing thing to see here is just how green Alice Springs is. With the tops of the trees having the most greenery, it's all I could see from above them. Behind this lavish see of trees rising up, separating itself from the rest of the landscape, is the magnificent MacDonnell Ranges in the north, easily seeing on this bright clear day, the range stretching far from the east to west. You can't imagine the impact this rolling mountain range has on you, there isn't many 400 mile natural formations that can be seen in the world. Most probably the biggest thing I had ever seen.

After another food shopping spree, we went to visit a couple that cared for injured and orphaned kangaroos. We pulled up at the house we were sure it was, as the car parked outside had a registration number plate that read ROO ZOO. But the kangaroos in the front garden were more of a give away. The thick wire fencing made sure they didn't escape into the road, to which they inquisitively came to see us. There were 2 small joeys and 2 bigger juvenile ones. After a little difficult petting through the wire, a nice middle aged woman came to the gate and invited us in, so we could greet the roos much more closely. The woman was shortly joined by her equally nice husband and they told use how they take them in caring for them, with the youngest she saved still needing a mothers pouch, which she successfully encouraging a surrogate mother to carry it. Something that apparently was not too easy according to one of her many depressing sad stories, as someone told her it was a possibility the surrogate mother would kill the joey. She was an interesting lady but she could've told us some stories that were happy. But looking around we could make our own mind up with that, they were well looked after and her garden looked nice, it was obvious she cared deeply for these guys. They had a few toys and other well kept pets, one of which was a massive dog that could be easily mistaken for a horse that was a soppy thing. She also had cats that seemed to be happy and at ease around the kangaroos and quite interested with each other, stretching towards one another sniffing, to a point when they were touching noses. I was expecting the cat to freak out at any minute and jump into the air. She brought a cloth shopping bag out to show us the best way to pick up a joey. She held the handles and opened the bag in front of it, bowing its head a little, it lined up with the hole and rolled into it to where it was then laying on its back, with its head, front paws and tail hanging out. The cutest thing! After several prompts from her husband that they had to be somewhere she finally stopped telling us her stories and we said goodbye. Mistakenly, we had thought they were a charity based organisation, funded by donations, which we wanted to help with what we could, as Sharon grabbed her purse to do her part the woman refused point blank and told us she doesn't accept donations. We thanked them for their time and went back to town.

It was getting late and we were all in need of food, so we took Dale and Sandra to *Melanka* hoping they wouldn't cock our order up again, taking a seat again close to the kitchen. I had the chefs special. A mixed meat dish of kangaroo, lamb chop, sausage, chips and salad for $8.50 (£.3.54). Is that wrong going to a kangaroo sanctuary and then eating one immediately after? Apart from the roo being a little oily it was a good dish.

We spent the last part of the evening at the *Sounds of Starlight Theatre*, to experience the pulse of Australia with Andrew Langford. An inspiring guy who had been playing the didgeridoo all his life, he had an uncanny resemblance to the comedian Billy Connolly. Tall, with a gentle calming aura about him, I got the instant feeling he was a connected person to this ancient art and the Aboriginal life. His show started with telling us how he had spent a good deal of time living in the bush with local Aborigines to learn their culture as well as the didgeridoo. Although this is something that is not seen so much with the Aborigines, with most of them living in towns or settlements, there is still a large proportion of indigenous people that are still very much attached to their ancient beliefs and culture and will go bush during spiritual times.

His show had many aspects on how the didgeridoo is played and the sounds that can be made, showing us an array of different shaped ones, with his iconic stance played level at head height on a stand, to where a microphone picked up the sounds. He is recognised internationally in this field, after he founded this 100 seat theatre in 1996 to where he now holds daily classes on the didgeridoo, and holds a spectacular multi media show of sounds and pictures that evokes the heart of Australia's red centre, attracting some 20,000 visitors a year. I enjoyed his talks on the instrument while he showed us his excellent skills. Obviously he is a very competent player, showing us several of his pieces as a solo and also with a band with drums, with one of his party tricks showing us how fast he can play this instrument by circulating his breathing accomplishing over 120 beat per minutes. One part of the show was interacted with the audience, where he asked people with skills in playing drums, bongos and another didgeridoo to play with him on stage, improvising an interesting melody that worked quite well. The show concluded with some of his recorded pieces with a projection of pictures from the area that was lovely to see and quite moving. One very memorable part of this visual show was of Ayers Rock when it rains, showing various pictures of water cascading down it in streams, and the animals that come out during this time, surprised to find out one of them, is frogs. We had a while after the show finished to mingle with him and ask questions in the shop, where there were many CDs, DVDs, instruments and cultural items. He also took the time to show us how to play the didgeridoo, with the opportunity to have a go on several of them, finding the children picking it up much better than us.

We left around the time we became to light headed to blow anymore and went back to *Melanka*, this time we wanted to see the band that was supposed to be on, after waiting a while with no sign of starting and getting a little late, we left Dale and Sandra there as Dale wanted to watch another football game, while we got our provisions for the next day, then driving to the football to where they said they'd meet us, we were expecting them to be later from drinking the night away.

Miles driven – 39

Chapter 15
Dreamtime on the big rocks and dreaming inside others.

Sunday 1st May.

    We were woken by our 2 drunken companions at 4am getting into the campervan, which then took me half an hour to get back to sleep.
    I got up a few hours later at 6.40am hoping for an early start as we had a long drive ahead of us to Ayers Rock, or Uluru as it is known to the Aborigines. Most people, including myself thought Uluru was close to Alice Springs, and to the locals it's only just up the road but in reality it's 290 miles from there. So we had our breakfast, filled up with fuel and headed out. Dale and Sandra were wiped out from the night before so slept in the back for most of the way. Sharon was also tired to drive so I took the driving seat as driving first thing is my best time, managing the first 250 miles. As we left Alice Springs we saw an unusual site, something you don't see in countries like my homeland England, it was the mileage board to the 2 main places in the direction we were going, one of them was Adelaide which is at the bottom of Australia, with the mileage of 1519km (943 miles), that would be like leaving Lands end in Cornwall, England, the most southern point, and seeing a sign post to John o' Groats in the most northern part of Scotland, which is only 837 miles. Does that give you a good representation of how big Australia is?
    There was very little besides the odd services to Uluru apart from more desert, until we stopped at a little homestead at Erldunda, 120 miles from Alice Springs where it marks the right turn to Uluru to top up with fuel before we turned off towards the big rock. We also took this opportunity to relieve ourselves in the public toilets, they had one of the most obvious signs for each sex, that I can't believe I hadn't seen it already. The men's were bloke's and the women's were shiela's. We made the last part of the journey to the big rock on this road, which was only another 158 miles, with still not much to see, so most of the time we were just scanning the horizon for something to look at. When we were within 25 miles of Uluru we saw this small rusty coloured mound in the distance, which wasn't surprising to be able to see it at this distance, as it's 2.2 miles long and rises above the desert by 348m (1141ft) However we would not be stopping here first but carried on past it, another 25

miles by road to the Olgas, also a name given by the first settlers, with its actual name given by the Aborigines of Kata Tjuta, meaning many headed mountain.

This group of 36 mounds is also sacred like Uluru to the Indigenous people and is much larger. Its highest point is 546m (1,791ft) above the desert. The first sighting of Kata Tjuta by a European was in 1872 by Ernest Giles who was exploring the country about 50 miles to the northeast of this site. Gile's progress towards Kata Tjuta was barred by a large lake, which he later named the lake, and the Kata Tjuta rocks after Spain's King and Queen at the time, Amadeus and Olga. Giles returned to explore the area again in 1873 but was beaten to Uluru by William Gosse, who sighted Uluru earlier in the same year, and named it after the Chief Secretary of South Australia, Sir Henry Ayers. He was also the first to make the climb to the top of Uluru.

As we approached the giant mounds of rocks I couldn't help but notice how strange they looked, so large but at slight angles to each other, that looked like singular hills. The 36 domes were once a huge slab of rock, similar to Uluru. When this part was being folded and faulted, vertical joints or fractures cracked through the rock. Water seeped down the cracks and over 300 million years or so the rock eroded away, to form valleys and gorges that split the rock slab into blocks.

We parked up next to the intimidating rock and took one of the easier and shorter routes, although an interesting place and I would have liked to spend a day exploring it, but we were always on a tight schedule and needed to priorities our limited time. The walk we took was the shorter of the 2 here, although there is nothing stopping you making your own route or walking round the entire group of mounds. We took the 1.6 mile *Walpa Gorge walk*, a route that takes you between 2 of the longest and highest domes. It was an easy going walk mostly flat even ground with a track to follow a few metres wide, lined on either side with simple lines of small rocks, the ground was also a little smoother, which may have been due to the amount of people using this route and literally polishing it with their feet through simply walking. This walk between these domes has been made possible from millions of years from natural erosion, of sand blown by the wind and rain, in a way we were walking on the top of this rock, it just happens to be a little higher than the desert. I was amazed again at the amount of plant life here in the dry place, more surprisingly it was growing on this giant rock. We walked for quite sometime, which was hampered by the strap on the back of my sandals breaking, allowing it to flap around, but I still managed. The towering walls were pitted areas of all shapes and sizes, caused by softer material in the rock formation, which falls away and crumbles as it erodes. All along the domes are black streaks that are caused by rain cascading down it during the wet season to form this black algae that look like to me streaks of tears. As we got further nearing the end to where 2 mounds join there was an abundance of healthy green shrubs and grass. A lot of the ground in this grove looks like it has been melted and is littered with pebbles, rocks and boulders that hides many different creatures, which we got to see one of them as we started to make our way back. I noticed a small snake dart across our path and under a group of rocks, so naturally I wanted to investigate, I like snakes and wanted to get a closer look. Carefully I moved the rock it was hiding under where this small snake of about 50cm (19") long was hiding, and then immediately jumped back a metre or so, which it reacted quite aggressively to and reared up at me with its head in the air, it was a beautiful light brown snake with 2 distinctive black bands round its head. Again after the fact, I have found out it was an Eastern Brown Snake, according to *Australian Geographic* it is the most deadliest snake in Australia and ranks 4th in the world. Again, I know it was stupid, irresponsible not to mention dangerous to the extent of the possibility of death if it had bitten me, but it was a calculated risk. I know I'm no snake expert but I kept a good distance from it, besides it was better to know where it was than to accidentally step on it. I think it was also a young snake due to its small size, which usually makes them non lethal to humans until they are about 3 years, but most probably making you feel quite ill!

We got back to the car park with Sandra keen to do the much longer route of 4.5 miles, of the *Valley of the Winds* on the north side of the domes. We really didn't have the time and I may have come across as rude and abrupt when I dictated we were going to Uluru, we didn't arrive here until 1.30pm as it was, and there was no way we would get round the part of Uluru we had planed before nightfall if we didn't soon get going.

After we assisted a French couple bump start their campervan 3 times, we drove to the Uluru car park and took the time to look round the visitor centre to learn more about this historical site. The Aborigines of Australia are perhaps the oldest form of sacred geography, and one that has its genesis in mythology. According to Aboriginal legends in the mythic period of the beginning of the world known as *Alcheringa* or better known as the *Dreamtime*, ancestral beings in the form of totemic animals, which are an animal's spirit trapped inside these believers when they are born, humans emerged from the interior of the Earth and began to wander over the land. As these *Dreamtime* ancestors roamed the Earth they created features of the landscape through such everyday actions as birth, play, singing, fishing, hunting, marriage, and death. At the end of the *Dreamtime*, these features hardened into stone, and the bodies of the ancestors turned into hills, boulders, caves, lakes, and other distinctive landforms. These places, such as Uluru and Kata Tjuta became sacred sites. The paths the totemic ancestors had taken across this landscape became known as *Dreaming Tracks*, or *Songlines*, and they connected the sacred places of power. The mythological wanderings of the ancestors thus gave to the aborigines a sacred geography, a pilgrimage tradition, and a nomadic way of life for more 40,000, making it the oldest continuing culture in the world, the Aborigines followed the *Dreaming tracks* of their ancestors.

During the course of the yearly cycle various Aboriginal tribes would make journeys called walkabouts, along these S*onglines* of various totemic spirits, returning year after year to the same traditional routes. As people walked these ancient pilgrimage routes they sang songs that told the myths of the *Dreamtime* and gave travel directions across the vast deserts to other sacred places along the *Songlines*. At the totemic sacred sites, where dwelt the mythical beings of the *Dreamtime*, the aborigines performed various rituals to invoke the *Kurunba*, or spirit power of the place. This power could be used for the benefit of the tribe and the health of the surrounding lands. For the aborigines, walkabouts along the *Songlines* of their sacred geography were a way to support and regenerate the spirits of the living Earth, and also a way to experience a living memory of their ancestral *Dreamtime* heritage. It is a great belief and I really like the idea that after more than 40,000 years in the modern world, these values are still practiced and believed with all their being and I hope it carries on for many more thousands of years. But I have one question for debate, there is no written word of these walkabouts and *Dreamtime* quests, it is also not shared with non-Aborigines, with it only being passed down to the next generation while on these walkabout. This area has thought to be first inhabited at least for 22,000 years, surely in that time with only the word of mouth, some parts must have been misheard and changed. If a group of just 20 people were to play Chinese whispers reciting a single sentence, it can easily become unrecognisable by the time it gets to the end.

For all the people reading this book who believe entirely in the Aborigines explanation of the formation of these mythical objects, then it would be a good idea to skip this page, as scientific research now takes over.

Uluru is often referred to as a monolith, and for many years this was listed in record books as the world's largest monolith. That description, however, is inaccurate as Uluru is part of a much larger underground rock formation which includes Kata Tjuta separated from one another by approximately 16 miles. In various tourist guidebooks it is said that two thirds of Ayers Rock is beneath the surrounding land but this is not the case according to the science of geology, which explains that Uluru is only the exposed tip of a much greater mass of rock extending far below the surrounding plain as an integral part of the earth's crust.

This formation started building about 550 million years ago at the Peterman Ranges to the west of Kata Tjuta. These ranges were much taller than they are now, so this allowed rainwater flowing down the mountains to erode rock and sand and dropped it in big fan shapes on the surrounding plain. One fan had mainly water-smoothed rocks while the other was mainly sand, with both fans building up miles deep.

50 million years later, the whole area became covered by the sea, which is today 863m (2,800ft) above sea level. The generally accepted explanation for the high sea levels is a raised sea floor spreading rates. Higher rates mean hotter crust, which expands, displacing seawater and causing long term flooding of the continents. Sand and mud fell to the

bottom of the sea and covered the seabed, including the fans. The weight of the new seabed turned both it and the fans beneath into rock. The rocky fan became conglomerate rock and sand fan turned into sandstone.

100 million years later, the sea had disappeared and the whole of Central Australia began to be subjected to massive forces. The rocky fan tilted slightly, while the sand fan tilted to 90 degrees, making the layers of sandstone almost stand on end.

Over the last 300 million years, the softer rocks have eroded away, leaving the parts of the old fans exposed. Kata Tjuta is a hard part of the old rocky fan while Uluru is part of the sand fan that stands nearly vertical.

We started the *Mala route* at Uluru, this covers a small, but one of the most interesting parts of the west side. The first thing I noticed is that the surface is nowhere near as smooth as it looks from a short distance away, it is weather beaten and pitted with holes and gashes, ribs valleys and caves, much more than Kata Tjuta. From a higher distance it takes on another visual aspect, you only have to find it on Google maps to see this for yourself, it is covered with grooves diagonally from the erosion of time across it, some layers of akrose, the rock that makes up Uluru, are softer than others, and wear away more quickly that leaves the characteristic parallel ribs or ridges, evenly and unnatural. In time, Uluru will probably have several domes similar to Kata Tjuta.

One of the first parts we saw looked like something had been pored down the rock and solidified not quite making it to the bottom. Many other parts had this almost smooth looking complexion with small areas eaten away.

We came to a part that has always had much controversy, 'The Climb'. This one mile climb to the top of Uluru is discouraged by the *Anangu* people and ask that visitors do not climb Uluru, mainly because, in doing so, climbers have to cross a *Dreamtime track*, which has spiritual significance. This walk was made by some of the first indigenous people in this area on one of their many walkabouts. Unfortunately 25% of the 200,000 visitors per year still tackle the climb despite this. I too had first thought of climbing it, until Sharon pointed out the stark realisation of why I wanted to learn and visit so many cultural things. She was right and

I respected the local peoples beliefs. This climb has been a tourist attraction for many years but it is very dangerous, with at least 36 deaths, mainly due to heart failure while climbing Uluru, with a few of them plummeting to their deaths.

I now have mixed views on the reason for not climbing. Many people who come to Uluru have no idea of the 'no climb' wishes of the Aborigines, until they are handed their ticket at that gate with this request. *The Climb* was kept as part of the conditions when the Aboriginal owners received the title to the lands in 1985, which they hold in partnership with the local authorities for 99 years, to which it will be owned completely by the Aborigines. If it meant that much to them you would think they would have pushed much harder to have this part banned, after all there are parts that were agreed by the 2 parties to keep banned, like parts that cannot be photographed, which I will come to later. It makes you wonder how the government would leave one ban in like photographing, but refuse to abide to such a cultural request like walking on it. Could it be that without the climb it could potentially lose that 25% of visitors that make the climb annually? That's 5000 people, how much revenue would they lose from that? It's really sad that money and greed could be the only reason for not banning this! If they had to keep the climb, why could they not make another climb on the opposite side that is not along the sacred journey or *Dreamline*, the climb is on a small piece of Uluru, and it's a big rock! I feel if there was more of a detailed reason to why they would like you not to climb it, then maybe more people would respect their wishes, I think that maybe this vagueness is one reason to why some people ignore these wishes. But the reasoning it's of great spiritual significance and sacred, and it's a traditional route taken by ancestral Mala men upon their arrival at Uluru in the creation time, is a little vague, why is there not a sign at every sacred site, *Dreamline* and tradition across the country asking not to walk there as it is a sacred area? It is also unknown how polite Aborigines are and don't like to say a point blank no, although they do point blankly ask for money when begging or swear at you shouting 'up the Ozzies'. There are many more conflicting reasons behind this controversial dilemma, with many more questions that I think will never be answered.

This last section is not meant disrespectfully in any way, this is just some of the many discrepancies in the reasoning on this whole matter I have noticed while I was there, and in researching the information on

Uluru for this part of the book, and hopefully it is seen as some type of education on the area. If you ever have the intention of visiting Uluru, obey their wishes, as we do not know all the truth about this place that has been used for thousands of years, by the indigenous people before it was claimed by European settlers. I will finish this section with a simple comparison, would you enter a Buddhist temple in shorts and hiking boots? Or would you walk up to the altar rail in an English cathedral to take a flash photo of the communicants?

I still wouldn't climb it now in case the vague secretive reasons were true, and would like to respect their wishes and beliefs. Although I would very much like to for the only reason, to experience this cultural and spiritual journey, to know what it would be like to walk a *Dreamline* that so many other spiritual people had done, and truly be a part of it.

At the bottom of the gentle slope of *The Climb* that led up to the top, there was a large board with the pleas to not climb it, with the majority of it taken up with how to climb it if you do. A chain that was installed in 1964 snakes its way up, supported by a short post about every 2m (6ft) with many tourist hanging onto it, they looked like ants on a boulder from where I was standing. Moving on we followed the path round the edge of it by several metres, rounding the corner with the climbers out of site, we came to a great view of the rock that rolled majestically over itself that gradually ran into the ground. We walked past caves that perhaps formed by uneven flaky weathering. Small pits became bigger dimples, then hollows and finally the caves that have taken millions of years to form. They ranged in size and shape with some like an overhand piece separated at the front of it that drooped down to the ground, seemingly holding it up.

In some places a boardwalk with a barrier would stop us from getting to close to it of some cave painting, maybe made with ochre that we had seen in the MacDonnell ranges, these painting are still done today for certain rituals.

There was deep ridges as we carried on further to see more evidence of the black algae that has made its way down the rock, along the valleys it had carved out over millions of years wearing it down that also makes chains of potholes and plunge pools. Another over hang we came to looked like it had been eroded away by waves, and that is a possibility, but it may have also have been from the gentle erosion of rain water carving this much softer part out, to leave this gigantic overhang that looked like a wave itself, almost cresting, frozen in time with more vertical grooves along it, stretching to at least 50m (164ft) and at lest 6m (19ft) high. At the time I did not realise, along with many others that day, that this area was off limits to non-Aborigine and was a photographic sensitive area, it could not have been well marked as all 4 of us missed this warning. The reason for this is because it is gender related, woman come here to do some kind of ritual thing the men do not know about and are not allowed to see this area. By taking a picture of an area like this, it is thought there maybe a possibility that the opposite sex may see the picture and accidentally break their tradition of not looking at it. In my case these pictures will never be published, and if I did come in contact with an Aborigine, out of respect I would not show them my pictures or mention it, and so it would be very unlikely that my pictures would break their laws and traditions. Also there are many books and pictures on the internet of this cave, with them going into great detail on this area.

There are several of these wave caves that boggle the mind to how they were formed, another one we visited had several large rocks that sheltered the front of it like some of the rock was melted and poured on the top to run down over the front of these caves, hardening as it went.

We came across another area called Kantju Gorge, this had the black algae line coming down the side of the rock as well as several areas round it, where it had been captured by the natural groves of the rock, to come out here like a waterfall. At the top it was much lower then it's surrounding rock making it into a small valley, no doubt this is the makings of one of the first areas to become like Kata Tjuta's many domes.

We got to the end of the *Mala walk*, but carried on for a short distance round to the top to see the Warayuki and Tjukatjapi area, another camera sensitive area, only allowed to be seen by male Aborigine, which was nowhere as exciting, it was a very large patch of a worn rough area, on the side of the rock.

It had taken us nearly an hour to get here and it was starting to get dark, so we hastily made our way back to the campervan to get to one of the many lookout points, to see the changing colours of Uluru during this time. It is one of the most well documented must dos to see the changing colours of Uluru, so we parked up in front of it and for most of the time, we viewed this eerily quiet scene from our seating position on the top of our campervan. In reality the colours only changed slightly and very gradually over a period of about half an hour, maybe it was the time of year that made it less spectacular than you're led to believe. It didn't make it any less special though, I sat there at another point in my life humbled by such a beautiful natural wonder, that had been used and seen by man for such a long time, to think of the transformations this giant slab of rock has made over the 100's of millions of years, with me, in this blink of an eye moment in time.

We cooked our meal there while watching this great phenomenon with several other people having the same idea, along this long row of cars and campervans pointing at Uluru. We left after dark with the idea we could camp on the grounds campsite until we found out it was $13 (£5.40) each, so we decided to camp out of the grounds instead, finding a spot on a little turning at the side of the road a few miles away from site. After writing our diaries for the day we went to sleep, which didn't take me too long to get to sleep from the exhausting day.

Monday 2nd May.

We hadn't been to sleep long when we were woken, startled into life by some major banging on the windows, a little after midnight by the local rangers. Dale jumped in the front and wound down the window to see what the problem was, they were ok about it and said we couldn't sleep here. Dale asked them if there was anywhere we could sleep, which they then kindly pointed off into the distance away from the site down the road and told us, anywhere past the 110kmh sign about 1.5 miles away. Dale started the campervan with the rest of us still half asleep in our sleeping bags, and drove at some speed that I didn't really care about, as all I wanted to do was sleep. As soon as we passed the limits Dale came to an abrupt stop at the side of the road with a spray of stones and a cloud of dust, killing the engine and jumping into the back in one single movement.

After several more hours of undisturbed sleep we had intended to get up for sunrise, so I had set my little watch alarm clock for 6am but none of us heard it and slept straight through it. Luckily Dale woke up 45 minutes later and it was still dark, so we jumped in the front, leaving Sharon and Sandra in the back still dozing and took a swift drive to Uluru. Dale at this point realised he was missing a shoe, I was so happy and thanked my lucky stars that I wouldn't have to smell those god awful shoes, I hadn't felt this good about his shoes since we were in Sydney when he lost one out of the window of our hostel. I didn't think leather could rot and smell that bad once it had been machined into a shoe, but Dales were, and after us moaning at him every night since we had the campervan we convinced him to leave them on the step of the side door, far enough away from our noses so we didn't feel nauseous all night. I knew one of them must have fell out of the door while we were turning in for the night at our previous location before the troopers moved us on. I kept quiet hoping he hadn't made the same connection and would be forced to buy a new pair. But unfortunately he did realise and stopped on the way back to Uluru where he was united with his shoe that was a little dusty and flattened from being run over when we left in a hurry last night. Getting to the gate we had to present our tickets that had cost us $25 (£10.40) each for our 3 day admittance, the girls kept their heads down even though they had paid for tickets the same as us, we just wanted to get in as quickly as possible. It took a little longer as Dale had his finger over the date that the eagle eyed attendant spotted, so she quizzed him why he was doing that and scrutinised the ticket much closer, she paid great attention to detail as long as she didn't have to get out of her Booth. After she was happy with us she let us in once she verified it wasn't faked. She wasn't as good though at seeing 2 people in the back though, which would have been a potential $50 (£20.80) they would have lost. It was quite fun smuggling 2 people in who were paying customers, shows how easy it can be, I wonder how many times that has happened with not so honest people.

We enjoyed the sunrise from another location that much closer this time, to see Uluru once again change through a group of different colours, but this time around the orange hue. It was incredibly quiet again as everyone else enjoyed this great spectacle of natural colours. We took a short walk near the rock after this, and by about 8am I was amazed at how many people were already there, making the hike to the top of Uluru along the spiritual path. I took a photo of this that gives a very good size representation of the sheer scale of it. This picture was taken directly to the side of the first part of the slope at the beginning of the climb, the tiny people can be clearly seen in a line silhouetted against the sky, I counted at least 70 people along this part which is about a third of the climb. Another part that was of great interest was a part of Uluru that has been eroded from water into a bowl, seeing several of the black streaks running down it that meet at the bottom to make this bowl, that then meet to one stream that must come down with a great deal of force when it rains.

After taking a drive round the entire site of Uluru, we left this massive part of Australian history with a better view and headed towards Adelaide, passing another slab of rock, Mount Conner or Attila, 50 miles or so from Uluru. Mount Conner is about 1.5 miles long and is 300m (984ft) above ground and is part of the same vast rocky substrate thought to be beneath Uluru and Kata Tjuta. This flat topped, horseshoe shaped mountain of rock doesn't get any recognition of any kind, it's not even accessible by road, the closest you can get is by a narrow dirt track that leads you to within 2 miles of it. I'm sure it has many wonders and strange formations similar to Uluru and Kata Tjuta and no rules on climbing it. If I had another day I would have loved to explore this interesting place that few people have seen, to me that would be something worth looking at just for that reason.

Our route from here to Adelaide would have one more stopover where we'd spend 2 days at Coober Pedy, a little town of 4,000 people which I'm surprised that it's this small, considering it is referred to as the *'Opal Capital of the World'* because this area produces about three quarters of the words opal. Opal has been mined here since it was first discovered by a 14 year old boy in 1915, and has grown to be the largest opal mining area in the world with 70 opal fields. Our journey to here from Uluru was a long and boring one due to Dale and Sandra being crap company as they dozed and slept for most of the way, we also completely missed the South Australia sign somehow to let us know we had entered another state, so no photo opportunity here of this big slab of brown smooth rock with a darker wedged piece in the middle of it. It may have been to the boring long desert roads with nothing but a few services. We stopped at a few services on the way, with one such services we stopped at had a pickup truck parked on the fore court of this petrol station by the door to the kiosk, it was so frightful you couldn't miss it. The equivalent in England would be a van with a symbol stuck on the back, with an almost cartoon look to it warning you that this vehicle was carrying a dangerous item, that looks a little funny, which doesn't seem so scary as the pickup we were looking at. There's something about the word EXPLOSIVES in 30cm (12") high red letters the width of the roof that makes you think, 'Yep, don't want to get too close to that!' We were that mesmerised by it that Sharon got me to take a picture of it, at which point the occupants came out and insisted having a picture taken with Sharon, I can't think why they didn't want me or Dale in the picture. Dale got a bit concerned here after we filled up as there was also a cop filling up a few pumps away. After he pointed it out to me I really didn't make the connection, and my answer of 'so what' led Dale to explain a little further, what he was concerned about was the fact 4 people were getting into a 3 seated vehicle. The cop really wasn't paying any attention to us as he was going about his business, so I hurried them in the campervan and we went without so much as a glance from the law.

Back on the road after some more desert followed by more desert, the scenery started to change, with the sparse trees and shrubs becoming fewer with the desert colour changing to a hint of red that gradually became deeper. As we got closer to Coober Pedy we started to see an array of large white and red mounds of soil, which rapidly became more frequent and regular before it took up the entire landscape on both sides of the road. I woke the 2 sleeping beauties in the back by telling how they were missing all the giant molehills. That soon got their attention and after a few moments they were peeking out of the curtains to see what I was on about. The conical piles in question were spoil or mullock heaps, the stuff what's left after it's been processed for its precious minerals, and by the looks of it they'd been busy.

Sharon and I were looking forward to staying in one of the many underground B&Bs to experience life as more than half of the locals do in a dugout. So many of these underground homes are built in this manner as it's so hot here, with the highest daytime temperature reaching 47°c (117°f), it's nice to retreat to a hole that is an average cool temperature of 23 – 25°c (73°f - 77°f) all year round. This way of living and the name of the town also has a link to the Aboriginal language, Coober Pedy is taken from the Aborigine term kupa-piti, with 'kupa' meaning either boy, uninitiated man or white man and 'piti' means hole or rock hole. Thus Coober Pedy is a description of what the local Aborigines regarded as peculiar activities of both mining and living underground, and so the town means 'white men down holes'.

Our first taste of an underground building was the visitor centre, the entrance was striking with its wide rectangular corridor lined with large boards with various pictures and points of interest in the area, which gave us some great ideas on what we were in for in this strange world. The visitor centre had several B&Bs on their books and we managed to get into one for this evening at *Anne's B&B, Koska Hill Dugout* for $85 (£35.40). We drove along the dusty red streets and made our way to the well disguised home we would be staying at for the night. Amongst the piles of ground up rock in the front yard, where we would usually have a fence or a hedge, was the simple B&B sign on a wooden stake to show us we were at our destination. The only part that is recognisable as a house, was the veranda at the front lower section that protruded out from a mound of rock, but the give away something lies beneath is the ventilation shafts dotted around on top. Entering the B&B owned by a lovely couple, Anne and Joe, it looked like any other house, expect the walls and ceiling were a little rougher as the machines that dig out the holes leave deep gouges. The ceilings were a little uneven and I hoped someone had done their maths to make sure too much hadn't been removed, I didn't want that lot falling on my head while I was asleep! We passed the kitchen and bathroom that were both very ample in size, with the interior looking very similar to your own kitchen with shelves, cupboards and a breakfast bar. Entering the lounge we passed one of the load bearing walls that must have been at least 60cm (2ft) thick with rounded corners that flowed into the ceiling to another ample sized room, this easily fitted two settees and an armchair that we were seated at while they chatted to us. They chatted to us for a while, I guessed to establish we were ok to be sleeping in the same house as them. There was one wall in the lounge that looked very odd, which was a brick wall that had been built to separate one of the bedrooms from the lounge. In one of the 3 bedrooms we would be staying in had more than enough room for the double bed and a wardrobe that was flushed into the rock to leave the room rectangular. There were also 2 shelves cut into the walls that were decorated with old pictures of mining and dugouts, as well as a small pickaxe, with the ceiling dominated with a big square hole that was the large ventilation shaft that stretched up about 3m (10ft) to the surface, where we could see a bit of sunlight reflecting in.

We made ourselves at home and showered the 515 miles of desert journey off in the also adequately sized bathroom, with a walk in shower that was plenty big enough for the both of us to get in. It was nicely tiled out and we used the size to our advantage, by washing our clothes while the other one washed themselves. We made a point of having our meal at an underground restaurant, directed to by our B&B hosts across the roofs of their neighbours dugouts, we didn't have to scale the side of a house or anything like that, it was a gradual slope up and over to the town that everyone used as a path. It was strange to think how alien it was to be going into different buildings underground with no windows and how soon it became second nature, not worrying about the hundreds of tons of rock above our heads. We were seated at a small table beside one of those thick load bearing walls that was much deeper than at our B&B at twice the thickness, where I polished of a very good chicken diane under the warm, miner type looking of electric lanterns, that were all connected to by cables that were visible strung across the wall between them, giving it an authentic look.

It was getting late but we had time for a drink in another underground establishment that Dale and Sandra should have been meeting us at. By the time we got there I think they must have got bored and had moved on, Sharon and I on the other hand liked the look of it and stayed for a drink and a game of pool. This bar had the similar grooved makings on the walls and ceiling as our B&B, apart from it having a higher ceiling with sharper corners and had been sealed with a darker substance, which brought out many different colours of browns and reds. This sealing process is vital to any living areas, otherwise most of your time would be clearing up dust.

We wandered back over the rooftops to turn in for the night at our B&B, under streetlights and past the ventilation shafts that looked more like the old type of metal dustbins, making us aware we were on someone's roof, wondering if we were going to overhear something we didn't necessarily want to hear.

Tuesday 3rd May.

We were up at 7am beaten by our host which was a good thing, as we were then offered anything we wanted for breakfast, opting for a fry up which was ready by the time we had washed.

After our lip smacking first meal of the day we were off to see the main attraction of the town, but without Dale and Sandra there Joe was kind enough to give us a lift to *Tom's Mine*. We were there a little while before the tour of the mines, which gave us just enough time to do a bit of noodling. No, Sharon and I weren't getting a little frisky, it really is a mining term which is basically rummaging through the spoil heaps. We climbed on one of the loose piles of dust and rock that we soon sank into ankle deep, even with sandals full of dirt, grit and little rocks we still happily picked our way through the waste that had been chucked out of the ground and already meticulously sieved through, but we were optimistic and after quite some time our perseverance paid off. We found a piece! One small precious piece of opal, well precious to me as it was very low grade of opal that wasn't worth anything.

The other 6 people arrived for the 10.30am tour and we ascended into the neatly cut out doorway all kitted out in white hard hats. My thought of a mine conjures up visions of rough holes, uneven floors as well as ceiling that are low making it a cramped place. This one however is a modern mine that has used modern day tunnelling machines, that have either a rotary cylinder with nasty teeth to chew away at the rock that makes those familiar gouges we saw at the B&B. The other is a circular rotary cutter that has several of these circular cutters to make one big circle from about 1m (3'3") upwards to giant tunnelling machines of several metres across. These circular tunnelling machines were obviously used extensively in this mine, showing one such circular pattern on the way in to this mine, as well as the first tunnel in the mine that was arched at the ceiling 3m (10ft) high. All this made the tunnels neat, safe and perfectly flat floors. The guided tour took 75 minutes and was very informative with all the modern day machinery showing how it is mined today, as well as the working conditions and tools used in the first mines in this area in the early 1900s. We strolled through the corridors that led off into two various others, there were shafts descending down with a mannequin at the bottom in the cramped conditions, showing what is was like for those first miners. There were many hands on tools that we were shown, the first one we got to try out was a bosun chair, basically a plank of wood suspended by a rope which looked like a playground swing. We all got turns to take a seat with a small pick to chip away at the rock face, and feel what it was like for those first miners to be lowered down a shaft and work. It was a little tricky to steady yourself and swing the pick and make any kind of impact on this hard rock, mostly because of that law of motion by Newton. There were many mining facts and how they find it in the rock, which was found in many places in this mine. There was a large slide in one of the walls once we got a bit deeper, a diagonal line showing two distinct colours, technically it is a large fault in opal dirt that is associated with opal formation. Another show of how the first miners worked, was a square hole into the rock that had been roughly cut out with a pickaxe that laid in the corner in the dust. One of the modern day mining examples was in a tunnel that had an electric powered jackhammer for extracting the more delicate pieces of opal in this long circular tunnel, with a UV light laying next to it in the rubble. UV light is the best way to detect opal as it will slightly glow white to bluish brown or green, making it show up very well in the rock. There was also several parts in the rock where it had been chipped out to show a seam of opal under a UV light. It's crazy to think they go to all this trouble digging deep into the ground, to extract these seams with this one in particular only about 60cm (2ft) long but worth thousands. Further and deeper underground where the temperature was now at 18°c (64°f) while the surface temperature was around 30°c (86°f), we saw another great example of a slide, this time it was a wedge of white rock amongst the dirty cream colour that went from ceiling to floor that no doubt had opal somewhere in it. Opal is formed from a solution of silicon dioxide and water. As water runs down through the earth, it picks up silica from sandstone, and carries this silica-rich solution into cracks and voids like this slide we were looking at, caused by natural faults or decomposing fossils. As the water evaporates, it leaves behind a silica deposit. This cycle repeats over very long periods of time, and eventually opal is formed.

Another area of explanation was the explosives used in the mines, as this is one of the easiest ways of excavating the rock out, not to mention quick, as long as you don't bring the tunnel down on your head. They had some of the drill bits on display that are used for this, leaning against the wall with a large heavy industrial drill on the end of it. It was as tall as me at 1.7m (5'7") with a diameter of 10cm (4") at a large opening in the wall, where several of the holes were drilled and stuffed with a bit of explosives to be detonated, making it much easier to chip away as it opens all those little fractures, where it is then shovelled into a pipe which we also got to try out. A metal pipe that was laying on the ground about 30cm (12") across took the dust and rocks to the surface, he pressed a button and we heard the rumble of an engine on the surface, followed by the pipe becoming one of the strongest vacuum cleaners in the world. We then all had a go at shovelling the dust into the pipe to see each shovel full disappear instantly. Another job that I'm sure is back breaking after a few hours, but most probably much easier than the method used in mining in the early days. What we were shovelling in was taken to the surface by a blower, which we were shown later being processed and those pretty little gems picked out of it. We were taken down several more circular tunnels that had the electric cables neatly strung along the ceiling and walls that had come from the surface through more neat little holes.

One of the questionable ways of finding these opals is with the aid of divining rods, also known as dowsing rods, which is something I had always thought was a load of old bollocks, as most of the time when you see someone do this on the surface, they will walk along holding these 2 rods of varying material about 45cm (1'6"), long bent at one end to make a handle to which they are held horizontally pointing forwards, when you apparently walk over a precious metal, stone or water they will cross or part. They will then say, "There! Right there is some precious material!" and they say it works, they don't dig into the ground to prove it, noooo, we have to take their word on it that there really is something there. They could be right, as there is many miles of soil under our feet and there's bound to be something down there they're looking for, and there is always water, it's called a water table! So as you might guess I'm a little pessimistic on this ancient art, as it has also been scientifically proven several times that it is no better than chance. One scientific test was held in Germany where pipes were buried 50cm (1'7") under a level field, the position of each pipe was marked on the surface with a coloured strip.

The dowsers had to tell whether water was running through each pipe. All the dowsers signed a statement agreeing this was a fair test of their abilities and that they expected a 100% success rate, but as with all the other ones before them trying to prove this works, were proven it was also no better than chance. So when we were presented with these rods by our tour guide, I was eager to have a go. After seeing several people walk down a corridor where a seam of opal was clearly visible, I saw every one of them have the rods turn outwards to the walls as they came to the opal. I took a go and made sure to keep them as level as possible with my arms tucked in, concentrating as hard as I could to make sure I wasn't mentally turning them myself because I knew where it should turn, but to my dismay, I had to eat my hat on this occasion as no matter how hard I tried, I had no control over it turning towards the seam.

Moving on to the next item we got to try our hand on, as I was picking hat out of my teeth, was another electric jackhammer. It was similar to an electric drill but a lot bulkier with a chisel on the end that pulsed back and forth at a tidy rate. The guide handed me the heavy item and pointed to a part in the rock that had been used by many visitors before me, so I could give it a go myself. I placed the chisel along one of the many uneven groves in this large hole and pulled the trigger to get shaken vigorously to a deafening rattle that bounced off the walls. I couldn't imagine holding this lump of metal rattling away in your hands all day, I'm sure you'd get strong arms from using it. I slowly chipped away a small piece after the guide showed me a more efficient way of doing, and after a few seconds of rattling away I managed to chip off a sizable lump much quicker and easier than a pick would.

At the end of the tour we were shown into one of the largest underground rooms in the complex, it was feeling more like some underground lair from a James Bond film, here we were shown many of the different rocks with the precious opals in it. Back on the surface we were shown the other end of the blower, an old large pickup truck covered in dust and rust with the suction motor on the back of it encased in a cage, which he started once again for us so we could see what happens at this end. It was linked to the large pipe we had seen below ground, extending up an arm from the back of this pickup and high into the air, to a large short cylinder with a lid on the bottom of it, this opened slightly to allow the debris to fall out of it gently to the ground. From here it was passed onto a conveyor belt that fed onto a shorter one through a small tin box room, which may have just been able to fit 2 people on the steel bench inside. This room is where the opal is sorted from the crushed up rocks, under a UV light in the dark. We had the opportunity to be shut in this cramped room to feel what it was like and how dark it was, as well as how intensely hot it was. I couldn't imagine home much you would have to endure in the summer when it was much hotter than this.

Dale and Sandra knew we were going to be here this morning and came to pick us up, after they had a sneaky peak at the mining equipment while we were finishing our tour. Once finished, we took a look at an opal shop to see what kind of items are turned out from these precious stones, basically any form of jewellery you could think of had an opal slapped on it, changing the style dramatically showing these multi coloured sparkly stones stand out.

We drove round the barren town a little more to find some more of the strange sites and attraction it had, one of which we stumbled upon that was a simple house in the making. We could see the perfectly cut doorways and windows in the front of the large solid hill that now had a cavity inside that will one day be a home to someone. You can dig a house out by hiring a machine here for about $25,000 (£10,400) which is much cheaper than buying a house on the surface, also you don't need to think about air-conditioning.

Along one desolate street, we found an abandoned prop left over from the film *Pitch Black* that I was excited about seeing, as I quite like this film. It was a spaceship that was made to look old and broken down like it had just crashed here with a good degree of rubble in front of it. It was massive at about 8.5m long and 3.5m high (28 x 11ft) making me look quite small next to it. Several parts of the film were shot here, as it portrayed the sparse alien planet with no vegetation quite well that Vin Diesel was marooned on. This is one of many films that have been shot here such as, *Queen of the Desert, Red Planet, Opal Dream,* Mad Max one, two and three and *Down & Under fire in the stone* to name a few.

We got back into the campervan realising how horrible and depressing it is here, with the red sand getting into everything, the campervans dashboard was covered in red dust with red soil all over the floor from our feet that were covered in it too. There was very little plant life here, any signs of life was grown in pots outside peoples houses making it look all the more of a dead town.

We visited the underground Saint Peter and St Paul catholic church, built in much the same way as all the other dugouts in this town. The wall to the front of the building was built in flint as well as the short open tower immediately to the front of it finished with a cross on the top. The front of this flint wall was dominated by a lovely stain glassed cross window, which was the only source of daylight that reached inside the building. Entering the church there was a notice board leant against the outside wall, chalked on it read; *'No mass this 1/2 May weekend. Father has gone to Birdsville to bless the cattle run to Maree'*. And Birdsville was 500 miles away from Coober Pedy! The foyer to the church was quite small but well lit from artificial lighting as well as the stain glass window with a heavy solid white door to enter the church. Inside, the church was similarly carved out as the B&B I had stayed in, giving the walls and ceiling that distinctive look of many shades of browns and reds, the lighting was adequate giving it a lovely warm glow. It wasn't very wide, it had normal chairs with only 6 rows of chairs across the entire width of the church, leaving a small isle in the centre. The first thing I did was to take a seat at the front to think about the religion for a moment and pay my respects, taking in the moment in this church. The altar was made from solid rock, faced with flat stone, behind it was two alcoves with religious statues inside, this was an usual look but very stunning.

Before we left this dusty town and after my chocolate spread sandwich I knocked together for lunch, Sharon and I wanted to see another mine that was much different to *Tom's mine. The Old Timer mine* originally dates back to 1916, but these miners for some reason concealed its existence by back-filling the shafts. The mystery is why they never returned to dig out the opal that remained. It was not until 1968 that the hidden mine was discovered by Ron Gough when he was digging an extension to his underground home and broke through, exposing three large seams of good quality opal, as well as opalised seashells which are still there today. Can you imagine how happy you would be after buying this piece of land to make a house and find an opal mine that still had this much riches in it.

We took a self-guided tour which was very well thought out, as it has many signs with descriptions of what we were looking at, also items used in mining past and present with several mock ups of miners going about their daily work in the cramped conditions. This mine is how I expected a mine to look, there was still pick marks on the walls and some very cramped working areas where the miners had gone into the rock, maybe following a seem. Some of the corridors were very low and narrow, which we made good use of our hard hats with us both taking several knocks to the noggin, which I'm sure would have been quite painful due to the rugged surfaces. Some of the corridors were so small we had to resort to crawling through some places with others unable to get to at all, as there was only a small hole to squeeze through that would lead into an open area. One of the first items to catch our eye was a large amount, of what looked like to me, was good grade opal in the rock face. Several large chunks of opal about 50cm (1'7") long that was worth over $20,000 (£8,300), that was found in the first half hour of tunnelling into the rock, while building the souvenir shop in 1987, that's one expensive exhibit for a museum! There were several areas of this opal close to the surface that looked like we could pick out with a pocket knife, but we were reminded we were on camera several times along with the signs of no digging.

There were also many exhibits showing how the minors worked and lived in the mines, figures had been put in certain relevant places showing this, one showed how they took the chiselled out rock to the surface with a mannequin pushing a low barrow with a 25 gallon drum on it. There were also many minor figures using drills or pickaxes, one figure was climbing up a shaft that led to the surface several metres above us, with his feet either side in foot holes showing how they used to get in and out of the mine. Another area of great wonder was the opalised sea shells that were on display in the walls and ceilings, covered by Perspex to protect them. These shells are what's left over from the time when most of Australia was under the sea, where the sea creatures and little gastropod lived in the sea, after it died and sank to the bottom it was buried by sediments which turned into rock over millions of years. In time this left voids in the rock where fossil shells had been, these filled up with opal and this was what we were looking at. You can clearly see the small domes of where the shelled fish had come to rest and long disappeared, leaving this outline of opal. One of the seams of opal in the wall had a sign beside it telling of how it was missed by the original miners in 1918 by 25cm (10"), and carries on into the rock by another 1m (3ft).

This museum shows how miners, usually working alone, how they dug the shafts and blast holes and winch the dug soil up to the surface, all by hand with only candles and carbine lamps for illumination. Ron Gough was one of these miners, and it was he who realized the potential for opening the mine as a tourist attraction, his family's underground dugout home was added and set up as a display home to show what life was like living underground from the 1920s to the 1990s. I was quite happy to find out that we could actually walk round most of these show rooms so we could get up close and personal. The bed in the 1920s room was part of the rock, basically one part wasn't excavated out leaving a shelf to sleep on with an opal safe underneath it. There was also an old black and white picture at Christmas time showing how basic their standard of living was, with a basic table and chairs was the only thing visible in the main room. The bathroom in this 1980s house was a little different to the one at the B&B as it didn't have any tiles, leaving the rough walls round all the bathroom make it look completely unfinished. Also in the museum amongst the many different types of rocks and opals there was a projector that was used in this town up until 1980 at the drive in movie theatre, as they didn't have TV transmitted here until that time and this was the only form of moving picture they had.

After a quick stop at the internet café that took forever, as they obviously didn't get much business and all the computers were turned off, we finally got under way for another long drive to civilization. By now it was late afternoon and wanted to get underway to get as close to Paul's house in Adelaide as I could tonight, but that was going to depend on how many miles collectively we could do. I was glad to be leaving as it had just started to rain and I thought how all the sandy dust was going to turn to mud. I did the first stretch of about 120 miles until Sharon took over the drivers seat for another 90 miles, until she suddenly saw a couple of sheep grazing at the side of the road as we were leaving the sandy landscape behind us, and little by little we saw more vegetation. After her little scare of sheep I took over again, several miles later I noticed we were getting rather low on petrol. We had opted not to stop at the last petrol station as we had only used a quarter of a tank of fuel, but as one of my philosophies stated earlier, always be prepared, and we were not prepared for the fact there was a large distance between this service and the next, so we should have filled up regardless. Now we were suffering for our self inflicted misfortune, I was driving as economically as possible as we all watched the needle get lower and lower until it was on the red. At this point we were discussing who was going to hitch hike to the next petrol station, as it was getting dark Dale nominated himself to do it, which in a way I was glad about, as I had visions if I thumbed a lift I'd end up getting in some strangers car who would be a complete weirdo. We drove for another 40 miles on the red expecting to run out any minute, with us all signing a big relief when the services came into view. Filling it to the brim we wasted no time and got going again and didn't stop for quite sometime until the next petrol station, not wanting to risk running out of fuel again we filled up even though we had only used about a third of a tank by that point. It was just the right time for our evening meal at this fill up, so we thought it would be best to stop here to cook it as it may be a little hazardous while driving along. We had parked up next to a pickup truck who's owner was sat near by, while serving up our meals he overheard us talking about where we had been and asked what the price of fuel was in Alice Spring. He was heading that way and was deliberating weather to fill up where we were, but with it being a bit more expensive as all the petrol stations were in the outback, he was going to wait until he got there as the fuel was much cheaper, making it possible to travel such a distance non-stop as he had a 200 litre fuel tank, that 43 UK gallons!

We started the final push out of the outback and towards civilization into the night, Dale and Sandra weren't much help as they fell asleep again after a short while, leaving Sharon and I to manage the driving. Admittedly, it was more for my benefit as I was the only one who wanted to see Paul in Adelaide. Sharon drove again for a while, and we kept wondering how much further it would be before we were out of the outback, even though it was still very arid. After 100 miles Sharon was on edge again and started jumping at the shadows at the side of the road, she was sure there were more sheep, as this isn't the best way to be driving I took over again ignoring them, and fortunately they were nothing more than shadows, or I should say they didn't start moving causing us to crash. Sharon dropped off to sleep shortly after our change over, without a peep from the other 2, leaving only me awake which can cause a problem, as sleeping people in a vehicle is catching, so I made sure not to fall into this trap and got some music in my ears on my mini disc player. I listened to lots of different tunes, making sure to skip all the slow ones and sing along to myself to the fast ones, driving well into the night searching for any signs of civilization, I didn't start to get into built up areas until I was within a few miles of the coast. I made it to Port Augusta about 50 miles from Paul's house, this is where I finally pulled over for the evening a little after midnight, I turned off the main road, driving a few metres further pulling onto the side, covering 480 miles today. That's like driving from my house in Norwich Norfolk, to Aberdeen in Scotland. I was starving hungry but was too tired to do anything about it, everyone stirred a bit and realised how late it was saying how well I had done to get this far. We did our evening ritual of cleaning teeth and spitting it out at the side of the road, and turned in for the night, managing to get off to sleep within a few minutes.

Chapter 16
The tale of two cities, and many parts in-between.

Wednesday 4th May.

I was awake at 6.30am despite my tiring long drive, to a beautiful red sunrise, as I wanted to get going I told everyone else it was 7.30am. I got out and walked to the back of the campervan to find one of us had left the rear door open all night. I drove on a bit further to Adelaide while they were all waking up, and stopped at a petrol station to get directions. I noticed they had some toilets here and after a quick peek seeing it was well equipped, we all took turns in using the facilities.

We found Paul's house at about 9.00am without too much difficulty and had a good chat and catch up, he was the same old Paul I had always known and grown up with. He was working today so we said goodbye until the evening and went to see what sights Adelaide had to offer. The first thing was to drop Sandra off at a hostel so she could book herself in, as we would soon be parting company, Dale and Sandra went on their way for the day while Sharon and I headed into the city for a walk and to see what we could find.

Our walk around the city seeing the sights was like any other old city, with nothing too exciting to write about. We ended up walking past the *Art Gallery of South Australia*, which has come a long way since this Victorian building was opened in 1881 when it had just 2 rooms. Today it has been extended several times and now houses 35,000 exhibits, not that we realised that at the time as we only got round half of it and thought there couldn't be that much left. This gallery is renowned for its collections of Australian art, notably Indigenous Australians, British and Colonial art. The Building had that same old feeling that most of them do like this in Australia, with large pillars at the front. The inside was spacious with many of the rooms having the pictures taken up on the walls with the odd statue in the middle of the room. It couldn't have had much impact on me, as I didn't write anything specific about the paintings.

Walking round the city centre we also came across the town hall. The front had several arched window built into it with a tower in the middle at the front of the building that was square at the base where it housed a clock, above this it turned into a hexagon and then a domed roof. We had limited areas we could view in this building that was built in 1863, taking just 3 years to complete. We were able to view the 1,100 seat concert hall that housed an English built organ, the biggest of its kind to be built in England for more than 100 years at the time. It was to be replacing the original that was installed in 1875 and was beyond modernisation by 1987 when it was replaced by this 64 stop over 4 manuals *Walker and Son*. I don't know exactly how big that is, but the statistics sound impressive and it certainly looked big, with its 40 pipes that we could see across the stage and was nearly the width of the room, as well as nearly touching the ceiling! This building is also used for all sorts of concerts, meetings and banquets.

A strange sight we came across in the town centre at *Rundle Mall* was some very well placed pigs, they weren't living in a pen, it was 3 life size bronze pigs officially known as '*A day out*'. One is looking in the bin, another is sitting while the third is standing which made a good seat that many people used casually like any other. There were some other interesting points that stuck in my mind besides the pigs, like the 1.8m (5'10") teddy for sale outside a shop in the mall and two buildings, one was an English pub called the *Elephant*. It was a corner building with that typical old style of wooden beams across the front of it, even though it looked a little fake and new looking. The second building was just a wall of a building with some fantastic artwork painted on it, to make it look like an old corner building that appeared to be a sheet draped over it, very clever!

We next visited the botanical gardens that was in the middle of the city, for some reason we kept finding ourselves looking for these in every town or city that we could, there was something nice about taking a walk round these gardens as we always found something different and new at each one, and this was no exception with the most unusual water feature. Slabs of glass were stacked together on end at least 2m (6'6") deep to make an arch that was bigger at one end that flared out of the top, most unusual. After finishing our walk along one of the longest growing archways I had even seen, at least 5m (16ft) wide by 50m (164ft) long, we found on the edge of the gardens The *National Wine Centre*. Being the wine connoisseurs that we are, we took a tour round here and got to see the machinery used to make the wine and stacks of bottles in racks, I was in my element with all those bottle in perfect lines, only being able to have a small sample at the end of the tour, unfortunately that was the highlight of the tour.

    We made our way back to Paul's house in rush hour that took us forever for the evening managing 118 miles today. I met his children Megan, Hailey and Tyson who last time I saw were babies and toddlers, and had a lovely evening showing him pictures and talking about where we had been. He cooked us one of the best meals we'd had in a long time of a very fulfilling homemade pasta bake. I called home to hear some bad news this evening, my mum had kept in regular contact with her second husbands mother after his death in 2003, she was a dear old lady I loved to visit who thought the world of me, she had became quite ill and declined very rapidly, she was then in hospital with only days to live. Being away from home at a time like this is one of the hardest things to cope with, I thought a great deal of her for the rest of the evening.

    We finished our evening chatting about nothing in particular until 1am, where we retreated to the campervan in his drive to go to sleep.

Thursday 5th May.

We were up at about 8am and started to fill Paul's washing machine, only to get caught by Paul as we had filled it much to full, he then helped each one of us in turn to do most of our belongings, you can only get your clothes clean to a certain standard with a bar of soap in the shower. Dale's white shorts had become a little more on the dirty cream side and wanted to give them a good going over, after using several different detergents soaking them he chucked them in the washing machine, with Paul sticking a double dose of detergent in with it that did indeed wash out 8 and a half months of travelling and brought them back to their former white, I hadn't seen Dale this happy about an item of clothing since he was reunited with his stinky shoes back in Sydney.

We finally managed to get into town much later than we wanted at midday, to meet up with Sandra to spend our last day with her. Our group activity today was to visit Haigh's chocolate factory to participate in the free tour, which we were sure would involve some kind of tasting at some point. Haigh's chocolate was founded in 1915 when Alfred E Haigh opened his doors to the public selling his chocolate covered fruit centres, which is still one of the items that is sold today. By 1919 business was going so well he expanded by building a factory behind his home, which is now the visitor centre where we got to see random items in chocolate making and the history of this sugary delight. In 1922 he moved shops to where it is today on Beehive Street and has grown even since, to 14 Haigh's shops in Australia which is now run by forth generation Haigh's. On our tour we were led down a corridor by a lovely and informative lady, although she did have a bit of a scary teacher look about her which was shown quite early on in the tour, while having our attention telling us of the history of this factory and how chocolate is made, Dale and Sandra were peeking through a window to watch some of the workers in the factory, Miss Tourguide firmly and abruptly directed a command at them to pay attention. Dale snapped round just like I remember when we were at school when he used to get told off, which was quite often. We were eventually aloud to know what was going on at the other side of the glass with the hand finishing of decorating the chocolates and packing, another nice piece of information was that many of the employees there had worked there for many years, one in particular had worked there for 33 years, which shows how the long running family business is also close to their workers as well as their family. There was a massive array of different kinds of chocolate that looked beautifully finished, which you could tell were of the higher class that were not in the budget range. By the end we were all salivating and gagging for the free sample of cherry coated chocs and also something very similar to a mars bar. If I had been visiting as a tourist on holiday sense of the matter, then I'm sure I would have cued up with the rest of the tour to buy several chocolate items, one of which that is sold in large quantities is one of their 'novelty' chocolates, The Frog. These come in various sizes and flavours and is well known and one of the cheapest items, clever idea having a free tour and novelty chocolates at the end to take home as a souvenir.

We parted company with Sandra after leaving here, it was lovely having her along for part of this trip and it was good fun being with her, making our trip that little bit different, we said goodbye leaving Dale to catch up with us later.

After our goodbyes Sharon and I thought we'd tackle the rest of the art gallery again, to find how much bigger it was than we thought which I was getting a little bored of as it was very much the same as I had seen last time, so instead we thought we'd concentrate on some of the cultures we had not seen already, which was the Chinese, Japanese and Aborigine which were all a refreshing change. With a few hours to spare we decided to take a look in the South Australian Museum, as it was next door, finding it to be a place that need much more attention than the 2 hours we had spare. The South Australian Museum is renowned for its world-class natural history and cultural collections. The museum is home to the world's largest collection of Australian Aboriginal cultural artefacts in the world, with over 3,000 artefacts on display. The *South Australian Biodiversity Gallery* has a wealth of information in the form of interactive elements with touch screens.

The *South Australian Museum* was founded in 1856 and today occupies 2 buildings, permanent galleries are full of objects drawn from the Museum's extensive collections, from different areas of natural and cultural heritage. The Museum's permanent displays give visitors an opportunity to see examples of the real thing as well as actual specimens from the collections, that are researched by Museum scientists and are an important piece of South Australia's past, present and future. As our time was limited and we were in Australia, we thought it only natural to explore as much of the Aborigine artefacts as possible.

So we cut our cultural visit short as time was getting away with us and I still needed to find a dentist, so it was back to *Rundall Mall* to get turned down at the first dentist but they did recommend 2 others. Finding the first one they recommended closed so I kept my fingers crossed for the second one. I was very pleased to be greeted with a straight teethed smile here and I was booked in for the next day.

We got back to the campervan for our arranged time to meet Dale having to wait a while as Dale was late, he too had been to seek out some medical advice but not as painful as mine. He had started to notice his eyesight wasn't quite right so had it checked out at the opticians, they had thoughts he might have picked up something from South America.

Breny's philosophies in life:
Backpacking, the clue is in the name and it's the most important part.

We headed back to Paul's for the evening managing to clock up 37 miles round the city, with my main priority to sort my backpack out to send all the items I wasn't using back home, as in 2 weeks I would be in south-east Asia and I would more than likely be doing much more walking with my backpack, unfortunately I hadn't spent an excessive amount of money on this very important piece of equipment for this type of travelling, and my shoulders were paying for it as the backpack had no type of back support at all so it sort off hung off me instead of on me. Paul was waiting for his girls to get home after they had been in trouble at school, and I got the distinct feeling it may be a little uncomfortable so we went out for dinner finding a Chinese at a food court, I got a wok in a box that was surprisingly satisfying.

Getting back to Paul's we found he'd sent his girls to their mothers for the evening, which left a spare bed for Sharon and I for the evening. We finished our second load of washing and chatted for the rest of the evening until about midnight, where Sharon and I retreated to the now vacant bed that belonged to one of the girls, to notice how small this single bed was.

Friday 6th May.

I was up at 8.30am, which wasn't the first time I had woken in the night as I had several startling occasions when I woke up from nearly falling out of the small bed. Sharon showered first while I went to get the coffee started, to find Paul had very kindly hand washed our towels and had hung them out before he went to work. Paul was quite upset with one of his work colleagues who he had covered and swapped shifts with several times to help out, to find the favours weren't reciprocated as he wanted to swing a day off while we were here to take us round the area to show us the sights.

One place he suggested to visit was at Adelaide Hills a 30 minute drive out of Adelaide, where a little German village was founded in 1839 by Captain Dirk Meinertz Hahn, he sailed here with 187 emigrants to start a new life and create a settlement. This community of several different skills purchased 4,000 acres and it was named Hahndorf, which is now the oldest surviving German settlement in Australia, attracting over 750,000 visitors a year. We parked at one end of the street to walk the length of it, the village had as you would expect, a very German feel to it with its 1 or 2 storey, brick or stone buildings lining the street, many of which had those lovely wooden beams that crisscrossed the outside walls. The street was filled with large trees down each side, which created some picturesque shadows along the many buildings with verandas, many of which were covered in hanging baskets overflowing with colourful flowers. A few places of interest we stopped at was an art gallery which I would've expected to see more German artists, but the most memorable painting were cow pictures. I made sure to stop in a bar that had recently had new pokies added, or fruit machines to you and I, we stopped long enough to have a German beer. Our last stop on the street was at a café for lunch where I had a slice of German cake, I tried a Bienenstich cake, or the English translated version is bee sting cake, mostly because I liked the look of it, and for once my visual taste matched the actual taste and I really like it. It was made up of a sweet yeast dough base with a baked topping of honey glazed caramelised almonds, filled with vanilla custard and cream. After my delicious cake it was back to the campervan, stopping briefly to see an amusing advertisement board, which read; '*The home of the famous Hahndorf Mettwurst (sausage) and the legendary Bavarian bum burner'*. I was interested in just how much it burnt your bum as I could withstand quite hot foods by now and I quite like the odd sausage, but we had no more time as it was nearing my dreaded dentist appointment.

We got back to Adelaide with time to spare, so we parked up where I went to the dentist and Sharon went to meet Dale. I've always been a nervous dental patient due to the fact of having a high decay rate, and having a lot of treatment as a teenager by a butcher that somehow got into dentistry. Needless to say I tend to jump a little at the pain inflicted during treatment, as my teeth are also incredibly sensitive. Having this chasm in my mouth for a few weeks had also left it vulnerable to the elements so I was getting to the stage where I was pleased to get it filled. After one full syringe of Novocaine he went to work, stopping shortly after when he had to peal me off the ceiling to give me another syringe of the numbing stuff. I could still feel it but it stopped me jumping so much as he hacked away with what seemed to be a Black and Decker drill on hammer action. It was filled and I went on my way after parting with $160 (£67) to meet Dale and Sharon with most of my mouth numb as well as my tongue, nose, ear and the back of my throat making it difficult to eat or drink anything. And how did my friends sympathise with me when they met me back at the campervan? They bought 2 bloody great novelty doughnuts, which looked so delicious! They were iced and shaped into insects, Sharon had a bee with lots of chocolate sprinkles and Smarties, with Dales enjoying a ladybird that was also extravagantly decorated with lovely mouth watering chocolate things, they looked so nice and I really wanted one but I could barely drink water yet alone eat, but at least I could no longer get my tongue into one of my teeth.

We'd driven 75 miles by the time we got back to Paul's and after my mouth had come round he cooked us a lovely Sunday roast, just like your mum makes it with heaps of gravy that left us stuffed and sleepy. He had been a fantastic host and took us all in to look after us just like one of his own. I gave mum a call to wish her happy birthday and to ask her to send me a picture so I could print it off at Paul's. It was a picture of my Grandpa from my mothers side at the Taj Mahal, he had visited here while he was on leave in the second world war, having his picture taken standing inside the front gate with the Taj behind him. I had meant to take a copy of this picture with me before I left home as India would be the last country on our list, and no doubt we would be visiting this magnificent monument.

Paul and I finished off the evening with long chats and a cigar before we got to sleep another night in a bed, hoping that I would be better at not falling out this time.

Saturday 7th May.

I woke at 7.30am to use the toilet, which I later found out that this was the time that my step dad's mother had passed away, I crawled back into bed and overslept until 9.30am. We had a quick shower got our things together and left our body boards at Paul's for his daughters as we were sure we wouldn't be using them anymore. Our last sightseeing item in Adelaide was *St Peter's Cathedral* that was built after some difficulties in purchasing a piece of land to build it on, Bishop Short brought the funds with him from England to purchase the one acre of land, that would fund most of the building of this cathedral, laying the first one ton foundation stone on *St Peters day* in 1869 in front of over a thousand people, which then took 8 years to complete construction where it had it's first service in 1877, with it's final completion of the towers in 1902. The stonework was supplied from local areas, which for some reason was rejected by one of the architects, that disliked it so much that he withdrew from the project, strange idea, but I think it makes the building much more special being built from local sourced materials. There are a few steps up to the front of the cathedral to the front doors where it has two tower spires either side that reach 51m (168ft). Inside it stretched on for 62m (203ft) and 18m (59ft) wide. The most striking part of this cathedral was the altar and Reredos, that could be seen dominating the centre of the building about 4m (13ft) high, made of wood with 20 large elaborate, wooden saint figures behind it carved into it.

We then hit the road with Dale doing the first stretch to Mount Gambier, which is about half way between Adelaide and Melbourne near the coast, most famously known for its sink holes. I dozed for most of the way in the front of the campervan, which is not the most comfortable of areas to do this as I kept getting bumped about and woken up. Sharon took over driving the second half of the journey while, I dozed some more with Dale retreating to the back to join me, to read and have a little doze himself. By the time we got to Mount Gambier after travelling 361 miles, it was getting late and we were just in time for our evening meal, after a quick stop at *Woolworths* to restock on water, fruit and bread we found *Hungry Jacks*, that had an uncanny resemblance to *Burger King* with its legendary *Whoppers*, but it did also have a few different items on the menu, one of which I plumped for was a BBQ burger meal, we only endured this kind of evening meal, as it was the only quick thing to eat before we went in search for a pub, so Dale could watch another Norwich city football match. Dale found a bar to satisfy his needs near a side street that ended up near an old railway track, which was also the perfect hideaway place to sleep at. Sharon and I left him there to go in search of our own entertainment, finding a bar that would have a live band on at a cost of $15 (£6.25) each, so we gave that one a miss and instead we turned in for the night to the campervan, to watch another slightly amusing film in our boxset of The *Family Plan* with Leslie Nielsen, while we waited for Dales return hoping his team would win so he wouldn't be a gloomy git for a while.

Sunday 8th May.

We were up a little later than we expected this morning, after a pee on the railroad tracks I was then looking for an important piece of mine, I was rummaging through the campervan looking for my sunglasses as it was another fantastically bright day, while Dale was annoyingly filming randomly round the campervan, while narrating to the camcorder where we were and how Norwich had won their game last night, no wonder he was so jolly! After watching me doing this for a while he asked what I was looking for, "My sunglasses" I said a little grumpily, no one likes looking for something first thing in the morning, especially when I hadn't had my morning coffee. Dale replied, "Oh, I have them." the penny still hadn't dropped and I had to ask where they were, to which he smugly told me. "They're on my face" The cheeky bugger! He gave them up and we went on our merry way to find sinkholes, but not before I got some wake me up coffee.

Dale had seen the *Cave Garden* last night so we thought we'd give that a quick look in the daylight. It's something that could easily be missed as it's in the middle of the town surrounded by a wall and several trees. Inside you are led down the spiral stairs to about 2 thirds of the way to the bottom, where a look out point protrudes about 5m (16ft) into the centre. It has many different plants and shrubs clinging onto the walls, some of which had been placed here, making it look rather nice and almost a purpose built hole. The reason why there is no access to the bottom of the 20m (64ft) pit, is because when there is sufficient rainfall, there is a torrent of water spewing out of the wall into the bottom of the pit and disappears.

We next visited a much deeper and more interesting sinkhole that had a series of underwater caves at *Engelbrecht Caves.* Arriving here we found a small hut at the top of a well, fortified sinkhole that had nobody there. Thinking it wasn't open, Dale and Sharon thought that'd get a little free glimpse at it, showing it wasn't all that well fortified by scaling the locked gate and hopped over the fence next to it. I on the other hand thought that there may have been only be one guide, who was already on a tour, which Dale and Sharon found out by the time they were half way down the steps, hearing a voice that was obviously of some importance to this site. They turned and ran back up the steps, scaling the fence once again, as they landed the other side the tour guide with 4 people in tow came into sight without a clue of the recent fence jumpers. We had a little chat with the tour guide in the little hut where there was a map of these underground tunnels showing where we were at the sink hole, with tunnels which stretched 100m (328ft) one way and about 300m (984ft) in the opposite direction, passing under several houses, where it opens up to chasm several metres under the Jubilee Highway. New parts of these tunnels have now been exposed due to the underground water level dropping considerably, allowing visitors to walk into it to view it. Along the tunnels there are several solution tubes that connect the tunnels to the surface, where they were used for more than 100 years from the late 1800's as a dumping ground for waste products from various establishments, from breweries to butchers. It wasn't until 1979 the *Lions Club of Mount Gambier* took 3 years to clear out all the debris and rubbish, after several explorations of the tunnels, to deem it profitable enough to be opened as a tourist attraction.

We took the spiralling steps down to the bottom of this sinkhole and into the tunnel, where we saw the solution tube that had been used as a chute for all sorts of refuse. The tube itself was stained a deep black, with old pieces of bones, bottles and various unrecognisable pieces of metal rusting away strewn around on the floor beneath it. The rest of the tunnels were interestingly sculptured, as this 100m (328ft) thick sandstone was formed here about 40 million years ago, with a good deal of this time that had some amount of water flowing through it, and like anywhere there is water flowing, it takes the path of least resistance, which is how these tunnel and sculptured parts were formed by the natural erosion of the weaker parts of the sandstone. Some parts of the ceiling showed signs that where I was standing was once full of water, with the current swirling through it causing several perfectly conical shapes that seemed like they were man made with some kind of drill. It's always hard to believe when standing in a place like this that a few hundred years before would have been impossible, due to the amount of water flowing through it. Other parts looked like large portions had been melted away in various directions but obviously had taken thousands of years of constant wearing from nothing but water.

Another part we were shown by our tour guide was a set of steps that led down to a clear pool of water 27m (88ft) below the surface, that disappeared down into a dark underwater tunnel, which was now at, the mannequin dressed as a scuba diver hung over it needed no explanation, that this was the entrance point to the rest of the tunnels and chasm that stretched under the highway, for the cave divers that come and go here regularly, unfortunately this was not one of those days. Prior to 1916 the water table was much higher then it is now which meant that almost all of the tunnels and caves were filled with water. Now cave divers can explore this complex much easier as there are several large pockets of air with many of the tunnels free from water allowing them to see the caves interior much more easily. We concluded our 50 minute tour with a short video of cave diving in these tunnels. Something that intrigues me, but I think I'd be a little apprehensive in the really tight areas where you would have to take your tank off to squeeze through.

On the outskirts of this small town we took a look at the towns reservoir, Blue Lake. This is an inactive volcano that is now filled with 36,000 million litres (8,000 million gallons) of steel grey water, which turns to a brilliant turquoise blue from November to March, this strange phenomenon has baffled scientist for many years and is very unique in how much of a dramatic change there is in colour, to any other lake. It is now generally considered to be caused by calcium carbonate to precipitate in the warmer months, enabling micro-crystallites of calcium carbonate to form which removes any water-borne impurities, resulting in the blue wavelengths of light to be scattered, giving this lake it's brilliant blue appearance.

This volcano is thought to have last erupted more than 6,000 years ago which created this perfectly oval crater that is 1,200m (3,937ft) long by 824m (2,703ft) wide, and for a long time it was claimed to be a bottomless lake but has bow been measured at an average depth of 77m (252ft) with an incredible 197m (646ft) at its deepest point. With a little over 2 miles round the rim it really does feel big, with the size perspective fortified by the pumping station on the other side of the lake to where we were stood, that seemed like a toy house from a train set, halfway down the crater. This crater is actually one of 3 next to each other in this area, making the entire combined crater rim of about 5.5 miles. Even stood on the rim of the Leg of Mutton lake, the middle of the 3 craters and the smallest which is also the last of the 4 volcano's here to erupt about 4,500 years ago, I still couldn't see the floor on the other side of the third crater, which was much larger than Blue Lake crater. It's another hard to believe fact that if I had been stood here several thousand years ago, I would have been in a massive turmoil of molten rock, unlike the picturesque and tranquil area it has been made into today, with the abundance of trees, water, children's play areas and picnic grounds, showing that something as volatile as a volcano, in time can become something as nice as this.

We didn't walk down to the Leg of Mutton Lake, which at the moment has a little misconception in the name, as it is a dry lake although it may return one day, as once in 1859 it was nearly dry but the water table rose again, until about 1978 when it dried up completely. Even with the water gone you can still make out why it is named this, as the area that was once the lake is not grown over, unlike the walls of this crater making it still appear like a leg of mutton. I would have very much enjoyed walking and exploring this area, but that would have taken more than a day given the sheer size of it. Moving on to our next destination meant we didn't get to see the third crater, bigger than the 2 we had already looked at, this larger crater was home to 2 more lakes that were once also volcano's, one of which, Browns Lake that is also dry on the opposite side from where we were, with Valley Lake that is about half the size of Blue Lake and much greener. Which makes the phenomenon of Blue Lake more unique as it lies just 400m (1300ft) from Valley lake that does not show the same clarity or change of colour.

So we cut our viewing time here short and moved onto another smaller lake of 70m (229ft) across 10 miles towards the coast, Little Blue Lake. Named so as it too once changed colour annually, however due to the pollution of agricultural fertilisers, this has increased the nutrient levels to the extent that they now remain a year round green colour, which also means at times there is a presence of blue-green algae and swimming is now discouraged as the effects from exposure to this, and even more so from ingesting the water can result in many illnesses, mostly the digestive problems as well as blistering and rashes. Although I didn't know this at the time, I was very tempted to follow suit to a bunch of travellers like ourselves, that were there jumping in from the rim into the water about 8m (26ft) below. This lake is almost perfectly round due to it being a sinkhole that is about 38m (124ft) deep. Although I could see it was deep from the way the adrenalin junkies were disappearing into it, I was a little apprehensive to try it out myself, I am fully aware at just how dangerous this sport can be, even from this seemingly small height. It would only take a slip on take off or landing wrong in the water to do myself some serious damage, not to mention hitting the wrong area of the water to find something much harder than yourself just beneath the surface, to seriously mess you up or even kill you. I really wanted to do it, and yes I missed this opportunity to try something amazingly thrilling, but I also wanted to make sure I could see more sights likes this in the future, so I watched with envy instead wishing I had a little more disregard for sensibility. It was a strange area and a place that could easily be missed, as it is perfectly sunk and level with the surrounding field, with almost vertical walls that had many plants growing from it. There is easy access to it by a large opening from the road with steps leading you down to the waters edge where there is a pontoon with steps into the water for easy access for swimming, which Dale was using to jump off in various poses while I was taking pictures. I would like to bet that if the germaphobe had known about this blue-green algae threat, he wouldn't have been so happy in the pictures I was taking of him at the time.

We then headed towards Melbourne stopping 2 miles up the road at something else that caught our interest. Mount Schank could clearly be seen a mile away from the road we were travelling, which is not surprising as this cinder cone rises 100m (328ft) above the ground and approximately 400m (1300ft) across. But as I had already said, time was getting on so we sadly had to make do with looking at it from the road that circled it before we headed off again, stopping at another town 60 miles closer to Melbourne and in the next state of Victoria, that was even less enthusiastically sign posted than when we entered the state of South Australia with a simple road sign like any other. We thought Portland had much more to offer than we presumed from what we had read in our guidebook. Portland is a major fishing port with more than 60 fishing vessels that use this port and can accommodate many larger vessels and tankers, as this is the deepest port between Adelaide and Melbourne that are 620 miles apart by sea. The most interesting thing we did here, and something I doubt I'll ever get the chance to do again involved an unusual short drive, Lee Breakwater Road takes a sharp right turn onto a pier that's nearly half a mile long. We drove to the end along this road with several other cars that were most probably sightseeing like ourselves. It had an additional jetty halfway down that had a fishing vessel moored up to it, with it ending in a tight area to turn around in that circles a streetlight. Straight on from here across the water roughly 200m (656ft) away, was another pier that had a large tanker moored along side it, with this pier at right angles from the end of Lee Breakwater Road to join the mainland, making this port an ideal shelter from storms out at sea. We made a quick stop at the end to take pictures and take in the area, the road either side was piled to the edge with large boulders that disappeared under the waterline that I guess were used to break the incoming waves.

This was all we had to see here so we moved on to Warrnambool another 60 miles further for the evening, bringing our mileage for the day to 171 miles, with our first stop here to get our provisions for the evening meal, which I went for an easy option of noodles and bread. We spent the night at Logan's Beach where it is well known for its, whale viewing platform that overseas the Southern Right Whale nursery. We went up to this platform with great enthusiasm hoping to catch a glimpse of these giant creatures that can reach up to 15m (49ft) and can weigh up to 46 tons, with a creature this big we were sure that if there were any here we would surely see them. But on this calm night we didn't see a single ripple that would indicate there was something there.

We retreated back to the van to cook up our meals and watch a couple more of our bargain buy comedy DVDs. Dale wasn't all that enthusiastic about '*Fortune Hunters*' and laid back, taking some time to work on his beauty therapy after hacking a couple of slices of cucumbers off and laying them on his eyes. I saw this as a photo opportunity by taking the other half of the cucumber and held it over is mid section pointing upwards, I know it was a boyish and childish act, but if you were to see the photo with the big cheesy grin on my face holding said item, then you would know just how much enjoyment I got out of this. Dale got a little more interested in the second film, '*Fart*', as he could have stared in the film himself with out the need of any sound effects as I'm sure he could fart on cue. Even though this was a little more humorous they both fell asleep by the end, leaving me watching it by myself. Sharon woke at the end of it as I was putting the laptop away, we then both cleaned our teeth and took a walk to the lookout point again, with only another moonrise for entertainment as the whales were still being a little shy. It was a very unusual moonrise this evening, in the fact it was very bright behind the clouds, which, was shining streaks of light through over the sea. We crawled into our sleeping bags, taking only my trousers off to sleep, as it was quite a cold evening compared to what we had been used to.

Monday 9th May.

We woke late again even though it had been a cold night at around 9.30am. The first thing we did this morning, was to try one last time to catch sight of some whales, we stood for a while at the look out, scanning everywhere between us and the horizon, wondering if we really were in the right place. Just as we gave up and headed back, a policewoman arrived and told us she came here often, recently seeing 2 calves in the surf. We disappointingly and unluckily walked back to our campervan for breakfast then carried, on our way along the *Great Ocean Road*.

Our first sightseeing feature for the day was a big one along the *Great Ocean Road*, which was the first of several rock formations we would be stopping to marvel at that stretched along 30 miles of coastline which was mostly cliffs, making it difficult to access the few beached areas. The first formation was The *Bay Of Islands*, several islands varying in sizes were scattered around this bay, some of the smaller rock stacks showed a much more interesting form of mother natures constant power. One particular smaller cylindrical shaped stack close to shore was once, along with the rest of the formations we would see today, were part of the mainland. This entire area was formed 10 to 20 million years ago while it was still under water, as the sea retreated it left large cracks in the ground that helped form the path of the seas destruction of what was then mainland, from about 6,000 years ago at the end of the last ice age when the sea advanced again.

Slowly the sea has eroded away everything around this rock stack, one of these formations looks like a pile of rocks defiant of the waves, still standing showing its scars from the test of time. This lone formation was curved slightly away from the sea showing how the waves had slowly nibbled away at it, leaving this white rock that had been constantly cleaned showing its natural colour, with the top a much darker colour showing mostly untouched settled dirt and debris. It clearly showed the sedimentary layers of several millions of years, with definite lines of the most hardest parts circling it like ribs that protruded out the furthest, that looked like it was trying to fight back and not wanting to become washed away. The stresses on this particular formation must be quite great when the waves are high, as it narrowed to about half the diameter at sea level showing this was either the weakest part or has had the most erosion from the sea, I'm sure that long before the top part is dissolved away, it will snap like a twig, becoming another strange sightseeing attraction of a large rock laying in the surf.

A short drive later and we were at The Grotto. A spectacular limestone cave that has been carved out by the sea making an archway I was able to walk over. The wooden steps led us the 700m (2,300ft) from the car park to the top of this arch, and down into the open cave that had been worn out. The sea had carved this perfect arch within a cove, with a constant pool of seawater underneath it, that due to the low tide and calm seas today, we were able to walk up to, peering through to the inside of this 3m (10ft) high arch that gave me a good view of the horizon at sea level.

Another short drive and our next formation was London Arch, until 15th January 1990 it was known as London Bridge because of its similarity to it's namesake. On this day the 25m (82ft) long arch closest to shore unexpectedly gave way, leaving 2 tourist stranded on the part that was left, just think how lucky they must have felt, being a few minutes out either way would have resulted in a much worse outcome than a ride in a rescue helicopter. The main arch collapsed along joint lines as its weight became too great from the erosion, for the arch to support itself. In time, the same fate will become of the second 50m (164ft), long arch that will eventually become 2 stacks.

The next unusual formation was The Arch, this 8m (26ft) high arch stands alone at about a 45 degree angle from the cliff face. What makes this arch unusual is firstly it's a smooth, almost symmetrical arch, with a platform beneath it a metre above sea level, that must be incredibly hard rock to withstand the seas unending attack, compared to the hole that has been punched through the limestone above it. The arch was showing visual signs of ware, as a few large boulders were lying beneath it that must have fell from inside the arch. There was no beach access to this one, so we had to admire this from the top of the cliff face.

The next stop was Loch Ard Gorge, this series of larger island close to shore has created several sheltered alcoves, caves and beaches. When I visited here in 2005, in the centre of this inlet was taken up mostly by a large arched island that seemed to be well established and would be for some time. This however proved me wrong as the Island Archway collapsed in 2009, leaving what appears to be 2 unconnected pillars. The area is named after the clipper ship *Loch Ard* that ran aground nearby on the 1st of June 1878, as it approached the end of its 3 month journey from England to Melbourne. Only 2 of the 54 passengers and crew survived this shipwreck that were washed up on shore at this location. Two beach areas next to each other are accessed by wooden steps, one of these semicircular coves had a bizarre and interesting formation dripping down from the overhanging top of the cliff towards the beach. Stalactites have formed from water running through the limestone and across the face causing this strange upside down, knobbly multicoloured candles hanging there. The beaches looked inviting with an abundance of trees, plants and shrubs that would have taken a long walk to fully enjoy it, signs here recommended at least 3 hours to take the different walks in this are, not to mention the extra time that would have to be allowed for me to take pictures and enjoy the scenery. As with everywhere we were visiting we had to appreciate what we could see and had time to do, so we moved onto to Thunder Cave nearby. This cave was once much longer, but due to the test of time the cave got deeper, and the entrance became further from the sea as the roof slowly collapsed toward the mainland. The mouth of Thunder Cave is now about 100m (328ft) inland with many large rocks that have fallen in from the erosion of time, making the sea swirl and tumble as it pours into the cave, disappearing for a short time before the weight of the wave runs out as it rolls back to meet another wave that carries on this process, that will cause this cave to continue inwards and outwards. This cave has been given the name of Thunder from the sound it makes during times of high waves, as a wave enters the narrow inlet, it opens slightly to narrow once again to the small cave opening, speeding up the wave to fill the cave, with large waves these will fill the entire cave at speed causing a loud rumble or bang, maybe due to air being forced and compressed by the waves as well as the sheer amount of weight behind the wave crashing into an enclosed area. Today there wasn't much of a swell so we had a very quiet rumble, but I would have very much liked to have experienced the natural noise of natures power with something as simple as a wave.

   Our last rock formation was the 12 Apostles, this is a collection of 12 examples of rock stacks that were all once part of the mainland like the rest of the formations we had seen today. These turned into arches that collapsed, leaving only these stacks that vary in width and height of up to

45m (147ft), which seem to majestically rise out of the water to stand the test of time. These too had the very unmissable ribs and multi coloured sedimentary layers, showing millions of years of the cycle of the earth that is slowly being washed away. These layers were mirrored on the mainland cliff face that curved back and forth towards the sea, We spent a good deal of time here admiring the formations, after a short while I realised I could only see 11 of them, maybe one was obscured by another or I needed to be at a better advantage point, I'm sure there were 12 Apostles and will be for some time to come, I wonder if one of them would disappear into the sea if it would be renamed. It was rather cold at this high point along the cliff, and we were debating weather to brave it out to the lookout point along one of the outcrops of rocks that made a natural jetty, while this contemplating was going on the sun came out that seemed to warm our bodies and spirits dramatically, so we took the short walk to get a better look at this fantastic sight.

We left our appetite for these rock formations fulfilled, and headed for our destination for the evening at Melbourne. Sharon drove from here and it wasn't long before something caught her attention, well several things caught her attention in the form of some excited professional photographers with large camera lens's pointing up into the trees, I soon realised what everyone was so excited about and told Sharon to pull over as I grabbed my own little camera and jumped out of the campervan, to take some pictures of an animal we hadn't seen in the wild. Up in the treetop was a lone koala slowly munching away on leaves.

Moving on I carried on being a passenger, taking this time to have a little doze. I found when travelling in this manner, some days when you have used a lot of energy or up early, you utilise every moment, you can to grab a nap to refresh you for your next possible major energy expenditure. Which was the next time we filled up with fuel, as it was overcast and quite dull Sharon had been driving with the lights on, and as most people do at some point in their lives when stopping somewhere in the daytime, you tend to forget you have the lights on, by the time we had filled up we realised the mistake by how the battery was flat was when Sharon tried to start it. I decided at this point it would be a good idea to check the tyre pressures as we pushed it off the pump and to the airline, to find out they were all about 10lb short of what they should have been. We were fortunate that this petrol station was on a hill that would assist us in bump starting our vehicle, Dale and I thought we were the strongest of the 3 of us so it made sense we'd be doing the pushing, until Sharon pointed out she had never bump started a vehicle. For most people this wouldn't seem a big deal, but I appreciated that without doing this before and just going for it could end up in a little bit of a disaster given the area we had to do it in. So I gave her a quick and to the point instructions on the principles of bump starting a vehicle, making sure to explain what to do once it had started, not as easy as it sounded as the area we had to pull this off was restricted to this small forecourt before it ran onto the busy road. Dale and I huffed and puffed pushing it back up to the top of this small incline with out a single offer of help from the public. Dale and I got into position and then pushed with all our might. I had timed it at what I thought would be the perfect balance between speed and safety before we ran out of room, at the right time I shouted for her to dump the clutch, and with one turn of the engine it fired into life, with a sigh of relief and a cheer from us all, Sharon came to a controlled stop with room to spare. What a result! Happily we carried on our way without any more dramas all the way to Melbourne, with Dale driving the last 60 miles or so we drove straight into the centre of town by 6.15pm, to find something to eat in the china town area. Sharon was particularly fussy about where to eat this evening for some reason, I personally couldn't have cared less where I ate as long as it was reasonably priced and soon. We finally plumped for a bar restaurant where I got a $16 (£6.60) chicken schnitzel, and finished off with a pick me up double shot of espresso to kick start me back into life to see me through the rest of the evening, after our tiring day and our long drive.

Sharon and I had a short wander round this area before meeting back up with Dale as he'd gone to find a much cheaper, and most probably much more unhealthy meal. One of the things we stumbled across was the *Performing Arts Centre*, I say stumbled but we could see it from quite some distance away and was naturally drawn towards it. This performing arts centre has a 162m (531ft) metal spire of complex latticed and criss-crossed tubing, which replaced the original 115m (377ft) after it showed signs of deterioration in the 1990s just 14 years after it had been built. It was rebuilt along the same lines of the original designers spire. The metal webbing looks like it has been thrown over the entire roof and is being pulled up as it gathers together to the centre where the spire starts. This webbing and spire design are influenced by the billowing dress of a ballerina's tutu and the *Eiffel Tower*. The spire is illuminated with some 6,000m (that's 3.75 miles!) of optic tubing, 150m (492ft) of neon tubing on the mast and 14,000 incandescent lamps on the spire's skirt. Because of its complexity of this detailed and precise addition to the building, it was the first structure in Australia to use computer-aided-design (CAD). Besides admiring this, one of a kind roof decoration, we wanted to see if there were any expressive arts shows that would be showing during our time in Melbourne, and we were in luck as there was a showing of '*Tango Fire, Flames Of Desire*' that was described as 'A dance extravaganza'. In the circle of expressive arts this is, a well known performance, that tours the world and often has a sell out at most of its locations. The 2 hour story takes its audience on an intellectual journey through the history of tango, from its roots in Buenos Aires before illustrating its rise on the global stage to become a much enjoyed contemporary dance style, that is enjoyed or at least appreciated, by many age groups and walks of life. At the time we had no idea at just how big this performance was, but we gathered that this was a popular and highly skilled show from the price of the tickets, which were well out of our price range at $87 (£36), something we couldn't justify although I know I would have very much enjoyed this show.

We met up with Dale and before driving out of town I called home for half an hour. Our search for a place to sleep was a little difficult for some reason this evening, when we did find a little spot by a reservoir bringing our total mileage for the day to 236 miles, that we thought was out the way, it turned out to have had several complaints by the locals from unruly people performing wheelspins and handbrake turns, we found this out from the local police that turned up shortly after we arrived and moved us on. So we drove off and parked on the other side of the carpark out of sight from the cops, getting off to sleep shortly after to an undisturbed night.

Tuesday 10th May.

We managed to get up earlier than we had recently at 8.30am and it was still bloody cold, we wasted no time shivering in the campervan and I drove us into town. We pulled over at some public toilets briefly for a pee stop and Dale snuck in the drivers seat, not that I was really that bothered but there was just a little bit of muscling me out without asking that pissed me off a little. Like I said, I didn't really care who was in the driving seat as long as we got there in one piece, and as none of us had showed any signs of really bad driving, except me of course on that gravel road in New Zealand, I was really not worried about Dale driving. We carried on into the city centre along a dual carriage way when Dale proved me wrong with the bad driving bit, A slight lapse in concentration as he was making a lane change meant he didn't see someone in the right hand lane stopped to turn off, Sharon and I screamed stop in several different ways that really shouldn't be repeated as we were both pushing our imaginary brake pedal as hard as we could. Dale instantly caught on to what we were trying to explain and stamped on the brakes, stopping a few centimetres from the car in front in a cloud of squealing tyre smoke.

He paid a little more attention for the rest of the drive round the suburbs of Melbourne. We were driving round aimlessly looking for the street that is used in the TV show *Neighbours* that Dale was sure was in the area he had taken us to. I thought it was futile and a waste of time as I was sure we were in the wrong suburb. After about half an hour he reluctantly gave up and we parked up in the city centre, to book tickets on the official tour of the *Neighbours* set at the Information Centre at $30 (£12.50) each, which I thought was reasonable considering we were getting transportation, a guided tour of the street and a video while on the bus.

In the meantime we had some time to kill until after lunch for our most anticipated tour, well it was for Dale and Sharon's excitement more than myself, I just wanted to see the set of the longest running drama series in Australian television. We parked near the *Wicked* campervan depot after unsuccessfully trying to get parked on their forecourt for free, but got a space on a street nearby for $3 (£1.25) for 4 hours which was exceptionally good, considering we were fairly close to the city centre.

We walked into the city that took only 30 minutes, on our way an advertisement caught my eye, it wasn't something I needed I might add but this was so bold and out there in true Ozzie style, it had to have a mention. A massive billboard that spanned the entire roof of a 3 storey building, in bold letters read, *'Stronger, Longer, Donga! Improve your sex life.'* with a freephone number that was set up by the *Advanced Medical institute of Australia*. I was so amused that an organization like that would use such a combination of words to describe a Viagra pill.

I stopped off at a post office to send some items home I wouldn't be needing, in an attempt to relieve the stress on my shoulders. I sent the latest collection of pictures I had saved to disc thanks to the laptop I had been lugging around, along with all the tickets and brochures I had collected on the way through Australia, that set me back $34 (£14.16) for a kilo (2.2lb) by airmail, and sending a second parcel of 3.5kg (7.7lb) by land at $42 (£17.50), making it much cheaper per kilo, which were items I wasn't too concerned about getting home in a hurry, this was a few clothes and my power converter as there wouldn't be any more need for it. It had been very helpful in the campervan here in Australia and the car in New Zealand, to charge the laptop. As we would soon be handing the campervan back we wouldn't be using the converter again, which was something I didn't really want to be lugging around with me for another 3 months. The pictures on the other hand were more of an importance to me, as I had a dedication and almost obsessive need to name and sort the pictures I had taken on a daily basis on my laptop, I needed to make sure they got home as quick as possible as hard drive space was very limited on my laptop. Back in 2005 laptops didn't have a huge amount of internal storage, and this one had a measly 40gb, which didn't take long to fill it to capacity at the rate I was going. This was my back up system by burning them all onto CD, no DVD burners on your everyday laptops back then either, and sending them home to my mum where she would check them all to make sure they weren't damage in the post, after I got the green light from her and I knew they were ok, I'd delete them off the laptop.

It was then breakfast time at Starbucks for a coffee and some of my own fruit, which they didn't seem to care that I was eating it in their café, they also didn't notice how long I took in their very clean, spacious and well equipped bathroom that I used to wash all of my important bits.

Our next visit was a common occurrence that we did in most big cities, of visiting its Cathedral, *St Paul's* is one of two cathedrals in Melbourne and it certainly wasn't a disappointment. It is noted to be the home church for Anglicans in Melbourne and Victoria, which was built on the site of the first public Christian services in Melbourne, led by Dr Alexandra Thompson in 1836, just one year after the first official settlers established a community in Melbourne. Soon after this event a small chapel was built at another location while this area became a corn market until 1848 when it was made available for the building of *St Paul's Parish Church*. Consecrated in 1852 it held services here for the community until 1880, when it was demolished to make way for the present cathedral, a move that was decided as its location is in the centre of Melbourne, and opposite flinders Street Station, which was the transport hub of 19th century Melbourne and it still is an important and busy place. I would think the decision to build this large and elaborate cathedral was made possible due to Melbourne being the most economic and richest city in the world in this time period, from the gold rush that had been thriving here since 1851, which caused a huge influx of money and people. The original church that was built here was demolished and the *St Paul's Cathedral* was erected in its place. The Cathedral is a revival of style known as *Gothic Transitional* and designed by the distinguished British architect, William Butterfield, who was noted for his ecclesiastical work. The first foundation stone was laid in 1880, but it had a slow and difficult build in the beginning from Butterfield refusing to visit Melbourne and the building program, which was plagued with problems that arose from the management of such a task with Butterfield living in England. He finally resigned in 1884 and it was completed under the supervision of Josef Reed, who is responsible for the designs of many of Melbourne's public buildings, nonetheless the design remained as William Butterfield's. It only took 11 years until the completion of the Cathedral that was consecrated on the 22nd of January 1891. But this is not the end of the construction and not the image that is seen today, the construction of the spires did not begin until 1926 under the designing expertise of John Barr of Sydney, using the original design of an octagonal central tower and gable west end towers of William Butterfield's. These three spires are obviously of a different material and time period to anyone looking at them. The dark grey, square front of the building, has an optical illusion of the 3 red, 8 sided spires being next to each other, when in fact there is 2 at the front and one in the middle towards the back, that are greatly different to the first original sketches by William Butterfield, with the Moorhouse Tower towards the north face of the building, being higher than the other 2 that stands at 96m (314ft) above street level, and holds the record as the second highest Anglican spire in the world. *St Paul's* is unusual among most of Melbourne's other 19th century public buildings, in that it is not made from bluestone, the city's most popular building material. Instead it is made from sandstone from the Barrabool Hills and limestone embellishments of Waurn Ponds limestone, and as the spires are made from Sydney sandstone some 30 years after the initial construction, they are of a different colour.

Besides Sunday and weekday Eucharist the cathedral maintains the English tradition of a daily choral *Evensong*, the only Anglican cathedral in Australia to do so, which was brought to our attention during our tour by a very nice gentleman, when we stopped at the magnificent pipe organ which accompanies the choir at choral services. The organ was built by *T C Lewis and Co* of Brixton, England, and over £6,500 was spent on its construction, shipping and installation, before it was played at the Cathedral's opening in 1891. Various modifications and maintenance works have been carried out since then, to a grand sum of $726,000 (£302,500), with the help of a *National Trust appeal*, with the restoration completed in 1990. In its restored state, the organ now has four manuals with 44 stops and pedals with 9 stops, all with electro-pneumatic action. Again I have no clue on just how good that is, but from my research I have found several references to being a *'must see to any organ enthusiast'*. Our tour guy too was very enthusiastic about it telling us how loud it is 'when it really gets going' with all its pipes, as this was the period of it being re-tuning, some of the pipes were missing as they had been sent to the UK for this tuning process, but still very much in use and still able to punch out a good deal of sound. The most memorable image I have of the inside of the cathedral besides several high windows that let in ample light, was the brick work and pillars that stretched to the ceiling, that had a unique large banded affect of black and yellowish stone. The interior and exterior has been well maintained and kept, as there has been extensive work carried out in the 1960s and more recently in 2009 after $18 million (£7.5 million) was raised to restore the spires and interior once again, under the guidance of Falkinger Andronas Architects and Heritage Consultants, to a very high standard.

We grabbed a quick lunch before jumping on the bus for the tour to Ramsay Street. Unless you have lived under a rock all your life I will not need to go into great detail on this long running Australian TV soap. The 3 hour tour would take us to Pin Oak Court in the suburb of Vermont South, on a small blue bus with *Neighbours official tours* plastered all over it. We saw an old episode on the way that was amusing entertainment for us, as it was fun to remember how good we thought it was when we watched it as teenagers, and for Dale and Sharon who watched it into their adulthood. We first stopped briefly at *Erinsborough High School* on Eden Drive that is actually a real school that has been used on several occasions and in the real world it has been threatened twice with closure until it was merged with both *West Waratah Tech* and *West Waratah High*. The school itself didn't seem to look like your typical school, or what I would expect it to be. It seemed quite small from the angle we were at, we weren't allowed to wander round it either as it was a school day and several children were hanging around probably feeling like an exhibit. It was a short stay here, but long enough to get a picture of us outside it, and for Dale to catch my enthusiasm on camera where I was making reference to my excitement, shown in the way from the loss of bladder control on the bus on the way over. A short drive later 3.5 miles away we arrived at the main attraction, catching a couple of guys playing cricket in almost the same place as in the opening credits of the older episodes as we pulled into Pin Oak Drive, which I thought was something this organisation must have gone to great lengths to do just for a small thing like that. We disembarked and soon all mingled about snapping away happily at all the characters houses while the tour guide filled us with several interesting facts and trivia, as well as reminding us of who lived in which house. One of the most staggering facts was that the actual residents of the houses used in the TV show, get compensated $20,000 (£8,333) a year for their inconvenience of allowing them to film outside their houses. If I lived there I'd be over the moon to get paid that much for that slight inconvenience, although they are restricted in any cosmetic changes they want to do to the outside of their house. Every change has to be passed by the producers of the soap, in one case a resident wanted to have a new front door put in, and so they incorporated it into one of the episodes, I presume they did this so it wouldn't confuse any of the viewers to how a door can just change colour! Yes, that was sarcasm. We also got one of the Ramsay Street signs passed around so we could all pose with it, I had my picture taken outside number 22, which at the time I was watching it as a teenager, Lou Carpenter was the resident here, this was my favourite just because I have always liked the look of the house and I always remember the opening credits, where a car in the drive is being washed while various comical antics were going on around it, in the most jolly and happy way that the Ramsay street neighbours always are. Dale and I had a little on the spot acting in an Australian acting kind of way, outside my favourite house, like most bizarre things I participated in with Dale it's usually him who's the instigator, and on this occasion it was something I am not very good at, especially as we had a gathering crowd from the tour to watch us, most probably for the comical aspect, Dale had a better experience doing the same thing with Sharon after my failed attempt that went a lot better. I thought the time they allowed here was just the right amount, everyone got ample time with the sign and a leisurely walk round by the tour guide was just right. We concluded our tour by driving round the back of the street where the crew park up and have most of their equipment, as most of the houses have access to this carpark, as well as to Toadies house which has the pool in the back yard that has been used in numerous stories and the opening credits. On the rest of our return journey on the bus we had another showing of a *Neighbours* episode, this one is by far the most memorable one of the fairytale marriage between Charlene Mitchell, played by Kylie Minogue, and Scott Robinson, played by Jason Donovan. I was not one of the 20 million people in 1987 in the UK to watch this episode, I didn't even watch it then but like most people, I did know about the wedding.

Arriving back we sent emails home and then back to *Saint Paul's Cathedral* to witness first hand how good the organ and choir were, as they would be performing their evening prayer song this evening. The guy was correct in his description of it being something worth seeing, and I'm glad we took the time to see this special gathering, as it was the only one of its kind in Australia. The choir performed brilliantly singing their set of songs beautifully, with the organ played professionally until the end, where in my opinion it sounded liked someone else had snuck up and pushed a load of random keys. For the most part it sounded perfectly adequate and didn't seem to suffer at all from the missing pipes. I don't know what got into Dale at this point after our religious choir did their bit, maybe he was 'in the moment' of such a magnificent place of worship and such a beautiful choir. What ever it was, after the service there was a kind of special prayer being held for people to participate in at the end that Dale stayed for, I was quite surprised to see him standing there with the vicar speaking posh and respectfully, like we all do when faced with someone of the cloth. I should have known something was up when he got up and took great care in combing his hair with a side parting, just like the stereotypical religious types. All joking aside Dale enjoyed this special prayer and was very sincere about it, while he was relaying what he did back to us later on, telling us how he said a prayer for his mum who he was very close to and missed dearly.

Sharon and I made our way back to the campervan to cook something to eat, I heated up a pan of ravioli on the one ring gas cooker and browned some bread off on it to go with it, and finished off with noodles which turned out to be plenty for me. We walked back into the city to meet Dale who turned out to be 15 minutes late as he'd had a tough time finding something cheap to eat. We stopped off in a bar for a drink that had music videos for entertainment, where Dale and his shirt drew the attention of one Australian, at first he started taking the piss out of him and then Sharon for knowing one of the country songs that came on the TV, then really ruffled Dales feathers by moving his insults onto his beloved home football team. Fortunately Dale didn't start a bar brawl, as it turned out the guy actually liked Norwich after all, we finished up our drinks soon after this before any more trouble ensued and headed back to the Campervan. On the way back Dale was drawn to one of his favourite past times that seem to attract him as soon as he's had a drink, and which he finds even harder to turn down than another drink, but this karaoke bar was appointments only and his name wasn't on the list so he wasn't allowed in, so we went to a book store instead. I picked up the next most important book for our next venture as our time in Australia was drawing to a close, the '*Southeast Asia on a shoestring*' by '*Lonely Planet*'. This would be something I would refer to almost every day to help guide us for 75 days after we left this great continent through Southeast Asia.

Back at the campervan we drove to another quiet street to sleep, only clocking up 16 miles for the day.

Wednesday 11th May.

We were up at 8am, which is a good job as it took us an hour and 45 minutes, to clean the campervan from boot to bonnet and find all our belongs that had hidden themselves in all sorts of places over the past 40 days, and filled our backpacks to capacity once again. We handed the campervan back and said a sad goodbye to our home, even though it had a shocking pair of dictators so boldly painted across it that we initially hated, but this was what made it all the more memorable. Our little campervan had been faithful to us for all this time and by far the best way to travel and experience Australia on a budget. If I had more time I would have wanted to travel this entire continent in this way, I found it to be one of my best experiences and one of the most memorable. We had clocked up a massive 6,818 miles averaging 170 miles a day, and that was with exploring only half the country. To give you an idea on just how far that is, at the widest part of Australia from Sydney to Perth is 2,445 miles. It's like driving from New York to San Francisco and back again, and still have a 1,000 miles left to drive! It's also the same as flying from London to Singapore or London to Mexico City. That's a lot of miles and we barely scratched the surface of this massive country, but compared to the average backpacker from what we had observed, we had been to many more places than most and experienced much more too.

We were walking once again with all our possessions on our backs, to the *Firefly* bus station where we would be taking an overnight bus the 450 miles back to Adelaide, where we would be catching the *Indian Pacific* train to Perth on the west coast, which would be our last destination we would stay at in Australia. I always liked overnight buses for 2 reasons that are both as good as each other, firstly as it's overnight I didn't have to pay for a nights accommodation, secondly from a travellers point of view, there's usually not many sightseeing attractions to be seen at night time. So it's a win win situation that made me so happy, I was skipping along the 3 miles to the bus terminal, I was so happy in fact I decided to show my bravado to Dale saying I could even outrun him with all this weight on my back. So he put me up to the challenge and started to jog so I had to kept pace not trying to show I was trying really hard, for some reason Dale and I were always trying to compete with each other in a friendly sense of the word, I don't know why I even attempted to compete in a running competition with Dale, as he had participated in several races and mini marathons in the past. Fortunately for me I saved face as we were relatively close to the bus terminal, any further and I would've had to admit to him that he was better than me on this occasion. After our exhilarating sprint we checked our bags into a locker for a staggering $12 (£5) for the rest of the day, managing to get all 3 rucksacks in one locker so it made it much more reasonably priced between the 3 of us. We checked in for the bus and made sure it was still on time and everything was ok with that, we also had to verify our train ticket 48 hours before our boarding of the *Indian Pacific* which we were a little concerned we had missed as it was 31 hours before we would be boarding the train in Adelaide. When I asked the lady behind the counter she told us that it wasn't possible, as the train hadn't left Sydney at this point so there was no way of checking. So we left the bus terminal a little baffled to as when we could verify our ticket and went in search for a morning Starbucks and post some postcards back home.

    For the rest of the day we would be basically sightseeing round Melbourne, we stopped to look at many of the old buildings as well as taking time to admire the modern day building and feats of engineering. One thing I noticed plenty of in this city, was trees, they stood out more than usual as they were displaying something most unusual to me at this time of year, as we were in the opposite hemisphere to my home country it was autumn, and we were in May! A little strange to say the least for someone who was used to seeing green trees in May, not kicking dead leaves down the street. Dale went off to change his dates on his Thai Airline ticket while Sharon and I checked out the National Gallery of Victoria. Like us Dale had pre dated tickets that could be changed at anytime, we had discussed between us all the dates we would need them changed to, with Sharon and I changing ours 6 weeks before.
    Founded in 1861 the *National Gallery of Victoria*, NGV, is the oldest public gallery in Australia and maybe one of the most interesting to get into, the front door was in a large semicircular arch in the middle of the entire length of the front of the building, it was a featureless grey wall 150m (492ft) long with no other else except for the water fountains that were evenly spaced along 3 sides of the building. The entrance through

the arch was made of a glass wall that had a shimmering wall of water flowing down it, looking out of the wet window to the outside world looked even stranger as everything was distorted and morphed out of shape. Inside the gallery was well spaced out with some spacious rooms with others packed out that displayed different sections of culture, ages, pottery, glass ware, furniture, clothes, Roman, Egyptian and Columbian artefacts. In the international arts section I got to see my first real painting of *Constable* and *Rembrandt* pencil drawing, of course I had seen reprints and original paintings on TV, but never in an art gallery so that was quite special. You stand there looking at a picture that was created 400 years ago, by a person who would have had no clue on just how much his work would be revered by people like me, and holding a firm place in the history books, or how much it would be worth. We spent about 4 hours here having a stimulating overload of cultural arts and exhibits that was well documented, that kept my attention and was most enjoyable, but my hunger was just that little more on my mind than the countless more items on display.

    We sat outside by the one of the water features where I had a chocolate spread sandwich made up from the last of the items from our campervan's food stock, I actually had some more choccy spread left but I'm sure it would have spoiled after a short time getting lugged about in my backpack, so my sandwich ended up with a large amount of spread stuck between the bread. We took a walk to the *Royal Botanical Gardens*, by the time we got there we had about an hour before it started to get dark, so we took a leisurely walk round trying to cover as much as we could, but it may have been wishful thinking as it covers 38 hectares (380,000 m^2) that includes over 10,000 individual species of native and exotic plants as well as a herb garden. This swampy marshland was selected as the Melbourne's Botanical site in 1846, which is not hard to believe it was once a wet area that has been moulded and made into, the well kept ponds, marshes and gardens we see today. We walked past and over several of the 11 named, tough wearing lawns that is also a non-native grass that were also very well kept, it was picture postcard standard. We saw several buildings in the grounds, and there were many more monuments and buildings we didn't get to see that can easily be hidden away. One example was of a 2 storey building that we nearly missed, an 1856 Georgian mansion that has also been kept to high standard and in beautiful condition, it holds venues of all descriptions and can seat 68 guests. We could only see the top balcony of the second storey that can seat 20 of the guests, behind a tall hedge that was hiding this lovely house, along with its second building, and the marquee that can accommodate up to 160 seated guests on its immaculately maintained garden. We passed many great trees that had been here for many years, overlooking the continuing changing gardens with several of them inhabited by grey-headed flying foxes, a breed of bat. There had already been attempts to move them on as they caused a lot of noise and were detracting the garden's beauty from the musky odour they emitted. In 2001 there were attempts to move them on as the population had grown to 28,000 and had caused a great deal of damage to the plant life, when we came through in 2005 there was still evidence of them here as there was an abundance of them hanging in the trees. I quite like bats, but if a colony is allowed to get too big it can have a devastating effect on the environment around it. When I was there it seemed ok with nothing too smelly, but by 2012 the bat colony had grown to 5,000 and were claimed to be responsible for the loss of 28 trees and 30 palms, with a further 60 on a critical list. And so there was an attempt to move them on once again. The garden's are home to many other animals and fish, in one of the lakes we saw some black swans that were one of the 50 species of birds that were residents here, there are also fish, turtles, eels and frogs in the many ponds. The insects here, which I would expect to greatly increase with the demise of the bats as there is 533 types of insects flying about with 400 species of butterflies. One of the most unusual residents here that many people are unaware of is the small population of foxes.

One of the last unexpected sights we stumbled across in one of these perfectly kept lawn gardens was the *Sidney Myer Music Bowl*. It was opened on the 12th of February 1959, and is able to accommodate an audience of over 2,000 seated and 10,000 people standing. It is cleverly made using the natural lay of the land to utilise this to its best ability, built into a natural depression the undercover stage is 27m long and 19m deep (88ft x 62ft) with the canopy that seemed to resemble a large sheet that had been thrown over the 2 posts that are 21m (68ft) high making an opening in the front, with the surrounding edge of this shell like building tethered to the ground. The canopy is actually 4,055m^2 (43,648 ft^2) of weather proofed 12mm (½ inch) plywood sheeted on both sides with aluminium covering, with a lattice of cables anchoring it down to the ground around its edge. The bowl is also registered on the *Victorian Heritage list* for its cultural importance as the largest, purpose built, permanent outdoor performance venue in Australia.

Due to the very successful businessman Sidney Myer, who upon his death in 1934 left a large portion of his estate, to establish a fund that would guarantee the Myers families continuing connection with the community, from this the *Sidney Myer Music Bowl* was built at a cost of $500,000 (£208,333) that won prizes for its unique design from the architect Barry Patten. The venue was opened by, Prime Minister Robert Menzies, where 30,000 people attended. Soon after this the American evangelist Billy Graham attracted over 70,000 people. Since then there has been many performances of all kinds and genres, with one of the most notable venues in 1967 when The Seekers performed, packing 200,000 people into the park, which I'm sure a large majority of didn't have a good view. There are too many great bands to mention, but among the many were bands such as *ABBA, AC/DC, Metallica, Wings, Blondie, the Czech Philharmonic Orchestra The Beach Boys, Dire Straits, Neil Diamond, Bob Dylan, Paul McCartney, Red Hot Chili Peppers, and R.E.M.* Among the most recent bands to perform here are *Bon Jovi, Soundgarden, Guns N' Roses, Lenny Kravitz, blink-182,* and *Swedish House Mafia*. Walking through this very empty and quiet park makes you realise how important something like this is to the community, the revenue and the history made here in this simple park is huge beyond comprehension to the normal every day person like myself. It was a great feeling to think I was standing there in an area where many great legends had been.

This is also used every year to hold 'Carols by *Candlelight*' where thousands turn up for this long standing Christmas eve tradition, that has been celebrated since 1938 that has top entertainers performing a mix of the season's contemporary and traditional favourite carols.

We strolled round as much as the light would allow us before we left this autumn feeling wonderland, that was making me feel rather festive, in May? We had a long walk back to town, while randomly walking down roads and across one particular bridge near the arts centre,

I saw a fantastic photo opportunity in the dusk Melbourne skyline, I set my camera up on the wall of the bridge that crosses the Yarra River, with just a 0.6 second exposure, which was just enough in what little light there was, to bring out the skyscrapers with 2 of them that had cranes on them, there was also the beautifully old Flinders Street train station with its clock tower in the foreground, illuminated in a warm glow. The other significant building that stuck out in this picture was the 19 storey, Victoria University, that was also bathed in a warm light, although this one was a much newer building. I also managed to get the streaking headlights of a car as it went past. This is another one of my favourite pictures that made a memorable image in my mind that will be hard to forget, and is one I have hung on my wall at home.

I took my time to look for a cheap place to eat as we had 2 hours before we had to be at the bus terminal, which I succeeded in when I found ham steak and chips with a bottle of fosters for $12.50 (£5.20) that I also took my time over before leaving for some more leisurely walking, stopping in a few shops for no particular reason except to waste more time, I think there's nothing worse than sitting at the place of your departure for any amount of time, watching other people going on their merry way while you're sat there for hours on end trying to amuse yourself. I ended up only buying water as nothing else peaked my interest, making it to the *Firefly* bus terminal with about 30 minutes to spare.

Dale joined us a short while later, we booked in and boarded our overnight bus by about 8pm, and were greeted with a funny little speech from our very nice driver of the do's and don'ts on his bus, one of which was not using the toilet except in emergencies, which Dale and another chap used before we had even left the station, I on the other hand went before I got on the bus, silly rule though considering we would be on this bus for 10 hours, although there would be one stop at around midnight where we could disembark and have something to eat if we wanted. We were underway a little after 8pm, with our first film of the night *Meet The Parents*, one of my favourite comedies for entertainment. I can't say what other films were screened as I was off to sleep shortly after the first film. Buses are incredibly uncomfortable to sleep on and even worse than planes, which I found out several times in the night waking up with various limbs numb or sore, also waking up dehydrated and gasping for water, which fortunately I had bought before on the way to the bus, I had left it close by, so it was a simple reach out with minimal movement for a few gulps before I was back off to sleep.

Chapter 17
The great train tour of the Australian desert.

Thursday 12th May.

We arrived at Adelaide at 6.15am for a second time, something that would be quite rare in the entire 6 months of my travelling. I collected my things and left Dale sleeping thinking he was pretending just for laughs, as it turned out he really was in a deep sleep and hadn't realised we were at our destination, very nearly disappearing off with the bus to wherever it was going next. It was quite amusing seeing him suddenly jumping up realising he was the only one left on the bus, grabbing his possessions in a disorientated state and joining us. As it was so early nothing else was open, so we utilised our time the best we could at the bus station, spending 2 hours in the bus café for breakfast, using their bathroom that was surprisingly adequate enough to wash in, and caught up with our journals over several cups of coffee to try and bring us back into the land of the living.

We made our way out into the daytime, feeling strange as I hadn't actually been to bed as such, and I was off to find what could amuse me in Adelaide for a second time. The first thing we had to do was to get rid of our heavy backpacks at the train station where we would be leaving from tonight. You would think a train station such as this one that links one side of Australia to the other in a major city would be well signposted, well that's what we thought and we walked straight past it. We were pretty quick to work out we were no longer heading towards the train station, when we could see that the tracks behind us. So after a little bit of common sense, we found where we had to go and talked the staff into letting us leave our bags there while we went in to the city for the day. It was about that time on the way to the city for cake and coffee for a little energy boost and we were ready to tackle the parts of the museum we didn't get to see last time. And talking about something that had been tackled before, my well broke in sandals were showing increasingly worrying excessive wear on the well improvised pop riveted strap Paul had tried to fix them with, and it had held quite well, but the constant walking was just too much for it so I dropped it off at a shoe repair shop in *Rundall Mall* to see if they could be resurrected. The guy probably thought why the hell did I want them repaired instead of buying a new pair. Well it was because I liked them and they were well moulded to my feet as they had covered many miles by me so far, and besides it was cheaper, so I dropped them off and it was into the museum once again.

This time we were much more leisurely with our intake of museum facts of all kinds, for 2 reasons, firstly we had plenty of time and this was pretty much all we had on the agenda for the day, and secondly we were feeling a little lethargic after our uncomfortable overnighter. One of the first items I was amazed at and taken by was a meteorite that was on display in the foyer. At a metre (3'3") long and about ½ a metre (1'7") round it had an amazing presence to it and felt incredibly solid. It was great that it was purposely situated for visitors to touch, after all it wasn't something that would be damaged, from people touching it all day as it's largely composed of metallic iron-nickel and stony-iron, in other words very hard wearing. It felt incredible to think I was touching something billions of years old that had been floating around in space to come to rest here on maybe the only inhabited planet in the universe, to be found by someone and brought here to where I was touching it. It's astonishing it was ever found at all as it was 1,145kg (2,524lbs) of rock laying in the treeless Great Victoria Desert that is 77,000 mi^2 and at its widest part stretches for 684 miles. It was found in 1911 and is part of the Mundrabilla meteorite that had broken up on entry as, two more larger parts were found in 1966 and two more in 1979, along with several smaller ones in a 12 mile radius. This meteorite remains the largest total mass recovered in Australia with a total collective weight of 24 tons, with the largest piece weighing in at 9,980kg (22,000lbs). There is a large section dedicated to space debris with some of great interest, especially one sample that was claimed to have amino acids on it, this is the building blocks for, intelligent life, maybe we are not alone! Among this rocky part, from which you may gather was one of my favourite parts, as well as the 35,000 registered specimens of minerals with the oldest item found from 1865, there was many other very interesting items on display to learn and generally look at. Like most places of this calibre, many of the areas we learnt about have long diminished from my memory, but at the time I very much enjoyed my learning experience here that kept me intrigued for the entire time I was there. However some of the parts that do stick in my mind were the fossils, something that has always interested me since I was a young boy when I first went to the *Museum of London*, the fossil record here at the museum spans more than 600 million years of Earth's history.

After lunch in the café of rolls with pecan pie and coffee, we were ready to push on with the last of the museum, trawling through many areas of interest and countless glass cabinets that were very well set out, well illuminated and well documented. Another fascinating specimen I came across was a sea creature I had never known just how big it was until now. It was the giant squid, it is displayed in an old lift shaft made into a glass cabinet that stretched across 4 floors. Including its tentacles this 11m (36ft) long model of a giant squid, or *Architeuthis dux* is based on the largest squid ever recorded, found in New Zealand waters, complete with life-size models of other creatures that inhabit the murky depths. The real specimen can be seen in the *Science Centre*, preserved in alcohol. It was about this time we had taken the weight off our feet as they were seriously aching and fatigued, most probably from our acute sleep deprivation, we sat there with our heads on each others staring into nothing wishing we were sleeping, I willed myself back into a higher state of mind by suggesting we should get our blood pumping, I encouraged Sharon and myself to jump up and do something about it, with a few more encouraging words of 'come on' several times we sprang into life with a bang that drew attention to ourselves, with some of the other visitors wondering what the hell was wrong with us as we jumped, spun and thrashed our arms about for a good minute, which worked surprisingly well, making it possible to get back into keeping our attention span, to enjoy the rest of the exhibits we wanted to see.

We popped into the library to check our emails and was amused by the 3 coloured guys who were obviously of popular class by the stylish clothing they were wearing, it was also quite obvious on the type of music they were into from this style along with the back to front caps. The main guy of the 3 took position at the computer next to me and proceeded to look up the lyrics to a rap song he was very enthusiastic about, reciting it rapping the words to his friends, stopping momentarily every now and then to express how good the next line was, as we were in a library this was all being done in a whisper. After a very good rendition of one of the latest rap songs we wandered round a few more shops, the first of which was to where my sandals had been very expertly stitched back together by the over muscular guy in the shoe shop for just $7.50 (£3.12), which I was very pleased about. We wasted some more time looking round several other shops, looking for items I would need for the 2 night train ride, I bought a 2 way headphone jack so Sharon and I could listen to the same music on my mini disc player, as I was guessing there would be a lot of down time where music always helps. I also bought provisions for the journey too as I was sure their price of food and snacks would not be for the budget minded traveller like ourselves. I got snacks and lunch for the next day, as well as 2 bottles of wine that was on offer at $4.17 (£1.73), this was one of several that were on offer to taste, and I can say they were all palatable enough to get drunk on.

As we neared the train station, we could see our train sitting at the platform as we passed over the railroad tracks, some 250m (820ft) away, although it was at the station it also took up most of the immediate area, disappearing under the bridge we were standing on as the train is massively long that has tankers, car transporters, luggage, freight as well as the carriages we would be living on for 3 days. The train itself varies in length depending on what needs to be transported on the journey, it has a maximum length measuring 711m (2,332ft) which our train was about that length, as the 24 carriages alone on this trip made up 573m (1,879ft) of it. Arriving at the train station we found Dale and reclaimed our backpacks to have a good sort through, taking out what we would need for the next 2 nights, as we had to check them in just as you would on a plane but without so much security. We had our evening meal in the café at this station, with fish and chips being the cheapest on the menu at $8 (£3.30).

We had about an hour and a half at the station before we were called to board the train, the entire passenger list congregated on the platform where we were greeted by 10 of the staff, who were lined up in front of one of the carriages all very neatly dressed, they were represented by one lady who was obviously of a much higher authority than the others, she then proceeded to explain who the members of staff were and who would be looking after us, ending her speech with: "On behalf of

Victoria and Great Southern Railway, I have this great pleasure of welcoming you aboard this great train. Ladies and gentlemen the mighty *Indian Pacific* is now ready for boarding." There was a loud blast of her whistle in unison with the conductors that made up the crew on the platform, along with several cheers from everyone. It was a great experience and seemed all very exciting to be welcomed onto a train in this manner, back in England you'd be lucky to get a grunt off any of the train staff.

We had a bit of a long walk to carriage R where we were introduced to our day/night seats as we were travelling by the *Red Service*, which to you and I is really known as economy class. This service offers two abreast chairs with a generous amount of leg room, with each set of chairs able to swivel, allowing four travelling guests to face each other. The chairs also have retractable armrests and stowed tables with reclining seats to approximately 45 degrees, much better than what is offered in economy class on a plane. We had communal showers and toilets that are at the end of each cabin that had toiletries and fresh towels supplied. A few carriages away we had the dining car, the *Matilda Café* that had a sufficient range of freshly made salads, hot meals and Alcohol. I settled in to our little area before taking an early shower in the cupboard, it really was that small with just enough room to get in there with a small dry corner to hang your clothes. The toilet was just as claustrophobic with literally no space to turn around in but not unsurprising, as space is something of a commodity on a train. I settled down for the second night in a row to sleep in a seat on public transport, with a little visual entertainment in our carriage of the film The *Terminal*, screened from a row of TVs suspended along the centre of the ceiling, while I snacked on biscuits. It was a little uncomfortable as an alternative for a bed but much better than the bus ride the evening before.

Friday 13th May.

I woke several times in the night, not only from the slightly uncomfortable seating but also because I kept slipping down on my seat, which Sharon unknowingly assisted in my problem after deciding to lay her head on my chest in the early hours of the morning, pinning me down. When I did wake at a reasonable hour at about 8am, I opened my bleary eyes and looked out into the distance at nothing but desert to see a wild animal, that would be the only one of its kind I would see in Australia. A solitary camel stood looking my way with an expression similar to my own of starring in wondrous amazement. I thought I would have seen more wild camels considering there is over a million of them roaming around wild in Australia, another fact that shows how big Australia is.

We were now well into our journey at this point as we had already covered about 600 miles since we left Adelaide and were now travelling through the Nullarbor Plains, and soon we would be on the part of the *Indian Pacific line* that is the world's longest straight stretch of railway track, at 297 miles (478 km). We were tripping along quite nicely and we must have been near our maximum speed of 70mph although it averages 52mph on its 65 hour journey from Sydney to Perth, covering a total of 2,704 miles with just 24 stops, with our part of the journey covering 1,652 miles of it. We could have easily carried on driving in our little campervan to Perth as it may have been cheaper in fuel, but we didn't for several reasons, we were running out of time as our flight out of Australia was on the 20th of May, and unless we drove straight through it, it would not have left us much time in Perth, and it would have been much more tiring, but most of all we wanted to experience one of the longest, greatest and well known train services in the world. This epic journey would take us straight through in 40 hours with our travel time well utilised, as we would only be travelling for one full day, as we would be arriving the next day at 9.30am, so that was another 2 nights of free accommodation.

After our morning freshening up in the cosy little bathroom, we went for breakfast and coffee in a polystyrene cup in the restaurant car and met a lovely, 62 year old lady who looked more like 40, she was moving from Sydney to Perth, that's one hell of a move! Most of her belongings were being transported by road, and she decided to travel on this train with her car in one of the wagons at the back of the train. After breakfast we went back to our seats where I started a book Sharon had lent me '*On The Road*' that would hopefully keep me occupied until the next town. We took a break from the reading after a short while as our curiosity got the better of us, and thought we'd explore the more extravagant carriages. The top classes are rated with names of precious metals of *Platinum* and *Gold services*, with a lounge car with the name of *Outback Explorer* and a restaurant car called *Queen Adelaide*, and then there was us way down the class list at the back in *Red service*, drinking out of polystyrene cups and eating sandwiches out of a packet in the *Matilda Café*. For the money no object type of person, there was also 2 private carriages with executive provoking names such as '*The Chairman's Carriage*' and '*Sir John Forrest Carriage*', for 8 or 6 passengers to share, that has the luxury of full size double beds with en suite bathrooms, big TVs and a conference table. To rent one of these carriages as listed on the official 2014 fares guide of the *Indian Pacific*, will set you back a mere $19,511 (£8,129) for a one way ticket the full length of the journey. Compared to $868 (£361) for a full paying adult for the same journey in *Red Service*. We didn't get as far as the private carriages but we walked towards the front of the train for several carriages. We got to the *Gold Kangaroo* carriage that had sleeper cabins on one side like an old fashioned train carriage, with a corridor you could almost pass someone on, these rooms had single twin beds in a bunk bed formation that would be classed as cosy with an en suite bathroom, but still a little boring after a while in such a small room. We then passed the little cabins through a weaving corridor that you couldn't realistically pass someone on, without getting a little intimate with them. The private little rooms along this part that looked seriously depressing and had their doors open, most probably so they could see something more interesting passing in the corridor than what was in their dreary room. The rooms varied in size but all quite cramped, in the smallest one we could see there was a small table they shared with a seat either side, and that was the room, on your own with just desert to look at! And their view is only on one side of the train, from my seat I was able to look out of several windows both sides and had room to swing a cat. We got as far as we could when we arrived at the busy posh restaurant car where there wasn't a polystyrene cup, sugar sachet or a sandwich in a box in sight. This upper class café sported separate booths with a pressed tablecloth draped perfectly with china plates set out and flowers as a centrepiece on each table. We started to get a look off one of the waiters, (no self service here!) so we thought it was time we headed back before we got told to stop looking at the people with the money.

After a little more reading we arrived at our town where we were able to get off at to stretch our legs. I say a town but it was actually a ghost town that now has a population of just 4 people, after it was effectively closed in 1997 when the railways were privatised, as the new owners didn't need a support town here, although overnight accommodation for train drivers is still there along with the diesel refuelling facilities, which I made good use of to get some pictures as the train driver was refuelling. Cook is the only scheduled stop on the Nullarbor Plain and has little other than curiosity value as we walked through this deserted town that looks like it has been abandoned. Immediately as we got off there was a huge step down of about half a metre (1'7") as there wasn't a platform so we had a 2 step box that had been pushed up to the carriage doors. Every aspect of the town said it had not been maintained for along time, with the train station sign of Cook looking scared and worn that a good lick of paint wouldn't go a miss, although there was a nice modern new one that was pointing to 5 areas, 2 of which were a little to far from here to be any use, as it pointed either way along the track to Sydney and Perth, 1,458 miles and 970 miles respectively, with the other 3 pointing to the school that was no longer in use, but at one time did teach up to 30 pupils. Another sign pointed to the toilets that I thought were probably delightful and worth a miss, with the last one pointing to the only real attraction at this town, the souvenir shop. Something that you might guess is only open at times when the *Indian Pacific* is stopping, and that's not very often as at peak times it comes through here just twice a week and only once off peak.

My real attraction here as a photographer was the dilapidated and run down buildings and various pieces of debris, preserved by the extreme dry desert heat, along with the arid surroundings. I first took a walk to the front of the train, looking into the distance along the track we were headed, to see the tracks disappearing into nothing as far as I could see. I was amused at one signpost near the front of this train, where it was quite clear that walking any further would result in a lot of nothingness, the word shop with an arrow pointing back along the train on a rusting red 25 gallon drum, I soon found this wasn't the only barrel signpost pointing to the shop, as they were dotted all over the town. I couldn't get a photograph here in anyway that showed the sheer length of the train as it seemed to disappear into a blur of pixels, so I had another idea and went in search of a better view point. Walking through this little town you can imagine how it once did have a busy, thriving population, another item of many that peaked my interest was a white steel square tank that had painted on it, *'Our hospital needs your help, get sick.'* And on the other side it carried on with, *'If you're crook, come to cook.'* The bush hospital is now closed but the town still maintains some medical suppliers for emergencies.

There were several other, hand written graffiti signs that made me smile or bewildered me, on the school house there were several signs that seemed like they had no where else to put them, so they thought 'Here's a place, it's as good as any.' The signs included:
Caution speed humps. Cook, ghost city of the Nullarbor. No entry without train control authorisation. Road closed. Shooting prohibited. Trespassers will be prosecuted. And *no food or fuel for 862km Kalgoorlie'* which was 535 miles at the next town along, which makes you realise just how far you are in the middle of nowhere, which made me also think how I would be making sure not to miss the trains departure, it certainly wasn't an area I wanted to be stranded at, and I think the other passengers were thinking the same as no one ventured off very far in our 30 minutes we had to take a look around. We really were in the middle of nowhere and to give you an idea just how remote this town is from civilization, I took the time to find some mileage references, although it was a little tricky as Google maps doesn't even recognise any of the roads around it, so I had to improvise and do a little measuring to get a rough distance. Southwards we were actually relevantly close to the coast at 75 miles, although all that was here was the A1 Eyre Highway, and apart from the odd house there weren't any towns east from this location for another 175 miles. West along this same road you would still see nothing but road until you reached the neighbouring town to Kalgoorlie 500 miles away. Northwards from cook there is only desert and dirt tracks for 400 miles until you reach Uluru.

The sign that I was most drawn to at the school was on a corrugated drum that was as high as the roof at this 2 storey school, a large painted picture of an old man with a bushy grey beard and eyebrows wearing a typical Australian hat, with the a train that most probably symbolised the *Indian Pacific* behind him on the tracks with a hand written sentence. '*Murray Sims. Cooks longest serving railway worker. 28 years, died at Cook.*' Is that a sad life? Living in this desolate town, serving a handful of people passing through on a train a few times a week. Or is it commendable that someone would dedicate their life to helping a major train route at a station that is still very much needed, all be it for 30 minutes at a time. Inside the school it seemed like a quick lick of paint and a clear up, and you could use this as what it was intended for within a day of hard work. And that's the feel I got from most of the buildings here that they had just been abandoned in a hurry, like everything was going fine and then they all said at once 'Grab everything and lets go!'

I walked through the empty town, past the 2 Historical Gaol (jail) cells of Cook, each one was a square corrugated box about 2m (6'6") on each side and 3m (9'9") high with a pyramid hip roof and a very dry, thick wooden door. A small square hole in the door and a small barred window at the top of the door was the only source of light into this confined prison cell, and if the thought of sweating in there for your crime wasn't enough to deter you from wrong doings, the sight of the 50cm (1'7") rusting bolt and thick hinges that looked like they came straight from a castle that implied you would never break out of it, just might make you think again. I carried onto the outer part of the town which only took a few minutes, passing a large garage with a long drop at the back of the yard and 2 old pickups parked neatly, that had obviously been used as spares with a surprisingly small amount of rust eating away at them with most of the tyres still full of air, amazing how the dry desert air can preserve something like this. The buildings abruptly ended into a vast opening for another 25m (82ft) where there was a row of trees and the houses that once held a small community, the landscape stretched off east and west as far as I could see, and this was the only angle side on to the train, approximately 100m (328ft) away that I could get the full picture of the train and the unbelievable size of it, it is so long that I had to take 3 photos side by side and stitch them together to get the full length. I would have liked to spend a day here exploring the old deserted houses and surroundings, maybe even taking the time to try out the grassless 9 hole golf course and take pictures from the possible infinite angles of the countless items on display. 20 minutes after we had arrived, a few people were then making their way back to the train and I was getting a little insecure myself from the distance I was away from it, I could imagine seeing it start to pull away and running with all my might and not making it because I was that far away. So I made my way back to leave this old town behind, it dates back to 1917 when the railway made its first continual link from coast to coast, with the town being named after the 6th Prime Minister Josef Cook. The first trains to complete this transcontinental route took longer due to the difference in track gauges, with passengers having to change trains 5 times because of it. It wasn't until 1970 when the first train made an uninterrupted journey on the standard gauge line from Sydney to Perth, arriving on the 27th of February to a crowd of over 10,000 people.

Back on the train and with everyone accounted for we were underway again, trundling along slowly to start with while we cleared the 1,800m (5,900ft) passing loop, and we were soon up to our usual speed to Kalgoorlie. We set our watches back by 90 minutes at this point, as that would be the time zone we would be in at this next destination where we would be able to get off and have another short time to explore a town. We found out consuming our own alcohol on board was prohibited, a stupid stipulation as this was probably only enforced so they would make more money from selling it to alcohol dependant travellers, which was most of them once they'd been staring at the walls on the same train for 24 hours. But that didn't stop Dale improvising to get into our bottles of wine, by pushing the cork back into the bottle for us, resulting in having to drink the whole bottle otherwise it would have spoiled. The only thing worth mentioning of interest as we watched out of the window beside the odd 4x4 jeep and a surprising amount of green bushes, was that we saw it rain for a short while, making the desert even more uninviting as it turned into a quagmire.

We arrived at Kalgoorlie with no rain at 7.30pm which had a much more civilised undercover platform to get off at, rushing into town to get the most of the 3 hours we would be there. As soon as I cleared the platform I realised that Kalgoorlie was much bigger than I thought and that we were getting back to civilisation and only 367 miles from Perth.

This town has grown considerable since 1893 when the first lucky discovery of gold, by prospectors Patrick Hannan, Tom Flanagan and Dan O'Shea who had stopped in this area after a horse had cast a shoe, while carrying out their repairs they discovered signs of gold and decided to stay. A few months later they filed a reward claim that resulted in hundreds of men swarming to the area. 5 years later that population had grown to 2,000 as more areas of gold were discovered. Today this town has grown to 31,000 people with the gold industry thriving and is home to the multi million dollar Super Pit. This massive hole in the ground that was once several mines has been made into one giant hole 2 miles long by 1 mile wide, and uses some of the most modern and biggest machinery to pull on average 670,000 ounces out of the ground which is 18,994 kg or nearly 19 tons, a weight and value beyond comprehension. This particular mine is estimated to produce this amount until 2017, at which point it will be abandoned and the groundwater allowed to naturally fill it, which will take about 50 years making a man made lake that will be visible from outer space. It's a shame we didn't have a day to learn about this gold mining community as this is one of my interests, I couldn't imagine what it would be like to stand at an open mine this big.

However we only had 3 hours and most of us made a beeline for the bars, I'm sure all the bars and restaurants has a substantial peak in business thanks to the *Indian Pacific*. The first bar that would be profiting from us was a quiet little bar next to Woody's, which Dale would be meeting us in after he'd purchased some wine from Woolworths. After Sharon and I had our half in the quiet bar, Dales idea of the more lively and interesting one seemed much more appealing. We were greeted by many lovely ladies in all types of outfits, some of which were topless with just a small star or heart covering their nipples, I was in my element with these beautiful ladies swanning around much to the delight of Dale and I. Some of the other waitresses were dressed in a particular outfit, one of which I liked especially was the cowgirl outfit who was modelling Daisy Duke shorts that were undone which were so low I can't believe I couldn't see her goodie basket. Dale had his eyes fixed on another waitress that was in a tarty nurses uniform, she was wearing a short white silky dress and lacy red bra and knickers. Dale is usually over confident with women but on this occasion he was showing more than a lack of it, probably because this is his most fantasised outfit, and maybe a little embarrassed that his friends were seeing him in this degree of visual ecstasy, his nerves had got the better of him so he wouldn't ask her for a picture with him. So I got my camera out and Sharon stopped the waitress to ask if she wouldn't mind if we could get a picture of her with our friend. Dale soon overcome his embarrassment once she said yes and jumped up and put his arm around her, I'd hate to think what was going through his mind at that moment that was making him smile so big. We had one more stop at a hotel bar that we initially entered with a genuine intention for another drink, but once inside we realised it was a strip club that was also holding a raffle. We wrongly presumed it was for a free lap dance that I didn't dare be interested in until Sharon said she was ok with it if I wanted to have one, after all you can only look but not touch in this place. Unfortunately like I said the raffle wasn't what we thought and just a general raffle. So we had a drink instead and watched 2 girls dancing very seductively with a little fun mixed in, with one of the girls giving a guy a lap dance and managing to get one of his teeth caught on her outfit. I can't understand why but time had run away with us and it was 10pm, so it was a brisk walk back to the train making it there for 10.20pm with 10 minutes to spare until we would be on the last leg of our journey.

Once we were underway we had a shower that was now starting to smell distinctly like pee, which isn't surprising as there was only 2 toilets for the whole cabin that were under constant use at this time of day. We were then ready for bed and decided to follow Dales lead from the night before where he had a much more comfortable nights sleep than us. We went back a couple of carriages where we found a completely empty carriage that we claimed for the night, we spun one of the seats 180° so there was 2 sets facing each other, using the second set to rest our feet on, giving us much more of a bed like position to sleep in, which made it adequately comfortable that would give us a decent sleep that we hadn't had for the past 2 nights.

Chapter 18
The Final City of our Australian Journey.

Saturday 14*th* May.

Sharon woke first to a glorious sunrise, waking me to ask me for my camera so she could get some pictures. I slowly opened my eyes to become aware of the clickety-clack of the train, that had been constant for the last 9 hours as we were in our deep slumber, it really was a fantastic sight that no picture can ever come close to how it made us feel. The orange glow on the horizon gradually turned to a dark blue the higher it got, that would soon be invaded by daylight and would signify the start of another day where we would be exploring and learning a new place. The glow of the takeover was showing up the silhouettes of the odd tree in the desert as it dashed past our window and into the distance. What a great view to wake up to and by far one of the most memorable and beautiful sights I had seen on this entire train journey, I carried on looking at the horizon, enjoying the view while I dozed a little more as there was nothing to get up for, which was a very unusual luxury that I was taking advantage of. When I did finally rouse myself once the sun had made its appearance, I had some more of the fruit I had bought in Adelaide for breakfast. A short while after this I found out customs were coming through to check travellers bringing fruit into Western Australia, as I had paid for it myself I wasn't going to let someone else take it away because it might contain fruit flies, so I ate the rest of my cache of my daily healthy intake. In hindsight I could have just said I didn't have any, as I'm sure he wouldn't be checking everyone's bag on the off chance, or just let him have the spare apple and banana I had stowed away for later. These laws are in place for a good reason, as all types of fruits can be effected and this is to stop the spread of devastating crop diseases or insects that could wreak havoc across entire farms. I was now full of goodness and energy and ready for the day, after we were given the all clear by the fruit man we got all our possessions together, making sure we were leaving nothing behind as we arrived at the station at Perth at 9.30am.

While standing on the platform feeling rather full of fruit and possibly several fruit flies, waiting for our backpacks to be slung out of the cargo carriage, we had a little commotion on the platform that was a little sad as well as worrying, a 14 year old girl was escorted off by police, we were told by another lady that she thought she had ran away from home and someone had obviously realised this on the train and alerted the authorities, that's one long way to run away to and a desperate measure to go so far, that makes you wonder what the reasons were behind it.

Claiming our baggage we walked towards the city centre, within a few minutes we found more than enough backpacker hostels to choose from about 2 miles from the centre, that had a free train service in to the city, so we decided to stay here and chose one of these hostels, knowing that the ones closer to the centre would be much dearer than the ones on the outskirts. We chose *Rainbow Lodge* that looked ok from the outside for $15 (£6.25) a night. As there were so many hostels in this area and that we would be staying for several nights, making it the longest we had stayed in one place since I started this trip nearly 3 months ago, in the end we managed to beat the price down to $12 (£5) each a night, which made the shock of the cramped, tatty and slightly unclean rooms look a little better for the price we paid. The rooms were very close together, having to walk through another room that had several bunks in to get to our own little room. But we weren't really that worried on the layout, as all we wanted was a place to have a good nights sleep on a bed. We took a quick shower that was in a communal block that we got to in the back courtyard, another cramped facility that worked well enough for the price we were paying and it didn't have a hint of pee smell. After our freshening up we were ready to find out what Perth had to offer while Dale was ready for bed, apparently he didn't have such a good nights sleep for some reason, even though he was adopting the same sleeping position Sharon and I had recommended by him. On the way out we found there was a BBQ being held at the hostel that evening for just $5 (£2.08), how could you go wrong on that! The hostel had many free services with tea and coffee but more importantly information on the city of Perth.

We decided to take in the views and walk the 2 miles to the city centre, it was a pleasant walk as it was a nice warm day with a few clouds to shield us from the full sizzling Australian sun, making it quite comfortable. The walk was a much better idea than the train as we got to see this lovely city for the first time at a much more leisurely pace. Perth is another similar story to many other cities around Australia in its history of settles taking over a piece of land they liked, as it had been inhabited by the *Whadjuk Noongar* people for over 40,000 years, this is dated from archaeological findings on the Swan River that runs through the middle of the city. The slow expulsion of the aborigines started here in 1829 when it was founded by Captain James Stirling, gaining its city status in 1856 which saw a substantial sudden increase in the population from the discovery of gold in the surrounding area. In the early 1900s most of the easy to find gold on the surface was gone and so mining was moved underground, pulling even more gold that was processed at the Perth Mint from 1899, putting the city on the map for potential prospectors for the first go to place when starting out. The city carried on growing to the 1.9 million residents of today that has claimed over 2,079 mi^2 of land. Which I'm sure has pushed all evidence of the indigenous population out.

Our first stop today was *Saint George's cathedral*, which had a striking exterior but not for what you would expect from a cathedral, as this one was unusually built from brick. This cathedral is the principal *Anglican Church of Western Australia* and the mother church of the *Anglican Diocese of Perth*. This Gothic Revival style cathedral is made from local handmade clay bricks from Queens Garden and Victorian blue stone pillars, on footings of Fremantle limestone. It was designed' by Sydney architect Edmund Blacket and consecrated in 1888, built near the site of the first church built in 1829 shortly after Perth was founded. At the time of our visit, a 3 year scheme had been undertaken to extensively renovate the cathedral, which has included the cathedral's castellated bell tower that was damaged in an earthquake in 1968, subsequently earthquake protection has been installed on 2 of the walls. The tiles we had seen it with, have now been replaced with much more cleaner, stylish slate as well as many other renovations inside, along with Burt Hall and the Deanery building that adjoins the cathedral. Inside, the interior walls showed the same bricks as the exterior, making it look much higher as we are all used to seeing much larger blocks for cathedral walls. As the brickwork continued down the cathedral, it forms several arches either side of the nave supported by the blue stone pillars, with bright lights that illuminated under the arches. The high altar was elaborately partitioned by a wrought iron piece of black and gold arches of detailed metalwork, shaped into 3 tiers, with the centre one topped of with 3 arches to mimic the 3 stain glassed windows behind it. We were very lucky this day as the cathedral was being prepared for a wedding, so it was being decorated with flowers, as well as a gentleman singing hymns. He was singing effortlessly and professionally, making himself easily heard throughout the building, on a specially constructed gallery at the West End of the Cathedral above the entrance next to the organ. The West Organ was installed in 1993, and dedicated on Advent Sunday, it has casework made from Tasmanian Oak with burnished tin pipes. The organ has 4 divisions, 48 speaking stops and 3,516 pipes, arranged in several enclosures in a semicircular arrangement to fit round the rose stained glassed window. The organ is one of the largest mechanical-action instruments to be installed in Western Australia, and sounds incredible easily filling the cathedral acoustically.

After a photo shoot of the seagulls that were getting in the way of the exterior of the cathedral, we spotted some bronze sculptures across the road at *Stirling Gardens*. This is Perth's oldest public garden, which was named after Governor James Stirling, originally being used as an acclimatisation garden where many of its mature specimens were raised from seed. Grapes and other important fruits were first grown here, by 1845 it was opened as a botanical garden with some of its original trees that were planted at that time, still stand within the Gardens today. A shallow pool snakes along the front of the lawned garden where 5 life size kangaroos of different heights are standing, each in a different pose, one of which was taking a drink, bending over forwards where I posed along side in almost the same stance for a photo opportunity.

We carried on towards the centre and came across another unexpected series of bronze sculptures that are very unique, with an interesting insight to the recent history of man, commemorating the 175th Anniversary of Western Australia. *The Footsteps in Time* are 5 bronze men that were unveiled outside St Martins Centre in 2004, they symbolise the businesspeople who built this thriving central business district. This site was chosen for these 2m (7ft) sculptures, as it was the location of the first businessman's club of Western Australia. The 5 larger than life characters start with a Dutch explorer, who were responsible for the discovery, mapping and naming of the Swan River from 1697, dressed in what is best known as outlaw clothing. The second man is Anglo Celtic (English), dressed in a top hat and much more presentable clothing who colonised the Swan River settlement which is now known as Perth, from 1829. Next in line were the discoverers of gold, from 1885 which, brought money and people to Western Australia. Second from last is the post, Second World War days from 1945, where the state once again experienced a large influx of people. The last is the modern day man, with a short haircut clutching a mobile phone to his ear and like all the rest, was carrying a bag from that era, with our modern businessman holding a brief case, although I thought he was missing one important piece of modern day clothing, so I tried him out with my sunglasses that finished him off. I took them back once I got his picture, but wonder how long they would have stayed there had I left them on him.

We carried on looking for what we came to see in the first place, a little piece of England nestled between 2 high-rise buildings. London Court has been designed using the architectural features present in 16th century Elizabethan times. Its friendly and inviting atmosphere soon beckoned us in through its portcullis arch into the narrow street of this oldie world street. The front looks like an old English 4 storey building that has those lovely wooden beams fronting it. Above the arch are 2 items that draw your attention, a large gold clock that chimes every 15 minutes, which if I was working in the vicinity would seriously piss me off, having a constant reminder of the time when I'm working will make my day drag! And I'm sure I'm not the only one. The second item above this clock is a static sculpture of George and the dragon, which at the time I was not aware that at the opposite end of the court at the Hay Street entrance, there is a similar sculptured entrance with 4 mechanical knights joust in the window above the clock at every 15 minute chime, known as '*The Tournament of Armoured Knights*'. Icons of past English themes was something of a feature of this court, I suppose it was to make it as English as possible. As we walked into the court we passed under a statue moulded into the entrance on the inside of the court of Dick Whittington and his cat, to see every shop and café in this narrow open air street with striped canopies stretching out over the front of their shops. Every façade adorned the typical look of detailed carved woodwork and Tudor windows comprising of many small panes of glass held in place by lead frames. Many of the shop windows on all floors were decorated with ornate window boxes, with every corner and space filled with crests and gargoyles. We stopped at one of the cafes for an afternoon coffee and take in the atmosphere of a little bit of home, the only thing missing here to make it any more authentic would be a pub and waste water being thrown out of the windows, although no matter how authentic this would be, I'm sure it wouldn't be appreciated in anyway by the people caught in it.

After spending an hour drinking coffee, rabbiting on about nothing and window shopping down the whole arcade, we left via Hay Street totally unaware of the mechanical jousting show as I stopped briefly to get a picture of them, sitting quietly like as if they were meant to be in that position. Like most cities we visit we found the information centre in a pedestrianised square at *Forrest Place*, a box at one end of the square with 2 very helpful people inside ready to direct us to many more places of interest in the area. On our approach a very stoned guy crossed my path and nearly walked into me, quite clear the lights were on but no one was home as a result of something he had ingested, he walked round to the other side and was being helped by the nice and helpful lady that allowed him to use their phone as he had some problem with his bank, and was unable to draw any money out. While his heated conversation was going on, the other very helpful and nice gentleman was finding all sorts of leaflets and filling us with lots of information for us to take away to make our stay here more memorable. Once we had more than enough leaflets to keep our interest, we thanked the guy as we were stuffing them into our bag, at this point stoner guy on the other side had reach his ability to be a thankful citizen to these people that were trying to help him out, as he showed no respect for the phone he was holding or the information centre, as he proceeded to thrash hell out of it with the handset in a fit of rage as he was using just about every swear word under the sun to the person on the other end of the line. I shouted across to him to calm himself down, which I have no idea if he heard or if he cared what I was saying. I really felt for this 2 people of the older generation, they stood in this little room everyday dealing with allsorts of people to get treated like that. Unfortunately the poor woman was so panicked from this mans behaviour she couldn't even uncover the safety switch of the panic button to protect it from accidental pushing. By the second round of the assault to the Perspex window the gentleman that was helping us uncovered the button and pushed it for her. The stoner finished off with one more volley of swearing before he threw the receiver down and left it dangling. Quite frankly if he hadn't stopped there or turned on the helpful people trapped in the box, I would've been inclined to show him what it was like to be on the receiving end of that phone at the same velocity. I couldn't believe how quick the police arrived, stoner guy was still fuming from his unresolved issue strutting away while we were walking in the other direction, when he was accosted by 2 policeman and led off.

We met Dale here for a while as he had been exploring the city by himself, he was most interested by a large stone Kugel ball here, made from granite weighing several tonnes, it is suspended by the power of water pumped from underneath it, creating a thin layer it sits on making it slowly rotate. I became just as interested in it as Dale was and decided to see how fast I could spin it, I pushed on the perfectly rounded and polished sphere, trying to put just the right amount of pressure on it to spin it rather than fall of the slippery surface which didn't work out every time as I intended, I got it up to a fair speed that naturally kept turning at this speed for sometime, still spinning as we walked away a few minutes later.

We left Dale once again as *Heirisson Island* wasn't high on his list of places to visit in Perth, a place to finish off the day until it got dark, brought to our attention by the lovely info people. A 2 mile walk towards the Swan River and we were at *Heirisson Island*, accessed by the Causeway that links East Perth and *Victoria Park*. The island sits in the middle of the river and occupies and area of 285,600m^2 (3,074,000ft^2) making the island 1,200m (3,937ft) long and 300m (984ft) wide. Prior to development, it was originally 2 islands surrounded by mud flats, which has been made into a single island over the years from dredging and reclamation. We entered the island through a secure gate that came apparent why it was a sealed enclosure shortly after we arrived, as we started our walk on the 1.2 mile path round the island. We soon came across these inhabitants of the southern part of the island, to see several Grey Kangaroos hopping around that have been introduced to the park. We sat there for quite sometime peaking at them through the trees and bushes as they merrily hopped about leisurely eating.

After we had sufficient viewing time of the roos, we explored a little more, finding many strange budding flowers, my favourite being the bright red pompom looking flower with yellow tips known as a *Eucalyptus Macrocarpa* or *Mottlecah*, which is a native of Western Australia. We also found the statue of a naked man with a spear across his shoulders, this statue is one of controversy, and sadness, it is of a Noongar leader Yagan. Yagan was responsible for leading the Aboriginal resistance against European settlement of Western Australia in the early 1800s, after a string conflicts mostly from the settlers fencing off their lands and hunting grounds, in turn the Aborigine stole food and livestock from the settlers to survive. After several more run ins with the law, Yagan was exiled to an uninhabited island, from which he escaped from and declared outlaw. That same year he was killed in 1833 and decapitated, his head was smoked to be preserved, then taken to England where it was exhibited at private parties and at the *Liverpool Royal Institution*. The head was kept in the Liverpool Museum's storage until 1964 when someone started to think along the right lines of humanity, with it being buried in an unmarked grave. It stayed there until a group of Aboriginal Elders, led by Ken Colbung wanted to rebury the head with Yagan's body and demanded Yagan's remains to be returned to his homeland. In 1997 Yagan's head was exhumed and finally returned home, but to date the head has not been buried, as all efforts have failed to locate the body of Yagan.

During the mid 1970's the Noongar community lobbied for a statue to be created as part of the 1979 sesquicentennial celebrations (150 years) in Western Australia. The advise by a local historian was that Yagan was not important enough, the then Premier of Western Australia, Sir Charles Court, denied the request. But the Noongar community would have their way and set up a Yagan committee and began fund raising themselves, eventually raising enough money to commission local artist and sculptor Robert Hitchcock to design a statue and was unveiled on 11th of September 1984, by Yagan Committee chairperson Elizabeth Hanson, in honour of Yagan who was a prominent Noongar leader.

Unfortunately that is not where this sad story ends, a week after Yagan's head was returned to Perth, an anonymous vandal who claimed to be a *British Loyalist*, beheaded the statue of Yagan and stole its head. The statue, was restored only to be beheaded a second time in 2002.

Our walk finished by one of the lakes on the island that strangely has an island in the middle of it, we saw a heron here in the failing light sitting on one of the fences by the water, seeing a second a little further on which is where I saw a rare photo opportunity unfolding as it began to take off. I knew it would have a hard job getting airborne quickly with its 2m (6'6") wingspan, so I ran further on to get a picture just in time of the big heron flying low, almost touching its wingtips in the water reflecting nicely on the almost still lake. We walked along the shore on our way out of the park to find several jellyfish in various degrees of lifelessness, deciding to rescue a few by flipping them back in the water with some empty shells, in the unlikely possibility they did still have some life in them.

We had an uneventful walk back to the hostel to meet Dale again, and for our long awaited BBQ that was way more filling and more than I could eat. I stuffed myself of hotdogs, burgers and potato bake while we wrote our journals. They also had a few boxes of red wine to go with our BBQ, while one of the owners served up a glass of Australia's best cheapest wine for us, a fly landed on his face to which he frantically tried to waft away. "Those dirty fucking things," he began quite angrily "probably just came from a dirty niggers arse and now it's on my face!"

I couldn't believe the strength of his racism, stemming from a few in the area that were renown for being very dirty, smelly and drunk most evenings, small pockets like this is something that is common to find in most cities, it was unfortunate that they had made a bad name for themselves here, as we were also warned not to walk the back roads at night as these characters would sure to cause trouble for us if we did.

After this bellyful of meat we were ready to hit the nightlife at our first night in Perth, Sharon had heard of a bar called *Guitar Legends* that sounded good to me, but we were soon turned away because our sandals did not fit in with their dress code, with the only other type of footwear we had were trainers that weren't eligible either, we had no chance of us getting in. So we relented and joined the rest of the hostel at *Black Betty's*. Dale commented on us being mad as soon as he saw us, coming to a place like this with open toed shoes, which he must have had much more experience than us on this matter as we soon found out how many times your toes get trod on in a place as packed as this. We paid $5 (£2.03) with a coupon from our hostel, this allowed us a jug of beer that worked out to about a pint and a half, making it a fantastic price. The second fantastic item here was the band, who were a rock band playing covers extremely well at ear blistering level, they pulled off several greats such as *Franz Ferdinand, Metallica* and *Bryan Adams*. It was a real spit and sawdust establishment, with a sticky floor and chain link fences to partition several parts, and getting a drink took guts and determination, having to fight your way through several rows of people. Looking back I can see why it ended up being the most violent venue in the area, but that's what made this place so appealing and memorable. The night was quite uneventful with plenty thrashing about on the dance floor enjoying the music. As the venue came to a close the band was thanked by the lead singer, as they were all playing a line that loosely sounded like something else, the singer thanked each one in turn who then gave a blast of their own rendition of the song they were all playing, as he got through them finishing on the drums, I was sure one more song was coming as I a distinct suspicion they were going to break into the song Black Betty, which is one of my favourite rock songs. Sure enough as they finished playing their small part they broke into Black Betty in the style of Ram Jam, and it was truly awesome and probably one of the most memorable songs played by a band on my 6 month tour! This song marked the end of the evening ending in a flood of lights on the stage and a massive cheer from the entire venue, the clubs lights then came on showing how tacky this place really was as we left to head back to our hostel as it was now past midnight and we'd covered a good deal of Perth on our first day here.

On our walk back, avoiding the back roads we came across the strictness of drinking in the streets, as one chap found out drinking his last bottle of beer of the evening on his way home, to be stopped by the police and having it tipped out into the gutter. Getting back to our hostel we found no one there, thinking we'd get off to sleep much quicker being quieter that usual. But our last challenge of the day being tired from our long day and a little drunk, was to find the light switch, how hard could it be? Well quite difficult to us, after a few minutes of searching the walls in and around our room I gave up and took the florescent tube out and stood it in the corner.

Sunday 15th May.

My trusty digital watch woke us at 8am, as we wanted an early start, knowing Perth had much more to offer. We started off with a shower to wake us up before we had our complementary breakfast of toast, jam and coffee with my first malaria tablet. We were then ready for the day but Dale wouldn't be joining us for a second day, as he was still worrying about his eyesight and had an eye test at lunchtime, so we left him to explore the neighbouring town of Fremantle by ourselves where we would be spending most of the day. With me dawdling to the train station meant we had to run to catch the train as it had that look it was about to leave, but the very nice new Ford Falcon pick up truck was a must for me to get a picture of, as I had owned an older version myself in the UK 3 years before. The train took us southwards about 15 miles in a relatively short time to a little town on the coast, known for it having the largest collection of heritage listed buildings and also as the world's best preserved example of a 19th century port.

Our first item in this historic town was the indoor public market, that was packed with people most probably because it had started to rain, with the odd busker and over 150 stalls, all crammed into this building that's over 100 years old that one way or another has always been the scene of market sales, with trees growing in it what peeked through the few openings in the roof. The stalls were on top of each other selling their wares of every type, attracting all kinds of people for their needs such as clothing, jewellery, souvenirs, home goods, fresh food produce, vegetables and many internationally prepared foods from Turkey, Japan, Vietnam, French and of course more local foods to which I went for. I had been feeling ill all morning from what I thought was a mixture of alcohol, hunger and late nights, it took until I had consumed my lunch to realise it was the malaria tablet I had taken that morning making me feel so queasy, something I was hoping to get more accustomed to soon. We searched through the stalls looking for nothing in particular, with a few items really grabbing my attention. A stall selling prints of all sorts was one stall I liked, as there were several scenes of large old sailing ships being tossed about by high seas. Another item that interested both Sharon and I was a stall selling small polished stones that were harbouring a

fossil, we were amazed at this little spiralled shelled fossil that was supposedly 350 million years old. We couldn't help ourselves and we picked each one up carefully to feel the contours of the stone, it was fabulous to think I was holding something so old. We were having a great time until the owner of the stall spotted us among the crowd and asked if we had seen the sign, "Yeah, a little expensive." was my reply,
"No, the other one that says do not touch!" he said rather abruptly.
We had completely missed that one in our excitement and put them down immediately and made a hasty exit. In a place that was packed with items supposedly so expensive, it was a little silly in my opinion having them in the open like that. Not just from imbeciles like myself but it could have easily been knocked on the floor as it was so precariously placed, not forgetting the incredible value of them that would make them an easy target to thieves. Some years later I found they were extortionately overpriced as I could get the same thing off eBay for £50 instead of the few thousand this guy was asking.

After our hasty getaway we visited the *Western Australian Museum - Shipwreck Galleries,* this is a maritime museum that is recognised as the foremost maritime archaeology museum in the southern hemisphere. Housed in an 1850s commissariat building that has been restored to its former glory, the gallery houses over 24,000 relics from ships wrecked along Western Australia's treacherous coastline, and has done for 120 years. Ships and boats are one of my favourite pastimes, owning a 3 man sailing dingy myself as a teenager, I have also sailed many different types from a one man sailing dingy to a wherry, and I have also been on many powered boats from a 2 man speed boat to a luxury cruise liner, I have a natural calling to all things that float and very much enjoy them. So the 2 hours we spent here was definitely a favourite of mine and with a $2 (83p) entrance fee, it was a no brainer. One of the first permanent exhibits we came across in the entrance was an anchor that is stood up on end, and is so tall it occupies 2 floors. It belonged to the *Trial,* captained by James Brookes and is the earliest known ship to have been wrecked in Australian waters. There are many factual accounts of this ship even though it came to its end so long ago on the 24th of May 1622, as 44 crew members made it to safety in a lifeboat and a skiff, leaving the remaining 93 to perish as the boat broke up and sank on a reef, now known as *Ritchie's Reef,* which contain the infamous *Trial*

Rocks. Captain James Brookes wrecked his ship from a navigational error whilst following a new course, *'The Brouwer's Route'* to the Indies, by sailing too far east. Dirk Hartog made this same mistake of sailing too far east along this same route a few years earlier, as a result he was the first explorer to have discovered the west coast of Australia.

Although four museum expeditions have visited the site of the remains of the *Trial* since the discovery in 1969, no evidence has been found to identify the site conclusively, although circumstantial evidence indicates that the wreck site is that of the *Trial*. In total only 20 items have been recovered from the wreck site of mostly anchors and canons, with no sign of the rest of the ship that had a cargo capacity of 500tons.

The *Woodblock Gallery* is dedicated to artefacts, charts, documents and books from Australia's early Dutch explorers and their journeys of Dirk Hartog through to Willem de Vlamingh, showcasing 100 years of Dutch explorations of Australia. On display in glass cabinets are several replica galleon ships about a metre long (3'3") complete with rigging, sails, canon, anchors and finished to a high detailed, some of which were 400 years old. The *Woodblock Gallery* also features the *Willem de Vlamingh Plate* that commemorates *Dirk Hartog's plate,* these plates are one of the most historic items of the discovery of Australia and the oldest known written artefact from Australia's European history. Once Dirk Hartog discovered Australia, he spent three days examining the coast and nearby islands. When he left, he affixed a 36.5cm (1'2") pewter plate to a post, on the plate he had etched a record of his visit to the island. Its inscription translated from Dutch for the ease of us people who are not fluent in the language read;

1616. On the 25th October the ship Eendracht of Amsterdam arrived here. Upper merchant Gilles Miebais of Luick (Liege); skipper Dirck Hatichs (Dirk Hartog) of Amsterdam. On the 27th ditto we sail for Bantum. Under merchant Jan Stins; upper steerman Pieter Doores of Bil (Brielle). In the year 1616.

The Dutch Captain Willem de Vlamingh left Holland to search for the *Ridderschap van Holland,* a VOC ship lost en route to Batavia. (VOC is abbreviated from *Dutch East India Company,* the translation from its

Dutch name is, *Vereenigde Oost-Indische Compagnie*.) Willem de Vlamingh was also to chart the southwest coast of New Holland, as Australia was then known, to improve navigation for merchant shipping. When he landed at the same spot and found *Dirk Hartog's Plate*, though the plate was badly weathered and the post had almost rotted away, Willem de Vlamingh copied the record on to another plate, added his own inscription and nailed the plate to a new post that he erected. Willem de Vlamingh then took the *Hartog's plate* to return it back to the Netherlands.

Willem de Vlamingh's inscription added to Dirk Hartog's read;

1697 The 4th February is here arrived the ship The Geelvinck for Amsterdam. The Commodore and Skipper Willem De Vlamingh of Vlielandt, Assistant Joannes Bremer of Copenhagen Upper Steersman Michil Bloem of The Bishopric of Bremen The Hooker The Nyptangh Skipper Gerrit Colaart of Amsterdam Assit Theodoris Heirmans Ditto Upper Steersman Gerrit Geritson of Bremen The Galliot The Weeseltie Commander Cornelis De Vlamingh of Vlielandt Steerman Coert Gerritsen of Bremen Sailed from Here with our fleet the also The Southland Further to Explore and Bound for Batavia.

The original *Hartog Plate* is on display in the *Rijksmuseum* in the Netherlands. The *Vlamingh Plate* was later removed by French explorer, Lois de Freycinet in 1827 and the French government presented the plate back to Australia on the 28th of May 1947.

This section also displays a replica of the original *Pelsaert's journal*, which documented the horror of the *Batavia* mutiny. The *Batavia Gallery* is the centrepiece of the Shipwreck Galleries, housing the reconstructed remains of the VOC ship *Batavia*, excavated by archaeologists in the 1970s. There is an elevated viewing deck to look down inside the stern of the *Batavia*, which gives you a real perspective of the size of this once magnificent ship. The history of the *Batavia* is a very interesting one, made famous by the subsequent mutiny and massacre that took place among the survivors, and the ships demise. It was the VOC's flagship from Holland on her maiden voyage to the East Indies and sailed under the command of Francisco Pelsaert, a very experienced merchant. The ship of 57m (186ft) and 650ton cargo capacity was carrying among other items, silver coins, antiquities and a prefabricated sandstone blocks for a portico Façade to be erected as a gatehouse in the city of Batavia. There are many factors that came into play on the fateful voyage until it struck *Houtman Abrolhos* on the 4th of June 1629, a group of 122 islands near the west coast of Australia about 300 miles north of Perth. Most of the 322 crewmembers managed to get ashore the island with about 40 crewmembers drowning. As food and water was very limited, some of the passengers along with the captain made a failed attempt to find fresh water on the mainland in a 9m (33ft) longboat, after their unsuccessful attempt they abandoned the other survivors and headed north, in a danger-fraught voyage to the city of Batavia, now known as Jakarta, a journey which ranks as one of the greatest feats of navigation in an open boat. Batavia's Governor General Jan Coen, immediately gave Pelsaert command of the *Sardam* to rescue the other survivors, as well as to attempt to salvage any riches from the *Batavia*'s wreck. It was 2 months after leaving the crew, did they arrive back at the island, only to discover that a bloody mutiny had taken place amongst the survivors, reducing their numbers by at least a hundred.

After the ship was found and raised, an extensive treatment and restoration process took place, taking a few years, the remains of the ship's stern were rebuilt in this gallery. The water logged look has been preserved in this process and has been re-assembled perfectly, showing the rear section of several metres long and about 6m (19ft) high with each plank of wood slotted together as it had been when it was built over 400 years before. This part of a ship is all held together by a metal frame with the rear section mostly accounted for and slowly diminishes further forward like the front has been snapped off. This gallery also featured a skeleton of one of the people murdered on the Abrolhos Islands, a replica of the impressive portico façade that was carried as cargo to be used as a grand entrance to the city of Batavia, a reconstruction of the Captain's cabin and numerous other artefacts recovered from the wreck.

Other parts of the museum included many more artefacts from the Dutch shipwrecks *Zuytdorp, Zeewijk* and *Vergulde Draeck*. Another really great experience we were fortunate enough to be able to do was to handle several artefacts, thanks to the help of an employee who talked for sometime with us. She presented us with some of those thin white gloves you see in any documentary where someone is holding or touching something incredibly old, which made the first item of a canon ball all the more challenging to keep a hold of, with other items much easier to hold were of wood, coal and nails.

By the time we left it was raining much harder and it was time for dinner, taking shelter in the fish and chip shop *Cicerello's*. This must be one of the most interesting fish and chip shops in the whole world and not to mention incredibly busy. It has been an iconic eatery in Fremantle since its founding in 1903. It isn't so popular and interesting just for the large variety on the menu of items such as Battamundi, local Garfish, muscles, local chilli crab, prawns and oysters. What attracted me the most along with every single customer that passed through, was the row of fish tanks at least 12m (39ft) long that separates the queue from the restaurant seating area, that is home to over 50 species of tropical fish all from the Fremantle area. It was a visual overload to see so many colourful and interesting fish, such as a sea snake over 2m (6'6") long that was completely yellow with a black fin that ran the full length of its body that looked nasty and pissed off. There were large round fish, small shoals of fish, Nemo and Dori were there, more commonly known as a clown fish and a regal blue tang fish, crabs, lobsters, starfish and even a shark. The fish and chips were really good too. But as I sat there I couldn't help but think if we was being cruel, happily eating fish in front of fish. Lets take a moment to understand what I was thinking. Imagine that by some strange quirk of an alternate reality, humans were caught and put into captivity for the viewing pleasure of some creature that has a much higher intelligence, as well as higher on the food chain than us humans, in their restaurants while they ate another human being! A little bit of a strange thought but a thought none the less that makes you think, what if… Well, the what if probably doesn't apply here as fish don't recognise such things as battered plaice as part of their own kind, or have a consciousness like that of us humans.

We took the same trip back to Perth and despite the rain that had turned to a light drizzle, we went to the *Supreme Court Gardens* as there was a celebration that is observed and held here in Perth every year, the *Buddha's Birthday and Multicultural Festival*. Buddha's birthday is held on the 8th day of the 4th month in the Chinese lunar calendar, typically only observed in East Asian countries, but we were lucky enough to be part of it this year and would become another one of those memorable moments of my travelling, that left me thinking and feeling a huge connection to a culture. Not only were there Asian cultures celebrating this day, but also many other cultures as well as a large proportion of Australians of all ages.

We walked around the many oriental stalls selling all sorts of items related to this culture, with several stalls making items such as hats, animals and grasshoppers all made from a simple palm leaf. There was also a bouncy castle, a big wheel, miniature pagodas, foods from many Asian countries and the centre piece of Buddha, sat high undercover with strings of Chinese lanterns hanging down each corner of this high portable undercover building. Buddha was sat at the back among several tiers that had items of fruits, vases, books, ornaments and flowers on them. But the main item here that was getting the most attention was the several statues along the front of miniature infant Buddha's, this ceremonial item was *'the Bathing of the Buddha'*. Since ancient times, Buddhists all over the world celebrate Buddha's birthday by using fragrant water to bathe the image of the infant Buddha. There is great significance in the act as the fragrant water is poured over the statue of the infant Buddha three times. It symbolizes the cleansing of our body, speech and thoughts to eradicate anger, greed and ignorance in order to purify our minds, to cultivate merits and wisdom. This ritual performed with reverence and a purified mind is said to improve harmony and inner balance, leading to a flourishing, fulfilling, blissfull and enlightened life. It was something that I found very interesting, and in the moment being surrounded by religion and the people who obviously very much believed in it, I would have like to have participated in it to feel what it was like and be a part of it, to take a part of this religion and be involved in such a spiritual ritual. But it was not my religion and I would have felt I was not only being unfaithful to my own, but I would also be participating in a religious act that I would not have whole heartedly believed in, making me feel I may be insulting the Buddhist religion. But the flipside to that is being a multicultural person and accepting and experiencing other peoples ways of life. Instead I stood there on the water logged park, with soaking wet feet appreciating what I was seeing of those who were engaging in this lovely sight.

Nothing much was happening at this point and it started to rain heavier, so we went across the road to The *Lucky Shag* pub to shelter from the rain until the festival livened up, while we had a beer and caught up on our journals. By 5.30pm it had almost stopped raining so we went back to the park to hear the most professional voice singing, once we found the source of it we found it was coming from a 10 year old girl. This part of the celebrations was more multicultural with different groups singing, one of which would have a profound effect on me along with most of the people watching, something I really wasn't expecting. A group of 4 women of 2 young girls in their early teens and 2 older girls in their 20's who sang beautifully. The song they were singing was *'I am Australian'* made famous by The *Seekers,* which has become unofficially Australia's national anthem after it was one of the contenders, being beat by *'Advance Australia Fair'*. After hearing both versions I think *I am Australian* is more relevant to the modern day Australians. I have gone into great detail in this book so far on the Aborigine race and the first European explorers. I would like to take this opportunity in this book, along with the lyrics to this song to acknowledge the modern Australian and who they are.

Man has an insatiable urge to travel, explore and find out the unknown, from the deepest ocean to the furthest reaches of outer space, and exploration in this manner is no different to the earliest man, and how the Aborigines came to be the first settlers over 40,000 years ago in Australia. The first point in modern Australia that signified the beginning of Australia as we know it today, was the landing of the European settles, the first verse of the song is dedicated to the Aborigine race at this time;

I came from the dream time, from the dusty red soil plains,
I am the ancient heart - the keeper of the flame,
I stood upon the rocky shore, I watched the tall ships come,
For forty thousand years I'd been the first Australian.

The first verse needs very little explanation of the meaning to the words in it, it evokes thoughts of the spiritual aborigine's being the real discoverers of Australia who had claimed it a long time ago when it was uninhabited. Several European explorers sailed to different parts of Australia in the 17th century and mapped out and documented much of the coastline. It wasn't until 1770 that Captain James Cook chartered the east coast and claimed it for Britain that the exploration of Australia really started. This new outpost was soon put to use as a penal colony and on the 26th of January 1788, the first fleet of 11 ships carrying 1,500 people, half of them convicts arrived in Sydney Harbour who had committed a wide range of crimes from stealing an orange to murder and high treason. Penal transportation ended after 80 years once 160,000 convicts had been deposited on the shores of Australia.

The free settlers began to flow into the country from the early 1790's while the 1000's of prisoners had an extremely harsh life with re-offenders brutally flogged and could be hung for something as petty as stealing. Female prisoners were outnumbered 5 to 1 and lived with constant sexual exploitation. By the 1820's soldiers, officers and convicts turned land they had received by the government into flourishing farms. It wasn't long before the news of this new land spread across the world that had cheap land and bountiful work brought more and more boatloads of migrants.

The second verse refers to this part of the Australian history;

I came upon the prison ship bound down by iron chains,
I cleared the land, endured the lash and waited for the rains.
I'm a settler, I'm a farmer's wife on a dry and barren run,
A convict then a free man, I became Australian.

The first line really made me think about the 1000's that had been shipped here for something as petty as stealing food, most probably because they were starving or to feed their family. For this they were shipped across the world to serve their sentence, only to be let go into the land they had been dragged to with no way of getting home, making this their new home. It's amazing that the Australian population turned out to be such a diverse and good willed group of citizens, from a large portion of them in the beginning being built from convicts once they had served their time, along with migrants that flooded here on a whim for a better and easier life, many coming from a deprived country or lifestyle themselves as the cost of emigrating was very low. At this time it wasn't an easy life and the work was hard with many failures, but for the ones that worked the hardest were rewarded the most and did very well.

Gold was first discovered in central Victoria in 1851, which lured thousands of adventurous young men and women, from colonies all over Australia. This also soon paved the way for prospectors from nationalities all over the world to find their riches, bringing gold fever, wealth and an economic boom. The country had grown so big by 1901, Australia's 6 states became a nation under a single constitution, gaining independence.

The *First World War* had a devastating effect on the population, as at the time there was only 3 million men in Australia with 400,000 of them volunteered, with an estimated 60,000 of them dying in battle. From this in the 1920's there was a big increase in cars, cinema and music, until it peaked resulting in the *Great Depression* that lasted 3 years from 1929, by which time 32% of Australians were unemployed. The recovery of this depression was not fully resolved in some working roles until the 1940's. Since then, Australia has shown a dramatic increase in their economy with more migrants arriving from the Middle East and Europe, demand grew and carried on to grow for their exports of metals, woods, meats and wheat.

The third verse has many references to this part of its history showing the diversity in Australia;

I'm the daughter of a digger who sought the mother lode,
The girl became a woman on the long and dusty road,
I'm a child of the depression, I saw the good times come,
I'm a bushy, I'm a battler, I am Australian.

The last line in this verse refers to all working classes that are seen as the same, the opposites of working people, from someone who works in the bush (*bushy*) to the working class in the cities (*battler*) who feel they must work hard at a low paying job to earn enough money.

The 4th verse is dedicated to some of the Australian greats that made this country what it is today, and shows how historically interesting Australia is, and they are remembered in this verse;

I'm a teller of stories, I'm a singer of songs,
I am Albert Namatjira, and I paint the ghostly gums,
I am Clancy on his horse, I'm Ned Kelly on the run,
I'm the one who waltzed Matilda, I am Australian.

Teller of stories is most probably from the countless accounts of riches, hero's and historical events from the modern Australia, and maybe also referred to the Aborigines *dreamtime* and the many stories of the creation of certain areas and mythical creatures

Albert Namatjira was one of the most talented Aborigine artists. If you were paying attention at Alice Springs you will know this anyway.

Clancy is a drover (cattle driver), and a city office worker who longs for the bush, an all round good helpful guy and an excellent horseman as depicted in the poem, *The Man From Snowy River (1890)*.

Ned Kelly is one of the most renowned outlaws who came to his death by hanging in 1880, for a string of offences of stealing cattle and horses, dating back for most of his life, many of which he had served time for. His end came after one of the largest manhunts, after a failed arrest by Constable Fitzpatrick on his brother for cattle rustling to which Ned supposedly shot at the arresting officer, even though he wasn't at homestead at the time, Fitzpatrick then accused the rest of the family of assaulting him, and it seems most probable there is a great deal of false allegations by the constable in question, as in later years he was dismissed by the force for being a liar. From this action, the 2 brothers went on the run and were joined by 2 friends Joe Byrne and Steve Hart for 2 years, who swore revenge and became to be known as the *Kelly Gang*, who committing bank robberies and murder to add to their list of offences and securing an £8,000 bounty upon them.

I'm the one who waltzed Matilda refers to the song *Waltzing Matilda*, another contender for the Australian national anthem. The phrase Waltzing Matilda is believed to originate with German immigrants, derived from the term '*auf der walz*' which means to travel while learning a trade. Waltzing Matilda came to mean to travel from place to place in search of work with all one's belongings wrapped in a blanket or cloth on your back, as in the first line of the song that talks about a *swagman* who is a drifter.

The 5th and final verse is reference to the diverse Australian environment and the extreme opposites that is respected and embraced by all Australians;

I'm the hot wind from the desert, I'm the black soil of the plains,
I'm the mountains and the valleys, I'm the drought and flooding rains,
I am the rock, I am the sky, the rivers when they run.
The spirit of this great land, I am Australian.

The chorus that is sung through out this song;

We are one but we are many,
And from all the lands on earth we come,
We share a dream,
And sing with one voice,
I am, you are, we are Australian.

I found this chorus to be of great importance and full of meaning despite its simplicity. No matter what nationality you are, you too can be part of the Australian community and belong to it while being accepted yourself, and conveys a great sense of belonging and individuality from the people who have moved here from all over the world. It shows the joining of the same goal in life and to become one.

I couldn't believe that I had been all round Australia and it took until this point, hearing this song that made me realise the hardship and unison of this country, what it took to build this nation of some 200 nationalities and has grown to a population of over 23 million. The atmosphere we had been embracing this evening, on such an event had made me feel a little more religious and caring than I would usually be, I felt a little saddened from the words of this song with the hardship, but enlightened and happy on other parts of it and to see the many cultures around me joining in with this celebration. Like myself, most of the other people were silent just listening to this song, even though it had started to rain again.

A short while later it was time for the performance of the Chinese Lion Dancers where the girls had been singing. The first record of this type of performance, is a form of the Lion Dance that dates back to the early Ch'in and Han Dynasties (Third Century B.C.) The dancing lions express joy and happiness, and in traditional China lion dance groups would tour from village to village. The Chinese Southern Lions we were seeing today were 2 men suits that were very elaborate and highly detailed, each costume was lavished in a different groups of bright colours which denotes a different age, with white fur being the oldest and black being the youngest, they would move in speed and agility according to their age. Their fluffy fur ran from front to back in waves along its body to its tail where it was shook and waved by the guy at the rear in time with the music, with the front man holding his arms up to control the head, manipulating the mouth, eyes and eye lids. The show was fantastic to say the least, held in front of the Buddha stage, they danced on a wooden black tile platform that was glistening in the lights as it was now dark and still very wet. The 3 lions danced to music performed live by several men behind them, with drums and symbols of various sizes that somehow made an endless array of notes and tunes that seemed to merge into the dances of the lions and become one. Each lion danced, jumped and span with martial arts characteristics and precision, not putting a foot wrong, or slipping on the wet platform or bumping into each other. The glistening black stage had become reflective under the bright lights that added to the majestic dancing. The lions moved uncannily, mimicking animal traits as the head were lifted high and low, while moving it in all directions, as the music became faster the lions danced in a more frenzied way, accentuating the lines of curved fur that moved naturally, with exerted thrashes of movement from the head or body in time with the loud crash of the symbols. At parts of the performance the music would stop, bringing each lion to a different pose that then looked round the audience, clacked its mouth shut and blinked a few times before it sprang into life again as the music started. The most amazing part of this act that intrigues me was how well they danced in these costumes, as their field of view must be seriously obstructed but they still managed to dance in time with each other, as well as with the other 2 lions.

We carried on our religious path for the evening with the *bathing of the Buddha* and *world peace prayer*, that we wanted to participated in. The diverse faith groups took turns to say a prayer while everyone of us was holding a small tea light candle held in a small bowl, that reflects everyone united as one in peace and harmony of all the different societies, not just here but the world over. It was, a very enlightening experience that change my understanding of faith a little, to be able to feel and understand another religion a little more.

There was another drop in activity at this point as they prepared for the last part of the celebrations. We took this time to use the public toilets and try to find a little shelter while we waited, which we found at the side of the toilet block that had a slight overhang. We stood there for several minutes looking at a broken umbrella lying on the ground, before I thought I'd claim it for myself that I attempted to fix. After some degree of success we braved the soggy field once again in time for the fireworks, because of the extreme damp it produced a lot of smoke but we could see enough to enjoy it, with it finishing with a volley of large rockets screeching high into the air that seemed to go on forever.

After the fireworks, drenched and a little cold we made our way to the train station for a dry, short trip back to the hostel. We grabbed our washbags as soon as we arrived back for a long, hot, warming shower to wash away the evenings unpleasantness of the cold rain and to also wash our unpleasant sandals as they were in a bit of a state from standing on a boggy field for most of the evening. Warmed up and clean we slipped into bed for a well deserved rest after another tiring day that for a good part of it, had been spent on our feet, and once again falling into a deep sleep quickly.

Monday 16th May.

We initially slept ok for the first 3 hours until Dale had came in and woke us, saying something about booking the TV to watch a match at this early hour between Norwich and Fulham. Norwich lost 6 – 0 which we couldn't have cared less about, as we were already asleep again before he left the room. We woke again at 8:30am to hear it still raining hard, we looked at each other and both had the same idea and went back to sleep without saying a word until 9:30am. We all met in the hostels café for our toast and coffees before we went out into the now fresh city, after the rain had finally stopped. Strolling down the main road we came across a house that was more unusual than most, in fact, I don't think I have ever seen anything like it and probably never will again. A man had been feverously slapping paint on various pieces of wood, cardboard and plates writing warning signs that made him seem a little more than eccentric, this also stirred wonderings in our minds to what had made him write these strange captions. Most of the signs revolved around being warned by *Frederick (or big Dick) and big John*. Other warnings read;

Watch out for the big cat, he danger, you been warned.
Beware of the snake, you been warned.
Beware of the giant, you been warned.
Been ware of the gorilla, you been warned.
John got eyes on you, watch out, you been warned by the cops.
Bathroom seating capacity for one, Frederick.

As you can see he really wanted to warn somebody, but there were other slightly less stranger notices of *god bless Australian Frederick*, and *keeping Perth cleaning Australia Fred.* There must have been 50 of these signs that all differed from each other and were growing each day, filling every space possible. This guy had some grievance and was something we weren't going to get too involved with, and so took our pictures to remember this strange spectacle of information and moved on into the city. As we neared the centre we walked past a bus stop on the other side of the road that was occupied by several Aborigines, one broke away from the rest and approached us. The general description of this type of homeless Aborigine I had been given by many locals all over Australia, did not portray them in the best light. I took the advice and was just cautious when in their presence, and really I wasn't all that worried. I think the problem really stems from the Aborigines being westernised and introduced to alcohol, contrary to public perception Aborigines do not have an intolerance to alcohol, surveys have in fact found that proportionally fewer Aboriginal people drink alcohol than whites do, but they are more likely to drink at more higher levels of dangerous quantities, leading to this misconception. The belief there is more by percentage unemployed of indigenous than non-indigenous people are true, a figure that changes from year to year depending on economic growth, but this is an unfair observation to make, as I have said before, if it wasn't for the interference of the white colonist 250 years ago, 100% of Aborigines would still be unemployed and living off the land. Western society pushed them into this lifestyle by taking their land and obstructing their nomadic ways that were imperative to the survival of this way of life. Most of them had no choice but to live a modernised life that I think as a culture wasn't ready for, something that may be missed by many people. It is nice to hear though that even the Aborigine office workers will still go bush from time to time, especially in times of spiritual significance. The Aborigine that approached me today was obviously unemployed and from a poor background, as his clothes were a bit tatty and in desperate need of a wash, but he approached us with a cheerful face and an inviting smile. He started with, "Don't worry I don't want any money, I would just like one straight tailor made." poor guy was only looking for a little treat for himself, and was maybe quite unhappy at his employment status, many people may have been abrupt or scared at his appearance. I just smiled back and replied, "Sorry, non of us smoke I'm afraid." he was quite happy with my reply and went back to his friends. Looking back I wish I had gone and bought him a pack of cigarettes for a bribe, to chat to them to hear about this part of Aborigine life.

  We carried on to our original destination that was the Perth *Art Gallery of Western Australia,* which Dale decided he was going to join us, a place he hadn't been to with Sharon and I many times, as he had been to so many places similar to this and had got quite bored of paintings and arts, I always saw it myself as an opportunity to see an insight into that cultures artistic history, and the further I got into my travelling, the more I wanted to go to these places. There were many different artists at this gallery, with a large section that was Aborigine, a style that I had now came to recognise. Other works that caught my interest was a bunch of pencil drawings, one style had been drawn in pencil and then rubbed out, creating impressions and shading on the paper, to be finished by drawing over it once again. We were reminded a little bit of home too as there was a British section, one of which was by an artist 'Robert Bagge Scott' that lived and worked in my home city of Norwich, a painting of large sailing boats off shore with people waving them off from the beach. The gallery went on forever, finding more rooms and buildings, we then found there was an upstairs that showed a series of courtrooms, holding cells and offices. There was also a collection of art from the late 19th century to early 20th century, as well as prints from a much more recent time of the 60's. One of the several rooms we explored left us wondering what it was all about, it was a room with a bench in it, and that was it. We took a seat and stared at the wall for a moment, thinking there may have been a hidden picture in the plane cream wall. After we all agreed there really was nothing there Dale thought it may be a room where you make your own modern 'living art', so Dale took his position against one of the walls and performed several poses for us, getting quite inventive at one point that would definitely have passed as modern art to be shown in a place such as this, as he stood there with his shoes on his hands in a comical pose.

We had a spot to eat there where they served me up a nice piece of lemon meringue and a coffee and we were ready for the last piece of the arts and crafts section. This had several life size models, one of which Dale managed to attract the attention of the security guard, not once but twice! A creation of a white dove in a nest that was extremely life like, that also had a proximity sensor on it, so not to be damaged by anyone who wanted a little piece of the exhibit. We found this out when Dale got a little too inquisitive as he got a closer look, setting off the alarm to which none of us were expecting and jumped quite considerably. Admittedly we did find it quite amusing as we were chased off by the security guard, only for Dale to set it off again as soon as the guard's back was turned, which was so obviously intentional as I couldn't imagine him being that fascinated, to have to study it at 5cm (2") away. So we thought we'd better make a swift exit and into the next room, this one had people art in the centre of the room, with a taped area on the floor to signify a no go area making the exhibit out of reach. We all thought it looked incredibly life like. The mannequins were of a naked woman holding a sheet in front of her that didn't really cover anything, behind a clothed man with plaster spatter all over him and the chair he was sitting on, holding a plaster cast of a human head. We weren't sure what it was supposed to represent, and while we stood there pondering about this, our minds turned to weather the statues were actually 'living art'. I scrutinised every aspect of it and was amazed how like life it was, short of throwing something at one of them to see if they would flinch, I decided to stare very obviously at the woman's 'lady bits' in an attempt that if she was real then she may feel a little uncomfortable, making her move her eyes or something. After a few minutes intensely doing this I conclude that the pubic hair looked like a piece of carpet that had been stuck on, so maybe they were just paper mâché after all and I was just a weirdo staring at a statues mid section.

After the art centre Dale and I had to go and get tickets for one venue that would top anything else we had seen so far, we would be seeing the newly released film and the last in the series of 6 that Dale and I had followed since we were children, and most probably part of every boy in the 70's. We would be seeing the film *Star Wars: Episode III – Revenge of the Sith*. We then idly took a walk round several shops, one of which was an opticians for Dale as his eye test showed a slight and unusual condition that glasses would help, Sharon and I tried on several ourselves while we were waiting for him, that gave me some good ideas for my self as I needed a new set once I got home, and Sharon just looked like a geeky librarian.

Wandering around we found ourselves passing *St Martin's Centre* to find it was open, so took a look inside and up to the revolving restaurant on the 33rd floor, to find ourselves a little underdressed to say the least as it looked extremely posh, and at $65 (£27) per head just for a meal meant it was way out of our reach for tonight. So we had a little slink about and enjoyed the views hoping not to get chucked out too quickly. They were actually very nice and pleasant people who worked there, and didn't seem to bothered about our presence while we took a few pictures of the skyline, which wasn't all that interesting with very few large buildings to speak off, but it did give a great view of the entire city.

So we moved onto to the greasy Chinese food court for a $5 (£2.08) meal, it tasted good but greasy as always. We caught the train back to finish the day off with writing diaries and loading the days photos onto the laptop, whilst getting on with all this I noticed a little mouse go scurrying across our doorway in the room adjoined to ours, I wasn't really surprised to see rodents here, after I heard the management discussing which parts to fumigate in that room earlier that day, as there were some unwanted bed bugs visiting. When I enthusiastically informed Dale about our new room mate, he told me that he had also seen it the night before and had left some nuts out for it, to which it ate and went into hiding again until now. Sharon was a little more disappointed as she was the only one of us that hadn't seen it, so we moved and banged things about until it came running out and past Sharon into our room. So as I laid there trying to get to sleep I held onto my camera looking out from my bunk across the floor, to see if I could get a picture of the cute little critter.

Tuesday 17th May.

I woke at 8am still holding onto my camera and no picture of the mouse I was hoping for, so we had a quick breakfast and then got started on the day, with our first stop at *Perth Mint*. Built in 1899, this building shows typical signs of designs from that era, with a large square 3 storey building where the front entrance is, that has stone pillars at the front of the upper 2 floors balconies. The balcony changes in the adjoining 2 storey buildings either side of this in a symmetrical style, to a much more open bright white wooden balcony and large limestone arches and pillars, with the ends of the building having a square 2 storey building with the similar arched design windows, it has a presence that makes it stand out, which I'm sure was intended considering what it brought to this area as there was very little in the way of money back then, as miners would exchange their gold for goods and services in the rapidly expanding population in this area, western Australia had a population of 48,000 in the 1880's and ballooned to 180,000 by the time this building was constructed. The centre piece to finish off the front of the building was a life size pair of bronze figures named *The Strike,* The statues paint a picture of William Ford and Arthur Bayley in a pose of digging for gold, with one of them holding a sizable gold nugget in one hand and a pan that had a few coins tossed into it with the other, with the second man standing with a pickaxe beside him looking as astounded as the other. It was sculptured by Greg James whose involvement with art began at 18 years old when he enrolled at *Claremont Technical College*, where he studied *Fine Art* and majoring in sculpture. This monument of every gold diggers dream, was made in 1991 and has a very informative plaque that leaves very little else to be said. It reads;

This sculpture depicts the gold strike near Coolgardie by prospectors William Ford and Arthur Bayley in 1892, which unleashed the gold rushes that secured the future of the struggling colony of Western Australia. Established one of the State's most successful and enduring industries and led to the foundation of the Perth Mint in 1899.

Perth Mint was actually the 3rd such building to be built in Australia by the *Royal Mint of London*, due to the rapidly increasing finds of gold deposits throughout the country. The first was built in Sydney in 1855 followed by Melbourne in 1872, to deal with Australia's gold industry and to mint gold sovereigns of which 106 million were struck, with 735,000 half-sovereigns made for the *British Empire*. Inside, the first most obvious room we came across was the jewellery store that was incredibly expensive but very nice, one such item was a pink diamond at $30,500 (£12,708) superbly hand set into a 1oz (28g) 22 carat pink gold bullion ingot, crafted by The *Perth Mint*. Another item that would have been very nice to own if I had the money, was one of the many old gold sovereigns used as currency in Australia before the British abandoned the gold standard in 1931.

Our main attraction here today was the very informative and historical tour of the mint itself, our tour guide was a little bit strange to start with and had an obvious attraction to Sharon, something I wasn't really that concerned about. This became even more obvious at the start of the tour when he grabbed Sharon by the arm and told her 'for security reasons she would have to stand with him', which didn't last long, and she soon broke away to enjoy the tour with me. I'm not sure if there was some jealousy after this but as we came up to one particular part, he announced very loudly for the rest of the tour to hear, that if we wanted to know what a Olympic medal looked like there was one round the corner, in a very sarcastic insulting way as if Britain had a total failure that year. The *Royal Australian Mint* in conjunction with the *Perth Mint* had produced the *2000 Summer Olympic* medals. At the time I wasn't aware of just how many the UK had won in the Olympics that year in Sydney so I didn't have much of comeback, as it happened we had won 11 gold medals that year and ranked 10th, whereas Australia came in 4th place with 16 gold medals. Everyone made the same sort of sound as we did, with a sharp intake of breath, so hopefully he made himself feel a bit of a dick.

There are several accounts of large nuggets found round the world with Western Australia being one of them, one such story is of when the 16 year old son of Jim Larcombe in January 1931, on his father's claim at Larkinville, near Kalgoorlie, discovered what is known as The *Golden Eagle*, named because of the shape it resembles. This 35.5kg (78.26lbs) hunk of gold was melted down and sold to the State Government for £5.438, a price that is shadowed by the gold prices today in 2014, where the same piece of gold would be worth £878,444. However this isn't the largest record nugget ever found, the largest is the *Welcome Stranger* found at Moliagul, Victoria Australia in 1869 by John Deason and Richard Oates with a returned weight of 71kg (156.52lbs), I couldn't imagine what it would be like discovering something like that! In one of the courtyards in the complex of *Perth Mint*, there was a mock up of an early gold miners camp and a replica of the *Golden Eagle*, it had a pickaxe beside it that I couldn't resist picking up for a photo opportunity, the nugget is massive, its 67.5cm wide and 29cm high with a thickness of 6.4cm (26.5 x 11.5 x 2.5 inches). The camp showed the living conditions of the early miners, hard to believe a worker who could be making a fortune living in such squalor, a cloth tent open at one end, with a simple low bed made from canvas, that I saw as another photo opportunity, that was also a little insight into how these people slept every night after a hard day of digging, and it wasn't that comfortable either. The cooking facility was nothing more than a pot over a fire suspended from branches that would have been sourced from around the campsite. All very minimalistic, which I would presume was because they may have moved around the outback to several different areas covering 1000's of miles to find that lucky pay streak.

The next part of the tour was in the smelting room that had been used for this purpose since the building was completed. 2 guys were standing by one of the furnaces while a crucible was heated to about 1,300°c (2,372°f) inside it, sounds pretty hot but what was even more amazing, was that the crucibles could withstand 2,000°c. (3,632°f) They told us some facts on gold and how it is processed, with one of the most notable pieces of information about the renovations that had taken place in this 19th century building, there was originally 15 furnaces that several were renovated while the others were removed, but before they threw away any of the bricks they were processed for any remaining traces of gold dust, to which $250,000 (£104,166) was reclaimed, with more gold dust and particles found in the ceiling, roof and walls adding up to another $200,000 (£83,333). It came to the traditional gold pour, where they grabbed the giant heavy pair of tongs to pull out the red hot crucible, pouring it into a mould that formed a solid gold bar that was quite obviously heavy, as he banged it out and held it in one hand while wearing a massive pair of gauntlets that must have had one hell of a heat resistance, as the bar was still a bright red. It was at this point anyone was aloud to hold the gold bar, which for some reason no one volunteered. They dipped the bar in cold water that soon came down to room temperature, but needed a good polish to make it look as shiny as the gold we are used to seeing. Our tour ended with us finding out what our weight in gold was, I was worth $1,293,110 (£538,795) at the time. We also had a lucky break in the penny coin press where we gave this machine $2 (83p) to press a coin that pumped out 2 instead of one. I got to lift a gold bar in a box that only weighed 12.54kg (27.64lbs) but worth $230,000 (£95,833) that was 99.99% pure. As we were departing the tour, our guide couldn't leave without one more pass at Sharon, saying how I was Stirling but she was fine. We left the randy little bugger to find a few more items on display on the way out, of some Roman coins, with the oldest being a ¼oz (7g) coin that dated back to 400 – 500 BC as well as different gold bars and gold leaf.

We next headed to *Kings Park* stopping off at the government building first to have a look at the lovely gardens, which had grass that was unbelievably spongy that gave us a little spring in our step as we walked across it. This 2 storey mansion is an early *Jacobean Revival style* building, constructed mostly by convicts in 1859 that took 5 years to build, situated on 32,000m² (344,445ft²) of English Gardens. They did a fantastic job too with characterising it, by the use of stonework on all the corners and pillars with bonded brickwork, evenly sectioned with 4, high square ogival capped turrets that define it with such uniqueness. It also shows signs of Victorian Revival style with its thin gothic arcading on the ground floor. It is the official residence of the Governor of Western Australia, who must have had a lot of visitors staying over as there are 16 rooms on the ground floor, and 25 more upstairs. But we didn't get to see the extravagance of the interior today but were allowed to freely wander around the gardens with the ground keepers, who were making sure to make the gardens look perfect. Everything was well kept everywhere we looked, there was a small lake at one end with a simple water feature in the centre of it that had a few ducks swimming round, many rose bushes and plants of all kinds that were in perfect condition as well as the arched bushes leading off into others as equally nice parts of the gardens. One of the most incredible trees here were the palm trees, one of which was grown almost into a 10m (32ft) high bush that had a dozen or so trunks grown from the same point. Another equally interesting palm tree was completely the opposite, a single palm tree grown to a tremendous height that must have reached at least 12m (40ft), topped with an afro of leaves.

We left the extravagance of government and moved onto the public domain of *Kings Park* and botanical gardens, which required a lot more exertion than we had banked on getting there, as the park is on a large hill above the city that gave us a fantastic panoramic view of the skyline and the Swan River. The park covers nearly 1,000 acres (400 hectares) of land making it one of the biggest city parks in the world, which had been used for 1000's of years by the Aborigines as an important ceremonial and cultural place for the *Whadjuk tribe*, who camped and hunted the grounds in this area and used the natural spring for their all year round water supply, now known as *Kennedy Spring,* an area that was noted by one of the first European visitors, Willem de Vlamingh on the 11th of January 1697. The park was first exploited for its woodland properties in 1835, which continued until 1871, when the newly appointed Surveyor General, Malcolm Fraser persuaded the governor to set aside a large portion of what became *Kings Park*. By 1890 it was enlarged to the size it is today and was officially opened on the 10th of August 1895.

The park is packed full with many items of interest, but being so big Sharon and I didn't see anywhere near as much as we wanted, I should think you would need 2 days to take everything in and enjoy it fully. There are several memorials dedicated to wars and loss of life at places such as the bombings at Kuta on the Indonesian island of Bali. There is more than enough walks to keep you occupied, one of which we walked part of is the 620m (2034ft) elevated walkway of metal and glass that took us high in the tree tops, giving us a unique view of the woodland tree tops and park area. The central part of the park has large lawned areas and a sizeable long lake that is themed and decorated in many ways as it weaves across the park, from water features, to modern art and children's play areas. We were lucky enough to see a few of the 80 species of birds. One special species we got to see quite tamely jumping around in front of us was a laughing Kookaburra, we also saw Australian Wood Duck, a Western Wattlebird, Magpies and one of our favourites, the Australian Ringneck. We also met an older couple from Dorset in England who were feeding them, they were so tame with some of them eating nuts out of the woman's hand. The guy was saying how clever they were as he threw several nuts in front of them that they eagerly ate, as he threw a piece of apple down that looked very similar as he told us they didn't like it and the bird would leave it, which it did without even sniffing it.

The park is home to over 3,000 species of the State's unique flora with 2 thirds of the park protected as bush land, allowing a variety of natural diversity to flourish, a part we barely saw due to the sheer size of the park and the impending darkness. We did however see some unusual plants and trees that we stopped to study, the boab tree is one of the parks trees that stands out more than the others, as it has a one of a kind bulbous trunk that swells to store large amounts of water to use in the dry season, and is one of the few trees that sheds its leaves at this time. The hard fruits, or pods known as *monkey bread* or *cream of tartar fruit* that it grows are rich in vitamin C, and were used by the Aborigines for medicinal purposes. The trees live to a great age and are found in many hot countries due to their unique way of storing water, the oldest tree in the world is a *boab* in South Africa, known as *Big Baobab*, with a circumference of 47m (154ft). The example has been carbon dated to be 6,000 years old, once they reach 1,000 years old they start to become hollow in the centre which gets bigger with time, the centre of *Big Baobab* is so big it has a bar inside and can accommodate 60 people. Other plants we found of interest were the *Yellow Kangaroo Paw* that has bunches of finger like buds that look similar to that of the animal it suggests. A close relative to this was the *Flaming Kangaroo Paw,* which is the same as the yellow one but a fiery red, a name I'm sure took a lot of thought and consideration. There were also many of the *Mottlecah* flowers we had seen at *Heirisson Island*, but these ones were in several different stages of emerging from their hard obconical husks to turn into the large bright red flower with yellow tips.

As we left the park we walked along the road that verges through the park named *Lovekin Avenue,* that has been planted with eucalyptus trees, in front of each one is a plaque honouring those service men who died during action or as a result of wounds received during conflict, to which there is now over 1,100 of these plaques.

Night time fell as we walked back into town, after spending 3 hours exploring the park, and was about the right time for our evening meal where we found an old English pub where I was a bit more extravagant choosing from the menu and treated myself to a lamb special with some gorgeous garlic spuds, complimented with a pint of Old Speckled Hen, something I hadn't sampled for quite some time as it's a well known beer in England I had drank on several occasions. After a quick stop off at the hostel to change and freshen up, we went back to the city and stumbled across *Charles Hotel* that was advertising a few bands on for the evening, so we set up there for the night and it was well worth it. Although blues isn't my first option when I turn my iPod on, I do appreciate this style of music and tonight was no exception. The first artist we saw this evening was advertised as the headlining act, Lloyd Spiegel. Unbeknown to us at the time, he is one of the leading performers in this genre and now has 8 albums and has toured all over the world, performing in some of the world's best known blues venues and festivals. So to find him in this little hotel that had free entry was quite a lucky treat. And he certainly wasn't a disappointment either, taking the stage with just his signature model *Cole Clark* guitar. All his music played this evening were solo performances that felt to me a very modern version of blues and kept us entertained, his fast strumming and that well known tapping on the strings and body of the guitar that gives blues that unique sound, was perfect and he didn't miss a beat or chord. Lloyd played one particular song that amused everyone in the bar as he sang another blues song written by himself. It was a story of how he had been married for 37 years, and found he had become a lot less happier with her to say the least, and if he'd killed his wife at the beginning he would be out of jail by then, and a free man. The next band was also blues that consisted of a bass and lead guitar with the drums that was also really good and current in their songs. I had only one pint all evening as I was enjoying listening and watching the world go buy seeing everyone else dancing, something I tried myself from time to time through the evening with some degree of success.

We stayed here dancing and enjoying the atmosphere until the venue closed at midnight, it then took us nearly an hour to get back to the hostel as I had an attack of the munchies and had to find a 24 hour garage where a bit of trouble was brewing for no reason. This SEP wasn't going to get in the way of my pie, and it didn't, I just ignored it and put in my order through the little kiosk window. Back at the hostel I got off to sleep as quick as I hit the pillow, with a huge aching in my legs that made me know how much I had walked today.

Wednesday 18th May.

I was up with a surprising bounce in my step at 9am considering how active my day was yesterday, and today was going to be as packed so it was a quick wash and into the canteen for toast and black coffee, and I hate black coffee! As there was no milk I had no choice but to have it black, but better than no coffee at all for me first thing in the morning. It was raining again, and the hostel staff were nice enough to lend us an umbrella, which was very much appreciated as we had already had several soakings since we had been in Perth. We caught the East Perth train that was close to our hostel to Fremantle, as there was another 2 very interesting attractions to see there, the second attraction we were seeing today Dale had already seen so Sharon and I left on our own. Usually we would have walked into town first to catch the train as it was closer to Fremantle to save money, but as it happened the ticket machine had no change on the platform and so we intended to pay the conductor when he came through, but no one showed so we got to ride for free.

The first attractions I was surprised Sharon enjoyed so much as she wasn't going to go in at first, but as it was raining she joined me round the *Motor Museum of Western Australia.* I was in my element at this attraction, as I love cars of all ages and anything to do with them, even if I didn't completely understand something about them I would still try and take interest in it. Cars are a big passion of mine from not only driving many different makes of all shapes and sizes, I have always gone to car shows when I have the chance. I'm also mechanically minded and have worked on cars all my adult life from changing a bulb to rebuilding an engine, I also have a 1969 MG Roadster that I have lovingly and slowly restored and something I have enjoyed every minute of. On entering we were greeted by one of the staff that was obviously one of the more experienced members that worked here and maybe had close ties to the ownership, which will become more apparent later on in the visit. I soon got chatting with him and it didn't take him long to gather I was a car enthusiast and so we had an interesting chat. As we entered he told us to enjoy ourselves and if there were any cars we wanted to sit in we could, as long as they weren't one of the more fragile exhibits that was labelled 'do not touch' I was even more excited now, seeing one from the inside gives you much more of a feel of the history of it and have a little more insight on what it might be like to drive. The museum has a large range of cars and motorcycles from the early 20th century to the present day. Some of the vehicles had a local and historic story attached to them with a handful of cars that are so rare there are few examples left in the world. The museum was opened in 1995 and was dedicated to the late Percy Markam in his appreciation of his contribution to the historic vehicle movement in Western Australia.

Entering the exhibit I immediately found it to be almost overwhelmingly big as it contains over 130 vehicles, sectioned into different, areas of post war, sports and performance, racing, pioneer, veteran, models, vintage and post vintage, Bentley and Rolls Royce, motorcycles, Holden display and Australian and American muscle cars. I enjoyed every minute of this display as there was so much to see, the walls of the museum, were taken up by many signs, pictures, information and posters of all kinds. One poster I was surprised to see, was one advertising, a very small English car, the Morris 850, which I hadn't realised, had been sold in Australia. The picture of this tiny 3m (10ft) long car on the poster was at the seaside with 6 very cool looking young people, who obviously didn't all arrive in the same vehicle as you can barely get 4 people in it, they were accompanied by 2 surf boards on the roof. There were captions in the descriptions such as *What could be more swinging,* with another hard to believe caption to describe the vehicle of *Exciting to drive* with the best one of them all *The car that goes with sun and fun.* Fun certainly wouldn't be the first thing that sprung to my mind as the little engine only puts out 33bhp, that would make the performance and handling something of a myth from the description of this advertisement. Good job companies couldn't get sued for false advertising back then. But there must have been something in the little car that people love as over 5 million of them have been sold worldwide.

One of the smallest record breaking vehicles displayed here was a rocket powered drag kart, built and raced by Australian Rosco McGlashan who drove this hydrogen peroxide rocket car to a speed of 253mph on a quarter mile drag strip in 5.97 seconds in 1980. The kart was no bigger than a regular go-kart with the 2 large tanks either side of the driver that held the very volatile fuel. Several sections of the wall were racked out to take many of the motorcycle displays, some stacked 3 high utilising the space of the entire museum. We hopped in and out of several cars, one treat was the Piero Taruffi or Tarf II, built in 1951 and has held many land speed records in its time. I squeezed myself into the open drivers seat of the radically designed 'bisiluro' or twin boom vehicle that looked like 2 silver rockets side by side with a fin on each. Originally it harboured a 1,720cc Maserati four-cylinder engine with two-stage supercharging, developing 290bhp, with independent front suspension, and chain-driven live rear axle. Once inside it my shoulders wedged on each side, I couldn't imagine travelling at the high speeds it has achieved, looking in the cockpit was very basic with 2 dials, a red and green light and a switch, and steered by 2 levers that were close to the floor. This simplicity was all it took to break the record for the *Flying Mile* at its fastest recorded speed of 185.49mph. This was one of 7 speed records this car would achieve after winning the *Flying Mile.* Sometime after its speed records the engine was replaced by a 195 bhp, 2,418cc Ferrari 246 Dino, DOHC V-6 engine, with three twin-choke carburettors, and stayed at this museum for another 3 years after I saw it. Recently it was put up for auction and sold for €89.600 (£74,289).

    We sampled the seating of several more vehicles of interest, an old 1907 Fiat America Latina Torino was one of the older ones I liked that had running boards and a 3 litre engine that produced a mere 20bhp with a near perfect interior, as well as one of the more modern vehicle of a Ferrari. There were very few visitors here today so we pretty much had a private viewing and were enjoying the insides of the cars as well as respecting the 'do not touch' signs, which we viewed from a short distance. While Sharon was climbing out of one of the cars, 2 middle age men happened to pass by us and remarked in one of those annoying posh voices that he didn't think they would like us sitting in them, mentioning one of the owners names so he was obviously a regular. We told him we had already been given permission to do so to which he looked down his nose at us and said "I don't think so". I wasn't going to be talked to like that from someone who clearly presumed he had much more insight into the company than he thought. So we went straight to the front desk and spoke to the same guy who we had seen on the way in, to inform him of our little run in with toffee nose inside and to make sure it was still ok to carry on what we were doing. I wonder if this guy didn't care much for the attitude of the dickhead trying to throw his weight around inside, as he accompanied me into the museum asking which one of the more special cars I would like to know more about. One of the cars I wasn't able to access was a Lancia Stratos. this is one of the most well known rally cars of all time. The nice guy showing me it disappeared for a few moments to get the key to open it, as we both climbed in, the over confident know it all was walking past with a not so smug look about himself. The guy showing me this car was a very knowledgeable man, and we had a long chat about the car as he had personal experience with this car himself, as he had driven it several times taking it to car shows. This rally car was the first purpose built car to compete in rally driving, everything about the design was built and engineered entirely for rallying and it was certainly built well, fitted with a mid mounted v6 Ferrari engine that won 3 world championships consecutively from 1974, and going on to win many other titles. This particular car sported the iconic green and red striping, 4 extra spotlights on the front of the bonnet with flared wheel arches.

There were several sections that were mocked up to display an era, such as 1950's diner, with another section of a circa 1940's petrol station with a car and a motorcycle of the time. Before we left the nice guy who had shown us round the cars said there was a workers canteen there that we were more than welcome to use, that would be much cheaper than eating anywhere else locally, to which we did, filling myself with a cheap and good tasting hot dog.

We next revisited another part of the *Western Australian Museum – Maritime*, which was close by to the *Shipwreck Galleries* we had visited 3 days ago. The main item we would be seeing here was something you cant really miss, as there is a 90m (295ft) black submarine parked outside. We got our tickets for the next tour inside the sub, which gave us just enough time to see the underwater gallery pictures and some of the cameras that are used to capture these. This is a type of photography that is something of an interest to me, mixing 2 of my favourite things was something I had only been able to achieve on this tour round Australia, and it would be something I would get much more into by the time I would return home.

The tour of the HMAS *Ovens* was an hour long, which I was wondering how we would fill that much time in a tube. This sub sits proudly on a slipway next to the museum, which was built to service submarines during *World War 2*. During that time over 160 subs served from Fremantle, making it the biggest allied submarine base outside Pearl Harbour. The sub sat at ground level on some seriously heavy duty bogeys, braced with steel girders that also had several steel wedges jammed up beside the underneath of the sub. Apart from the wedges the sub was only supported by something that looked like a keel that ran underneath the sub for about three quarters of it along the centre, that was only about 1m (3'3") wide. This keel and those steel wedges were all that supported this hunk of steel that has a submerged displacement of 2,030tons, and we were about to get into it. I was sure it was fairly safe as it had been in this position since 1998 when it was donated to the museum, also the team at the museum are very dedicated to the upkeep of the sub, inside and out to make sure it will be in the best conditions for many years to come, to preserve this piece of historical information, and to stop it from falling over into the water. This sub is one of the 27 *Oberon class* that were built from 1956, with the one we were exploring today being launched in 1967 from the *Scott's Shipbuilding* in Greenock, UK where it was built, during its career this sub covered a distance of 420,000nm (483,327 miles).

We boarded the sub at the front via a metal staircase, it zig-zagged back and forth on itself 4 times before we reached the top of the sub about 9m (30ft) up. Even though it was raining I stopped here for a moment to take in the sheer size of it, from this perspective you start to wonder how it could actually move itself underwater being this long and 8.1m (26'6") wide, not only had we just climbed the equivalent of a 3 storey building, there was still another 5m (16ft) of steel perched on the top, better known as a sail. We descended down a steep purpose built ladder, through a heavy circular, water tight door and we were then in the torpedo room. The first thing I couldn't help but notice in this room besides the cramped conditions, is the amount of what is best described as clutter. Admittedly every lever, switch, pipe, gauge and handle was an integral part of the workings of the torpedo launchers, and I couldn't conceive how the crew could remember what every one of them did. What we were looking at crammed into the nose from floor to ceiling were six, 53cm (21inch) torpedo tubes in rows of 2. This took up the entire bulkhead with all these working parts around the torpedo hatches, as well as the walls and ceiling. One of the torpedo hatches was open, which showed the depth of the tube and the thickness of the 25mm (1") torpedo hatch door, with another tube had the rear end of a mark-8 torpedo sticking out of it with 2 propellers, one behind the other, this particular sub would change what type of torpedoes it carried depending on the mission, some types it had carried were sea mines and anti-submarine torpedoes. From the open tube we could see they must have been big, they are actually 6.6m (21'8") long, making it one of the longest in its class and has 365kg (804lbs) of Torpex packed into it, this explosive is 50% more powerful than TNT per volume. The whole torpedo is a whopper weighing in at 1,566kg (3,452lbs) and can hit a top speed of 41 knots (47mph) and has a maximum range of 8.5 miles. The maximum complement for this sub is 20, given the size of these torpedoes I couldn't work out where they would have put them, as immediately after the torpedo room walking through the corridor at every available place were bunks, also known as racks stacked 3 high, with the bottom rack actually on the floor with no mattress to speak about as they were only about 5cm (2") thick, with everyone of them fitted with a seatbelt, and just enough height inside to turn over. Most of the racks faced fore and aft along the curved hull of the sub. If you were a searider for the patrol, or under training, you had a rack in the forends, which you may have shared with one of the torpedoes. Not something I would be happy sleeping along side, but then again if it was to go off, you wouldn't know anything about it or die from drowning, something the rest of the crew would succumb to.

  We meandered through the corridors and more water tight hatches and past more bunks, this sub has every part of it utilised with these bunks in every nook and cranny as unbelievably it had a crew compliment of 64. Even the captains quarters were cramped, once you were in the room, you could either turn around or sit down on the couch/bed, but we do have to keep in mind this is no luxury liner and this was built for combat. One of the messes we viewed in this area was unbelievably small, this too had a stack of 3 bunks in it with several other small seats just big enough to sit on, along with a small table barely big enough for 2 people. Another room just as small was the sick bay that was also the chief engineers cabin, with little room to attend to anybody who was unfortunate enough to get ill while aboard.

  We carried on towards the rear of the sub passing the toilets, which I'm sure was a mission in itself to use, as there was no way of sitting up straight as it is against the outer wall and sloped inwards, and if we hadn't been told by our guide we would not have seen the shower, a small sprinkler was hooked onto the toilet roll holder and that's where you'd sit while showering yourself, although this was restricted to once a week for the majority of the crew with only the cooks permitted to shower every day. A little further on was the ships kitchen which was a lot smaller than I expected, here meals would be cooked 4 times a day, there was something very apparent as soon as we looked into the small room, that it was small with enough room to take about 2 paces while you ducked under the utensils hanging from the ceiling. The kitchen was manned by 2 chefs as the sub obviously operates 24 hours a day with the extra meal in the middle of the night, as there is no room in the kitchen for anything but cooking appliances and utensils, the food is stored away in refrigerators under the floors in the corridor that could supply the 64 crew members with 8 weeks worth of food, along with 30tons of fresh drinking water. The crews meals were eaten in their individual messes or their own rack, which can be quite a troublesome chore if your living quarters where in the aft section, which would mean after collecting your meal you would have to travel through half the length of the sub, through the drive room that would sometimes be in 'black lighting' with all the lights switched off except for the illuminated screens and controls, you would then pass through the engine room and through 3 watertight bulk head doors.

    The next major part of this sub we came to was the control room, at several metres long it was like the rest of the sub with instruments, gauges and levers of all description in every available places, with one section that had an array of what looked like large water taps, but these simple taps where what would let the water into the ballast tanks to submerge the sub. There was also the odd seat that was neatly attached on an arm, for one of the 13 crew on duty in this room. Other positions here was the sonar station, as well as a station that had 2 screens with something in the region of 100 switches above them, this was where the torpedoes would be fired from. Two parts here needed no explanation to what they were, the first was the periscope, a vertical cylindrical tube that extended through the floor in the centre of the room that could be seen to reach the bottom of the hull. The second was a large aeroplane type of steering wheel surrounded by gauges of all description and sizes, with the largest the size of a dinner plate. From here, once the order has been given, the sub could be completely submerged in 90 seconds and able to dive to a depth of 300m (984ft), while submerged it could reach speeds of 15 knots (17mph) which seems pretty slow to me, but apparently this was about average for the time, with the fastest sub in the world today only capable of 47 knots (51mph).

The next room along, through another bulk head door, was the engine room, this had a walkway through the centre with the massive engines either side. These 2 Admiralty Standard Range, supercharged V16 diesel engines are not what you would call a regular engine, as each one is 5.5m (18ft) long, weighs 21tons and produces 1,840bhp each. The superchargers are nicknamed *'screamers'* as these are driven mechanically off the crankshaft that is turning at about 850rpm, which is fairly slow in normal engine terms, from the crankshaft the 850rpms are put through a 4 stage gearbox that then turns the supercharger at a blistering 16,700rpm, to force air into the engine to produce this huge amount of power, and this is how it becomes incredibly noisy claiming its name and probably not one of the better places to work. These engines however are not what powers the sub directly, as it's a little difficult to operate an engine while submerged, not only would it use all the air inside, but it would also kill everyone on board from carbon monoxide poisoning. The engines would be started when the sub had surfaced to charge 2 banks of 224 lead acid, single cell batteries, with each cell producing just 2 volts which doesn't sound a lot, but that makes 2 outlets of 480 volts, that then powers the 2 English Electric motors that produce 4,500bhp each at the propeller, which is huge! That would be the equivalent power of 90 family sized saloon cars. The weight for these 2 items is also huge, the 448 batteries weigh in at a little over ½ a ton each, making the 2 banks a total of 300tons, and although each one has only a little more voltage than an AA battery, they carry much more amperage, so they can sustain much longer periods of use with something as power draining as a 4,500bhp electric motor. There was one of these batteries on display in the museum, it is 1.2m (4ft) tall and ½ a metre square (1'7"). There is also a lot of fuel onboard, when it's filled to capacity, that is the equivalent to about 12 fuel tankers. All this allows the sub to stay submerged for 3 days at a time without recharging, or to give you a better idea on what that equates to in terms you or I could compare it to, it would be the same amount of power used by 3 suburban houses for 12 months! With the ability to snort it can run just under the surface utilising its snorkel to expel stale air and the fumes from the engines, it could stay submerged for several weeks at a time. The engine room, as you can imagine is filled with gauges to monitor the 32 cylinders for pressure, heat, volume and volts to name a few.

Directly behind the engine room was the electrical control room, that was more like 2 walls of volt metres, here 2 electricians would be on duty at all times. At this station they would control and monitor the electrical equipment on the sub, also they would control the main motors that drove the sub by adjusting the speed from orders they would receive from the control room.

The last section in the aft of the sub originally housed, 2 rear facing torpedo tubes, after the development of wire guided torpedoes that had the ability to steer, made these tubes redundant and were removed in one of its refits. The last incredible fact on subs we learnt in this section, was a visual example of how the sub would be squeezed under the immense pressure of sea, at 300m (984ft) the force exerted on every square centimetre of the hull is 30kg (432psi), once every square centimetre is added up across the whole sub it's a phenomenal amount which probably involves a lot of zeros. To break it down a little, if we were to take a 1cm (3/8") strip of the length of the sub, at a depth of 300m (984ft), there would be 270tons of pressure on that one strip. This visual representation of this pressure is something the crew did when they submerged. By the super strong hatch that kept the sea out where it met the reinforced hull, a thick steel bar would be placed in this gap to further enforce the hatchway, here a crew member would place a nickel coin which turned out to be much harder than steel, this has left a perfect impression of a 5 and 10 cent piece in the thick steel hatchway, as a result of this hole being squeezed from the pressure against the bar. Another surprising fact about the hull is that it's only 25mm (1") thick, to withstand this pressure there are several ribs and bulk heads to enforce the outer hull.

This concluded our tour, as the deck below is not accessible by the tour from it being too cramped and mostly taken up by the ballast and water tanks, the banks of batteries and the electric motors and propellers. Under the engine room there is also a small workshop where there is a lathe and, various other machinery, so the engineers could make some running repairs of the items they might need to make while at sea.

Back inside the museum there was a large section dedicated to the submarine, one of which was a torpedo that had been cut away in several sections to show the workings of it. We also found many exhibitions of Australia's love affair with water, from all era's old and new. One large exhibit was the *Parry Endeavour*. This actual sailing boat is displayed at a steep angle with the bow pointing downwards, so the deck was easily seen with a life-sized sailor on board to show the perspective of this small, 14m (47ft) yacht, in 1986 an Australian Jon Sanders, in this yacht single handily, circumnavigated around the world, non stop 3 times. This room also displayed the *Australia II*, a revolutionary design that caused much controversy, when it entered and won the *12m (39ft) class America's cup* challenge in 1983, which had been held by the *New York Yacht Club* since 1851. During trials, once the opposition saw the advantages of the Australian's newly designed 'winged keel', they challenged the legalities of this design, which fortunately for the Australians it was decided in their favour. I'm sure the other new innovative features such as a vertical sail, Kevlar running rigging and lightweight carbon fibre boom, also contributed to their success. From the ground level we had a great view of this simple design of what looked like a stumpy wing attached to the bottom of the keel to lift it out of the water slightly to reduce drag, a design that had never been used until 1983, and from the next level up we could also see the inside of the yacht that had a mock up of the crew inside.

Some of the older ships included an Indonesian fishing boat the *Sama Biasa,* a more modern sailing boat that the hull was the only commercially made item on the whole thing. As items such as rigging, sails and fishing items all varied in types and materials, that had obviously been sourced from anywhere they could get their hands on to make it work. It was the first boat the Australian's confiscated in 1980 after it was spotted outside the agreed fishing zone, in Australian waters near Gregory Island which is barely 20 miles from Australia's coastline, subsequently it was confiscated and donated to the museum. This is another sad case of a westernised country that has the power to do what they want, I was surprised to see a newspaper article alongside this boat telling the Indonesian's story. Before 'Australia' these fisherman once fished a wide area to preserve their fishing stock, but now the Australian government restricted them to within 90 miles of their island, making their own area a poor fishing ground. There are many un-answered questions on this boat when it was seized, as it was carrying 40kg (8lbs) of rice, 360 litres (79 gallons) of water, 10kg (22lbs) of dried fish, clam meat and squid, and approximately 250kg (551lbs) of trochus shell. It's hard to believe with all this weight it didn't sink this little 7m (23ft) boat. The consequences if they drift out of this area for whatever reason, after a second time to teach them a lesson, their boats are confiscated. But this is the only way their families and community are fed, leaving them poorer, hungrier and more desperate. I wonder if at the beginning of the Australian history, if the Indonesian government had restricted the Australian's to fish within 90 miles of their own coastline, if they would have been so obliging. Another older boat, but this time from the Australian history was the *Valdura*, a simple much more modern boat and one that you can get up close to below and above being able to walk onboard, this was one of the first ferries to work on the Swan River.

The museum also had historical and educational parts with some of the old Aborigine canoes, pottery and foodstuffs. We also came across another photo opportunity, 2 neck shackles joined to each other, that would have been used in the transport of convicts in the 1800's, these where attached to the wall that we quickly tried on round our own necks, stopping another visitor to snap this moment in time of us. Hard to think how I would feel after being in those for the 3 months voyage from England! This museum, like the *Shipwreck Galleries* was full of information that we could have easily spent a day in. But time was getting away from us and we were already late for meeting Dale, so we left with learning a good deal from this museum.

We arrived at the *Little Creatures Brewery* an hour late, something I dislike doing immensely, but I was sure Dale wouldn't get too upset having to wait for us in a bar, and he did look happy when we found him lovingly caressing a half of their own brewed beer, and besides he was 40 minutes late himself so we were all happy. I sampled 2 half's of the stronger ones on offer, and I can definitely say I could have drunk much more as they are up my street of beers I like to drink, and this brewery had several ways of keeping your interest and patronage from guided tours of the brewery to random games that were dotted around on the tables. We found hungry homer that was after the doughnuts we were trying to carefully pick out, that we had to do carefully to stop him lurching forward sending them everywhere. The huge silver beer vats were in plain view behind the bar that had a network of pipes running to and from them, and even across the high ceiling.

For me a beer dinner wasn't sufficient enough to keep me going, so we made another visit to *Cicerello's* to marvel at the beautiful fish once more, while eating some of their companions. Fully recharged we braved the outside again as it hadn't stopped raining, although we had the use of the hostels brolly, are legs were soaked and the wind had popped our brolly inside out a few times that was an easy fix to rectify but annoying. At least half of us were dry.

We boarded the train once again back into Perth, Sharon I got our tickets as usual at the station, it is an unmanned station with a ticket and change machine on the platform, Dale thought this would be like all the other times on board with no conductor and thought he'd save himself the price of the fare and not pay. Only to be busted when the cops walked on at the next stop, I sat there sniggering to myself while he very convincingly used the genuine excuse Sharon and I had a few days ago, as he held up a note telling them the coin machine didn't work. Dale's middle name should be jammy as they let him off with a warning. He nearly hung himself at that point as he put the note back in his pocket, which made a loud and distinctive jangling noise of a pocket full of coins.

The rest of the evening was taking up with naming pictures on my laptop from our packed day, writing emails and my diary for the day, getting finished by midnight where I fell into a deep sleep from another busy day.

Thursday 19th May.

I woke at 7am feeling a little over excited about this morning's activities, the long awaited, much anticipated last film in the *Star Wars* saga. Although not even this amount of excitement was enough to keep me awake at that time of the morning, from the busy last few days I had endured. An excited Dale woke me at 8.30am after I dozed off for a while and it was quite apparent he was as excited as I was.

We stopped off on the way to pick up a bottle of coke and huge pot of butterscotch popcorn for $4 (£1.66) to smuggle in, instead of the extortionate $10 (£4.16) for a smaller amount there. I was a little shocked to see there wasn't as many *Star Wars* fans there as I would have expected, considering it had been released that day, maybe it was too early for the average Ozzy. And this is all I'm going to say about the subject, as any Star Wars fan would say the same as I would, and it would be a little bit of an insult telling you fans on how good it was when we all know it was going to be fantastic before we even watched it. And for those who have no idea what I'm talking about, then you obviously have missed out on the greatest series of films ever, and you should go and buy the box set now!! Accumulatively these films have made £2.74 billion. That many people can't be wrong!

After being in our seats for 2½ hours and drinking that much coke we were desperate to pee, so we made a quick exit as soon as the credits began to roll, passing a gent who was sitting there spilling over 3 seats, excitedly watching the credits. He was obviously a die hard fan too as it looked like he'd had several cosmetic surgeries to look like *Jabba the Hutt*. We were a little shocked and surprised to see him entering the gents as we were finishing up washing our hands as I didn't think something that big could move that quick or get through the door. We squeezed past him to escape in case he had thoughts of throwing us into his pit, to be taken apart by his pet rancor for his own amusement.

Dale and I parted company here, as the thought of another museum was too much for him, I on the other hand was looking forward to it. It was only half a mile walk to the Perth *Western Australian Museum*, it felt a lonely one as this was probably the longest time alone by myself walking in a city, and the longest time I had been away from Sharon since I started this trip nearly 3 months ago. Sharon had amused herself this morning while Dale and I had been at the cinema, by visiting the *Swan Bell Tower*. If I had the time I too would have enjoyed visiting this huge bell tower, but *Star Wars* was much more interesting than anything else in Perth. The tower is beautifully designed and an architectural masterpiece made from copper and glass that stood at 82.5m (271ft) high making it one of the world's largest musical instruments. The bell tower is wrapped in glass that narrows down to a point at its highest point with a star at the top, with the lower half of the tower cocooned on more than half of it by copper tiled sails that also come to a point. What is most interesting about the 18 bells in the tower, is that 12 of them were donated by the *St-Martins-in-the-fields Church*, in Trafalgar Square, London, when they replaced their own with a new set in 1988, and donated them to Perth. Before they were donated these bells had been used to celebrate the New Year for over 275 years.

We had arranged to meet in the museum when we had both finished our mornings entertainment, I then had the challenge of finding Sharon in this monstrous building among the 4.5 million exhibits and artefacts. The museum was opened in 1891 at the site of the Old Gaol and known then as a Geological Museum. A year later their exhibits grew to include ethnological and biological and by 1897, the museum officially became the *Western Australian Museum and Art Gallery*. Today it is much bigger than when it was first housed in the Old Gaol, and had to expand to house more exhibits, the original building still holds most of the exhibits that is built in traditional style of that age, with a complete contrast of style with a very modern glass fronted section in the middle of these old buildings, that is in an L shape of 100m by 70m (328ft x 229ft) with 2 floors. So I knew it would take sometime to locate Sharon here but it was relatively easy after I had walked round the entire museum first, finding her on the ground floor in the *Mammal, Bird and Butterfly Galleries*, which was a great place to start. There were hundreds of these butterflies in every colour and shape you could imagine, but the one that caught my eye the most, was the Queen Alexandra's birdwing (*Ornithoptera alexandrae*) of Papua New Guinea, which wasn't eye catching for its impressive colours, as it was mostly brown with creamy brown patches on its wings. It is known for its impressive 30cm (12") wingspan making it the largest butterfly in the world.

As there are so many items on display, and way too much to read we had to limit ourselves to how many different categories we viewed as well as read. Some parts interested us more than others, being drawn to the Aboriginal story of the *stolen generation* that I had already learnt to some degree in Alice Springs, and took this opportunity to dive into this piece of history a little more. The variety of items to learn about here is immense, we searched for interesting items here of the prisoner of war camps from *World War 2* all the way up to space science which displayed rocks from meteorites, the Moon and Mars. Some of these space rocks were displayed under different types of lights, one of which was a UV light that change parts in the rocks to a luminous colour. Another rock I was drawn to for our visual pleasure, was probably one of the most sparkly precious stones I had ever seen. We took a break from learning at the café, indulging in a large coffee and a pie, and got back into the museum after a short rest. After lunch we went to the *Discovery Centre* where there was more space stuff where I saw a short film on spacecraft and their engines while Sharon read some other literature. We then had some hands on parts of fossils and various bones we were able to handle to, it was a great experience and nice to see incorporated into the many exhibits that were behind glass. Any museum would not be complete with out an animal and dinosaur skeleton section, which was one of the last sections we explored, with one particular animal skeleton that most countries don't have, but camels are in abundance here so there were several of them.

We managed to stay here for most of the afternoon, by the time we came out it was getting near to that time to eat, with our first choice packed out and an enormous waiting time, we moved onto Cottesloe for our last evening meal in Australia and to watch the sunset at the beach. It was an 8 mile train ride to this western suburb of Perth that has very little else here but a great beach and a relaxed lifestyle. We arrived just in time to see the sunset, but as it was a little cloudy it wasn't as pretty as we hoped so we took a bare footed walk along the beach instead, stopping to get several pictures of the many seagulls standing on one leg all pointing the same way, who weren't all that bothered about us being there allowing us to get some close up pictures, as I shuffled up towards them on my belly. We checked out a few restaurants but they were a little

above our daily budget for meals, but we did find a much cheaper alternative at a kebab shop for a burger and chips, and headed back soon after.

Back at the hostel I made a start packing my bag while Sharon phoned home until 8.45pm, when she joined me for a walk to remember my step dad's mother, as it was her funeral at this time back home. We ended up at the end of the train station platform on a bench chatting for an hour, talking about lots of nothing while I remember my step gran.

By the time we got back it was time for a shower before we turned in for an early night, each time I had used the communal shower block here since I had arrived, I had noticed several half or nearly empty shampoo bottles, lined up on the dividing wall in one of the showers, I had left them here like a good backpacker would in case they were owned by someone who was staying here and they had not realised of their misplacement. But after 6 days with them still not being claimed or moved, I thought it was a good chance they were now up for grabs as my own shampoo bottle was nearly empty. So I took a little from each bottle to fill up my own, hoping that I'd accidentally stumble across the best shampoo ever known to man. That didn't happen, but I did manage to acquire myself several more weeks of free hair washing. Cleaned and shampooed up with my new product, I finished off packing my backpack and got to bed a little earlier than we were used to, ready for our big culture change tomorrow.

Friday 20th May.

I had a sudden start being woken from a seriously scary dream of large buildings that had lots of people in it with all the windows smashed, which was also getting bombed. I hoped it wasn't a precognitive sight of things to come or had some symbolic meaning for what I was doing today. I was so shocked by the dream I laid there thinking it over for a while and didn't get up, I fell asleep again and missed my watch alarm, waking up very slightly late at 7.10am. I had a quick visit to the front desk to ask them to phone for a shuttle for us, as they had already said they would do this for us the night before after telling them of our early departure. Back in a little bedroom for the last 6 days I did my morning usual and packed the last pieces in my backpack. We stripped our beds and took the sheets to the laundry room before breakfast. We got there to find the staff had already got out our toast and coffee ready for us, showing their dedication to their guests even on their last day with them.

Despite our late start we were ready with ample time although the bus picking us up wasn't. I was getting more excited about getting going now to our next destination, which was the smallest province of Indonesia, today we would be in another country and on the small island of Bali. I had slight concerns about the culture shock I would be heading into, as so far compared to what I had ahead of me, I had been on holiday up to this point. Although I had concerns I also had great excitement of a challenging adventure through a world that would be alien to me, I would get to see sights of foreign lands that most people will never have the pleasure of seeing, it would be enduring but fulfilling. I also had the comfort of my 2 companions to help me with this transition into this unusual environment, as they had already had experience in this type of strange world to the average westerner, as they had already spent more than 3 months backpacking through Central and South America before I met them in New Zealand, which makes them practically experts in this.

While we were waiting for our illusive bus, one of the kind staff informed us they had heard that Bali had suicide bombing threats, which really wasn't something a first time traveller to this type of country wanted to hear, especially the threat of this kind as the 2002 Bali bombings at Kuta near the city of Denpasar, was still fresh in most peoples minds and will be one of the most horrific bombings that will always be known from the sheer devastation it caused, with the loss of 202 people and another 240 injured. Maybe this was what was on my mind this morning. We had a quick check on the foreign office website where we found out that all of Bali was under threat, but as there were no reports on any imminent bombings we thought it'd be alright, hoping history wouldn't repeat itself and something we were hoping wasn't going to effect our visit.

The bus was 25 minutes late, when we boarded we were thinking we would still have plenty of time to make our flight, but our relaxed journey soon changed to despair and our concerns rose of the possibility of missing the flight, when our route took us a long way round and had several unnecessarily long stops to pick up more passengers. Dale, who at times like this always looks on the worst case scenario, had done very well up until we got in a traffic jam when he immediately panicked and had lost all hope in making the flight, and started to check if he was insured against missed flight. I got a little grumpy with him at this point as although we were late for our 3 hour check in, we still would have made the gate even with an hour to spare, although the airport staff may have been a little unhappy with us.

As it happened we were only slightly late arriving there at 9.40am, which meant we had more than enough time to check our bags in and relax at the gate. Well Sharon got straight through, but Dale and I had a patting down and items confiscated for different reasons. I don't know why I had not put the adjustable spanner I bought, to attach the power converter to the campervan battery in my luggage, or why I thought I would even need it anymore and I could have sent it home with the power converter. But I hadn't and it pinged up on the metal detector and they took it off me, I don't know what they thought I could do with a small adjustable spanner on a plane, but I'm sure they had their reasons. I skipped through to see Dale having his knife and fork getting thrown away, for much more obvious reasons. He also got quizzed on the 1.5 litres of wine in a plastic bottle which he tried to make out it wasn't alcohol, by taking a big swig that didn't convince them and they still wanted it, so Dale chugged down as much as he could without making himself ill before handing it over.

Through the gate we took a look round the expensive shops, with only $10 (£4.16) left I could barely buy the toothpaste I needed, so I went to the café instead and blew it all on a coffee, a giant cookie and a chocolate bar that had a close similarity to a Penguin chocolate bar that is much more common in England.

Although I was now minutes away from boarding it seemed like it was taking forever, I was unbelievably intrigued to what the next 93 days and 9 countries would bring me, along with the diverse culture and religion I would be learning and this strange life I would be living. I knew it was going to be much harder travelling than I had been doing, with it being more of an endurance that would push me to my limits at some points.

We finally boarded the plane and my long awaited, second adventure was now starting with only a vague a clue on what laid ahead over the next 3 months, that would further mould my character to what it is today.

www.ingramcontent.com/pod-product-compliance
Lightning Source LLC
Chambersburg PA
CBHW071645090426
42738CB00009B/1433